D1432075

FROM CONTRACT TO COVENANT

From Contract to Covenant

*Beyond the Law and Economics
of the Family*

Margaret F. Brinig

HARVARD UNIVERSITY PRESS

Cambridge, Massachusetts

London, England · 2000

Library of Congress Cataloging-in-Publication Data

Brinig, Margaret F.
From contract to covenant : beyond the law and economics of the family / Margaret F. Brining.
p.   cm.
Includes bibliographical references and index.
ISBN 0-674-00216-4
1. Family—Economic aspects.   2. Domestic relations—Economic aspects.   I. Title.
HQ518 .B737 2000
306.85—dc21   99-054683

To the Marys and the Margaret:

Margaret Culkin Banning (1893–1982),
who let me use her typewriter and encouraged me to write.

Mary Banning Friedlander,
who gave me life and taught me women could do anything.

Mary Margaret Brinig,
whose birth filled me with the joy of creation
and whose growth instructs me about hope.

Contents

Acknowledgments

As with any project that takes many years to write, many people have contributed much to this book. In particular, I would like to thank those who have read all or chapters of it, making valuable suggestions. These friends include Pat Cain, June Carbone, Jane Cohen, Martha Minow, Allen Parkman, Richard Posner, Eric Rasmusen, Michael Trebilcock, and Anne Witte. I also owe tremendous debts to my various coauthors, in particular Michael Alexeev, Douglas Allen, Frank Buckley, June Carbone, Steve Crafton, Steven Nock, Carl Schneider, and Lee Teitelbaum. Many of my friends and colleagues have helped me sort out sticky points along the way. I thank particularly Frank Buckley, Lloyd Cohen, Karen Czapanskiy, Martha Fineman, Jennifer Roback Morse, Francesco Parisi, Mark Ramseyer, Mit Regan, Jana Singer, Jeff Stake, and Bob Tollison. Mary Friedlander and Mary Brinig have both given up vacation time to proofread multiple drafts. A number of student research assistants have helped with references and suggestions. The most involved have been Bryan Beier, Laura Fraedrich, and Cindy Rappaport. The referees and editors at Harvard University Press have made this a much better book. I thank Michael Aronson for his great wisdom and his patience with the project, and Amanda Heller for her careful attention to detail and precise language. Finally, Robin West and Bill Eskridge encouraged me to write this book in the first place, and by their examples inspired me to finish it.

FROM CONTRACT TO COVENANT

1

Introduction

Students of the family are preoccupied with divorce. They read about relationships in crisis, and use the fabric of lives worn thin and stretched to the breaking point to develop ideas about what families are, and even what they ought to be. In a way, of course, teaching devices like the Socratic method encourage us to see families as a collection of pathologies. Happily, many us live most of our lives in families that are healthy. We grow, we develop trust, and we dare to share ourselves with the special people in our inner circle. Much of the law that is in the broadest sense family law—and is frequently unexplored in class or in the literature—protects us and encourages us and sometimes pushes us to live in families in particular ways.

Although I consider troubled families in this book, I spend more time on intact families. I describe many characteristics of families using the legal framework alluded to in the title: the contract and the covenant.

Both terms, contract and covenant, suffer from some ambiguity because of their special connotations. "Contract" is used here almost exclusively in the legal sense of the term: a legally enforceable agreement. Covenants are those agreements enforced not by law so much as by individuals and their social organizations. Though rich in religious provenance, as used in this book "covenant" refers to the solemn vows that create and characterize the family. Enforcement stems from that solemnity and from the values of the family members. Thus, while some covenants draw power from religious values, today we find families whose covenants derive most of their power from the family members' mutual commitment to one another and to the preservation and protection of the family itself.

These two concepts have economic analogues. In many ways, the economic concept of the market is consonant with the legal concept of contract.[1] Similarly, the economist's model of the firm has some commonalities with the covenant paradigm espoused here.[2] Although market, firm, and contract are useful constructs for thinking about families, they fail to complete the picture of families as we experience them. In consequence, I also consider the limitations of economics for describing intimate relationships. Using the ideas of covenant and other legal notions to overcome these limitations, I offer some suggestions for creating a better fit among theoretical models, legal rules, and the state of Western society as one century ends and another begins.

The title also suggests that this book will not follow the rigorous approach favored by economists and others who write in the law and economics field. Because I hope the audience will include students of sociology and women's issues, for example, I have tried to write without presupposing mathematical or legal backgrounds but at the same time without compromising the quality of the analysis.

From a lawyer's perspective, and reduced to its simplest form, a market involves a sale of a good or service based on some type of explicit or implicit contract, or promise. Law provides the framework within which this transaction takes place as well as the foundation for enforcing the bargain should one or both of the parties not carry it through. Remedies for breaking the promise (or breaching the contract) typically take the form of money damages or an order requiring specific performance (completion as specified) of the contract.

The market in theory is composed of so many buyers and sellers that no one transaction has any effect on the market as a whole; the participants are price takers rather than price setters.[3] Each has perfect knowledge about all relevant prices and goods, and each acts rationally and individually. That is, each buyer or seller chooses in a way that will maximize utility; each also chooses according to the rule of diminishing marginal utility. This means that if a person acquires more of a given thing, he or she will value each additional unit less than the previous one. Thus, the first cup of coffee in the morning yields more satisfaction than the second, and the third less than the second. At the margin—which means a small change in the total amount—an increase (decrease) in price will cause a decrease (increase) in the demand for a good.

In the market, the consumer also has transitive preferences, that is, if A is chosen over B, and B over C, then A will be chosen over C.[4] In this theoretical market, prices will change instantaneously as supply and demand fluctuate, and consumers will seek out the best prices until the cost of additional search (the marginal cost) exceeds the expected price break. Contracts usually govern only a particular (spot) transaction.

The individuals who buy or sell may be either real or fictional (corporations, in law, are considered fictive persons), and may be relatively powerful or not. They are typically adults who are competent to make decisions and who know enough about the particular agreement into which they are entering to make its enforcement fair. The difference between these general markets and the ones I consider in this book is, of course, that markets in family law involve decisions about lifetime partners (if children can be called partners). Thus, courting couples and birth and adoptive parents necessarily know less about what will occur over the course of a lifetime than one can know about the market (price and technology changes), and usually know less about the other person than one knows about repeatedly purchased consumer items. And, obviously, people are already much more emotionally invested before they pursue these family-related transactions than before they purchase consumer goods or services.

Even with all these qualifications, the idea of market, with its legal analogy of contract, is useful in describing the law that governs parties about to enter into family relationships, for example, those concerning courtship and adoption.[5] To some extent, contract may also be an appropriate concept for framing the context of dissolving families: those disrupted by separation, divorce,[6] or termination of parental rights.[7] Nevertheless, contract law dragged out of its usual commercial context and into ongoing family relationships has serious drawbacks. The most obvious of these is that it does not have the right concepts or language to treat love, trust, faithfulness, and sympathy, which more than any other terms describe the essentials of family.[8] The second problem is that contract law implies the possibility of breach. When a better business deal comes along, it may be advantageous to breach the contract, pay damages, and recontract with the inviting third party.[9] When family members are involved, particularly children, paying damages does not really compensate. One's affections are not, and should not be, readily transferable. Moreover, continually being on the lookout for better family "deals"—better spouses, children or parents— would itself destroy family life and ultimately harm the community.[10] To describe the ties of ongoing families, then, a better legal term might be "covenant," which provides the organizing feature of the second part of this book.

A covenant, in ordinary discourse, is a particularly solemn agreement. Contemporary covenants characterize the priesthood and the Jewish marriage agreement, the *ketubah*. When a man begins a priestly vocation in the Roman Catholic Church, he is fundamentally changed, particularly by his ability to perform the sacrament of the Eucharist. His vow, which requires him to forsake marriage, lasts for his lifetime. Even though he may receive permission to be released from his vow of celibacy and pastoral duties, he remains in many ways a priest. The priesthood, and even more obviously the religious order, involves covenants with God and also with other members of the religious community, with whom the priest shares a common life and with whom he can seek self-transcendence. The priesthood, though also a vocation, differs from modern marriage because it is necessarily hierarchical: the priest must submit not only to God but also to his bishop and ultimately the pope.

The *ketubah* is a set of solemn promises regarding the mutual obligations of husband and wife. It is signed by the bride and groom in front of a community of witnesses, who promise to be supportive of the couple. The ancient *ketubah* protected the bride's rights as a married woman and ensured her care and protection by the groom. Even the modern wedding ceremony reflects many of the elements of covenant, particularly including a promise to love despite "the hurts that are to come," with a love "that embraces life and surpasses death." The concept of franchise, which will be discussed shortly, can be found in the *ketubah* promises to rear children "devoted to Torah, *chuppah* and *ma-asim tovim:* to Wisdom, love and good deeds." The children, reared in the Jewish tradition, will carry on the faith even when husband and wife no longer can. These aspirations are revealed in the following excerpts from the rabbinical prayers for the bride and groom, recited before they sign the *ketubah:*

> May the Source of all blessing,
> the Fountain of all Life,
> fill your hearts with blessing
> and crown your days with love. . . .
> May they be blessed with children
> reared in health and well-being,
> devoted to Torah, *chuppah* and *ma-asim tovim:*

to Wisdom, love and good deeds. . . .
The fires of love illumine the divine.
Water cannot quench love nor can floods drown it.
If we were to offer all we had for love
it would not be enough.
Love demands not only what we own but who we are.
To love without fear,
without holding back,
without illusion.
This is a love that
embraces life
and surpasses death. . . .
We are about to enter into a unique covenant,
a bond of body, mind and spirit.
We acknowledge the hurts that are to come
and pledge to keep our hearts forever open to healing.[11]

As these prayers demonstrate, the married couple is obviously beginning something quite different from a commercial contract. The joyful and solemn occasion marks a life together, a "little Commonwealth"[12] that will be quite different from what they have known even if they have lived together before. In many of its characteristics this married life, like the priestly life, resembles the legal partnership or firm and the community much more closely than the contract.

The firm is an association organized to perform some specific function, usually for financial gain. Although the participants retain their individual identities, they join together because it makes business sense to do so. Third parties often deal with the firm as a collective unit rather than with its individual members. When beginning a firm, the parties usually draft an agreement that describes the new relationship in general terms. This agreement does not purport to anticipate all future transactions among the firm members. In fact, one of the goals of the firm is the elimination of explicit interparty contracting and account keeping.

The economist sees the firm much as the lawyer does, as an entity designed to reduce the costs of contracting on the market, and organized in a way designed to maximize profit, which is the ultimate goal of the firm.[13] The firm takes inputs of raw materials, labor, capital (machines and tools and other technologies), and land (the physical location or plant) and transforms the raw materials into finished products or goods. The amount produced is chosen so that the marginal return on the last unit of goods (the price obtained for it) will just equal the cost of producing it. The firm takes advantage of specialization and economies of scale and scope,[14] that is, the costs saved because many similar functions are performed using the same equipment, say, or because the same materials and their byproducts can all be used to produce a variety of goods.[15]

Gary Becker uses these concepts drawn from the economic theory of the firm to build a model of ongoing families.[16] To the extent that the household is a unit organized to produce a good (children), his analogy is powerful. But when children are not involved, when marriage becomes less than permanent for many couples, and when women's opportunity costs of staying out of the labor market become too high, the model becomes problematic. Legal and financial incentives that would have encouraged the specialization of Becker's efficient household in the 1950s may now work to disadvantage family members, particularly women, in a less specialized marriage.

While the traditional theory of the firm may be ideal for explaining mid–twentieth-century marriages and an imperfect model for explicating more recent ones, it has still less predictive value when applied to parent-child relationships. For these, the firm model is more useful when combined with concepts of the new institutional economics, which emphasizes transaction and agency costs, reputational effects, and signaling. This newer way of depicting families comes very close to my own use here of the legal, historical, and religious concept of covenant.

Covenant embraces much of what is not covered by the concept of contract in terms of the non-financial, community-centered, and permanent components of family. A covenant carries with it a whole set of duties and obligations that reflect the needs of the community as a whole. Further, it is a compact or promise that cannot easily be broken even if one side does not perform fully or satisfactorily. It thus has durability beyond that of many firms and far beyond the time horizon of the market, where a transaction may be entirely episodic or discrete.

In this book I argue that covenant is a preferable concept for describing families that are well under way—for illuminating the relationship between husband and wife or parent and child[17]—for, in brief, the covenant implies unconditional love and permanence. Further, the parties are bound not only to each other but also to some third party, to God or the community or both.[18] Of course, law sometimes seems to contradict the permanence of the covenant relationship described here. When children reach adulthood and leave their parents, or when couples divorce, the law no longer binds them as a family. To be persuasive, covenant as it is used in this book requires a "post-firm" state. The device chosen here is the franchise, the concept that organizes the third part of the book.

Another possible analytical device might be the corporate reorganization, the legal device that allows the less than solvent firm to continue doing business because of the value (to consumers) of the goods or services produced.[19] Such an analogy aptly describes the different associations of couples who have divorced, and perhaps parental relationships that are also "insolvent" and are being dissolved through involuntary termination. Unlike the franchise, however, a corporate reorganization model does not fit the most common situation of the changed family, whereby children just grow up to become adults. Unlike reorganization, then, the ordinary life cycle change does not require that the family experience insolvency (or that liabilities exceed assets). The important point, though, is that in both reorganization and franchise, there are changed but continuing relationships.

"Franchise" usually describes a particular type of business structure in which at the outset the franchisor possesses something of great value, typically a trade secret or name brand recognition.[20] Because it is too difficult to manage a large number of retail outlets, the franchisor arranges for others to purchase the right to use the brand name or secret process in exchange for royalties and some assurances of high quality. In return, the franchisees may have to build certain kinds of outlets, may have to use intermediate products furnished by the franchisor, and may have to be available for frequent franchisor inspections. Thus, the resulting franchises create a particular kind of firm, independent in some ways but nevertheless having many things in common. The "family franchise," which stands under the umbrella of covenant, is what remains after the legal ties imposed by marriage or infancy are gone. In this specialized use of "franchise" (for commercial franchises are completely terminable), the family name remains important, as does whatever investments have been made in biology, career, education, or personal growth. The shared family history, which may be pleasant or not, does not disappear when the child turns eighteen or the divorce court pronounces the legal end of a marriage. Particularly when children are involved, divorcing couples never completely revert to a pre-marriage state. Nor do children leaving home entirely free themselves from their parents or siblings.

In this book I argue that thinking of the family in terms of covenant relationships will suggest ways for laws to strengthen ties among existing family members. To the extent that modern American law has become centered on the individual, and particularly the adult, it works against family covenants and, ultimately, against the institution of the family and its community function. The chapter on law reform with which the book concludes provides some explanations as to why family law has developed in the particular direction it has and advocates ways in which better legislation might be crafted.

In Part I of this book I show how the formation of family relationships (or pre-families) can be described according to a consumer economics, or market, model. When these consumer models are appropriate, law and economics scholars (and libertarians) suggest that unregulated, or private, contracts ought to be encouraged (by law and practice), tempered by conditions I hinted at earlier: questions of competence to contract, incomplete information, negative externalities, and rent extraction or hold-up. In these four sets of circumstances some degree of market failure occurs, which means that the most efficient contracting cannot take place. Cases of market failure typically require some type of state intervention in the marketplace.

In families we see many examples of all these contracting problems. The legal status of childhood means that people under eighteen are deemed legally incompetent for many purposes. As we shall see, some writers question whether people engaged to be married, surrogate mothers, or pregnant women considering placing children for adoption enjoy the kind of detachment required for a valid market transaction. Even when these family actors are considered competent, they may be plagued by information problems well beyond those most consumers face.

Examples of incomplete information, the second potential limitation on free contracting, abound in family law. They include, for instance, the notion that the typical engaged person faces a lifetime with his or her partner without knowing what kind of parent he or she will be. Similarly, parents must invest in a child without knowing whether the child will be a success in life or what their own old age will bring. A pregnant woman considering adoption or facing a surrogacy contract also confronts information problems, since she cannot know what delivering and then giving up this particular child will be like.

The third impediment to free contracting, negative externalities,[21] refers to a spillover effect on people who were not direct parties to a transaction. Take, for example, two people who are parties to a contract involving the making of cement. The neighborhood in which the cement plant is located suffers from the noise, dust, wear and tear, and danger presented by the cement trucks. The ill effects suffered by the neighbors are spillovers or externalities, and much of the law and economics (and economics) literature calls for making the parties to such a contract internalize, or absorb, these ill effects. Sometimes the internalization is effected through government regulation, sometimes by giving people in the position of the neighbors the right to sue.[22]

There are two primary kinds of externalities in family transactions. The first, and perhaps most obvious, occurs when there are minor children. In fact the market analogy itself is imperfect in adoption and surrogacy situations because the "goods" are themselves people who will be affected by the actions of the grownups. Whenever couples have children living at home, their actions must be taken with those children in mind. Constraints may include refraining from creating "secondhand smoke" or displaying sexually explicit materials. Investing in a career may have positive externalities because it gives the children a better parental role model or creates more financial security, and negative externalities because it takes the employed parents out of the home. The presence of children for divorcing parents presents a huge externality problem since children are usually worse off in a divorced than in an intact family. A custodial parent's moving out of state causes an external effect since relocation makes visitation more difficult for the other parent. Part of my argument in this book will be that because of such ramifications, or externalities, a marriage persists to a certain degree in spite of divorce. To the extent that it persists, the family still lives on as what I call the franchise.

The second type of externality we encounter with families is more diffuse. Because families are critically important to the way society functions, any change in family life has a much wider impact—an effect on the community. Although allowing free contracting for divorce, sexual or childbearing services, or the division of labor in the household may well promote individual autonomy, it also affects the quality of what is sometimes called social capital. Permitting such agreements arguably changes the quality of life for the rest of society, that is, the community.

Finally, when a wealthy suitor presents a restrictive marriage agreement on his wedding day, or a pregnant surrogate indicates that she will refuse to give up what she now claims is her child, families encounter the fourth problem, hold-up. Just as with some commercial contracts, if one side to a marriage or adoption agreement holds too many cards, the state becomes concerned that so much value can be extracted from the other that the deal should not take place.

Despite this very long list of objections, many of these issues, when properly analyzed, suggest that there are only a few occasions when the state should prohibit the parties from doing what they want, or even heavily regulate their activities. In most cases, leaving family members to work out their own problems proves the most satisfactory solution in the long run.

Hence, as we shall see in Chapter 2, "Courtship," with regard to adults there is legally a free marriage market except in cases where there are substantial information problems (where the remedy is annulment) or substantial negative externalities (leading to void marriages or unenforceable agreements, both of which occur because the social, or community, benefits of families are threatened). A premarital contract will be closely scrutinized and sometimes overturned when inequality of bargaining power suggests that free bargaining may lead to hold-ups or rent extraction.

In Chapter 3, "Becoming Parents," we shall see that in parenthood, externalities are always present because, although the contracts are between adults, at the same time they affect children. Moreover, both the (informal) community and the (formal) state have goals that reflect the importance of parenting. Much of the discussion (and litigation) involves problems of adequate information (about, say, what a birth parent is giving up, or what an adoptive parent is receiving) and market power, say, wealth extraction by one of the parties (hold-up) or by a third party such as an adoption intermediary. Additional concerns involve the costs of transacting adoptions and the effect on would-be adoptive parents. I also discuss other externalities that affect society as a whole more than the individual parties to a contract, including so-called commodification (making a person or a very personal act the subject of commerce) and incommensurability (the inability to value or measure or compare two experiences or things).

Part II, "The Family as Firm," explores families that are already formed, a situation in which the market model seems particularly incomplete. This time the relationships are described in terms of the economic problem faced by the firm, in this case the family unit. Here the legal analogy is no longer the contract, as in Part I, but the covenant, and the economic problem is to maximize the family "firm's" production or welfare in its broadest sense. The particular characteristic of covenant that is most important to this part of the discussion is the unconditional giving that typifies most families. The ongoing family also serves a vital function for the community.

The commercial firm's goal of profit (the excess of revenue over costs) parallels the family's goal of maximizing the utility (or welfare, or happiness) of its members. The factors that the firm must consider in producing goods, or the family in producing wealth and happiness, critically involve transaction costs as well as the costs imposed by externalities. The kind of transaction cost we will encounter most often in this portion of the book is the principal-agent problem: frequently, with very little or no supervision, one relative (the agent) must interact with those outside the family on behalf of another family member (the principal).

Mainstream economists see the family's "profit" as a maximization of household production. More recently, feminist economists have challenged the appropriateness (and accuracy) of that interpretation and suggest alternative goods of happiness, intimacy, and security. In Chapter 4, "Husband and Wife," I reassess Gary Becker's classic household production model. In line with feminist concerns, I acknowledge the limitations of the firm model (in fact, the limitations of economics in general) for describing much of what involves the family, and particularly the nature of people's tastes and preferences. Here I analyze the goal of maximum household production as well as the means of reaching it. Thus, the household production function itself is examined, with particular attention to transaction costs (the costs of bargaining) and also to the economists' rationalizations for marriage (specialization and the division of labor). The family unit, like the modern firm, particularly requires investments in capital— called human capital when it affects earning capacity—and these are also discussed here. Thus, although the firm is the central theme of the chapter, feminist concerns about divisions between the labor force and household economics will also play an important role.

Chapter 5, "Parent and Child," also looks at the goals of the family firm, this time in the context of children. I ask whether good ("profit-maximizing") children are those who will please their parents or those who will make model citizens, thus benefiting the community. Moreover, I ask what difference the answer to that question makes for the law, and from whose perspective we should approach this problem. Although all of Part II treats families as firms, Chapter 5, even more than Chapter 4, revolves around investment in what is called human capital, that is, the knowledge and skills that build future citizens, workers, and social beings. How these investments are made—whether by father, mother, or public authority—is of tremendous social importance as well as interest here.

In Part III I explore another ramification of the covenant model as an alternative to more conventional legal and economic views of the family: the fact that the agreement is perpetual. Here, although the family has legally ended—the law has decreed that the marriage is over or that the child is now an adult—we shall see that some important vestiges of the relationship continue. We can think of two different paradigms for the situation in which the family is no longer bound together legally. One—and this is the way contemporary law views such families—is closely related to the contractual framework that dominates Part I of the book. This I call the sovereign nation model. The other, which I propose as a more attractive heuristic, is an outgrowth of the principal-agent discussions in Section II on firms. It is what I call, for want of a better analogy, the franchise model. (As noted previously, when there are no children involved in the changed relationship, another analogy might be corporate reorganization.)

Chapter 6, "Families in Transition," considers the dissolution of marriages (and, briefly, emancipation) as a return to contractualization of the family. The question throughout is whether a legal decree can really terminate a permanent relationship: whether law is limited, just as economics is, in its dealings with families. Here I question what consequences flow from assuming that a divorcing couple can make a clean break. Because of the emphasis on contract thinking (thus the consumer model in Part I); this chapter revisits transaction costs (in terms of grounds for divorce), questions of information (in terms of property settlement agreements), bargaining power and equality (in divorce settlements), externalities (in terms of the effect on children and the stability of social relationships in the wider community), and hold-up problems (in alimony).

In Chapter 7, "Winding Up the Firm," I compare the contract and covenant models and make the case for a return to covenant-like thinking. This chapter begins with an extended discussion of the sovereign nation model from Chapter 6 and of the franchise, or vestigial covenant, as I use the concept. The problems identified for treatment as issues of family franchises are those involving relationships between divorcing persons, between elderly parents and adult siblings, and between birth parents and adopted children.

In the final chapter I reflect on the role of law and lawyers, asking: Which comes first, social change or law reform? What happens if the law does not accurately reflect what is empirically true (as with the post-divorce duties and obligations of fathers)? Should we return, as Louisiana suggests with its new choice of marriage regimes, to a rule of law reflecting covenant ideals, with the hope that society will follow? How would we design a legal system for families in a modern age? Would the goals we wish to maximize be stability, intimacy, protection, and nurturing of children, all of which are consistent with the ideals of community, or the more laissez-faire goals of individuality and autonomy? If the former, how can these goals be met without perpetuating gender inequality in the labor force or even, arguably, in the marriage relationship? How can these ends be accomplished without creating serious hardship for older citizens or children? Is it more sensible just to tinker around the edges of the present system so as to avoid dislocation, merely removing distorting incentives and reducing transaction costs?

Another way of explaining the plan of this book is to say that in the "market," or "before," chapters, both legally and factually the players function as individuals. In the "firm," or "during," section, both the law and the parties involved see themselves in the context of their relationship. In the "franchise," or "after," section, the parties have few legal bonds, but emotionally and perhaps in other ways they will be forever marked and changed by having been members of their particular family.

The descriptions of courtship as a market and marriage as a firm are not original. But neither of these ideas captures the permanence, stability, and intimacy that people experience in marriage. What is unique to this book is the association of marriage (a firm) with covenant and community, courtship (a market) with contract, and post-divorce relationships (arguably having characteristics of firm and market) with franchise, and the extension of the analogies to parent-child relationships. None of the analogies is perfect. Although some of the structure (particularly in the sections on contract) lends itself to the hypothesis-testing that is characteristic of the social sciences, the necessary empirical work is only partially complete. I suggest explorations for the future as well as ideas for law reform that naturally flow from the ways I conceptualize families.

Many of the ideas in this book will be quite familiar to a law and economics audience, for the discipline of economics sheds considerable light on family law. But I have consciously pushed the boundaries of the law and economics disciplines, frankly admitting limitations of both, but, I hope, presenting a truer, and perhaps more optimistic, vision of families as we experience them.

Although at first glance their contributions to this book may not be as obvious as those of the economists, feminist ideas are at the core of the analysis. They soften the rationalism of traditional law and economics and underlie the three central messages of covenant presented here. In particular my discussion of the roles of community, permanence, and unconditional giving is situated in the feminist tradition of Karen Czapanskiy, Nancy Dowd, Martha Fineman, Martha Minow, Carol Sanger, Jana Singer, and Joan Williams. The ideas about the relationship between family and market work that are so central to this book have been helped especially by the writings of Ann Estin, Gillian Hadfield, Arlie Hochsfield, Kate Silbaugh, Daphne Spain, and Amy Wax.

Markets in Family Relationships

2

Courtship:
The Marriage Market

In this chapter and the next, the defining concepts for thinking about family relationships are markets and contracts. As relationships (between husband and wife or parent and child) are formed, in many important respects people act as individuals. In making choices they may well take their own preferences as foremost. By definition, when couples are courting or parents deciding whether or which child to adopt, they are not yet in legal family relationships. Yet even here, there are limits to a strict application of law and economics concepts.

For example, engaged couples usually know each other quite well—perhaps very well if they have lived together—so they have pretty reliable "quality information" about each other.[1] They also, according to Lynn Baker and Robert Emery's 1993 study of marriage license applicants in Charlottesville, Virginia,[2] have rather complete knowledge of the legal regime surrounding marriage.[3] They apparently have no appreciation, however, that their own marriage may end unhappily. Does this lack of prediction change the nature of marriage contracting? In the parlance of modern economics, is this a case of "market failure"?[4] Most cases in which the likelihood of "market failure" makes regulation essential involve transactions not between two empowered individuals such as those about to marry,[5] but rather between parties who are (financially at least) unequally matched.[6] The couples studied were found to be engaged in a "willing suspension of disbelief."[7] The subjects knew that half of all marriages end in divorce, but each thought, "Not my marriage!"[8] They also knew that 60 percent of responsible spouses fail to meet all their support obligations, but they apparently thought that this figure didn't apply to the guy (or gal) they were marrying.[9] These reactions, of course, are only logical. If engaged couples expected their marriage to end badly, why would they get married? At this point, when the relationship is at its most ardent, why distrust their partner?

These questions exemplify the limitations of applying law and economics to the family. The couples in Charlottesville were "in love," and were thinking beyond their own self-interest toward the other and their future together. They were ready to engage in a set of promises that would affect not only themselves but also, ultimately, their children and the broader society as well. Contracts in general are a two-person matter. They are individual, they are occasionally selfish, they are "masculine" in some senses (as opposed to promoting the nurturing and caring values that many characterize as feminine).[10] Marriages, or at least most marriages, are not like these contracts or Chicago School law and economics efficiency-seeking venturers.[11] When marriages are good, they involve self-sacrifice, sharing, and other-regarding behavior,[12] perhaps a more "feminine" view of the universe.[13] They are relationships, not just relational contracts.[14] Regardless of the couples' statistical prospects and predictions, as a society we have tremendous incentives to promote the noncontractual, non-market view of marriage and to change the statistical success rate.

The societal incentives exist because what is being maximized here is not monetary wealth, although marriage does enhance financial well-being. People do not get married to make a lot of money. They get married because they believe (or know) that living with the other, sharing with the other, creating with the other, will make them happy. As we shall see in later chapters, the commitment that neither will breach the agreement even though getting out may be "more efficient" is central to marriage too.[15] It is this commitment, or as I have called it the covenant,[16] that promotes what Milton Regan calls "the pursuit of intimacy,"[17] as well as providing the best environment for child rearing. After a reasonably long marriage, a clean break is not possible even with one's spouses, let alone children, there is too much invested, too much shared.[18] In the final chapters of this book I will discuss what is left after these legal ties are broken— what I call the family franchise.

Despite all these caveats, I begin my discussion with market or contractual behavior in families, including several different views of family creation. I commence with the classic description of marriage markets by the economist Gary Becker.

Why Markets?

Gary Becker pioneered a discussion of courtship in terms of the search behavior that leads to what he called "assortative mating."[19] This term implies that people sort themselves and others on a scale of desirability, finally choosing the most desirable person they feel they can attract with their own attributes. "Desirable" does not usually mean identical, however. In addition to the legal requirement that the couple consist of a man and a woman, each seeks out a mate who will be a complement—who will have strong points the other does not possess. Young people usually begin the search for a mate after they have "played the field" for some time in order to discover what they want in a spouse and what they are worth to others. They then date to find out enough about the other person to see whether he or she matches the characteristics that hypothetically would make a good marriage partner.[20] Finally, each attempts to convince the other party that he or she is capable of fulfilling the other's expectations. Engagement occurs when the expected utility of getting married outweighs the expected utility of remaining single and continuing the search.[21] The way in which people conduct these searches has varied throughout history.

At all times, courtship rituals have enjoyed major significance. When property holdings were the basis for wealth, marriages were usually arranged by the couple's parents. In wealthy families at least, courtship involved an attempt by the two sets of parents to convince each other of the validity of an alliance. In ancient times, a marriage could be repudiated if the intended did not conform to "specifications" such as virginity or fertility that were needed to guarantee lineal descendants.[22] Presents were exchanged, and a dowry was paid to cement the bargain.[23] This practice of arranged marriage began to change as early as the twelfth century, when church reformers decided that marital unions "should be contracted freely by the parties themselves, not by their parents or families."[24] Affection, rather than property, now initiated the relationship.[25] In colonial America, the parents still had a role in approving the prospective son- or daughter-in-law and in providing the necessary means of support for the new household, but the choice essentially belonged to the couple involved.[26]

Until the early twentieth century, American courtship was mainly carried on in the woman's home, with the suitor making a "call" upon her and her parents. The woman could elect whether or not to receive him, and could serve him tea or small sandwiches.[27] He might escort her to church if the relationship became serious, and would call on her father to ask permission to marry before the engagement became formal. As the historian Beth Bailey points out, the woman had little control over whether the man would ever present his card, signaling his wish to call on her, but exercised almost complete control over the progress of the courtship thereafter.[28]

With the advent of the automobile, courtship changed. It left the woman's home and increasingly took place in public. At first there was little "pairing off" during dates: at dances a woman sought to be "cut in on" by a large number of men so as to demonstrate her attractiveness and popularity.[29] Her escort also wished her to be popular, since that enhanced his prestige in bringing her to the social event.[30]

Since World War II, however, this mating practice has changed. Although theoretically a woman is free to initiate a date or to pay for it, during the last half century or so, most dating begins with the man asking the woman "out" and financing the evening's expenses.[31] Once the relationship becomes more serious, in many cases there is sexual intimacy. More than half the men surveyed by Alfred Kinsey even before World War II reported having sexual intercourse during engagement.[32] Since 1970, an increasing number of couples have been cohabiting prior to (or outside of) marriage. The National Center for Health Statistics reported in 1990 that 47 percent of women aged twenty to twenty-nine had cohabited. This modern pattern of courtship gives the couple more opportunity to discover each other's good and bad characteristics.[33]

The later stages of courtship lead to significant reliance expenditures, meaning that these "serious" couples give up other opportunities. At the very least, the engaged person is removed from the marriage market for some period of time.[34] There may also be increasing specific investment in the other person: learning his or her favorite foods, establishing relationships with future in-laws, taking the other's career plans into account, beginning wedding preparations. If the reliance results in a marriage, there are weighty social and personal consequences. As we shall see, the consequences of reliance, either by becoming engaged or by marrying, have traditionally been more severe for the woman than the man.[35]

Until fairly recently, marriage was necessary to secure a woman's social position, for an "old maid" not only would be stigmatized as not attractive enough to snag a husband, but also would be disadvantaged in later life because she would not be secure financially.[36] Marriage was, as one writer noted, the "one career open to" a woman, and once she had made her choice of husband, her "options were suddenly, irrevocably gone."[37] Her options may have been drastically limited even by a serious relationship short of marriage. Particularly during the period between the two world wars, a woman was expected to remain chaste until the time of her engagement. Once she was betrothed, however, sexual intimacy with her fiancé reportedly occurred among nearly half of all engaged couples.[38] This was all well and good, but if the marriage never came about, the woman was irretrievably barred from offering an unblemished self to a new suitor,[39] and consequently she suffered a loss in "market value."[40] While a man could pretend inexperience, a woman's virginity or lack of it was usually a verifiable physical fact.[41]

Search and Fraud in the Marriage Market

Law and economics suggests that we examine the search process itself. When a man and woman become engaged, they do not tell each other everything. Sometimes they misinform or fail to inform each other about important personal characteristics. When returning to the single state is more attractive than accepting the other spouse's true characteristics, the disappointed spouse may bring an action for annulment of the marriage on the grounds of fraud.[42] Whether or not the action succeeds depends on the nature of the marriage market. Some of the incidence of fraud in courtship can be reduced through nonlegal means. To this end, one may limit the search for a mate to individuals with good "reputations" within the relevant community. This provides the single person with a strong incentive to establish a good reputation. Such incentives are particularly important in small communities where "everyone knows everyone else."[43] In general, reputation will have less influence in a large urban area, where one can conceivably take advantage of (cheat) any number of members of the opposite sex without ever being discovered. Mechanisms have evolved, however, in which reputation or other signaling devices once again become important.[44] This is why there may be so much dating within particular organizations (university alumni clubs, church "singles" groups, sporting or exercise groups, or even computer dating services). In circumstances where reputation is less effective in reducing fraud, other devices such as the "trial marriage" may be used. As Paula England and George Farkas note, premarital cohabitation is the search mechanism that provides the most relevant information about the likely performance of the other person as a marriage partner.[45] Note also that such additional search mechanisms imply greater reliance expenditures than more traditional courtship behavior. Paradoxically, though, the choice of marriage preceded by cohabitation apparently attracts some couples who are less committed than others to lifelong relationships, since these marriages end in divorce at a far higher rate than those not preceded by cohabitation.[46]

Despite the existence of non-legal fraud-reducing devices, marital fraud does occur, and it has to be dealt with by the legal system. Outside of the marriage context, the law regulates fraud through the contractual devices of mistake, lack of meeting of the minds (fraud or lack of capacity), and unconscionability. Contracts can be rescinded (that is, voided) if the parties, or either party, did not fully understand what was involved, could not understand what was being promised, or should not be penalized because the bargaining power was unequal and the results unfair. In the case of marriage, the parallel remedy to rescission of contract is annulment, which declares the marriage void or voidable and decrees that from the beginning it never legally existed.

An annulment was at first the only way (short of death) that a marriage could be terminated. The ecclesiastical (church) court granted an annulment when it found that one spouse had an incapacity to be married or to carry out the marital obligations. By declaring that no marriage had ever existed, an annulment freed either party to enter into another marriage relationship.[47] When the common law became part of American colonial jurisprudence, annulment jurisdiction passed to the courts of chancery (since there were no church courts in this country),[48] but the old grounds for annulment remained. Because of an increasing demand for ending "dead" marriages, jurisdictions with particularly strict divorce laws (such as New York, Illinois, and California) expanded the concepts of fraud that had historically been used in annulment cases. Even here, however, the device of annulment was used less often than the collusive divorce.[49] Like the divorce action, annulment ends a relationship. But since, unlike a divorce, the annulment decree states that no marriage, legally speaking, ever existed,[50] divorce can be thought of as analogous to an action for breach of contract (or termination at will),[51] while annulment is more like a rescission of contract. There are actually two kinds of annulments: the decree of nullity, which declares a purported marriage void, and the dissolution of marriage, used for voidable marriages.

Marriages are void when prohibited by law or when one party is unable to fulfill the contract. Such marriages include those that are void for incest (called marriages within the prohibited degree) or polygamy (bigamy). Marriages are also void when made between people so mentally retarded or mentally ill that they are deemed incapable of making a valid contract (idiocy or lunacy). Others include marriages between persons at least one of whom was so young as to be legally incapable of giving consent (non-age) and, for definitional reasons, those between persons of the same sex.[52] Although children born of void marriages are legitimated by statute, for all other purposes the marriage never existed. Third parties (usually parents or legal guardians) can bring the annulment action, and there is usually no ability to recover alimony or a distribution of property. Almost all such annulments are due to bigamy, usually resulting from the non-dissolution of a first marriage before finalization of the second.

Voidable marriages involve a defect in the contracting mechanism. The category includes sham marriages (for example, to gain admittance to the United States as a non-quota immigrant), fraudulent marriages, marriages contracted under duress ("shotgun marriages"), and marriages of minors who did not have the requisite parental consent. These marriages are valid until the court declares them "void *ab initio*" (void from the start). A plurality of these annulments are granted on grounds of fraud. In 1966, when California revised its laws to include no-fault divorce, annulments represented fewer than 5 percent of all severance actions. Of these, 47 percent were based on fraud.[53] If the asymmetry, or inequality, of information does not rise to the level of fraud, the remedy is divorce, not annulment.

A spouse may prefer annulment to divorce for several reasons. Annulment may relieve a spouse who would otherwise be forced to pay support or cover medical expenses incurred during the marriage. The spouse may think that a civil annulment will make a later ecclesiastical annulment less difficult to obtain. An annulment may also be quicker or easier than a divorce in a state that requires a waiting period before a divorce can be granted. Finally, it may be used as a device to circumvent a statute disallowing evidence of "marital fault" from entering into calculations of spousal support or property distribution.

Fraud in contracts occurs only when there is asymmetric information between the parties. The implications of fraud in the behavior of the potential contracting parties depend on the nature of the informational discrepancy. The economist Philip Nelson, writing in the commercial context, distinguished between what he called "search" goods and "experience" goods.[54] Search goods are those qualities that can be examined in a short time or otherwise at low cost to the consumer, who can therefore make an inspection before purchase. The qualities of experience goods, by contrast, cannot be ascertained until after purchase, as with a can of food. Nelson predicted, among other things, that there would be more monopoly among sellers of experience goods, and that buyers would seek the advice of others more frequently before purchasing them.[55] Thus the conversations that people inevitably have with friends before purchasing computers, say, or cars.

Michael Darby and Edi Karni introduced an additional category of "credence" goods, whose quality may not be easily determined even after purchase.[56] This category includes goods such as home heating systems: although they work immediately after purchase, this is no indicator of their long-term quality.

The good acquired through marriage has the characteristics of all three of these categories (and, of course, involves a person rather than a commodity). In the marriage context, as with the purchase of canned goods, there are some things that usually cannot be known for certain until after the promises are made: for example, whether the other party will ultimately want to have children; will be a good parent; will practice, as opposed to nominally belong to, a particular religion; or will generally be interesting or pleasant to live with.[57] There is, however, yet another significant difference between marriage and Nelson's experience goods. At least in theory, marriage is for life, and there can be no "repeat purchase" or purchase of another brand. This may be one reason for the legal intervention of annulment, as rescission of the contract in the case of marriage. Also, the nonrepetitive nature of marriage increases the importance of the credence goods aspect.

The search goods aspect of marriage is reflected in the fact that there are some things that a "diligent buyer" of a spouse can know, such as whether an admitted prior marriage was dissolved by death or divorce. Fraud about such matters will not lead to annulment (although a spouse's disillusionment may result eventually in a divorce).

There are also marriages in which, although there may be fraud, the deceived spouse is still getting the person he or she wanted, and the contract of marriage will be found valid. Typical of these situations are those involving assurances that one loves the other, or will be faithful, or even that one is a famous sports star. In other situations, although there is some fraud, the person on the whole will be so wonderful that the deceived spouse will not even consider filing an annulment action. It is, nevertheless, primarily in the experience goods aspect, where fraud cannot be discovered at a reasonable cost prior to marriage, that the law offers the relief of annulment.

In a study of reported annulment cases,[58] nearly one third involved misrepresentations of social standing that the innocent party might have discovered prior to marriage through diligent search. Courts granted annulments in only a small percentage of these, and all of the successful cases were decided prior to the enactment of no-fault divorce, at a time when the annulment doctrine was expanded to its limit. Six of twelve such cases involved concealment of a prior divorce and were decided in New York, where the only ground for divorce was adultery. The other cases involved concealment of a trial for murder and conviction for petty larceny, concealment of pregnancy by another man (three cases), and nondisclosure of four children of a prior marriage. All of these involve conduct that at the time was considered immoral and embarrassing.[59]

Most successful annulment suits involve concealment of some fact that cannot be discovered until after the marriage takes place. In one group of cases, one or the other party concealed a desire not to have children until after the marriage ceremony. Where the plaintiff proved that this intent existed prior to marriage, the concealment was grounds for annulment.[60] In another group of cases, one spouse was unwilling or unable to consummate the marriage. This was grounds for annulment in all cases except two that involved proof problems.[61] A last group of cases involved nondisclosure of religious preferences, usually grounds for annulment.[62]

Fraud that is undiscoverable and that will vitiate the marriage promises is fraud that "goes to the essence" of the marriage, warranting annulment. That is, it concerns an intent not to perform one or more of the terms of the marriage contract. Although it may not seem that marriage involves any concrete terms, it may be argued that they appear in the vows many couples exchange.[63] These vows,[64] although in archaic language, can be interpreted to mean that the couple intend to live together "until death," to support each other, to engage in sexual relations, and to provide the bundle of goods and services that is legally called "consortium." Some ceremonies also state that the couple "will welcome the children God shall give them."[65]

Undiscoverable fraud that does not involve such "essential terms" is not grounds for annulment. Such fraud is interpreted in domestic relations cases as failing to "go to the essence of the marriage contract." Here the court may be setting a threshold value for the difference between the reported and actual characteristics. For example, one case held that the fraud must be about matters vital to the marriage relationship, and must be capable of deceiving the ordinarily prudent person.[66] In broader terms, the nondisclosure or misrepresentation may involve the bundling of more and less desirable goods frequently seen when a seller possesses substantial market power, as in antitrust cases or restraints that are placed on property when it is sold.[67]

When most people marry, they do not believe that their spouse is a perfect individual, even though they may not yet be aware of what his or her flaws might be. Although the spouses can reduce overwhelming surprises by engaging in a lengthy courtship, by living together prior to marriage, or by participating seriously in premarital counseling, they can never completely know each other. For those hidden deficiencies not on the usual mental list of desirable or unacceptable characteristics, the law provides no relief through annulment. Should the spouses discover eventually that the "bad" outweighs the "good" in each other, the remedy is not annulment but divorce.

For example, in *Heup v. Heup*[68] a woman sued her husband for divorce on grounds of cruelty. He countered with the claim that the marriage was voidable on grounds of fraud because she had agreed before marriage to take birth control pills for only one year but continued to take them thereafter. The court stated that there was no proof that before marriage she had intended to remain childless. She was granted a divorce on the basis of her testimony that, among other things, her husband had called her "a sinner" and criticized for parting her hair on the wrong side, painting her nails the wrong color, planting the wrong flowers in the garden, and eating crackers in bed.

Spouses tolerate some amount of fraud as they realize the other benefits of the person they have chosen to marry. They accept some of these, despite the advantages of annulment, because of the relatively high transaction costs of obtaining an annulment as opposed to a divorce.[69] Some degree of fraud is found socially optimal in a court system that does not want to be concerned with *de minimis* mistakes. Certain frauds are intolerable, however, even under these constraints, and result in annulment of a marriage.

Cohabitation: Remaining in the Market as a Substitute for Marriage

Since the 1960s, many couples have lived together in a stable long-term relationship that resembles marriage but lacks the state sanction that marriage requires (Figure 2.1).[70] Some of these are "trial marriages" of couples who agree not to formalize their relationship until they are sure they can live together successfully. Some avoid marriage because they do not want the obligations it would bring.[71] Others cannot marry because one has an existing spouse. An increasing number of cohabiting couples are of the

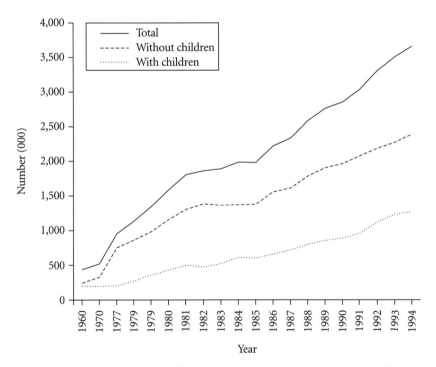

Figure 2.1 U.S. unmarried cohabitants, 1960–1994 (source: U.S. Bureau of the Census, Current Population Reports Series P20-495, "Household and Family Characteristics: March, 1996")

same sex and hence cannot marry.[72] Many elderly couples cohabit in order to preserve the financial benefits of being widowed or divorced. Some states nominally criminalize these marriage substitutes.[73] The majority tolerate them through recognition of express agreements to support.[74] A few jurisdictions have enacted "domestic partnership" legislation giving such couples some, but not all, of the legal rights of the married.[75]

Looking at this phenomenon through the lens of economics reveals several interesting patterns. The most obvious is that states want to encourage marriage, since only a very secure relationship leads to the kind of costly specific investment, particularly in children, that states consider desirable. They therefore penalize couples who do not wish to marry,[76] either directly, by making their behavior criminal,[77] or indirectly, by not protecting marriage-like investments without specific contracts. The costs of not being married therefore rise, so that on the margin, more couples choose to marry.

A second observation is that this informal marriage substitute is a pattern that has occurred before. Just as, in a general commercial setting, legislature-chartered corporations were "outflanked" by the less costly informal corporation substitute until corporate chartering rules were relaxed to permit private incorporation,[78] the nineteenth century also saw a parallel development in the law of divorce. When divorces were available only at high cost through the legislature, many husbands simply left their families, moved out West, and began "married" life anew.[79] The legislative response was to outlaw bigamy[80] and to cede divorce authority to the judiciary, providing the desired remedy at lower cost. State competition in divorce laws, like many innovations in state law, moved from West to East.[81]

One question raised by today's rapidly increasing rates of cohabitation is whether the rules governing marriage, like the earlier rules regulating corporate chartering and divorce, will need to take into account the "shadow institution" of cohabitation. The law might make cohabitation less desirable than marriage in order to differentiate the two institutions more clearly. The distinction could be made, for example, by penalizing the conduct (prohibiting cohabitation and adultery and enforcing these laws), not recognizing implicit cohabitation contracts for the exchange of services, or disallowing recovery for legal benefits (such as recovery under wrongful death or a tort consortium claim) that accrue to married people.

As an alternative to making cohabitation less desirable, the law might create benefits that make marriage more attractive in order to increase the marriage rate (see Figure 2.2). Some writers have suggested two forms of marriage, an option the states of Louisiana and Arizona have enacted.[82] The "default" option is a "lite" version of marriage for those who do not wish to have children; it entails very little in the way of state regulation and offers easy exit requirements.[83] The "covenant" option carries substantially heavier obligations in the event of divorce, including the requirement either of finding fault or of a lengthy separation period.[84] The so-called "marriage tax penalty" could also be lifted, making marriage more attractive for dual-earner couples.[85]

Economic Objections to Covenant Marriage Legislation

PRECOMMITMENT MIGHT LIMIT FREEDOM.   The covenant marriage statutes allow the state to take a greater role in determining reasons for di-

Figure 2.2 Marital status of U.S. males, 15 years and older, 1950–1993 (source: U.S. Bureau of the Census, Fertility and Family Statistics Branch, Series P20-484, 1995)

vorce, thus reducing the freedom of some couples to exit unhappy relationships. At the same time, however, this arrangement makes more
choices available at the outset. I have argued elsewhere that, sometimes,
proscribing specific sorts of behavior (in this case, no-fault divorces for
those electing covenant marriage) allows more freedom in a relationship.[86]
Covenant marriage, as Elizabeth and Robert Scott note,[87] will also lead to
greater investment in the sorts of things that make marriages better but
that might be too risky in the less permanent world of no-fault.[88] It will
promote marital autonomy (freedom from state regulation while the marriage continues), while permitting enforcement of whatever contracts the
couple wishes to make.[89] Frank Buckley and I have pointed out in the context of joint custody that the sort of precommitment made under the Louisiana covenant marriage option should lead, like other bonding devices, to
better choices later on.[90]

THE ELECTION CANNOT BE MADE BECAUSE OF INFORMATION PROBLEMS.
The sort of precommitment that covenant marriage implies must survive
the overoptimism critique made by Lynn Baker and Robert Emery,[91] which
I introduced earlier. Baker and Emery point out that most couples seeking
marriage licenses do not know much about marriage and divorce law, and
tend to be overly optimistic about the chances for success of their own
marriage, despite knowing the statistics on divorce.[92] Their confidence is
characteristic not only of marriage but also of the many long-term relational contracts that courts enforce every day.[93]

Another type of information problem is described in an important article by the economists Gary Becker, Elisabeth Landes, and Robert Michael.[94]
They note that unstable relationships tend to be those entered into when
the parties could not complete an optimal search for a new partner. Such
hasty marriages, which usually break up within the first couple of years, include those in which the woman is already pregnant or has one or more
minor children from a previous relationship, and those involving religious
or racial differences.[95] If the Louisiana and Arizona couples who choose
the covenant option were not required to have counseling before marriage,
this lack of information might have quite serious repercussions, especially
for young couples.[96]

Finally, there may be an objection based on signaling, or the implications of choosing one option over another. No one is certain how many
couples will ultimately elect covenant marriage, with its stricter divorce

rules, simply because *not* to do so would suggest that one is less committed to marital fidelity or longevity.[97] The argument is that this quandary "forces" couples into covenant marriages, therefore artificially inflating the numbers. Of course, there could be a movement in the other direction, with covenant marriage taken as political symbolism rather than an option many people would actually like to take.[98] Louisiana and Arizona would then merely have articulated a higher standard exemplifying the "expressive function" of law.[99] This is hardly a problem. Assuming, however, that the law does more than this, and that more than a token number will elect covenant marriage, more married partners will have an incentive to behave better to each other,[100] which seems a good thing.

WOMEN IN COVENANT MARRIAGES MAY BE HURT BY POWER IMBALANCES? The major feminist objection to the covenant option is that making divorce more difficult will enhance the power imbalance they find in many, if not most,[101] current marriages.[102] Women in deeply troubled relationships who would otherwise obtain no-fault divorces might not be able to prove fault, or might be afraid to seek a divorce based on fault grounds, particularly cruelty. Because women are generally in a less secure financial position than men,[103] they might not be able to get equally good legal assistance prior to divorce, including the expert witnesses they might need to prove cruelty or intoxication, for example. They therefore might have to "trade" property or other financial resources simply in order to escape. Or a woman might have to endure increasing amounts of abuse at her husband's hand.[104] These are all ex post power problems, and they are not new ones.

In the 1960s, before no-fault divorce was available, the definitions of fault expanded to meet the growing demand for relief. In Illinois, New York, and Texas, three large states that prior to no-fault had quite strict grounds for divorce on the books, "cruelty" could in fact be shown on what many would consider rather trivial grounds.[105] Presumably the expansion was necessary to relieve the pressure on marriage. Because covenant marriage states will still allow divorce after a lengthy separation period without proof of fault, and because American society is much more mobile than it was forty years ago, in practice divorce will be possible for all but the most indigent citizens. Women or others disadvantaged by lack of power in their relationships will nevertheless be able to exit them. Whether social mores in the states that provide the covenant option will be such that divorce is *practically speaking* impossible is another question. The "enslavement" of women in abusive marriages painted by opponents of covenant marriage and fault divorce is clearly not an attractive picture. My work with Steven Crafton[106] on the difference in levels of abuse between states retaining the concept of fault divorce and those eliminating it would at least cast some doubt on that possibility.[107] Our research suggests that alimony or other monetary penalty for opportunistic behavior both decreases problems such as child abuse and increases investments in marriage, such as having children.

One other question involving marital power remains: Would those who elect covenant marriages be more likely to abuse their spouse? The supporters of covenant marriage frequently come from conservative religious households, where marriages tend to be more traditional than among other groups. In such marriages, where the husband is by biblical fiat the head of the household[108] and the wife is enjoined to submit to his authority,[109] there might be more abuse and fewer complaints about it.[110] This, of course, is an empirical question, and one for which data will be difficult to obtain.

THE EXTERNAL EFFECTS PRODUCED BY COVENANT MARRIAGES MAY BE HARMFUL.   Legislation involving families typically produces results that range far beyond the husband and wife. Children are the third parties most obviously affected by marriage and divorce legislation. Two features of the covenant marriage would seem to benefit the offspring of such a marriage. The first is that since fewer couples will divorce, and, since divorce almost always harms children, children will benefit.[111] The other interesting feature of the legislation is the inclusion of abuse directed against a child as a ground both for absolute (fault) divorce and for *a mensa* divorce (or separation from bed and board).[112] The only other state as of this writing which allows fault divorces where it is not the spouse but the child who is physically or sexually abused is West Virginia.[113] Since parents have a duty to protect their children from abuse (and can be found responsible for child abuse if they do not prevent it when they could have done),[114] they ought to be able to terminate the marriage, ending the abuse of the child, or at least making it much more difficult.

Covenant marriage should also foster the kind of permanence that would allow specific investments in the marriage,[115] ranging from financing a spouse's advanced degree to investing in children.[116] Steven Crafton and I have noted that the divorce revolution had also produced considerable litigation involving investments in a spouse's education where the benefits were not realized before the marriage dissolved.[117] We posited that this increase in litigation was not coincidental, but that it arose primarily from increased awareness (among courts and lawyers) of the role human capital plays in creating wealth.[118] The litigation may also stem from the increase in no-fault divorce, for if there is no financial incentive *not* to leave (and behave opportunistically), more spouses with advanced degrees should be expected to do so.

In an important early theoretical and empirical article on the economics of alimony,[119] Elisabeth Landes noted that alimony payments were lower in states with no-fault divorce than in those without. These findings have been replicated in work by Marsha Garrison,[120] Yoram Weiss and Robert Willis,[121] and my own work with Michael Alexeev,[122] not only for alimony but also for property distribution. To the extent that women and the children in their custody are disadvantaged by divorce,[123] the persistent "feminization of poverty," should decrease in regimes affording covenant marriage. The decrease should result from the lower rates of divorce (since married families are by all accounts financially the best off) and from the incremental difference that fault divorce seems to bring. Of course, women "at fault" would do less well, at least where alimony was concerned.[124]

As a final positive effect reaching beyond the couples involved, covenant marriage makes law coextensive with emotional realities. Later in this book I will argue that law occasionally pretends to cut off relationships that are destined, for biological or emotional reasons even more than financial ones, to be lifetime commitments.[125] Where children are involved, parents carry a shared interest in their offspring regardless of their legal status. Even where parents are no longer jointly raising their children, their lives may become so intertwined (through what Gary Becker would call specific investments in the marriage)[126] that a "clean break" divorce is not really possible.

Of course, legislation as unusual as the covenant marriage proposals has its opponents,[127] and some of them will undoubtedly make their arguments on the grounds of externalities. The most obvious objection, and one that has already been discussed in the popular media, is the specter of a return to the hypocrisy of the pre–no-fault era.[128] Divorce lawyers, whose status has arguably improved since the mid-1960s,[129] might once again counsel their clients to perjure themselves or contrive situations from which the spouse can sue for adultery.[130] A decline in both the prestige of the legal profession and the moral climate of the country could arguably result. This is certainly the position the American Law Institute takes in its 1966 *Principles of the Law of Family Dissolution*.[131] But certain features of the Louisiana and Arizona legislation make these fears unfounded. There is, after all, a bilateral release provision and escape after a lengthy separation rather than a prohibition against any divorce for the party at fault. The migratory divorce is a much less costly alternative than it was in the 1940s and 1950s, with a generally robust economy and provisions in all states other than Louisiana and Arizona for relief.[132] Spouses seeking the no-fault alternative could well expect financial penalties, however, since they might be barred by jurisdictional requirements from later seeking spousal support in the covenant marriage states,[133] and would in any event be violating their valid covenant promises, triggering relief under any premarital agreement the couple made.

A more subtle objection is that covenant marriage will support "traditional" marriages in which the man works in the paid labor force while his wife shuns such employment in favor of domesticity.[134] In economic terms, covenant marriage would encourage too much specialization along gender lines to please many feminists.[135] More equality in marriage implies more economic power for women, which cannot be obtained when wives specialize in the marriage more than their husbands. At this point discussions necessarily veer from economics into the political realm. The principle that individuals ought to be able to choose their own balance between labor force and family provides at least a free market solution to the problem.

Implications of Economics for Same-Sex Couples

Quite a different facet of the relational contracting problem is seen in the contrast between heterosexual cohabitation and long-term relationships between couples of the same sex.[136] Heterosexual couples may write cohabitation contracts to avoid marriage default rules, and specifically the interdependence that marriage encourages. A minority will not be able to marry, and so will try to replicate the forms of marriage in their contracts. Most, or at least many, same-sex couples may also want to replicate marriage and the interdependence and intimacy it allows.[137] Some of these presumably are the same persons who seek marriage licenses.[138] Others may wish to adopt or otherwise raise children. They seek stability, the benefits of two incomes, and intimacy.[139]

The remainder of same-sex couples seeking marriage may actually shun traditional institutions and prefer relationships that encourage independence and individuality. They may be most interested in receiving the public benefits currently enjoyed only by married couples rather than the property rights or private support that could be secured by contract.[140] Given the current legal structure, contracting options for these couples either would be nonexistent or would resemble the cohabitation contracts of heterosexuals.

If this set of assumptions has merit, the questions then become very interesting. For example, one (noneconomic) problem with antenuptial contracting is that such micromanagement may itself harm the relationship. When people are in love, they do not want to get involved in complete contingent claims contracting.[141] Besides, predicting the future is impossible, especially predicting what people are going to be like over the very long term. Thus a minimalist approach is attractive, except that for nonmarital relationships, the default (no legal protection) is undesirable. The implicit contract expressed in a same-sex commitment ceremony may be recognized by the community.[142] What aspects of marriage are necessary, then, to promote interdependence and intimacy? Which of these can be the subjects of contract, or at any rate enforceable contract, for cohabitants? One way to approach this question is to examine the terms that married couples cannot (enforceably) agree to vary. The first two that spring to mind involve support: mutual support and support of children. These terms may be the most popular in cohabitation contracts of the quasi-marriage variety, for it is the provisions for mutual support that provide the security needed for interdependence, and many same-sex couples approach marriage-like relationships with the hope (or sometimes the reality) of being parents. As we will see in Chapter 4, it is parenting, even more than a division of household tasks, that causes opportunity losses in the labor market. Support terms are more apt to be enforced if the agreement is taken to court.[143]

Other terms that are central (though married people may vary them) but are less certain of enforcement include those of cohabitation and exclusivity. Some married people live on opposite sides of the country and meet occasionally. Some are forced apart by employment or service in the military. People in relationships write agreements mostly because they want to live together.[144] Similarly, married couples theoretically can have "open marriages" in which both are free to pursue sexual relationships outside the marriage. Even in states where this behavior is not criminal,[145] however, it is hardly reflective of the kind of relationship most married people want. In jurisdictions that retain fault concepts (and most of them do), breach of the core promises to live together and to remain sexually faithful will have consequences in terms of divorce or allocation of support or property, but will not typically support a suit in tort.

For same-sex couples, enforcement of these positive provisions is much more problematic. In some jurisdictions the underlying sexual relationship may itself be illegal.[146] In many others, though it is not criminal, the sexual component of the relationship cannot be a significant part of the contract in order for it to be enforceable at all. This may be because nonmarital sexual relationships are against public policy,[147] or because then the entire relationship is seen as akin to prostitution or payment for sexual services.[148]

Thus the cohabitant whose partner has breached may be left without the remedy of divorce (which is available to married couples, and which allows property division and vindication of innocence in fault states) or contract damages (which are available to most non-breaching parties to an enforceable commercial contract). Of course, specific performance of intimate behavior is not available as a practical matter to anyone.[149] What good, then, is the contract?

What the parties may be bargaining for is some sort of pledge or liquidated (preset) damages that would automatically be transferred to the non-breaching party, or for an automatic referral to a third-party neutral. Liquidated damages themselves would not work because they would require court enforcement,[150] which will not usually be available in cases of breach of the terms of intimacy. The enforcement mechanism must, then, be extrajudicial, though the mechanism itself ought to be enforceable.[151] The third-party neutral (arbitrator or mediator) I have suggested would be a member of the relevant community. He or she could be designated in advance, or a panel of such neutrals (or an interest group association given power to designate) could be referred to in the agreement. This third party could hold the contracting parties' bond in escrow and release it to whichever partner did not breach.[152] Or arbitration could be made binding, so a sum stipulated in the original agreement would be awarded or not as the neutral decided.

Why would this mechanism work when it is not used in marriage (except, perhaps, in cases where the parties agree to refer their differences to religious tribunals)? As Jennifer Brown has noted, members of the gay and lesbian community tend to have higher-than-average levels of education and at least a middle-class income.[153] (It may be *because* they are middle class that they seek to marry or otherwise become involved in long-term, committed relationships.)[154] There may well be greater bargaining equality for same-sex couples considering cohabitation agreements than for heterosexual couples considering marriage. As Gary Becker has noted, much of the differentiation in roles that will occur after a couple marries is encouraged by human capital investments made prior to marriage.[155] Many same-sex couples will have invested equally in the training and education typical of their gender, and whatever gender discrimination (or sexual orientation discrimination) is present in job markets presumably will affect each partner equally. Another reason why these couples may be more likely to be able to post bonds or stipulate to reasonably large damages is that they tend to be older than the typical heterosexual couple, and therefore will have accumulated more wealth.[156]

The mechanism for enforcement, and the need for contracts at all, will be influenced by what the parties hope to accomplish through the agreement and the relationship. One central question will be whether they plan or hope to have children, and if so, whether they want to provide for that possibility at the outset or through a later agreement. (Because the duty to support children is normally tied to biological relationships, most heterosexual couples do not have to include in their contracts provisions for support,[157] though they may if one of the parties already has children from a prior relationship and the other biological parent is deceased, uninterested, or unfit.)[158]

Once children arrive, even same-sex couples are more likely to specialize than if they remained childless, since, as we will see in Chapter 5, child rearing requires flexibility. It is possible, of course, for the parties to share child rearing and labor force responsibilities equally; it just does not occur often.[159] When the partners specialize, there should be provision for the spouse who does more child care and less work for financial gain.

For the rest of the same-sex couples, there will be a marked resemblance to the cohabitation agreements others have written about.[160] There may be provisions for children from prior relationships. The parties may agree on which property to keep separate and which to commingle. They may agree who is to purchase health insurance (if the partner can be made a beneficiary according to the employer or other insurance provider). They may agree on how their current income will be spent, and even on who will do the shopping, who the bill paying, who the car maintenance.[161] They may provide for vacations or for visits by family members or old college friends. But too much of this type of specification leads to bitterness rather than preventing arguments.

In the glow of love, it hurts to plan too much and to overanalyze. The haggling over terms may itself raise doubts about one's intentions (and is thus a kind of negative signal). People change over time, in any event, and these contracts are designed in the hope that they will endure for years. Finally, perhaps people simply need some territory over which to bicker in the future.

Remarriage: The Question of Secondary Marriage Markets

The secondary marriage market involves the remarriage of people whose previous marriage ended in death or divorce. Several studies show that most divorced people remarry within five years of the original dissolution, although remarriage is swifter and more likely for men.[162] The presence of children makes remarriage more difficult for the custodial parent, usually the mother. The presence of children from a prior marriage is also correlated positively with the breakup of the subsequent relationship.

In general, as Lloyd Cohen and others have shown, a first marriage ending in divorce enhances the husband's chances of a second marriage,[163] in part because the husband's nonspecific human capital (earning capacity) has increased because of support received during the first marriage. For a woman, according to Cohen, the situation is reversed. She frequently has expended her human capital or allowed her labor force skills to depreciate, particularly if she stayed out of the labor force for some time or accommodated her work schedule to care for children. For divorced people who hope to remarry, potential spouses may well be concerned about their ability to remain married.

Contracts Regulating Marriage: Antenuptial Agreements

Private agreements regulating aspects of marriage will be discussed in depth in Chapter 4. Most often they are executed prior to marriage, when they are called antenuptial or premarital agreements. Marriage contracts may also be executed during the marriage.[164]

For now it will suffice to say that there are legal and nonlegal constraints on any version of these contracts. Couples may not vary the essential terms of the marriage contract, such as mutual support during the marriage.[165] The contracts will be unenforceable if they attempt to regulate the couple's intimate behavior,[166] or if they violate public policy, for example, by "facilitating and encouraging divorce."[167]

Nonlegal barriers include the fact that these memorials of long-term contractual relations necessarily leave many terms incomplete for later interpretation.[168] Courts will infer the marital "default rules" (the standard provisions such as monogamy, fidelity, and mutual support) from the marriage vows whenever possible, but couples must understand that, as with Oliver Williamson's "bounded rationality,"[169] they cannot contemplate *ex ante* all aspects of their relationship.

In fact, as we saw at the beginning of this chapter, engaged couples may have complete knowledge of the frequency and effects of divorce[170] but no expectation that their own marriage may end unhappily.[171] Generally, worse-than-predicted outcomes will not justify contractual relief, even when the losses are extremely large, for the risks of nonperformance are supposed to be reflected in any contract's price.[172] In this situation, when there is no explicit pricing, the parties are engaging in a "willing suspension of disbelief," for it would be unreasonable for them to marry thinking that the likelihood of divorce in their case is substantial.[173] They therefore suppress any uneasy feelings about the impending marriage.[174]

The other extralegal constraint is that the very fact of negotiating the contract may be threatening to the relationship itself. It is unromantic to contemplate divorce and death and to haggle over a detailed agreement on the eve of a wedding, and to do so may signal undesirable qualities about one self. The couples that choose to do so are weighing these costs of negotiation and agreement against the benefits that may follow private modification of the default marriage contract. As the Virginia Supreme Court reasoned many years ago: "Not business or money, but wedlock is what the parties contemplate. They are, or should be, motivated by love and affection to form a mutual and voluntary compact to live together as husband and wife, until separated by death, for the purpose of mutual happiness, establishing a family, the continuance of the race, the propagation of children, and the general good of society".[175]

Once the parties marry, they enter into what the nineteenth-century commentator Joel Bishop called a status: "Marriage, as distinguished from the agreement to marry and from the act of becoming married, is the civil status of one man and one woman united in law for life."[176] When the contract to marry is executed by the marriage, "a relation between the parties is created which they cannot change. Other contracts may be modified, restricted, or enlarged, or entirely released upon the consent of the parties. Not so with marriage."[177]

Can Promises to Marry Be Enforced?

The breach of promise suit entitled a woman disadvantaged because her fiancé had broken their engagement to sue him in assumpsit for damages, including the actual expenses she had incurred in relying on the marriage, and, additionally, for her embarrassment, humiliation, and loss of other market opportunities.[178] The remedy belonged only to the woman because, as will become apparent, her losses on the marriage market vastly exceeded the man's. Damages in breach of promise actions where seduction (sexual intercourse) had occurred were far more substantial than in cases where no sexual intimacy was alleged.[179] The trials themselves frequently became public spectacles because of testimony regarding the woman's previous chastity (or lack of the same). By the beginning of the Great Depression, the breach of promise suit came to be regarded as legally sanctioned blackmail, a threat to marriage and the family.[180]

In 1935 a woman legislator in Indiana sponsored a bill abolishing the "heart balm" actions in that state. Almost immediately thereafter, fueled by a sensationalist newspaper campaign, similar statutes were passed in most of the other major urban jurisdictions, so that by 1945, sixteen states had eliminated breach of marriage promise.[181] Today, there are only scattered reports of breach of marriage promise decisions from those few jurisdictions where the action remains viable.[182] A contemporary commentator speculated that the explanation for the law abolishing heart balm actions including breach of marriage promise was probably a "realization of the failure of these actions to accomplish their original social purposes, and their non-conformity with changed mores concerning sexual morality, the status of women, and the functions of the family."[183]

With the demise of the breach of promise action, women gave up an important property right. The social impact of a broken engagement, however, remained the same: women suffered far greater opportunity costs than their fiancés. A very important promise was now no longer legally enforceable. What, then, would encourage engaged couples to marry, making the costs of breach more equal for men and women? One intriguing suggestion made by Yale law professor Anthony Kronman is that when a legal remedy disappears, one may expect to find a movement toward some nonlegal institution that would have the same effect: a bond, perhaps; the building of a relationship between the parties; a hostage taken; or hands-tying behavior.[184] In this case a particular type of collateral, valuable to any holder, had been theoretically available since the late 1880s: the diamond engagement ring.

An empirical study of the change in demand for the diamonds used in engagement rings relative to the abolition of the other bonding device, the breach of promise action,[185] shows a significant relationship. The data indicate that four factors explain much of the increase in the demand for diamonds in the period 1935–1960. The most important explanatory variable is the abolition of the breach of promise action, although the increased population of marriageable age was also significant. Diamonds were also used as investment devices during World War II. A "dummy variable" (a factor taking the value 1 during the war, 0 otherwise), however, was negatively related to demand, suggesting that the hardships and absences caused by the war had a greater effect on demand than the desire to purchase diamonds as investment instruments.[186]

An alternative way of testing the hypothesis that engagement rings serve as pledges is to see what happened to the demand for rings when social mores changed so that sexual intimacy was no longer confined to marriage and engagement. Although from 1965 to 1980 real per capita income continued to increase, the demand for engagement rings leveled off and actually decreased for the more recent period, when cohabitation of nonmarried couples was no longer a curiosity.[187]

Recently, the demand for engagement rings has changed because the wearing of a diamond symbolic of engagement is no longer a prerequisite to premarital intimacy, and because the cost to a woman of a broken engagement is no longer as significant as it once was. The marriage rate has declined as more women enter the job market and more couples postpone marriage until their education is complete and their careers are established. Since sexual activity for women is not so completely confined to marriage, the need for a bonding device before consent to intercourse is greatly diminished. Diamond suppliers have had to reach out to a new market, advertising wedding bands, anniversary rings, and other diamond jewelry. Recently, too, the action for return of engagement rings has become less settled. Some states now consider the ring a gift conditioned on marriage, so that it must be returned if the marriage does not ensue, regardless of who called off the engagement.[188]

Some couples do well without marriage, whether in the explicit market that constitutes courtship, the more focused exchange that takes place in long-term cohabitation, or in the extramarital partnerships governed by contract. We may well wrestle, then, as the California Supreme Court did in *Marvin v. Marvin*,[189] with whether marriage as an institution remains necessary.

One thing we know empirically is that cohabitation relationships (excluding monogamous same-sex relationships) last, on average, for a far shorter time than conventional marriages. According to demographers,[190] only one third of cohabiting unions last two years. After that, couples either break up or decide to marry. Marriages, even when they terminate in divorce, last on average over seven years.[191] This statistic suggests several ramifications. One is that cohabitants are reentering the marriage market and will presumably continue their searches for the ideal mate, hoping to reach a better outcome. This could be seen as a reason to encourage such relationships.

The other externalities are more negative. First, when couples end their cohabitation arrangements by marrying, the marriages are surprisingly statistically less stable: couples who cohabit before marriage divorce, on average, with a much higher frequency than those who do not.[192] This contradicts the information theory of Becker and his colleagues, who predicted more stability because of the longer and more thorough search.[193] Finally, if the cohabiting couple produce children and then separate, the consequences for both child and custodial parent (who is, even more frequently than after divorce, the woman) are sorry indeed.[194] The absent parent tends to become distanced from the child, and tends to feel even less responsibility to pay child support than those ordered to do so by a divorce court. The average custodial mother, who likely has a very young child at this point, will have difficulties pursuing a job or education. Because of the child's presence, she will have difficulties meeting or attracting a marriage partner. Marriage as an institution works far better for protecting children's interests as well as, secondarily, the interests of those who care for the children. Even though marriage may no longer be deemed important to protect chastity or family holdings in land, its other external functions—protecting investment in the relationship and ensuring the well-being of children—justify state intrusion into couples' marriage market decisions.

Because, strictly speaking, contracts cannot be enforced once the parties enter into marriage,[195] I will move to a new metaphor, the covenant, when I resume my discussion of marriage in Chapter 4. In this relatively unchangeable covenantal relationship, the individual interests of the spouses will still be important, but may be subordinated to those of the marriage itself, or of the couple's children. There is another area of family law where contract and market is still the dominant paradigm. In the next chapter, then, we consider the creation of the parent-child relationship, a situation in which the contracts, of course, apply only to the adults.

3

Becoming Parents

This chapter, like Chapter 2, deals with the formation of families. We have already seen in the context of courtship that before families are created, the people involved act primarily as individuals. They thus exhibit contract-like behavior rather than the firm-like behavior we see once their families are functioning. Although in this chapter we will again observe activities that in some respects resemble the search for consumer goods, we must recognize that people creating families are far more engaged and involved than even the most enthusiastic consumers. Further, the adults who determine the kinds of families in which their children will be raised are not simply contracting, for their decisions and actions will profoundly affect parties who are silent in the transaction: the children themselves.

When we think of babies, perhaps even more than when we think of marriage, we do not usually envision markets. In families where adoption occurs, however, there are explicit markets, as we shall see shortly. Even for the majority of parents who are able to conceive their own children, this involves economic behavior. For single women, for example, the decision whether or not to bear and raise the child is in part an economic one.

In thinking about whether to have children, married couples must consider the effect on each spouse's earning capacity. For some women, staying at home and rearing children will permanently affect their lifetime earnings as well as their current income. For even more women, the opportunity cost will be reflected in more flexible employment, with perhaps a temporary hiatus in labor force participation. Fathers may have to accept more work responsibility, work longer hours, or even begin a second job in order to support their dependents. Further, the Census Bureau reported in 1997 that when mothers work outside the home, 18.5 percent of child care is provided by fathers.[1]

In most families, then, the "market" for babies is already at work even before the child is conceived. Parents select the genetic qualities of their children when they select each other as marriage or sexual partners. They also exercise some degree of control over the type of offspring they produce by choosing the moment for reproduction, since the difficulty of conception and the incidence of genetic problems both increase with the age of the mother. Some biological evidence suggests that a woman can influence the likelihood of conception not only through the use of contraception but also through the type of orgasm she experiences during the intercourse leading to conception.[2] The timing of intercourse during the menstrual cycle also influences the probability of conceiving a male as opposed to a female infant.[3]

Other children in the family, consciously or not, may influence the incidence of conception, as they will compete for the same family resources once a new baby is born.[4] Nursing a child can delay the onset of menstruation, and thus the possibility of another conception. The very presence of a child in the family may make the parents more tired, so that intercourse occurs less frequently than before the child was born. Children may also attempt to monopolize the affections of at least one parent, interrupt the parents during the times when intercourse would otherwise occur, or even cause so much trouble that having another child is not an attractive decision.

Investing in Children: Fertility

A large volume of literature, beginning with the work of Gary Becker, analyzes fertility behavior among women of past and present societies.[5] The number of children born to American women declined dramatically once contraceptives became effective and abortion legal. Both of these medical changes were accompanied by legal changes, as the Supreme Court developed a right to privacy that encompassed contraceptive use[6] and abortion choice.[7] In this country, since the early abortion cases, most of the forces shaping fertility behavior have been economic as opposed to legal.

The traditional economic reasons for having large numbers of children (a high infant mortality rate requiring many births before a single child would survive to adulthood, or an agricultural economy requiring large families to work the acreage)[8] have been irrelevant for many years. As Becker explains it, what has replaced the need for *quantity* is an emphasis on the *quality* of children.[9] In other words, instead of having more children, we invest more time and money in the smaller number of children we do have.

Abortion aside, there are still some ways in which the law might profoundly influence fertility: no-fault divorce, the regulation of reproductive technology, legislation regulating public assistance for mothers of dependent children, and, theoretically, more direct policies such as those in place in China.[10] I will give some time to the question of single mothers later in this chapter, but it is worthwhile to note briefly the less than obvious effect of no-fault divorce on the birthrate.

In "Marriage and Opportunism,"[11] Steven Crafton and I found that holding time and the number of marriages constant, for the period 1965–1987, no-fault divorce had a significant negative relationship to the birthrate. We explained this result as evidence of a decreased investment by couples in their marriages as these became less secure. Another way of looking at the same phenomenon is to consider the thinking of a married woman considering or confronting pregnancy who realizes that her marriage is unstable. At a time when divorce was quite difficult to obtain and carried a substantial stigma, the birth of a child might have seemed a stabilizing influence. Today, however, most women would be reluctant to bring children into an unhappy family.[12] Bur perhaps more significant, the married woman might well elect not to conceive or bear a child because of the additional costs the child would bring should the couple divorce. Divorced women with minor children remarry less frequently than those without.[13] It is also more difficult for a woman with small children to be economically self-sustaining, since employment must usually be more flexible for the single-parent custodian.[14]

The Market for Babies: Adoption

Various factors have led to a decline in fertility. Many couples are now marrying later and are actively preventing conception until later in the marriage. Also, infertility may be induced by certain drugs taken many years earlier by the couple's parents (the would-be grandparents). These factors are counteracted to some extent by technological progress in the area of infertility, but in any event, couples are increasingly discovering difficulties in conceiving a child. As a result, the demand for adopted children has increased dramatically since the mid-1970s while, at the same time, the supply of available babies has decreased.

Probably the most important factor affecting the supply of children for the adoption market has been the ready availability of abortion.[15] Yet another cause is the increasing societal acceptance of unwed or single parenthood, encouraging women who might otherwise have given their children up for adoption to carry them to term and raise them instead.[16] Further, the modern emphasis on the rights of natural parents has slowed the supply of children available for adoption. Both because it has become so difficult to prove permanent parental unfitness[17] and because the social work caseload has expanded geometrically, making the investigation process grind more slowly,[18] there are fewer and fewer children to adopt. Instead, in the absence of sufficient evidence to terminate parental rights, the children remain in foster care, sometimes indefinitely, while the parents maintain a token relationship with them.[19]

The increased demand and decreased supply coincide in a market lacking the expected price increase that would equate the numbers of parents demanding and supplying children. All states prohibit the explicit selling of a child as well as any payments made directly to or through middlemen that are not directly connected to maintaining the well-being of the child. The result is analogous to other cases in which government imposes a price ceiling: a shortage develops, with a growing queue of parents wishing to adopt.[20] Typically, a market with such supply shortages also sees the rise of a black market in the scarce commodity. The market for adoptable babies is no exception.[21]

Richard Posner has suggested that a market in babies would rectify many of the problems with the adoption system.[22] His idea provoked a tremendous reaction.[23] Posner's critics proclaimed that the sale of children would reduce the children, or their mothers, to commodities.[24] Further, unscrupulous but wealthy parents might purchase children to abuse them.[25] Ultimately "baby selling" became a code word for the foolish extreme to which its proponents could carry law and economics.[26]

Posner's suggestion nevertheless did not usher in either a highly regulated legal adoption market or its byproduct, the black market.

What Posner proposed was that the legalization of compensation would benefit most of the players in the adoption market. In the free market he describes, the supply of adoptable babies would increase, given a legal market price.[27] Adoptive parents would acquire the children they so badly desire. Birth mothers would suffer less because they would be compensated for bearing the children.[28] Since the market would provide incentives for pregnant women to take better care of themselves, the children also would be healthier.[29] Arguably, fewer women would terminate unplanned pregnancies by abortion.[30] Finally, the children would go to the parents who valued them most, as evidenced by their willingness to pay the contract price, or by the mother's willingness to forgo the income should she decide to keep the child.

Although Posner's idea of an implicit adoption market received immediate attention, some of the other economic ramifications remain largely unexplored. Child custody statutes and decisions begin with a "best interests of the child" standard[31] but end with choosing the interests of one parent or one set of parents.[32] Some analysts accomplish this sleight of hand by presumption, but presumption is simply the law's condoning a certain set of adult interests.[33] Sometimes the rationale is more explicit: for example, according to *May v. Anderson,* jurisdiction to decide a divorce "does not give Wisconsin, certainly as against Ohio, the personal jurisdiction that it must have in order to deprive [the] mother of her personal right to [the] immediate possession" of her children.[34] Frequently the child suffers if the birth parent can change his or her mind numerous times or late in the process, keeping the child in foster care.[35]

Although Posner briefly addresses concerns about abusive adoptive parents[36] and a potential oversupply of older or handicapped children,[37] he concentrates on the benefits a market price confers on parents. Thus, although the adoption market would have many buyers and sellers, it would remain regulated by the screening agencies, in Posner's view. These institutions would reduce the chance that parents would acquire children to abuse them.[38] Agencies could also match birth and adoptive parents, reducing search costs for both parties to the transaction.[39]

Even though he is keenly aware of the costs of regulation in other contexts,[40] Posner does not spend much time discussing the welfare losses caused by adoption agency regulation. These costs are by no means unique to Posner's adoption market. They are also part of what makes the current adoption system so frustrating. In the current system agencies, not price, act to ration the scarce resource of adoptable children among the many potential parents who want them.[41] In Posner's system, price would be the primary mechanism for allocating children; agencies would serve only a threshold screening function rather than an allocating one.

Agencies do guard against abuse by adoptive parents, though in general they dramatically increase transaction costs for both sets of parents.

Agency investigations not only are expensive and annoying but also add greatly to the amount of time required for adoption.[42] And because only the final order of adoption prevents the birth parents from revoking consent in many jurisdictions, the six-month minimum waiting period while agencies investigate the prospective parents adds uncertainty to the transaction.[43] Thus, the transaction costs imposed by legislatures to protect natural parents' custodial rights and ensure suitability of adoptive couples may hurt more children than they assist. Virtually all couples trying to adopt children are found suitable.[44] Further, as Posner noted, we have no corresponding *ex ante* checks on natural parents who do not adopt.[45] Because there is no real way to predict what kind of parents most childless couples will make, agencies make errors of overinclusion and underinclusion, releasing some children who would be better off not placed with particular parents while preventing some fit parents from adopting.

Secondary Markets: Principals, Agents, and the Problems of Foster Care

Many children (several thousand in the District of Columbia alone) live not under their parents' care and protection but under that of state agencies. In the not so distant past, most children whose parents could not care for them would have remained in their families, living with uncles, aunts, or grandparents until they could fend for themselves.[46] In some parts of the country, boys in particular would have been apprenticed at a fairly early age to learn a useful trade. Only in cases of the very last resort would the family have relied on public help, and that would have come in the form of a foundling home or orphanage.[47] These institutions were grim enough to inspire a wave of nineteenth-century reform as well as immortalization in the tales of Dickens and the cartoon character Little Orphan Annie.

The reformers, many of them women also connected with the abolitionist movement, sought several improvements. First, they wanted to make the institutions themselves more palatable, eliminating vestiges of sweatshop labor and replacing work with education. On a more global scale, the reformers tried to eliminate some of the social conditions that had spawned the orphanages in the first place. They "resettled" immigrants, pushed for free public education, and later lobbied for a guaranteed minimum wage. They also sought to replace the asylum with community-based care as close as possible to the child's lost home. Thus the formal foster care system was born.

The idea behind foster care is that trained adults with experience as parents take in children from families unable to cope with them. They will tend the children on a temporary basis in a loving and stable situation and prepare them for their return to their own families, who have meanwhile been provided with community assistance.[48] In extreme cases, when parents are unwilling or unable to resume their relationship with their offspring, new (adoptive) homes will take the parents' place. The foster relationship begins with a contract between the state and the foster parents, one that assures all parties that the relationship is temporary. It normally provides that compensation will be paid to the foster parents, that inspection of the foster home is to be expected, and that the child can be removed for return to the natural parent or to another foster home according to the agency's discretion.[49]

Foster care was designed to be temporary, and was therefore never expected to be anything but a "second best" solution. Instead, for a tragic number of children who are never returned to their birth parents or adopted by others it has become a permanent way of life.[50] This seems to be especially true of African American children, who are frequently placed with relatives for "kinship care."[51] Foster children may be cycled through a number of foster families for reasons I will consider presently, so that they never gain a sense of attachment and stability.[52] In some metropolitan areas, the District of Columbia among them, the system has become overwhelmed by the scope and depth of the child welfare problem.[53]

From an economic standpoint, foster care presents a classic principal and agent problem, with the unhappy result being exactly what this model predicts where agents do not have appropriate incentives.[54] The theoretical solution for foster care problems is to correct the incentive incompatibility. But it is difficult to do so when the agents' duties involve vulnerable human beings and when the overseers are government agencies, which also have conflicting missions.

The definition of principal and agent given by economists is quite similar to that of attorneys. As Stephen Ross describes it,[55] an agency relationship arises between two or more parties when one, the agent, "acts for, on behalf of, or as representative for the other, designated the principal, in a particular domain of decision problems."[56]

The general idea can be illustrated by a simple example.[57] One summer my car's air conditioner stopped running. I took the car in to my neighborhood gas station and asked the mechanics to fix it. I did not know what the problem was: it may have needed only to have a fuse replaced and recharged with freon, or the compressor motor repaired, or the entire compressor replaced. These jobs cost $50, $129, and $691, respectively. Ultimately the repair shop replaced the entire unit.

In this relationship I, as the principal, engaged the repair shop as my agent. My intent was simply to have the air conditioner repaired as quickly and cheaply as possible. The repair shop's incentives were different. They wanted to make as much money as possible on this particular transaction while still retaining me as a customer. They succeeded: they chose to replace the compressor, and I have returned as a customer. In this and many other examples of contracts, a principal-agent "problem" arises from information asymmetry.[58] I could not know whether each component of the repair had been necessary; all I knew was that the air conditioner now worked.[59] While it is possible to get a "second opinion," or go to another repair shop, it is not always practical or financially sensible to do so. In addition, the repair might have cost too much owing to shirking—the gas station employees might have worked very slowly, requiring more labor hours than necessary—or they might have performed sloppy work such as not properly refastening the car's carpeting on completion of the job. The principal-agent problems in such contracts are usually worked out through the price, which will contain both fixed and variable components.[60] Finally, there is usually a guarantee: if the machine is not repaired properly, the work will be redone at a reduced charge.

The concepts of principal and agent, along with the theoretical solutions to the problem, have been extended to law primarily in the business context.[61] Reduced to its simplest terms, combining multiple workers[62] will take advantage of economies of specialization and scale[63] and will reduce transaction costs.[64] As we will see in Chapter 4, the firm has thus been described as a nexus of contracts.[65] Nevertheless, when the amount of effort each worker-agent contributes to the joint production of a unit of output cannot be measured, the rational worker will shirk, free-riding on the others because the loss in his or her compensation will be less than the reduction in contribution.[66] In order to reduce this tendency to shirk, managers monitor each employee's performance. If salaries are sufficiently higher than unemployment compensation, employees will work harder to avoid losing their jobs.[67] The theory is that the residual, or profit, should go to the one who employs the monitor: the principal-owner. In the partnership context this is the also the manager. In corporations the owners are stockholders.

In an extension of the principal-agent theory to the field of fiduciaries, Robert Cooter and Bradley Freedman have argued that the fiduciary is like the agent and the beneficiary like the principal.[68] The law has developed to discourage fiduciary misfeasance (the duty of loyalty) as well as nonfeasance (the duty of care). Cooter and Freedman suggest that compensation according to a variable rate for observable effort and a fixed rate for unobserved effort will discourage these problems.[69]

The concept of principal and agent promises to thin out the impenetrable foster care thicket. The foster parent becomes the agent of the birth parent (or the state, if the parent is permanently unfit) and also the child, who is something like a third-party beneficiary of the adults' promises. Like the agents in the car repair and business problems, the foster caretakers have incentives to shirk or even neglect the child in their care. They are held back by their own sense of duty, the effects of reputation (on potential for future foster placements), and, most important, the affection they develop for the child in their care. One interesting question revolves around the identity of the principal. If we emphasize the relationship between promisor and beneficiary, the child is seen as the principal. If we emphasize the intent of the contracting parties, the birth parent (or the state, where parental rights have been terminated) is the principal.

I would contend that both the parent (or state) and the child share the role of principal, acting rather like the two-headed monster on *Sesame Street* who often pulls in two different directions. When the two sets of interests coincide, the monster functions appropriately and the child is adequately cared for. When they differ, the beast is paralyzed, and the child suffers. If the interests of each head coincide, courts will enforce promises made on the child's behalf and duties that the agents ought to undertake. If not, however, the child will be without a remedy.

Another insight gained from third-party beneficiary cases such as the classic *Lawrence v. Fox*[70] is that one ought to determine whether there is constructive ratification by the third party (here, the foster child).[71] Ratification appears not in the attitudes of the foster parents but in the emotional bonds formed by the child. If the child is indelibly attached to the foster family, the state should not be permitted to move the child, particularly to another set of foster parents.[72] If the foster parents wish to adopt and the child concurs, concerns that the foster parents have "jumped the queue" should not eclipse the child's interests.

On looking more closely at the foster care question, we see two separate fiduciary problems. The first relationship is that between the foster parents and the state. Although both have an interest in seeing the child cared for, their incentives may not be the same. The custodial parent has day-to-day responsibility for the child, and the state (or the natural parent) cannot monitor the care effectively. The foster parent acts as a fiduciary, or agent, for the child's custody and the allocation of any money paid by the state.[73] The other perspective on the same problem, and the one that is most applicable for foster parent's rights, is that of the foster parent. From this vantage point, the state acts as an agent to provide guidance and support and to resolve any conflicts fairly. Finally, the child is always an implied beneficiary, or principal, looking to the foster parent for custodial services and to the state for support and resolution of the ultimate custody question.

Unlike the preceding analysis, cases and articles typically approach foster care from the birth parent's perspective.[74] The emphasis, then, is on parental rights, not on any harm to children that might result from their removal, or even their feelings about which set of parents would be better for them.[75] Occasionally, individual courts have changed their perspective to the state's, valuing whatever would advance the goals of the foster care system as a whole.[76]

When children are removed from a particular foster care placement, in many cases they do not have the same interests as any of the adults involved: their interests are not identical to those of the foster parents who have cared for them, the birth parents who may have abused or abandoned them or who may not have been "real" to the children for many years, or "The State," which may have removed them from the only home they ever knew and is now threatening to remove them again.

So long as the family remains intact, parents view the upbringing of their children as a joint enterprise, or "collective good."[77] They see how children thrive when they are appropriately cared for. They are rewarded by their children's smiles and hugs, and imitation of themselves as valued adults. When the family breaks up, however, and the children are placed elsewhere, the interests diverge. Although the parent may still love the child, and is usually required by law to support him or her, parent and child no longer reside together, and visitation may be infrequent.[78] The parent may be preoccupied with attempting to meet the conditions set before the child can return: securing employment, dealing with substance abuse problems, settling adult emotional relationships.[79] There are economic strains as well, in part because the family now maintains two households, eliminating economies of scale that were present before foster care placement.[80] Although income may stay the same, the parents are effectively poorer because of increased costs. Poverty, however, is not the crux of the problem; the difficulty is that the birth parents are no longer able to have day-to-day contact with their offspring. They cannot know exactly how the foster parents are caring for the child[81] and cannot watch him or her grow from close up.

Finally, because the birth parents live apart from their children and see them less frequently, even if not embittered by the removal of the children or any disputes regarding visitation rights,[82] the parent may lose interest in the children or become preoccupied with other things.[83] The parent would like to see the child happy in the new situation, but not so happy that the real home will be forgotten.

The state as agent has monitoring problems as well, although monitoring is usually required by the foster care contract. Too frequent visitation with foster parents, even if practicable from a staffing viewpoint, would disrupt the temporary family that foster care is designed to create.[84] The agencies are concerned, too, with "rehabilitating" the birth parents, and may also be overwhelmed by other truly horrible home situations in their caseload that require immediate intervention. Like the birth parents, the government agents are concerned that a good, but not great, relationship develop between foster child and foster parent. Thus the agency may be apt to remove children who have been with a particular family for some time, despite any harm to the child that may result.[85]

Using Cooter and Freedman's analogy to principal and agent,[86] we can say that the caring natural parent as principal fears that the foster parent, as agent, may shirk his or her responsibility, undermine the parent's standing in the child's eyes, or, worst of all, actually harm the child.[87] From the foster parent's perspective, the noncustodial birth parent is a complicated mixture of good and bad. At once the birth parent is the source of the child (who may be easy or very difficult to care for, depending on whether the parent was abusive or whether the child has other problems such as physical disabilities), the agent (for support), and source of the threat of removal. The state agency is placed in the difficult position of being at once an agent for the natural parent and an advocate (agent) for the child. Finally, of course, there is the child. If quite young, he or she may be a helpless pawn in this situation, desiring only love and some stability in life.[88] An older child may engage in substantial manipulation of the adults involved.[89] It is difficult to see how any contract could be written to give all these parties appropriate incentives.[90] Who are the "residual claimants"? Who can monitor compliance?

Here the noncustodial natural parent holds "title" to the child (except when rights have been permanently terminated or relinquished to the state), and pays (at least theoretically) for the child's custodial care.[91] The custodial (foster) parent serves as an agent for the provision of parenting services and holds "possession" of the child, to continue the property law terminology. The child normally cannot sue either set of parents or the state to terminate parental rights, change foster homes, or be reunited with the natural family.[92] One reason, aside from incapacity,[93] is that the child's side of the deal is not complete. The child continues to provide "child services" throughout minority. These include getting good grades at school, being obedient, and serving as good company. Because the *child's* performance is incomplete, courts will not enforce any of the various parental obligations.[94]

Moreover, as noted, the child and the various sets of parents do not have the same interests. Perhaps this is obvious, since children are concerned only about their own well-being, whereas parents must think about both their own consumption and the welfare of their children.[95] In the extreme, because giving up the child or having the child forcibly removed may have been very painful, the natural parent may want emotional distance from the child,[96] may avoid the child services agency, or may even want to hurt the child. If there is less visitation by a fit parent, both the parent and the child lose.[97]

"Bad" foster parents are those who care for children only to get the money they are paid by the state. They do not invest emotionally in the child, a failure that hurts the child. "Successful" foster parents are often at odds with state agencies precisely because they do invest and become attached. Since removal of the child will be costly for everyone involved, long-term foster placement will make adoption look tempting.[98] I agree with the amicus brief filed in the *Baby Richard* case, in which birth parents sought to overturn a long placement with prospective adoptive parents, that it is the child's vantage point that matters.[99]

To resolve the problems inherent in foster care because of its principal-agent problem, the law must make the players' incentives compatible. For the natural parent, there must be no "parental right" that will trump what is clearly best for the child. To prevent discretion and uncertainty from running amok, time limits must be set after which "rehabilitation" of the parent comes too late.[100] Making the agency's incentives compatible with those of either, let alone both, sets of parents (or even a third set if adoption is a possibility) is probably not feasible. But they could be made compatible with the child's interests in stability and safety.[101] This would require rethinking the goals of the foster care system. If it recognized that most children do not return successfully to their parents' care, and a time limitation were set, certainty could return to the system. Such a move would obviously require some new empirical work,[102] for there are questions without answers here. Questions that should be addressed in the future include: How many placements are voluntary? How many children return to their natural parents? Are these returns permanent? How often does abuse occur when families are reunited in this way? How many foster parents want to adopt the children placed with them?

A system with the types of reforms I have advocated, such as setting time limits and placing the emphasis on the child's preferences and best interests, might drastically reduce the number of voluntary placements. Apparently parents make "voluntary" placements in many cases because they feel that this is the only way to retain some control over the child, for otherwise the state might initiate action to remove the child involuntarily. If in fact "voluntary" is a euphemism in this context, reforms might increase the number of (costly) termination proceedings. An alternative solution, so-called open adoption, allows the placement to go forward without complete loss of the natural parent's relationship with the child. This possibility will be considered in Chapter 6.

Needless to say, children are not cars like the one my agent fixed in the illustration at the beginning of this discussion. Because they are not, the particular type of principal-agent relationship foster parents enjoy is fiduciary rather than market-like.[103] That is, the duties required of foster parents more closely resemble family duties than commercial ones: the foster parent, like the natural parent, must put the child's welfare before his or her own.

This hybrid relationship makes foster parent cases difficult for courts. Foster parents clearly differ from teachers or nannies or babysitters. Yet because the relationship is designed to be temporary, is incomplete ("title" remaining in the natural parent or the state), begins most often with a contract,[104] and carries with it some financial reward, foster parents do not have precisely the same rights and obligations as do natural parents.

Parents as Complements: The Single Mother

Children need parents to supply them with various kinds of material and emotional support: the basic necessities of life, education, good judgment, and a sense of trust and well-being. In a "first best" world, they need both a male and a female parent to fulfill their physical needs as well as their emotional ones. They need interested people to invest in their human capital in order to help them become productive in the future. Children are like subsurface minerals waiting to be mined. What is needed is the mine train and the mining equipment, but these require long-term contracts.

Men and women, meanwhile, are complementary factors in child rearing. Women may be more likely to perform their role without prodding (or channeling) than men. But, as Judith A. Seltzer[105] puts it: "For women, marriage and parenthood are distinct institutions. Women provide for children's needs, whether or not the women are married to their children's fathers. For men, marriage defines responsibilities to children. At divorce, men typically disengage from their biological children. When men remarry they may acquire new children whom they help to support."[106] Thus, men are likely to contribute in cash or in kind when they are certain of fatherhood, and when they can interact with the child.[107] They are more likely to invest when they have the ability to monitor the child, either through frequent contact or through trust of the maternal "agent." They are also more likely to keep their support commitments when they do not have a new family to distract them or drain financial resources. All of these reasons suggest why marriage, as opposed to some alternative family arrangement, is necessary for "first best" child rearing.[108] The distinct benefits of marriage suggest that children are not just factors to be ignored or non-actors whose preferences should be lumped in with their parents'.[109]

This argument accepts some of the premises advanced by writers such as Ira Lupu,[110] namely, that children rather than their parents ought to be central to any analysis of the family, and that having two parents presents advantages for the child. But after these agreements our roads diverge. Lupu sees the two parents as contesting and checking each other to ensure that the child is brought up well, with society intervening when they cannot or will not perform this mediating function. By contrast, I see the parents as complements working together and taking advantage of each other's differences: specializing, if you will.

The Price for Single Parenting: Welfare Subsidies

Despite the desirability of dual parenting and at a time when the overall birthrate has declined (see Figure 3.1), the number of children born to unmarried women (as a percentage of all births) has increased substantially since the 1970s, with the rate for white women nearly tripling and the rate for black women, always higher, continuing to increase (see cross-hatched lines in Figure 3.2).[111] During this period, many social commentators have argued that such trends were benign. Some touted the benefits of single motherhood,[112] while others argued that cultural conservatives should not impose their views of morality on indigent women responding rationally to their own environment.[113]

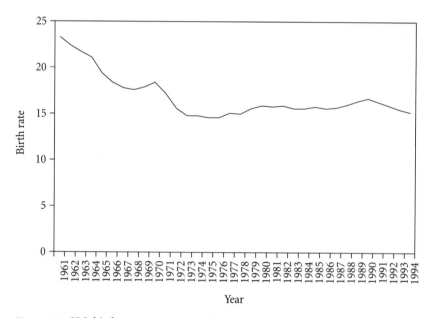

Figure 3.1 U.S. birth rates, 1961–1994 (source: U.S. Bureau of the Census, percent childless and births per thousand women in last year: selected years, 1976 to present; Internet release date, November 27, 1997)

There is persuasive evidence, however, that increased birthrates among unwed mothers should be viewed with alarm. The tocsin was first sounded in Daniel Patrick Moynihan's 1965 report on the decline of the black family.[114] Moynihan predicted that the increased birthrate among unwed black women would be followed by other social ills such as illiteracy, unemployment, crime, and drug addiction. Unfortunately, all of his predictions have come true. Reviewing these trends in the context of the 1995 welfare debate, Senator Moynihan noted that an "earthquake [has] shuddered through the American family" since the 1960s. "The rate of illegitimacy has nearly tripled in 30 years. No modern or ancient society has experienced such a situation."[115]

Studies suggest that the rise of unwed parenting is not benign. The absence of a father is seen as the single most significant cause of poverty.[116] Fathers who remain involved with their children provide strong role models, discipline, and a dependable source of income.[117] Without these benefits, children do much less well than those with married parents.[118] On average, girls born to unwed parents are either much shyer or much more promiscuous than those raised in two-parent homes.[119] Their male counterparts do worse in school,[120] are more aggressive,[121] and are more likely to break the law.[122] Children whose parents never marry are also more likely to become unmarried parents themselves.[123] Women who have children before they marry are more likely to have unstable marriages, perhaps because they cannot search as long or command as high a price on the marriage market as their childless counterparts.[124] Even if they divorce and remarry, a disproportionate amount of the apparent increase in child abuse occurs in second families.[125] Some research shows that children who grow up with stepfathers do not fare significantly better, at least psychologically, than those whose mothers do not remarry.[126]

The focus of attention has therefore shifted from the consequences to the causes of unwed births, and particularly to the role of welfare subsidies. The most direct subsidy to unwed parents in the United States was Aid to Families with Dependent Children (AFDC),[127] offering a cash subsidy to needy mothers of young children. In some states eligibility required that fathers could not be living with them, or in any case could not be fully supporting them. Most AFDC recipients were widowed or divorced rather than never married. Nevertheless, unwed births under the AFDC program rose dramatically, constituting about one third of all AFDC children by the time the program was abolished in 1996. In the District of Columbia at that time, about 80 percent of AFDC children were born to unwed mothers. In Virginia, the figure was 66 percent.[128]

From a basic economic perspective, it might seem uncontroversial to suggest that public assistance results in increased unwed births. Subsidize something and theoretically you will always get more of it. Critics of welfare reform argued, however, that AFDC cuts would not reduce unwed birthrates because they had not in the past, and so the cuts in welfare payouts would harm children without benefiting society.

The argument by some critics that the rise in unwed birthrates can be attributed solely to changing social norms is unpersuasive. First, the social norms might themselves be caused by increased births out of wedlock (what economists call endogenous effects), shaped in part by the welfare subsidy. Social norms were certainly stronger in the past, before the advent of public assistance programs. Brides were expected to be chaste when wed, and women who deviated from these norms paid a heavy social cost.[129] For many men, an extramarital pregnancy meant a hasty marriage.[130] But now the social sanction is far weaker for both men and women. Indeed, it becomes hard to talk of a social sanction in communities where more than half the births take place outside marriage.

Second, even if social norms are exogenous (not in any way affected by increased unwed birthrates), there is no reason to suppose that they explain all of the variations in unwed birthrates between states. It is as shortsighted to claim that economic incentives are irrelevant as it is to claim that social sanctions are irrelevant. Indeed, one would expect more unmarried women to respond to the monetary subsidy offered by AFDC as social norms weakened. When sanctions were stronger, the cost of single parenting was much higher. This path dependency argument might explain why unwed birthrates increased even while the real value of AFDC payouts declined after 1980: the decline in the social cost of unwed births had already altered the decision-making mechanism of the women in question.

Moreover, even though AFDC payments declined, the real value of other welfare payments increased (see Figure 3.2). Real per capita state and local public welfare expenditures (excluding those for education and for health and hospitals) increased from $209 per month in 1980 to $276 in 1989. Real payments also increased under federal and joint federal-state programs such as food stamps, school lunches, supplemental security income, and Medicaid. These increases largely offset AFDC cuts. For every dollar cut from AFDC between 1968 and 1984, a dollar was added to food stamps and medical benefits.[131]

The changes in welfare legislation, with the resumption of a work requirement for most public assistance recipients and the dramatic decline in the number of people on public assistance rolls, suggests that welfare does have incentive effects. This does not mean that there should be no safety net for parents who fall upon hard times. Rather, it means that any substantial redistribution of resources (and many other legal changes) will have predictable, if unintended, effects. I take up some such proposed changes in the conclusion of this book.

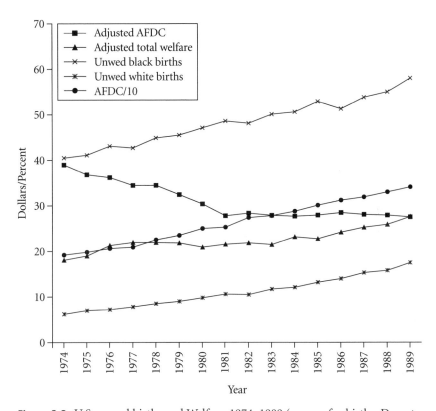

Figure 3.2 U.S. unwed births and Welfare, 1974–1989 (source: for births, Department of Health and Human Services, National Center for Health Statistics, Vital Statistics, 1949–91, Natality; for Welfare: Vital Statistics of the United States, AFDC and Other Payments, Various years)

Should the Market in Babies Be Regulated?

Every once in a while, someone proposes that would-be parents should be licensed,[132] or at least that they should be required to take a parenting course before their child is born. This would regulate the market in babies more directly than controls on the marriage process. Such a rationale may be one of the reasons why health insurers are now required to allow women who have just given birth to remain in the hospital for an additional day. A less successful effort to promote responsible parenting occurred in Wisconsin in the mid-1970s. In *Zablocki v. Redhail,*[133] the Supreme Court invalidated a statutory scheme requiring applicants for marriage licenses to prove that they were current on support payments ordered for their children from prior relationships and that these children were not in danger of becoming public charges.

Although there is little real regulation of the fundamental decision whether or not to bear a child,[134] once the would-be parents venture out of the realm of family autonomy and into the market for babies, they encounter significant regulation. The state is involved in carefully reviewing the birth parents' decision whether or not to surrender a child for adoption, and in protecting public and private agencies which may not disclose all relevant information to adoptive parents. (Also, of course, the state screens prospective adoptive parents.) Recent developments in regulating the birth market concern surrogate parenting, discussed in a later section.

Regulation and Transaction Costs in the Baby Market

As a society, we strongly presume that natural parents are the best custodians for their children.[135] By definition, then, others are not as qualified; their motivations are questionable, and third-party experts may intervene even when they may be acting in the child's best interests. More important for this discussion, the emphasis on parental rights to custody as opposed to children's rights to the best custodian may lead courts and legislatures to second-guess the birth parent's consent for adoption.

Birth mothers are not allowed to give binding consent for adoption until after the child is born.[136] This universal rule is advantageous because of the overwhelming bond between parent and child that occurs at and shortly after childbirth.[137] But even after the arrival of the child and a recovery period, courts scrutinize assent to adoption more intensely than they examine virtually any other transaction.

Looking at this judicial behavior charitably, we understand that birth parents placing children for adoption will feel tremendous regret,[138] a loss that compensation, as suggested by Posner, might palliate at least in part. It is more likely, though, that we allow revocation of this transaction because of the tremendous primacy we give parental rights, despite unquestionable harm to the promisee adoptive parents,[139] and frequently to the child as well. Although revocation does not occur very often,[140] the possibility introduces very significant uncertainty into the adoption process.[141] Incertitude creates major effects in the adoption market in much the same way that the very small risk of a catastrophe dominates the insurance market or many people's thinking about nuclear power.[142] There are, of course, other transaction costs to adoption, including the fees charged by social service agencies, the intrusive nature of the investigations, and the waiting period that frequently stretches for several years. As I have noted, many of these costs serve to "ration" the short supply of adoptable children, since price cannot. Fees may be charged on a sliding scale (so that higher fees are charged wealthier couples). Still, critics of transracial adoptions have charged that because of the biases of social workers toward placing children in materially comfortable surroundings, adoption has become a middle-class phenomenon.[143]

The fact that Posner and other students of adoption overlook children's rights is hardly surprising, given the history of parental supremacy. Cases involving child custody almost invariably invoke the "best interest of the child" standard.[144] Nevertheless, perhaps because the two contestants in adoption cases are parents and would-be parents, the court actually considers their interests rather than the child's.[145] A related reason for the focus on parental rights is the presumption, irrebuttable except when the parents are unfit, that parents always act in their children's best interests.[146] Finally, to speak of "best interests" is somewhat inappropriate. A more accurate standard is the placement that will cause the child the least harm—the "least detrimental alternative."[147] This test implies that the "best interests" standard cannot always be applied, since a loving two-parent home is always the best placement for children. Any other situation is second best to the arrangement I discuss in Chapter 5, in which parents act as stewards or trustees for their children, their most valued assets.

A few custody cases in the 1980s spoke of the child's right to parental custody rather than the parent's right to custody of the child.[148] In adoption and termination of custody cases, however, courts have extended the power of birth parents.[149] *Schmidt v. DeBoer*[150] illustrates the expanded power of natural parents, particularly unwed fathers, to withhold consent for adoption. In this case the birth mother had intentionally given welfare authorities the name of the wrong man as the baby's father, and he consented to the adoption in writing. She ultimately married the actual father, and the two successfully regained custody. The case was finally decided based on the procedural question of which state—that of the birth or the adoptive parent—had the ability to grant an adoption. Despite having lived more than two years in a suitable adoptive home, Jessica was returned to her birth parents, although it was her mother's deception that had created the loophole voiding adoption. The direct effects, particularly as portrayed in the popular press, reveal, among other things, the human costs of interstate custody conflicts. The dissent argued that "[t]he superior claim of the child to be heard in this case is grounded not just in law, but in basic human morality. . . . This Court, by ignoring obvious issues concerning the welfare of the child and by focusing exclusively on the concerns of competing adults, as if this were a dispute about the vesting of contingent remainders, reduces the PKPA [Parental Kidnapping Prevention Act] to a robot of legal formality with results that Congress did not intend."[151]

Thus courts, as well as legislators and economists, sometimes place greater emphasis on parental rights than on those of the children they purport to help.[152] We turn now to revocation of consent for adoption, where we will again see a pattern of concern for birth parents' rights even when these conflict with the child's.

Although some children enter the adoption market when their parents are found unfit, the vast majority begin the process after their parents voluntarily relinquish parental rights. This procedure is also called voluntary consent to adoption.[153] Because there is no federal regulation or even federal court review of child custody matters,[154] each state has enacted its own adoption system, and these demonstrate the tremendous variation (or natural laboratories) typical of family law.[155]

Although adoption itself is a creature of statute,[156] so each state can spell out the requirements of consent, the conditions for revocation are not always explicit. In states with statutes that leave room for question, the general consent law has been interpreted by judicial decisions. Some state adoption systems treat consent for adoption much like agreement to any other contract. In these states, once a parent has given valid consent (after the child's birth), it becomes irrevocable.[157] The rationale in these states, to the extent that it is expressed, is typified by the Mississippi case of *I. v. Natural Parents*[158]: "If a parent is allowed an unrestricted right to challenge his act of surrender, uncertainty and confusion among adoption agencies would undoubtedly result, making placement more difficult which would be detrimental to the children involved as well as to the public welfare. The statutory safeguards are themselves sufficient to guard against a hastily made decision."[159]

Next on the spectrum running from child's to birth parents' rights are the states that permit only a short time period for revocation, running from ten to thirty days after valid consent is given.[160] This allows some time for the parent to have a change of heart,[161] though not so much that either the child or the adoptive parents will be greatly injured by revocation.[162]

Another group of states have very strict revocation requirements but do not make consent irrevocable. Their statutes provide that there can be no revocation except in cases where consent was obtained by fraud, duress, or coercion,[163] where the consent itself is involuntary. The extent to which such states look to the best interests of children in rapid and certain placement depends on their definition of the exceptions to the no-revocation rule. If the states require a standard similar to the commercial contracts definition of fraud, for example, the defrauding conduct would have to induce performance, would have to involve a material fact, and would have to be performed by the other party to the transaction.[164] In adoption cases this other party is usually a state agency, but in direct placement cases it might be the adoptive parents themselves. A restrictive definition of the conditions in which revocation is possible tends to value children's rights as opposed to those of the natural parents. In fact, those statutes that provide for no revocation except in cases of fraud and coercion have restrictive definitions.

On the opposite or birth parents' rights end of the spectrum are states that permit revocation at any time before the final decree.[165] Since the adoption process may take years, and usually must take at least six months, bonds between the child and its adoptive parents are almost certain to have formed.[166] In such states a typical case will allow revocation in circumstances that would not suffice for revocation of a commercial contract. For example, commercial contracts allow revocation for duress only when there is a threat by the other party to the contract.[167] The threat must usually be of a severe physical sort that would clearly cause a reasonable person to enter into a contract where he or she would not otherwise do so. The threat cannot be one of ordinary economic circumstances. To quote again from *I. v. Natural Parents*,[168] a case not allowing revocation: "There is no doubt that John and Jane were not free from emotions, tensions and inescapable anxieties which resulted from her pregnancy during the time preceding their marriage. No doubt almost any person situated as they were would experience emotional trauma, but there is no law to the effect that surrender of a child is valid only if done without such distress. If such were the law almost any child surrender and subsequent adoption decree could be attacked."[169] Contrary to the preceding sentiment, however, in a "natural parents' rights" revocation state, duress may be the hardship most single parents of unplanned children experience.[170]

In between the two extremes are a number of states that allow revocation before final placement or within longer time periods following consent.[171] But physical or psychological harm to children (and to adoptive parents) occurs when birth parents are permitted to revoke long after they have given consent. In addition, there will be other, market-driven, effects. Some parents may be so wary of the market, particularly if they have gone through one unsuccessful placement, as to withdraw altogether. This prevents potential loving parents from benefiting children, and seems a particularly arbitrary sort of screening. Adoptive parents have other sources of children, including the black market, where virtual certainty can be purchased at a price. For $10 million, most unmarried pregnant mothers who were already inclined to place their child for adoption could be persuaded not to renege. Though not usually as high as this, the price must be quite high since, as in other black market situations, explicit payment of this sort is illegal and might well result in criminal prosecutions (at least for the birth parent and any intermediaries). Further, adoptive parents who are insecure about the stability of adoptions in their own states can look for children from other states or foreign countries. Because they are so eager to raise children, adoptive parents as a group tend to be exceptionally well informed. They will seek out placements initiated in other states, and so a quasi-legal intermediary mechanism flourishes.[172]

For example, in a 1994 case[173] a New Jersey couple sought a private placement adoption of a baby born to a New York mother located through a California intermediary. The adoptive parents' attorney drafted the consent provision, the birth mother signed in New York, and the consent form stated that the adoption would proceed in New Jersey. After forty-five days, the period when consent can be revoked in New York, the mother changed her mind, wanting the child back. Although the written opinion is resolved on a choice of law question, the court notes that "[t]he choice of law issue arises from the consent to adoption executed by the mother,"[174] since in New Jersey private placement cases parents may revoke consent "unless and until there is a judicial determination that they have forsaken their parental obligations."[175] The ultimate result was that the birth mother was able to retrieve the child nine months after his birth.

Alternatively, because of the birth mother's relative market power,[176] she can behave opportunistically, extracting consumer surplus from the adoptive parents.[177] These additional payments might range from concessions to visitation by the mother after adoption[178] to listing in an adoption registry.[179] Where legal, the payments might be more direct, such as increased reimbursement for prenatal expenses or loss of income.

Because there are alternatives to in-state adoptions, the economist can make several predictions about the adoption market as it is affected by the transaction costs of consent revocation. If birth parents find it relatively easy to revoke consent, there should be fewer in-state adoptions because the adoptive parents would not want to accept the increased risk.[180] There should also be more foreign adoptions and more adoptions from out of state. This last consequence is reflected in the ratio of in-state adoptions (as revealed by court data) to the number of children born in the state whose birth certificates are altered after adoption (revealed in data kept by state bureaus of vital statistics). In fact, some states are net importers of adoptees while others export them.

In an empirical analysis of the effect of adoption revocations on the number of adoptions,[181] I first categorized state revocation statutes for agency placement. When the statute provided a specific time period, this value was entered. Other states had no numerical provision but included language such as "in cases of fraud or duress." Some states had no statutory provision but had case law providing relevant standards. Each state received a numerical score ranging from 0 to 500.[182] States on the low end of the scale were heavily weighted toward the adoptive parents' rights, while those at the high end were birth parents' rights states.

The resulting data provide the basis for an empirical test of the effect of consent revocation legislation.[183] The dependent variable is the number of adoptions per thousand households in the state.[184] Obviously other factors besides revocation legislation affect the number of adoptions. The number of babies that are available for adoption changes with the availability of alternatives to adoption such as abortion or single parenthood. Unmarried women are more inclined to bear children as opposed to abort them when single parenthood becomes socially acceptable[185] and they receive adequate public assistance. The monthly rate for AFDC payments was therefore included as a controlling variable, as was the number of abortions in the state for 1987.[186] Factors influencing the desire to adopt included couples' income[187] and infertility, reflected in the number of married women in the labor force.[188] The results of regression analysis were that the best predictors of the adoption rate in a state were the number of unwed births, the revocation statutes, and median income.

If we assume that the uncertainty introduced by relaxed revocation statutes influences the rate of adoptions, the immediate question for legislators is whether it is appropriate to continue to focus on the rights of birth mothers. Once the state guarantees that the mother's consent is voluntarily given, a short revocation period should suffice. So long as the statute truly emphasizes "the best interests of the child," the exact wording of the statute makes little difference.

Fraud in the Adoption Market: "Wrongful Adoptions"

The idea that a "market for lemons,"[189] devised to describe the sale of consumer goods, extends to adopted children sounds at once abhorrent and seductive. Yet if we can stomach the idea that an adoption market exists, then some amount of fraud may be optimal.[190] Fraud, like the prohibition of a free market in babies,[191] may be one of the costs of placing less desirable children—those who are nonwhite, handicapped, or past infancy.[192]

Except for the philosophical problems associated with analogizing children to goods,[193] however, and the unusual amount of regulation,[194] both discussed earlier, this facet of the adoption market closely resembles the familiar "lemons" situation discussed by George Akerlof. A purchaser (here, an adoptive parent) acquires something (a baby) at considerable cost (in terms of cash, time, and emotional investment) from a seller (usually an agency in the reported cases). The seller possesses more information about the subject of the transaction than the buyer,[195] and in many cases[196] it is impossible for the adoptive parent to discover this important "quality information" (usually a handicap or emotional problem) prior to consummating the transaction.[197] (Some genetic diseases may not show any symptoms for many years. Such problems as fetal alcohol syndrome do not appear for months. Older children who were victims of sexual abuse by their parents may not show unusual behavior until they reach puberty.) The requirement of agency investigation of birth parents and adoptive homes is designed to overcome some of these information problems.[198] But since a higher price cannot be charged when the agencies comply, their incentives are to place the greatest number of children rather than to ensure the quality of the children placed.[199]

Once the child has been placed with adoptive parents and a major problem is discovered, the question becomes one of remedy. In some cases adoptions are annulled because of agency misrepresentation or nondisclosure.[200] In a growing number of cases, although the adoption remains intact, distressed adoptive parents have sued the placing agencies. Courts allowed recovery in eight of the fourteen cases reported before January 1999.[201] In three of these successful suits, the child had a life-threatening disease.[202] In all cases the agencies had deliberately misrepresented the child as healthy.[203] The parents were able to recover for past or future medical expenses even though the agencies were not guarantors of the child's health. The courts noted that although the agencies knew of the genetic or other problems, the parents could not have discovered the illness or disability through their own diligence.

In the other five reported cases, the parents' suits were barred.[204] In some, the defects were not substantial, although the parents would not have wished them. For example, one child was deaf,[205] while another turned out to be unavailable for adoption because his father had never given consent.[206] In others, although the agencies might have negligently failed to discover the problem, plaintiffs could not show fraud or prove that they would not have adopted the child had they known of the problems.[207] Perhaps the agency was also not the "least cost avoider." As one court wrote: "In short, to impose liability in a case such as this would in effect make the adoption agency a guarantor of the infant's future good health. . . . To do so would put adoption agencies in a quagmire because they want to continue to perform this service. Yet, they could not afford an unreasonable responsibility of guaranteeing the health of a child. Even natural parents are without this guarantee."[208]

Fraud in adoption resembles in several respects fraud in marriage, discussed in Chapter 2. Yet the fact that the cases involve children, who have their own interests if not their own rights, changes the set of possible remedies. In most cases, returning the children to their birth parents or the agencies that placed them (the equivalent of annulment) presents an unacceptable alternative. Children need stability, particularly early in their lives. Disabled children may need a stable, loving home even more than those without special needs. Rescission of the adoption contract therefore loses power as a device because of the third-party effects, or externalities, involved.

The special needs of hard-to-place infants create another barrier to recovery: a heightened burden of proof of fraud. Particularly if the adoptive parents expressed a willingness to accept a special needs child, courts will be reluctant to penalize the agency by a finding of fraud and concomitant damages even if the agency withheld some important medical or psychological information. If these "wrongful adoption" cases became routine, the government would have even fewer incentives to attempt permanent placement of disabled children, thus forcing still more to remain in permanent foster care.[209]

Finally, as in the "wrongful life" cases brought a generation ago, the courts in the adoption fraud cases confront situations in which damages are very difficult to measure. Even if the child has some trait that the adoptive parent would have wished to avoid, he or she is nonetheless a human being, capable of giving and receiving love. As with the "wrongful birth" children, the courts typically find that the positive aspects of having a child outweigh the negative. Taken as a whole, the child presents a net benefit to the adoptive parents despite the misinformation.

Contracts for Children: Surrogate Parenting

Legal recognition of surrogate parenting continues to be contentious in the United States. Several states have enacted legislation prohibiting or otherwise regulating surrogacy. Further, since the landmark case of *In re Baby M.*,[210] there have also been a number of important state cases applying common law principles to this new technological area. In *Johnson v. Calvert*,[211] for example, the California Supreme Court found that the surrogacy agreement between the genetic parents and the surrogate implanted with their fertilized embryo did not offend either the state or federal constitution or public policy. The surrogate was therefore not the "natural parent" entitled to custody or visitation with the child. The court suggested that the legislature resolve the public policy questions, for the court was "all too aware that the proper forum for resolution is the Legislature, where empirical data, largely lacking from this record, can be studied and values of general applicability developed."[212] State legislative responses to the practice have varied from a few that reluctantly acquiesce to a majority that find such contracts illegal and therefore unenforceable.[213] Several states enforce the contracts when they are regulated if there is no monetary consideration for the surrogate's service.

The chief product of all this state activity is uncertainty. As we saw in the context of consent revocation, uncertainty itself begets more litigation, higher prices to attempt to secure conformity with the contracts, and more opportunism on the part of all involved, particularly intermediaries. Litigation follows surrogacy just as it plagues other uncertain areas of the law.[214] The high prices charged by surrogates, and particularly the attempts to establish close relationships between the contracting parties, may thus be bonding devices where the contractual remedy is questionable or unenforceable.[215] Lack of certainty might theoretically produce a lower price (because the expected value of the child decreases with the lower probability that he or she will ever live with the would-be parent). The demand for biological children is very inelastic, however, meaning that would-be parents will go to great lengths to produce and raise children related to them. The fact that the prices paid (particularly "under the table" prices) are actually very high probably means that money is being used to encourage, if not bribe, the surrogate to conform to the contract.

On the other side of the transaction, the childless couple may become opportunistic, taking advantage of the surrogate's pregnancy and relative poverty to extract concessions ranging from restrictions on her behavior during the pregnancy to permission to film the delivery. It is more likely that the surrogate will behave opportunistically, however, since the couple's demand for their genetic child is very inelastic, meaning that they will still want the child even if the "price" is raised. She may therefore demand additional compensation, claiming that she is thinking about keeping the baby, or may ask for continued contact once the child is born.

What pushes some couples toward surrogacy, and what makes observers nervous about such arrangements, can be explained in simple biological terms. As Richard Epstein has noted elsewhere, we are driven by our genes to reproduce, and, more controversially, to behave in ways that will allow each succeeding generation also to be fruitful and multiply.[216] Infertile couples are tormented in part because of this unsatisfied and fundamental need. They choose surrogacy over adoption because they wish to have at least some of their own genetic code replicated in another human being.[217] Surrogate mothers are also affected by their biology. They too may desire genetic children that they cannot afford to keep in their own families, and so be attracted to surrogacy for this reason. They may simply enjoy being pregnant and the powerful feeling of creation that comes from giving birth.[218] But the dark side of these good feelings is that women are not programmed to have children and then part with them. A contract made beforehand, even though it may make the rational aspect of placing the child easier, cannot offset these biological drives. An ad cautions us that "it's not nice to fool with Mother Nature." Surrogacy contracts, by definition, do just that. This does not make them morally wrong; it just makes them problematic. The regret that such a placement causes does not pass away. It is large—probably larger than the $10,000 payment that a surrogate typically receives. And I wonder whether it can be anticipated beforehand.

If the surrogate has other children and therefore more information, problems for the surrogate's other children surface, too.[219] How do they know that Mommy will not decide to give them away if she needs money or if she feels that another couple needs them more than she does?

My final concern involves the placing agency. Like real estate agents who get paid by commission whether or not the closing ever takes place, placing agencies are compensated by the infertile couple upon signing the surrogacy contract.[220] They may not ensure that the surrogates have been adequately investigated or counseled. They may not do extensive checking of the infertile couple, either. From a practical viewpoint, they are dealing with very vulnerable people on both ends of the contract, and that may encourage "matches" between unsuitable players. What is more, I do not see that these middlemen are necessary. So long as surrogacy is legal, there is nothing keeping the infertile couples, who are already very well organized as a group, from creating a "clearinghouse" that, in effect, advertises their desire to find surrogates. There are already similar ads for private placement adoptions in California. Once the couple and potential surrogate have identified each other, they are then capable of contracting for home visiting or counseling by social service agencies. Since an adoption by the genetic father's wife is the desired outcome, social services will probably be involved anyway.

Now, let us reconsider these three primary objections: regret on the part of the surrogate, hardship on the surrogate's other children, and exploitation by for-profit placing agencies. In economic terms, these problems, all of which affect the enforceability of contracts, are those of imperfect information, substantial negative externalities, and rent seeking.

Economics, and particularly the "new institutional" economics, rests on an informational foundation. At its core, price theory depends on complete and instantaneous transmission of information about the qualities and prices of relevant goods. Rational consumers and producers capably process this vast stream of information. The law and economics of contracts floats on this informational sea, selecting its terms and the degree of specificity where transaction costs increase beyond the incremental value gained by the next good or the next term.

Contracting proves efficient regardless of the allocation of property rights so long as these transacting costs remain low. But there are limits to contract even in the world of law and economics, as we saw in Chapter 2. Some contracts are not permitted for moral or other societal reasons. Some become voidable (are less than perfect) because the parties did not have enough information beforehand to make rational efficient choices.[221]

IMPERFECT INFORMATION. The argument here is that surrogacy contracts are suboptimal because the surrogate cannot *ex ante* have perfect, or even minimally adequate, information. It is not, then, her *ex post* regret that drives the analysis. It is that she *cannot* have predicted accurately what the situation will be at closing time. She cannot have gauged precisely the long-term effects of what she promised before conception. Even in the case of the marriage contract, which society positively favors, specific performance of nonfinancial terms will never be ordered. As my colleague Lloyd Cohen wrote elsewhere, "[T]he marital duties are to be performed in a certain spirit, and no court can succeed in forcing an unwilling spouse to perform marital duties in a spirit of love and devotion."[222] In surrogacy, knowing during pregnancy that specific enforcement was possible could make the pregnancy a nightmare.[223] The woman who changes her mind after whatever the statutory revocation period may be has every incentive to hate and resent the child she carries. She might try to extract additional money from the intended parents to guarantee that she will not engage in

conduct that will harm "their" child. Such conduct might include participating in reckless activities such as skydiving, drinking excessive amounts
of alcohol or caffeine, dieting, or injecting drugs to numb the pain of her
predicament after the "turnback point."[224]

The information problem justifies at least some intervention into a free
surrogacy market. The state might require counseling or provision of mental health follow-up services. It might allow some reasonable waiting period after childbirth before consent is finally—specifically enforceably—
given.[225] It might simply change the contract from a "fully enforceable"
agreement to one where the remedy is the more typical one of money
damages.[226]

EXTERNALITIES.   According to modern economic analysis, contracts may
become less than fully enforceable where there are substantial negative
third-party effects.[227] Although most contracts affect third parties at least
indirectly, sometimes the contracting parties must buy off the affected outsiders.[228] So long as the compensation takes place,[229] the contract remains
efficient and enforceable. When the costs to the third party or parties are
too high, the contract may be prohibited criminally,[230] enjoined,[231] or just
not enforced.

As I will explain in Chapter 6, in the divorce setting there are frequently
third parties who are not part of the main action. These are the couple's
children. They suffer substantial negative externalities when their parents
separate and divorce, so much so that we make it more difficult for parents
to divorce than for non-parents. We try to make things easier for these
children by allowing child support up to the standard of living they would
have enjoyed had their parents remained together.[232] In some states the
court may order the divorcing parents to provide the children with a college education, a privilege children with married parents cannot claim.[233]

Although any negatives flowing to the child in a surrogacy situation are
probably outweighed by the benefits of existence, what are the benefits
of the contracted-for child's existence to the surrogate's other children?
One of the particularly maternalistic stances family law takes is to put
the interests of children first in the face of parental activities, witting or
not, that might seriously harm them.[234] In our fascination with the adults
involved in surrogacy arrangements, we seem to have forgotten some players. Whether we ought to compensate them directly, offer them family

therapy, or just question whether surrogacy is a good idea remains a policy question.[235]

RENT SEEKING, OR REGULATING THE MIDDLEMEN.   Finally, we come to the problem of the paid brokering agencies. In order to describe the law and economics paradigm, we must look a bit more closely at the market involved. As we have already seen, the adoption market, of which surrogacy is a subset, is characterized by extremely inelastic demand and very restricted supply. And as I have also already noted, the supply of adoptable babies is short primarily because of effective contraception, elective abortions, and the growing relaxation of the stigma attached to unwed parenting.

Middlemen, or finders, because they can reduce the transaction costs associated with search, are highly desirable in many contexts.[236] Where there are easy ways of obtaining information and making efficient trades, one would expect that the market would eliminate brokers because they were not eliminating costs in the system. There are, however, several features about this particular market that make this approach problematic. These all stem in some way from a substantial agency cost problem. The intermediary typically acts as agent for both the adoptive parents and the surrogate, thus creating serious potential conflicts of interest.

Several characteristics of the adoption market create incentives for brokers to enter the market (and perhaps to encourage enactment of high public assistance payments and liberal abortion laws). First, since there is an extremely inelastic demand for the "good" in question, the middleman may therefore be tempted to extract the "consumer surplus" from one or both parties to the transaction,[237] and may be successful depending on how many intermediaries there are and whether they need to pass professional licensing or other barriers to entry. In lay terms, "extraction of consumer surplus" means that the married couple would be willing to pay substantially more than the surrogate charges.[238] To extract the surplus, the middleman may engage in substantial "rent seeking," or looking for some sort of monopoly opportunities, through public or private mechanisms.

A second unusual feature is the legal uncertainty that has surrounded surrogacy. Because in most states the law of surrogacy has been unsettled, lawyers can offer what looks like a guarantee of success, a "watertight" contract. This, of course, may be a transitory phenomenon as more legislatures react to the surrogacy question. Ideally, once the law is settled (even if it says that money cannot be exchanged or contracts cannot be specifically enforced), the apparent (and illusory) "insurance" of a lawyer-drawn contract will disappear.

A third feature is that any "mistakes" will reveal the relevant information to prospective contracting parties only at the expense of existing children. That is, once the brokered contract fails, the parties' litigation itself will probably have negative effects on the child. These might be financial; or they could be emotional if the child is ultimately removed or the family experiences significant publicity. For-profit agencies may also act to *reduce* the beneficial flow of information between contracting parties, causing some "inefficient contracting." While state legislatures may be moved by reasons that do not include economic efficiency, it is surprising that commercial "baby brokering" is almost universally illegal.[239] That is, although the agencies may be paid for doing searches or for screening applicants, according to the statutes there can be no explicit payment either for the baby or for the go-between services provided. For example, the fairly typical Virginia statute[240] prohibits the "exchange of fees or other consideration for the placement or referral" in adoptions. The statute exempts licensed child-placing agencies that charge for their reasonable and customary services, and allows reimbursement for the mother's medical expenses directly related to the pregnancy, payment for transportation necessary to execute consent, and the usual and customary fees for legal services in adoption. In our jurisdictional market, if the use of middlemen in surrogacy or adoption were a good idea, presumably some state would have experimented with it.

I believe that surrogacy should not be outlawed, since a surrogate black market is a still worse alternative.[241] Let me explain what I mean. If surrogacy becomes illegal and there are still people on both sides of the market who want to participate in these transactions, as there will be, the law and economics literature predicts certain consequences. First, the price will rise, in part to cover the risk of detection and in part because measures must be taken to prevent detection. Illicit organizations that specialize in the black market activity are likely to flourish, and these will extract their price, whether for information or protection, from the participants. Finally, the black market would preclude any gathering and transmittal of information between the parties that legitimate state or private agencies would otherwise provide.

Just because surrogacy should not be precluded, however, that does not mean that the state needs to encourage baby brokerage. In surrogacy, the finder (broker) is frequently paid as much as the surrogate.[242] It would be preferable either for the surrogate to reap this consumer surplus or for the intended parents to have to pay less. There is no reason why brokers should extract this profit. Lawyers may be needed to handle the adoptions by the intended mothers, but they should charge only their customary—much lower—fee for this service.

Surrogacy may be a kind of "demerit good," one we view instinctively as harmful regardless of what the individuals participating in the transaction decide.[243] Society need not prohibit these goods, but may merely tax or otherwise regulate them enough to make them less attractive while not forcing them onto the black market.

Externalities and Equitable Substitutes for Parenting

Parents who undertake support of their stepchildren or begin an adoption process are occasionally estopped from denying parental responsibilities even though in truth they are not parents. In economic terms, the estoppel doctrine raises the costs for those who replace a natural parent and then attempt to exit. Another way of looking at the problem is in terms of the position the parent substitute has taken in the life of the child. The person, usually a man in the reported cases, is like a monopsonist: where estoppel occurs, he has been supplying parental services and support to the exclusion of all other males.

In several cases the prospective adoptive father has changed his mind and refused to continue the adoption once his marriage broke up. In two of these cases[244] the father's adoption was not completed, and he was not required to make child support payments following the divorce. In the third[245] the father was estopped under very similar circumstances. "The father's actions in bringing the babies halfway around the world" plus his "indications of financial ability and commitment to their upbringing" effectively estopped him from revocation, where the children's welfare might be in jeopardy.

The more typical cases involve a man who marries a woman knowing she is pregnant with someone else's child. When the marriage dissolves several years later, the woman often attempts to collect child support from her husband although he is not related to the child genetically or by adoption. Usually she is successful,[246] in the same way that the provider of a railroad line to an outlying mine shaft will be able to recoup his contributions, as will the manufacturer of a part useful only in a particular machine. As one court put it, "Georgia says that the biological father was never asked to contribute support for Michelle because Evan said he wanted to be her father."[247] Again, the legal remedy of estoppel acts to protect because there is no way to regain the custodial parent's opportunity cost.

But even more important from a law and economics perspective is the fact that every case of estoppel to deny parenting responsibilities involves an externality. In each of these situations there is a child who may be precluded (by the actions of the estopped party) from knowing a biological parent. In addition, or sometimes alternatively, the child may be unable to obtain support from his or her biological father because of the estopped custodial parent's actions. The law reasons that regardless of the problems with the estopped parent's actions, the child should not be allowed to suffer.[248]

Like estoppel, "equitable adoption" is a remedy ordered by the court when a fact situation does not fall within the adoption statute but nonetheless justifies relief. Like estoppel, the contract implied by the court runs between "adoptive" and biological parent. Unlike estoppel, the agreement to adopt is enforceable only by the child, not the parent. The economic reasoning is similar: the adults' actions are imposing external effects on the child.

In the classic case a couple promises to adopt someone else's child. They take the child into their home and raise the child as their own, but for some reason never complete the adoption process. One of the promising adoptive parents then dies, and the child seeks to recover the benefits owed an adopted child. In many cases, so long as the child is plaintiff, courts grant relief.[249] Not so, however, when the plaintiffs are the child's purported siblings or any persons suing on behalf of the would-be adoptive parents.[250] The fact that the child could use the doctrine of equitable adoption to sue the adoptive parents' estate does not preclude suit by the same child against the birth parents or their representatives. Because there was no adoption, the original relationship of parent and child remains intact.[251]

The economic view of equitable adoption runs much like the analysis of implied contract generally. Since it is a contract between two persons that is enforced by a third, the closest non-family analogy is to third-party beneficiary law. The law and economics position governing these situations is that one looks *ex post*, or after the fact, at what the contracting parties would probably have agreed to *ex ante*. Would they have expected the child to enforce their contract? If so, the courts allow the third party, here the child, to enforce the contract.[252]

In the law surrounding formation of parent-child bonds, perhaps the most striking feature is the competition between the various sets of adults involved. While this is consistent with a market or contractual framework, the rules are more troubling here than in the marriage market simply because children are involved. There is no intrinsic "problem" with marriage markets. So long as competition and contracting principles are confined to marriage formation (and, to some extent, dissolution), there is no cause for alarm. Markets in children do alarm us, as we saw with the comments to Posner's adoption proposal, because we worry about the human "goods" (the external effects of the parties' dealings) and what the market will do to them. Still, the children's interests are rarely represented directly, but more often are vindicated through government regulation. The growing tendency is for courts to appoint guardians ad litem for children threatened with removal[253] or involved in surrogacy disputes.[254] The legal system may be catching up with the economic reality of the substantial external effect.

Now, we have seen that markets involving family formation are similar to those resulting in commercial contracts. Yet families are different. In part, families are treated in special ways because they are so important. In part, family contracting differs because love—or the promise of it—is involved. Love is the factor that does not fit well into commercial economic models, and particularly not with regard to established families, as we shall see next in Part II. Frequently we will see that when the parties think they are in a family relationship, as opposed to acting "at arm's length," courts will assume that they are acting for love rather than with expectation of financial gain. The unconditional nature of family transactions is one major feature that distinguishes contract from covenant. Unlike in many commercial contracts, there will normally be no accounting of how much each family member has invested or contributed.[255] And unlike in even the relational contract, the benefits and burdens fixed by family connections will endure for the lives of the parties, whatever the law has to say about the subject. In Part II I will take up the first of these distinctions between covenant and contract, that of unconditional giving as opposed to more precise accounting, and in Part III the second, that of permanence as opposed to more transitory encounters.

The Family as Firm

4

Husband and Wife

We have now completed our look at family formation, the aspect of family relations for which the contract or market model may be used most successfully. Once couples have married and children are born or adopted, a new approach is necessary. In the terms used by some economists, this is because in families we develop "interdependent utility functions," so that what makes our spouse or child happy makes us happy. Although this interdependence undoubtedly exists in all families, we more typically say we love one another, we sacrifice for one another, we share with one another.

The family ceases in some ways to be a collection of independent individuals and takes on a life of its own, making it in many respects quite distinct from a contract situation.[1] As the common law put it, where once there were two, now there is one. This very special kind of relationship is what I call the covenant, with the firm its economic counterpart. Covenant differs from contract—and even relational contract—in a number of important respects. The most significant for this portion of the book involves the unconditional nature of marriage and parenting. Another, discussed primarily in Part III, involves the permanence of covenants, which persist despite the legal dissolution of the marriage or parent-child relationship. Both of these distinguishing features, in addition to the solemnity with which the relationships themselves begin, discussed in Part I, reflect the difference between what the parties are trying to do in contracts as opposed to covenants. In covenants, although other things are important too, the parties seek to maximize love. In contracts they have something else in mind, although the parties' relationship may nevertheless be important.

As with the discussion of the market, I begin here with one of the key concepts in Gary Becker's work on the family: the household division of labor. And as in the earlier chapters, I urge that there are limitations to the application of commercial law (firm) concepts to the family. Because members of families love one another, in successful marriages the spouses do not keep track of who has contributed what to the marital unit, or how much these contributions are to be valued.[2] As one court put it:

> [T]he fact that [the plaintiff] believed herself to be a wife excludes the inference that the society and assistance of a wife which she gave to her supposed husband were for hire. It shows that her intention in keeping his house was to act as a wife and mistress of a family, and not as a hired servant. There was clearly no obligation to pay wages arising from contract; and the plaintiff's case is rested on the ground that there was an obligation or duty imposed by law, from which the law raises a promise to pay money, upon which the action can be sustained.[3]

In other words, when we act as a spouse or parent, we act unselfishly and usually without expectation of a financial payback.

This difference over motivation seems to be the dividing point between legal scholars of the family and Chicago School economists, or, more generally, between feminists and those who adhere strictly to the Becker approach. What is being maximized in the family? Is it household wealth, as Becker[4] suggests (implying, as critics see it, that family goals might be given a pejorative financial connotation)? Or is it something far distant from wealth in the commercial sense? Milton Regan calls this "something" intimacy.[5] In a review of his book *Family Law and the Pursuit of Intimacy*, I likened the distinction between the intimacy of home and the calculated behavior of the workplace to that of the nineteenth-century "separate spheres" ideology.[6] We might also call what is being maximized love—an erotic love, to be sure, but also the particularly unconditional love identified with covenant. Something else the marriage might be maximizing is the best possible environment for raising children.[7] Modern family law seems to be at odds with the covenant model in ways I will discuss, and therefore acts to channel the family, and particularly marriage, toward fulfilling the individual self instead of toward goals of developing intimacy or raising children well.[8]

Whichever of the several goals dominates suggests which investments individuals should make prior to marriage.[9] For example, women might invest in themselves and their careers or, alternatively, in the type of human capital that will best benefit their future family. The choice of goals has a further implication because it defines the costs of marriage. For example, marriage might mean that a woman forgoes career opportunities when electing instead to marry and to earn money in a way that will most benefit the household. Marriage also serves in part as insurance—against the vagaries of the marriage market and against setbacks in employment. The relative importance of each of these goals will also be determined by one's purpose in marrying. The goals of a marriage also relate to the willingness to stay in a less than joyful marriage and the amount one is likely to invest in the relationship rather than in oneself. Critically, goals also shape issues of family law: how spouses control assets during marriage and at either spouse's death; how outsiders can sue family members individually (or, in the case of parents, vicariously); how easily family members can end the marriage or parenting relationships; how courts can divide children and assets at divorce. Obviously, the choice of a goal for marriage also determines what the marriage will produce in the way of property or investments in children and their human capital. Finally, the choice fixes the degree to which each spouse specializes in the marriage.

Specialization and Efficiency

Thinking of the family as a firm is not a new idea. Aristotle, in his *Œconomia,* begins his discussion with efficiencies in the household. Similarly, the Pilgrims spoke of the family as a "little Church, and a little commonwealth, at least a lively representation thereof, whereby triall may be made of such as are fit for any place of authoritie, or of subjection in Church or commonwealth. Or rather it is as a schoole wherein the first principles and grounds of government and subjection are learned; whereby men are fitted to greater matters in Church or commonwealth."[10] The nineteenth-century reformer Catharine Beecher described the family as a small economy where each participant specializes in particular functions.[11] More recently still, economist Yoram Ben-Porath wrote of the "F-Connection," where two of the "F's" are family and firm, and both are organized to avoid continual recontracting on the open market.[12]

Yet, as Ben-Porath recognized, the analogy between the family and the firm is imperfect. One obvious difference between the two lies in their reasons for existence. The firm exists purely to maximize profits for its owners.[13] The family's motivations are more complex. Although a marriage may be, in fact, more efficient than two individuals on their own, people marry and organize their families around different, or at least additional, principles. Values particularly important to families include altruism and commitment. In turn, these produce different rules for the ongoing family and its dissolution than those applied to the firm.[14]

Contracts in general involve only the signatories, and are not primarily ordered toward sharing, giving, and relationship.[15] Marriages, at least most marriages, bear small resemblance to these contracts or to Chicago School law and economics efficiency-seeking ventures. As one court found, "Not business or money, but wedlock is what the parties contemplate. They are, or should be, motivated by love and affection."[16]

When marriages are good, they involve self-sacrifice, sharing, and out-ward-looking behavior,[17] perhaps even a more "feminine" view of the universe: "A feminine view of human nature tends to be positive and the exercise of power by women more affirming. Such a fundamental optimism in a group that has been colonized and oppressed, often in very violent ways, is remarkable and perhaps accounts for the certainty of many feminists that we are unlikely to exercise power in the same way that our oppressors have."[18]

Marriages are relationships, not just relational contracts. This we have seen already in the public nature of, or community's witness to, family formation. Further, regardless of what the couple's prospects and predictions are *ex ante*, as a society we have tremendous incentives to promote the noncontractual view of marriage. In other words, an important external effect of each marriage is its effect on the rest of society. Societal incentives matter because what is being maximized here is not monetary wealth, although marriage does enhance financial well-being.[19]

Because there is such a strong external effect, because marriage implies such a long and complex commitment, and also because at times bargaining between the spouses will be difficult, law appropriately regulates ongoing marriages far more than it does commercial contracts. And the commitment that neither will breach even when getting out may be "more efficient"[20] is central to marriage, too.[21] It is the commitment, or as I have called it the covenant,[22] that promotes what Milton Regan calls "the pursuit of intimacy."[23] After a reasonably long marriage, a clean break is not possible even for spouses, let alone children; there is too much invested, too much shared.[24] These continuing relationships will be discussed in Part IV of this book.

Altruism aside, there may be limits in the family law context to the otherwise very useful law and economics work on the firm that conceptualizes the business enterprise as a nexus of contracts. Conventional theory of the firm maintains that the firm is organized to perform multiple tasks when the transaction costs associated with spot purchases in the market become too high.[25] Yet there are limits to the specialization and economies of scale facilitated by the commercial firm. Certainly part of the genius of the American corporate form, at least according to Oliver Williamson[26] and Alfred Chandler,[27] is that specialization is not complete. Thus in very large M-form firms, or firms with more than one product line there may be two sales staffs, two production staffs, and two central administrations, each performing similar if not identical functions.

In marriage, by contrast, according to Becker, even though the parties may have functioned quite similarly prior to marriage, they will begin to specialize once the marriage begins.[28] This specialization will occur as the couple realizes gains from each partner's comparative advantage in one or more functions. They will engage in two kinds of labor, which Becker calls market production and household production. The spouse involved in market production divides time between labor (earning money to purchase goods) and leisure activities (spending money, or at any rate not earning additional money). The spouse engaged in household production divides time between the production of household (or "Z") goods and leisure. In "Z" goods production, the spouse transforms purchased goods into ultimate consumption goods.[29]

It is because one spouse may have a comparative advantage at household production, however small,[30] that Becker predicts efficient spouses will specialize.[31] He argues that because only women can bear children, they have the comparative advantage when it comes to household production. This advantage increases because growing girls invest in human capital that enhances their efficiency at producing household goods,[32] creating a likelihood that they will follow a traditional path.[33] Future husbands, by contrast, will specialize in market production. They will choose the kinds of human capital investments before marriage that will maximize their production in the labor force. Pre-marriage specialization will also make each a more attractive mate.[34]

So long as the spouses remain together for life, this specialized system may in fact be the most efficient, at least for those goods and services produced by the marriage.[35] Once a spouse can exit from the marriage, however, Becker's model becomes complicated. It is usually the wife who has specialized in household production. To some extent, particularly in terms of caring for the couple's children, this specialization is "marriage-specific." Thus, she will be disadvantaged relative to her husband, who continues to employ his labor force skills after the divorce. As a result, institutions of fault-based divorce and the related invention of alimony were needed to protect the dependent wife from her husband's opportunism.[36] As we shall see in Chapter 6, when these institutions change (and divorce becomes no-fault, alimony rehabilitative), the incentive to specialize diminishes.[37] My own view is that specialization may not even be "efficient" in every marriage that stays intact. There are several points here, and they relate to the premises that proponents of specialization in marriage all use,[38] which in turn generate the particular, gendered, legal family law regime that prevailed until recently.[39] The predictions of the efficient specialization model include a fault system to protect against shirking, alimony to protect the wife's human capital investment in marriage,[40] the recognition that the husband makes important decisions for the couple,[41] and, perpetuating the system, the custody presumption in favor of the wife.[42]

I believe that five assumptions are most critical for the efficiency argument. First, the wife is better at child care than her husband.[43] This may be so for biological reasons or because she has invested more in nonmarket human capital prior to marriage than her husband has.[44] Second, the wife earns less than her husband in the labor market.[45] Becker notes the circularity of some of these arguments:

> If child care and other housework demand relatively large quantities of "energy" compared to leisure and other nonmarket uses of time by men, women with responsibility for housework would have less energy available for the market than men. This would reduce the hourly earnings of married women, affect their jobs and occupations, and even lower their investment in market human capital when they worked the same number of market hours as married men. Consequently, the housework responsibilities of married women may be the source of much of the difference in earnings and in job segregation between men and women.[46]

Third, there is specialization between husband and wife but not among women. These writers thus assume that it is not "efficient" to hire someone else to do the wash or clean the house.[47] Fourth, the only things that should be maximized are dollar income and the production of household commodities. Efficiency advocates do not count the wife's psychic costs when they calculate her opportunity cost of staying out of the labor market.[48] When the economists consider the husband's labor force production, they do not count the cost of working "to capacity" in the labor market at the expense of having close relationships with his children. Fifth, and most important for this discussion, there are no diminishing returns in this model but always gains (or at least no losses) from additional specialization.[49]

Let us assume for the sake of argument that the first three conditions are satisfied: women are better at child care than men, they earn less in the labor market, and it is not efficient for women to specialize among themselves. Let us also assume that women's and men's preferences work the same way.[50] Think, however, about what happens if we start counting psychic costs. If we assume that neither women nor men are as productive during their last hour of work as they were during their first,[51] the increasing costs and diminishing marginal returns eventually swamp the couple's gains from specialization. Once these two factors are taken into account, complete specialization does not lead to the most efficient outcome. Thus, even if many of the very strong assumptions made by economists hold true, specialization does not lead to maximum efficiency because neither spouse benefits from "all work and no life," as my teenage daughter puts it. The total benefit produced by the couple decreases, so that society loses.[52] The most efficient marriage, then, may well be the more modern one in which both husband and wife share labor force participation and household tasks—the more equally, the better.

The other assumptions of the specialization model include the postulate that the wife and husband have children (or plan to have them),[53] that the husband can earn enough to support the family,[54] that the children make no contribution to "household production," that steps must be taken to discourage opportunism in contract,[55] that there will be children living in the household for most of the marriage,[56] that the split between leisure and work time is equal between the spouses,[57] and that one should not deduct wasted human capital resources from the total household production.[58] Several of these postulates are questionable, particularly in America today.

Many critics of the specialization model advocate a more modern notion of marriage as a partnership.[59] This alternative assumes individualism within the marriage, equality between spouses, roughly equivalent earning capacity, and a need for flexibility over time. With these different assumptions, the predictable legal regime would include no-fault divorce;[60] no alimony, or rehabilitative alimony only;[61] no presumptions in custody favoring either spouse; and equal responsibility for child support. Behavioral predictions under this system would include more prenuptial contracts,[62] more variety among marriages,[63] more divorce,[64] more suits among spouses,[65] less investment in marriage,[66] more investment in individual human capital,[67] fewer children,[68] and fewer marriages.[69]

As we will see, particularly in Chapter 6, the legal predictions and many, but not all, of the behavioral predictions for decreased specialization hold true empirically. Part of the challenge for law reform, as we will see in Chapters 6 and 7, is the problem of helping people who began marriage in the older, more specialized system and are ending marriage in the newer, partnership one. The second challenge is equally difficult: deciding which of the outcomes of the newer system are desirable, and supporting these while discouraging behavior that detracts from healthy marriages and good parenting.

Empirical work I have done with Steven Nock[70] shows why one consequence of diminished specialization leads to marital instability. Couples studied in the 1987–88 national Survey of Families and Households[71] were asked, among many other questions, how many hours both spouses spent working each week in the paid labor force or on specific household tasks. Meal preparation, shopping, washing dishes, and doing laundry were among the traditional "women's tasks," while household repair and auto maintenance were among those defined as "men's work." The results for each couple were compared and found to be highly consistent. Five years later the same couples were surveyed again. Our study found that couples in which either husband or wife had spent more than the median amount of time doing "women's work" were significantly more likely to have divorced or separated by the time of the second survey five years later. These results remain robust even when the usual indicators of marital stability are held constant and even when labor force employment hours and income are included. By contrast, when either husband or wife had spent more than the median amount of time doing "men's work" in the earlier period, the couple was significantly less likely to have experienced divorce or separation by the second survey. Finally, couples who refused to answer the household labor questions (or who answered "0 hours" for more than three of the questions) also had more stable marriages.

These findings indicate that the early feminist predictions of successful egalitarian marriages need some rethinking. The most likely psychological explanations for these results are that "women's" jobs are distasteful or have lower status or are less goal-directed than "men's." The economic explanation for the difference between men's and women's work would seem to be that "men's work" contributes directly to marital assets (which have value outside the relationship), while "women's work" does not. This explanation suggests that marriages will be more stable if they rely on third parties (or advanced technology) for "women's work" while promoting or subsidizing "men's work" (to the extent that it is not favored anyway), especially if the couple works on cars or household repairs together. It also suggests that couples who are not keeping track of who is doing what around the house are happier. This finding, of course, relates to the theme of unconditional love that is one of the ingredients of covenant as I describe it.

Bargaining, Altruism, and Privacy: Households as Units

One of the questions I ask in this book is why households, not individuals, should be the basic building block of society. Part I provided a partial answer: society gains if households specialize in the particular two-person way that we call a marriage. But when couples marry, they do not give up their ability to be legal actors.[72] They continue to deal between themselves as well as with the outside world. They bargain about their respective household tasks; they earn money (which they may invest for the benefit of the marriage or separately), and they generally function as members of society, even harming others on occasion through their careless behavior. The relationship between these individual actions and those the couple takes as a whole are the subject of this section.

BARGAINING.   Once men and women marry, economists predict that they will stay in their relationship until the benefits from remaining married are exceeded by the benefits of separation or divorce.[73] Although many if not all marriages go through stages ranging from the "better" to the "worse" of the marriage vows, couples work out many of their disputes.[74] As with any other negotiation, the exchange can take place on many fronts.

Sometimes spouses may not reach bargains in the continuous reformulating of contracts that takes place in marriage.[75] In many of these cases they will divorce. The most common argument for why they fail to reach a solution is based on the difference in husbands' and wives' human capital and the specialization model discussed previously. Lloyd Cohen, for example, notes that women are likely to invest most heavily early in the marriage, when, at least historically, their children are born.[76] Meanwhile, husbands are building their careers; their investments will not be realized (and therefore their greatest contribution will not come) until later in the marriage, when they reach their forties and fifties. Because of this difference in the timing of spousal performance, Cohen's model predicts a large number of divorces instigated by men after women have made their initial investment but before the men fulfill a large part of their own performance. In fact, work I have done with Douglas Allen[77] supports this thesis, at least for extreme cases. The question, however, is why these potential divorces are not avoided by recontracting between husband and wife,[78] that is, why men do not offer more earlier in the marriage to induce women's performance, or why women cannot somehow pay more during the later period to keep their husbands in marriage.

One possible answer is suggested by Martin Zelder. He notes that children are public goods of the marriage, and that to some extent they are indivisible. Having one's children around on a daily basis is exponentially better than seeing them for "regular visitation." Zelder therefore predicts that when spousal conflict (over other things) ensues, access to the children becomes an asset that cannot be traded. That is, when both parents live with the children, access to them cannot easily be restricted, and having both parents around probably adds to enjoyment of and by the children rather than diminishing it. On the margin, therefore, where reduced costs of divorce are realized through no-fault and many couples lack substantial other wealth, couples are likely to divorce inefficiently. Inefficient divorce occurs when there are still joint gains to marriage, but owing to low transaction costs and the inability to trade on other fronts, the unhappy spouse cannot be "bought out" or offered some kind of concession by the spouse who wishes to remain married.[79]

Another interesting kind of bargaining that takes place within an existing marriage involves the spouses' relative market power.[80] In Becker's household model,[81] described at the beginning of this chapter, the dominant figure is the husband/wage earner, who is pictured as an altruist. Because he is altruistic, he will distribute resources, maximizing his own utility in the way most calculated to benefit the family resources.[82] Because of specialization, he will be at least the primary, and perhaps the sole, wage earner. He therefore enjoys substantial power over his wife and children, which ideally he will exercise with love.[83]

What happens if the financial power exercised by such a husband is diluted, or shared evenly, by his wife? Economists since Becker have modeled the effect of giving allowances for child care or income tax benefits to one or both spouses.[84] The idea here is that while family bargaining is seen as a cooperative game,[85] such transfer schemes change the relative bargaining positions if the threat point in a family argument is divorce. In other words, if the couple disagree vehemently over some issue, each spouse's option is to leave the marriage. If the husband earns substantially more than his wife, she will give in on a number of these arguments because she would be hurt more by divorce (as the likely custodial parent and the one with the lower-earning job). His threat to divorce (called his BATNA in the bargaining literature, standing for Best Alternative to a Negotiated Agreement)[86] is credible; hers is not. A required payment for child care, or a substantial tax subsidy for his income only while he is married, raises the price to the husband if the wife carries out her threat to divorce. This will help the wife as either a married person or a single person with custody because *her* threat to divorce if her bargaining position is not respected becomes more credible. She is therefore in a better position to insist on whatever she wants. She should "win" more of the time.[87]

Shelly Lundberg and Robert Pollack have refined the bargaining theory to discuss the difference in bargaining positions when a child care subsidy is allocated to the wife as opposed to the husband. The main difference in their model is that the alternative (or BATNA) is not divorce but a noncooperative position in the marriage.[88] This is less drastic than divorce but is still an unhappy outcome. Government policies directing payments to the wife not only increase her "threat point" but also have an "income effect." The noncooperative equilibrium is defined as "a division of labor based on socially recognized and sanctioned gender roles."[89] These will entail the wife's supplying household services and the husband's earning income, but with fewer "household public goods" such as meals and child care: in other words, a minimal performance done not out of love but out of a sense of duty and resignation. The responsibility for deciding how much of these "public goods" will be provided is socially "assigned" to one or the other of the spouses. Each will thus have a "separate sphere."[90] Absent binding premarital agreements, allocating the child care subsidies to one or the other of the spouses will change the "equilibrium" or final result they are likely to reach.

Another possible variation on these bargaining themes is suggested by the work on divorce I have done with Frank Buckley.[91] One of the questions we explored was the influence of increased labor force participation on the propensity to divorce. Two possible results could be expected. One was that since women were working, they would be investing in themselves rather than in the marriage. Divorce would therefore be less costly for women, and marriage correspondingly less important, so there ought to be more divorces.[92] The other, which was the result we found empirically, is that increased labor force participation by women *reduces* the divorce rate.[93] This could mean two things, either of which is consistent with Lundberg and Pollack's model. The first (the income effect) is that the wife's additional income makes the marriage more comfortable and thus reduces one kind of stress on the marriage that might lead to divorce. The second is that the additional income she earns represents a source of bargaining power for wives.[94] If the wife is given the power to allocate this income in her "sphere of influence," her threat point of a noncooperative, nondivorcing marriage becomes more comfortable for her. The bottom line is that she ought to win more arguments, and therefore ought to be more satisfied with the marriage.[95]

Still another possibility is suggested by sociobiology. Most sex research since the 1950s has concluded that a man's sexual drive peaks on average in his late teens or early twenties, and thereafter slowly tails off.[96] For women, however, the sex drive peaks in the mid-thirties.[97] Hence it is unlikely that the demand for intercourse throughout most marriages is ever matched exactly. Many husbands may feel that there is too little sex early on in the marriage, yet may feel that the wife is too demanding during the marriage's middle years.

Although in some marriages the husband may always have the greater sex drive, because of this difference in timing his wife's desire will likely either approach or exceed his during the middle years of the marriage. One way to think about this change in sexual interest is to conceive of the role reversal in terms of a gradual shift in the spouses' property rights over intercourse, or more precisely, a change in the marginal willingness to pay for sexual activity.[98] Assuming that intercourse within marriage is always mutual,[99] then the property right over the frequency of lovemaking belongs to the spouse who is less interested in intercourse—initially (in Region I of Figure 4.1) the wife. If a reversal in sex drive occurs—that is, if during the marriage the wife's demand for intercourse comes to exceed the husband's—then a gradual shift in the property right has taken place (Region II of Figure 4.1). If, later on in the marriage, the wife's sexual desire declines faster and becomes less than that of her husband, then another switch in property rights occurs (Region III of Figure 4.1), with the wife again holding the property right during the later part of the marriage.

This noncompensated transfer of property rights to the husband is significant because during this period (Region II of Figure 4.1), the wife is more vulnerable to divorce if the marriage is in trouble. If the husband decides to leave the marriage or behave opportunistically while he has the property right over sex, the wife has one less bargaining tool than otherwise to induce him to stay or to behave better. More wifely interest in and enthusiasm for sexual activity and intimacy has little or no value at the margin to the husband when he is less interested himself.

One of the unintended results of no-fault divorce, then, is exacerbation of this naturally unstable situation. Men, who currently enjoy more market

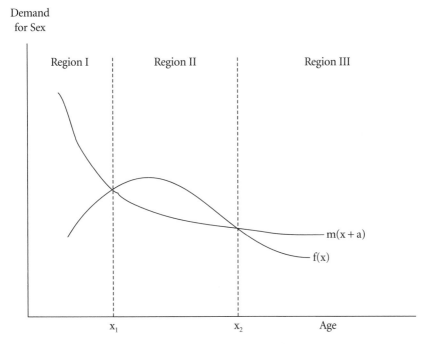

Figure 4.1 The demand for sex (source: Douglas W. Allen and Margaret F. Brinig, "Sex, Property Rights, and Divorce," 5 *European Journal of Law and Economics* 211, 215 and Figure 1, 1998)

power (in terms of earning capacity) than do their wives,[100] enjoy an increment of physical power greater than what they had prior to enactment of the no-fault statutes.[101] This occurs despite marital rape laws designed to offset husbands' physical power. From a biological standpoint, these statutes will on average protect women early and very late in their marriages. Spousal rape (to the extent that it is an expression of normal sexual desire other than an exercise of raw power and domination) should be less frequent in the middle period of marriages, when the wife's desire exceeds or approaches that of her husband. But it is during the period when husbands hold the property right, long called the time of the "seven-year itch," that many divorces and most adultery occur.[102] Divorce may ensue because one of the customary cards in marital bargaining (sexual intercourse) cannot be played. Thus, when other troubles in the relationship crop up, they may not be smoothed over as they were earlier in the marriage. Adultery may occur either because the wife is left sexually unsatisfied or because the husband finds that novelty in sexual partners piques his declining interest.

The other disturbing implication of differential patterns of desire is that biological distinctions, unlike socialized ones, are immutable. Even if society equalizes women's market earning power, and even if there is more sharing of child care between spouses, the biological differences will remain. Women will still be able to use their "property rights" early and late in the marriage to defuse potential dissolutions. They will not possess this ability during the middle period.

The middle period is also the time when many couples have small children. Women are therefore investing heavily in gestation, childbirth, nursing, and the care of infants, as Lloyd Cohen has noted.[103] One question is whether children will act as "little anchors"[104] or hostages keeping men in the marriage.[105] The relatively large number of divorces with children belies this premise, although hypothetically an extremely large number of "seven-year" marriages could be troubled, with only some dissolving to the point of divorce because of the preclusive hostage effect. My work with Allen and Nock suggests that this is true: marriages are more stable when there are minor children.

Of course, it is unwise to concentrate too much on these implications of biological gender difference. There are many other factors that simultaneously occur and influence the rate of divorce, and many of these will be discussed in Chapter 6. One is the investment by both spouses in careers, discussed earlier in this section, which reaches its height, but not its fruition, just as this biological time period begins.[106] Another is the fact that it is women who hold the ultimate power over reproduction.

My point in this section is that recontracting (or arguing, or what Joan Williams calls "gender wars")[107] takes place in all marriages. Whether these differences are resolved, and how they are resolved, depends in part on the relative bargaining positions of the parties (whether based on wealth, physical power, or sociobiology) and the alternative if they are not settled (divorce or "noncooperative marriage"). As we will see in the divorce bargaining section of Chapter 6, the outcomes (or what economists call the distributional effect) will also depend on the spouses' personalities, and specifically their attitudes about risk and altruism.

SHARING.   Armen Alchian tells the story of the fishermen who join together to take advantage of specialization and the economies of scale.[108] Eventually, even as they add units of labor and capital until the marginal product of each is equal to marginal cost, they encounter another problem, which he calls the problem of joint production. It is the same problem in miniature as the one faced by communist economies, as well as by marriages.

Marriage involves commitment and sharing. Experiences are shared, enjoyment is shared, work is shared, and income is shared. What, then, is the problem? The problem is that when more than one person works on a complicated project, at least a commercial product, so that exact input is hard to measure and one receives an equal share of the outcome, there is a tendency to shirk.[109] The more people involved, or the more complicated the task, the easier it is to shirk successfully. Eventually the risks of being caught are so small that only the saintly will resist the temptation and continue working to the maximum (according to his ability) to receive an equal share (according to his need). The economic term for this problem is principal-agent,[110] which I discussed in the analysis of foster care in Chapter 3 and will visit again in the child custody section of Chapter 7.

A different, and perhaps more familiar, view of the same problem is the Prisoner's Dilemma game.[111] In group enterprises, societies and families, happiness and wealth are maximized when everyone contributes 100 percent to the venture. Still, the actor knows that the best individual outcome is achieved by being the only shirker when everyone else is exerting maximum effort.

There are several strategies for reducing shirking. One is to employ a residual claimant who monitors those who exert effort and decides how much to reward each.[112] In the family, usually both spouses live in the marital home (i.e., they are residual claimants for or ultimate beneficiaries of housework). But they may have entirely different values for what is acceptable housekeeping. This results in the "gender war" of "I'd be glad to do the wash, but I don't mind not doing underwear for two weeks."[113]

This may be one explanation for the men's work/women's work effects observed earlier: "men's work" contributes to the value of externally verifiable goods such as houses and cars. "Women's work" contributes to the far more speculative (though important) value of increased comfort. We know that the contributions marriage makes to men's lives are quite considerable; married men do better than their otherwise equivalent single counterparts on every scale in areas such as employment, job responsibility and salary, health, longevity, mental health, and participation in social groups.[114]

The perception and reality here are the same: women disproportionately do housework even when both spouses are employed.[115] Income is shared if the spouses remain together. If they divorce, the spouse with the higher income keeps it or pays only a token or time-limited amount in spousal support. Some feminist writers believe that lifetime income sharing should be an integral part of marriage.[116] The part of me that believes in covenant[117] agrees but would not limit the sharing to finances. The spouses also are residual claimants for "parental consumption," and so should be dividing parenting responsibility more or less evenly as well. But here again, what succeeds in the commercial firm may not be a good analogy, since the spouses probably get entirely different levels of satisfaction from their minor children.[118]

In addition to establishing residual claims, another strategy to defeat shirking is for spouses to "pay by the piece," rewarding as each small job is done.[119] This works for routine or small tasks because the degree of effort is obvious and can be quickly assessed. Of course, assessment may come too late, as it did for two of my friends, both lawyers, who had their phone disconnected twice because the "spouse in charge," the husband, forgot to pay the bill. Strategic behavior may be involved here as well. The outcome for this particular couple is that the wife now pays the utility bills.

Piecework is related to a third shirking-reduction strategy, which is to divide the entire project into such small parts that there is no joint production except in the aggregate.[120] Although the monitoring effort is simplified, the gains from coordination are correspondingly diminished.[121] Obviously this kind of accounting is entirely unsatisfactory in marriage, as I point out in the introduction to this chapter and in my empirical work with Nock on keeping track of housework hours.

A final strategy to reduce shirking (or equalize work) is to create a very large incentive to maximize the joint effort.[122] This device is used by coaches giving pep talks to their teams. In marriage, the duration of the relationship and the ideal—if not the fact—of love give strong incentives to make the marriage work.[123] No-fault divorce has unfortunately diminished many of the values of these incentives, particularly because the legal residual claimant for some investments (such as children or professional degrees) is only one spouse.[124] Putting a spouse through graduate school, or accommodating the demands of a rising corporate star or military officer, or building a strong relationship with children will benefit the marriage only, or at best primarily, if it remains intact.[125] Consequently, the working spouse may well choose not to delay her own education or live at a reduced standard of living to finance her husband's education if she thinks it likely that the marriage will break up before the couple gets to enjoy the benefits of the increased earning ability. The father may choose not to spend tremendous amounts of time with his children if he feels that they will be "taken away" and his relationship with them sabotaged by a vindictive former wife.[126] By contrast, a joint custody statute that encourages relationships with children after divorce strengthens the incentives. Perhaps because the invested father values his children more and realizes that divorce is hard on them, there are fewer divorces where joint custody legislation is in place.[127] Some sort of guaranteed income sharing (whether or not the marriage continues) should work similarly to keep marriages together and counterbalance the distinction between more (men's work) and less easily verifiable (women's work) investments in the marriage.

COSTS OF SHARING. Becker's disciples and feminist scholars agree that one of the essential components of marriage is sharing. This, however, is where the similarity of their viewpoints ends. For law and economics proponents, on the one hand, sharing evolves naturally from comparative advantage and specialization.[128] Since the wife (specialist in household production) cannot recoup her human capital investments if the marriage ends, the husband, who retains his market investments, must compensate her with alimony. The more specialized the couple, the more efficient the marriage. According to this view, alimony is a permanent feature of the marriage landscape. For some feminists, on the other hand, income sharing is at best a temporary expedient, at worst an anchor to an inequitable system in which men exploit and dominate women.[129] If men and women were truly equal, they would not so much specialize as share household and market work.[130] Both husband and wife would participate in the marketplace to the extent that this made them happy, and both would participate in child rearing and in any other household tasks for which the market did not provide a satisfactory substitute.

The consequences of sharing take a tangible form in the concept of alimony and property distribution, which I will address again in Chapter 6. Feminists agree that realizing the dream of sharing has remained elusive in the vast majority of marriages. Women still perform most household jobs, and consequently earn only about three quarters as much as their male counterparts.[131] Here the feminist group splits. Some maintain that alimony should serve as a transitional or stopgap measure for homemakers displaced because of the change in legal and social regimes. Because they grew up, married, and stayed home with children in the reasonable expectation that either the marriage would continue or they would be awarded alimony, basic fairness requires compensation for the changes wrought by divorce reform and gender equality.[132] A minority argues that the promise of alimony discourages potential wives and mothers from investing in their own human capital to the optimal extent, reinforcing dependence, male oppression, and a society in which women can never be players without handicaps.

The characterization of sharing matters because it so dominates the rationale for alimony and property distribution, as I will show in my discussion of the marriage franchise in Chapter 6. The couple's investment in the reputation of their marital family, as well as its material goods, will continue to bear fruit even after divorce. (Thus, many years after his divorce, one of my colleagues confesses to true pleasure in his former wife's successful legal career. He is also very proud of their joint achievement, their adult son.) These ongoing portions of the marriage covenant are what I refer to as franchise. Arguably, the part of the relationship that continues (though the relationship is no longer recognized by law) should be taken into account in determining alimony. If we compensate according to the franchise nature of the post-divorce relationship, the key concept will be the investment in one's spouse or in the relationship. If we do not recognize franchise interests, alimony will instead either compensate for opportunities forgone or act as an incentive mechanism to promote optimal marriage behavior.

Apart from the fact that sharing in some form is central to marriage, it is obvious that the feminist ideal of shared housework has not been realized even when most married women work outside the home. Time studies chronicle the daily behavior of husbands and wives, mothers and fathers, and unmarried cohabitants. In each of these situations, labor is sharply divided even when both spouses work at full-time jobs. Most routine household tasks are done by women, who also perform most of the child care and associated functions.[133] Couples divide financial management and grocery shopping more evenly. More men than women take care of cars and yard work, roughly dividing "inside" and "outside" tasks. As Joan Williams has written,[134] the labor market expects an "ideal worker," who is almost invariably a married man with a homemaker wife who takes care of most of the behind-the-scenes work. Because women still perform these tasks, which eat into their leisure time, they cannot do as much in the paid job force as the men to whom they are compared. Thus they earn less, progress more slowly, and have lower opportunity costs from engaging in household production. That is, their employment sacrifices are more rational than their mates'. In order to change this pattern, either the ideal worker concept (characteristic of the labor force) or the (non)sharing of housework (characteristic of the household) must change. There is some evidence that both are in fact changing gradually.

PRIVACY LIMITATIONS ON SHARING.   Spouses do not share everything, despite their vows to "share and share alike." They retain some private spaces as individuals. Some of the things that remain private involve their innermost thoughts, obviously not the subject of legal proceedings. Some touch on questions of the appropriate involvement of courts "behind the marital veil."[135] Some concern such intimate matters as the wife's choice whether or not to carry a child to term.

The first category of privacy issues includes time-honored questions. For many centuries, spouses could not sue each other in tort because to do so would violate the "marital unity."[136] In other words, when they married, the two became one person, and a person cannot sue himself.[137] Although this marital unity has disappeared largely from the realm of property law,[138] it still retains some validity in tort, not so much because of the "unity" concept as for reasons of privacy. For example, in the nineteenth-century criminal case of *State v. Rhodes*,[139] the court found that a state could not hold the husband criminally responsible for beating his wife with a stick "no bigger than his finger":

> Our conclusion is that family government is recognized by law as being as complete in itself as the State government is in itself, and yet subordinate to it; and that we will not interfere with or attempt to control it, in favor of either husband or wife, unless in cases where permanent or malicious injury is inflicted or threatened, or the condition of the party is intolerable. For, however great are the evils of ill temper, quarrels, and even personal conflicts inflicting only temporary pain, they are not comparable with the evils which would result from raising the curtain, and exposing to public curiosity and criticism, the nursery and the bed chamber. Every household has and must have, a government of its own, modelled to suit the temper, disposition and condition of its inmates. Mere ebullitions of passion, impulsive violence, and temporary pain, affection will soon forget and forgive; and each member will find excuse for the other in his own frailties. But when trifles are taken hold of by the public, and the parties are exposed and disgraced, and each endeavors to justify himself or herself by criminating the other, that which ought to be forgotten in a day, will be remembered for life.

Courts are afraid that for them to interfere even in more egregious cases involving intentional torts might encourage suits for such day-to-day problems as the "unwanted kiss,"[140] and thus return spouses to the accounting (contract-like) behavior characteristic of the market rather than the firm. The "inviolate veil" of family autonomy derives from high, perhaps infinitely high, transaction costs. It is nearly impossible to recall the context of everyday family affairs, particularly when minor slights and adjustments go on for years. Nonetheless, modern courts have abrogated the doctrine in the case of simple, unintentional torts, such as automobile accidents and household injuries,[141] where the parties are covered by automobile or homeowner's insurance.[142] They have been more resistant to abolishing the immunity for intentional torts, although some courts have allowed suits where the action complained of was "outrageous" and destroyed any hope of marital unity.[143]

The second privacy concern involves individual rights on a constitutional level. Despite his obvious interests in and connections with his unborn child, a husband cannot interfere with his wife's right to choose whether or not to carry a pregnancy to term.[144] In recent abortion cases, practical interests, such as the progress women have made since *Roe v. Wade* and concerns about abuse, have outweighed the interests of the husband. In another context, a court rejected a husband's attempt to enforce a contract made prior to marriage that limited the couple's sexual intercourse to once a week (the wife insisted on more).[145] This last case reveals concerns about both family autonomy and individual privacy. Courts are loath to pierce the marital veil by entering the marital bedroom (and an inquiry into the frequency of intercourse, or requests for intercourse, would have had to accompany the husband's suit). They are also reluctant to second-guess individual decisions about marital sexuality, a matter over which each individual spouse has complete control.

Although the strongest claims of marital privacy supported the concept that a man could not rape his wife, violent sexual assault violates covenant promises such as the injunction that the husband is to "love his wife as his own body."[146] Once married women were accorded rights as people and citizens,[147] the ancient common law immunity from marital rape charges[148] necessarily disappeared as well. The assent to marriage was no longer seen as blanket consent to intercourse at the husband's demand.[149] Once the abortion cases fixed matters involving sexuality firmly within individual control, the husband's immunity from rape became a dead letter,[150] though there are still distinctions between marital rape and stranger rape in many state statutes. (Of course the proof problems, troublesome in most sexual assault cases, become still more intractable in marital rape cases.)[151]

The last several paragraphs have described the privacy concerns surrounding married couples in legal terms. The same phenomena may be analyzed in an institutional economic framework as well. The first set of problems—involving overregulating the marriage—are rather like the concerns leading to the concept of "bounded rationality" as a limitation on the complete contingent claims contract.[152] In other words, spelling out all the terms of a contract, and enforcing each minute detail, would itself be destructive of many long-term relational contracts,[153] whether commercial or marital.[154] In marriage this point explains why there are not more antenuptial (premarital) agreements: the necessary negotiation and specificity take some of the bloom off the most romantic relationship.[155] In the commercial parallel, if managers or employees of a business firm had to be continually afraid of lawsuits over the most trivial of matters, much worthwhile business simply would not get done. Similarly, overregulating a marriage, or what Milton Regan calls "the outside view,"[156] hurts marriages by encouraging a constant reexamination of whether continued confidence in or loyalty to the other spouse is worthwhile.

As we have seen, even if all eventualities in a marriage could be foreseen, specific enforcement of marital promises might be harmful. Finally, some of the qualities that make up a good marriage are simply incommensurable,[157] so courts may have difficulty dealing with them because they are at the same time such wonderfully familiar and incalculably worthwhile attributes.

COUNTERFORCES: MARRIAGE AS A NEXUS OF CONTRACTS.   One of the common ways lawyer-economists look at firms is as a collection or nexus of contracts.[158] If the firm, or the family, is nothing more than a collection of contracts, there is no reason to treat it differently from any other contractual arrangement. To the outside, the marriage is two, not one; on the inside, partners should be free to remain individuals, retaining all their juristic personalities, even between themselves.[159] This is market behavior, of course, and is therefore incompatible with the idea of marriage as covenant, since it violates the principles both of unconditional love and of perpetual duration. It is, however, compatible with the view of some scholars that couples should be entirely free to regulate the marriage contract: that marriage is essentially a private matter.[160]

The idea that privacy pertains to the marriage, not the individuals, does not sit well within this contractual framework.[161] And, as Milton Regan points out, this postmodern (contractual) family is not the sort of sanctuary in which intimacy can thrive.[162] The modern family member may feel alienated and alone despite being "in" a marriage or parent-child relationship. Thus, according to Bea Smith,[163] the partnership theory of marriage (with all its modern trappings of contract) fails to protect either the marriage or the people in it, despite the noble ideals of remedying gender inequality and counting the contributions of the homemaker.

In contrast to the business firm, there is more to marriage than merely a decrease in transaction costs. The love and intimacy that characterize marriage are quite unlike the economies of scale and scope that the firm generates for its owners. These qualities are hard to categorize, as Gary Becker noted in his Nobel acceptance speech.[164] They are the reasons why privacy exists, and are closer to the firm modeled by the new institutional economists than the law and economics paradigm. Yoram Ben-Porath, in his article "The F-Connection,"[165] wrote of firms and families whose names stand as a shorthand or symbol to the outside world of all the special qualities of the entity. Thus the firm (and the family) will develop a special reputation within the community for fair dealing, honesty, or quality.[166] Similarly, the marriage, as I see it, is shorthand for all the positive (and occasionally negative) attributes of the spouses as a couple. These qualities will be reflected in the concept of family franchise that is at the center of Chapter 7. They will, I argue, continue to hold the couple together even if the marriage ends in divorce.

Specific Investments in Marriage

One of the features that characterize successful marriages is the specific investments the spouses make in each other and in the marriage itself. As I have argued elsewhere, the increase in divorce in general, and specifically the costs of investment associated with no-fault divorce, decreases such investments.[167] These investments primarily include three types: investments in careers, investments in "public goods" (children), and investments in the relationship itself.

The legal literature has paid enormous attention to the first of these types of investments, and specifically to the professional degree or license earned during marriage. Most states hold that this token of advanced educational achievement (which of course is an investment in human capital and will typically produce some future earnings stream) is not marital property.[168] Elsewhere I have argued that to encourage such investments, alimony should at least reimburse the investing spouse if the marriage ends in divorce before the investment is recouped.[169] I will take up these claims in detail in Chapter 6, in the discussion of one spouse's entitlement on divorce to shares in the other spouse's earning capacity.

The second type of investment, investment in the children of the marriage, is perhaps the most obvious. Children are widely perceived to be the most important product of a marriage.[170] They are also the ones most likely to feel the effects of family problems, for example, lack of contact with the grandparents' generation[171] or their parents' divorce.[172] Martin Zelder has argued that children are a species of public goods: investment in them by either spouse does both spouses good without extra cost so long as the marriage continues. The children, or time with them, cannot be easily divided or bargained over to prevent a parent from leaving the marriage.[173]

Finally, but by no means least important, comes investment in the relationship. As I mentioned before, Lloyd Cohen has reminded us that some things must be done in a certain spirit to be worth anything.[174] Investment in the marriage, whether by lovingly cooking the spouse's favorite meals, working on the other's car, remembering anniversaries or birthdays, or graciously accommodating clients who come to dine, makes the marriage much more enjoyable for both spouses. When either spouse must be constantly anticipating injury by a divorce, there will be less of this type of investment. The spouse will invest more in his or her own career, and will have less time and energy for the family, or as a newspaper article surveying dual earner couples calls it, "for life."[175] He or she may also be constantly checking in the marriage market to make sure no good alternative is missed.[176] As Regan notes, our reliance on the family to gratify psychological needs holds the seeds of its own destruction.[177] We ground the family on "inherently dynamic emotional states."[178]

Products of Marriage: Autonomy and Intimacy (Marriage as Community)

The foregoing discussion is not unequivocally positive about privacy. Although the doctrines and the reasoning behind them establish what amounts to a presumption that the couple should be left alone by the state,[179] there are times when the individuals who are also spouses will be disadvantaged by this "hands-off" attitude.[180] Privacy operates to the advantage of the party who is stronger, and, like no-fault divorce,[181] will give rise to opportunistic behavior by this advantaged spouse. Thus, the doctrine of privacy erected the "veil" that prohibited prosecution of the husband in the nineteenth-century marital assault case cited earlier. The more disadvantaged spouse will usually be the wife, who is physically less strong and whose opportunity costs of leaving the marriage (even an unhappy one) are higher.[182]

On balance, and in the vast majority of cases, marital privacy, or the encouragement of a shared life together without the constraints of continually having to reassess whether the marriage remains "worth it," represents an opportunity for the kind of growth and freedom that will benefit most couples and their children.[183] The law, however, needs to be sensitive to the potential for opportunism that the doctrine creates. Abolition of interspousal immunity for intentional wrongdoing would prevent much of the harm, as would recognition that there will be consequences for a finding of fault upon divorce.[184]

Sharing has salutory effects not only for the individual spouses and their marriage but also on the national economy. Because it allows economies of scale and scope[185] in the production of important products that Becker calls "household production,"[186] as well as savings because resources such as housing and utilities are not duplicated, marriages enhance the gross national product. (In fact, a number of feminist scholars now assert that women's production in the household should be treated like any other, that is, it should be taxed and used as the basis from which to generate benefits such as Social Security and employment compensation.)[187]

Changes in the national economy itself are related to the tremendous influx of women, and particularly married women, into the labor force.[188] Wages in this country have historically been high in part because the majority of households had only one breadwinner. The fact that one's wife could afford to stay home and be a homemaker added to a man's status for over a hundred years.[189] Thus Becker's household production contributed immensely to the wealth of the country as women made men "ideal workers."[190] Of course, now that the pattern is changing, men complain that they are out of work because women (and minorities) are employed.[191]

As I noted briefly in the previous section, another and very substantial effect of the sharing done within families is its impact on future workers' (children's) human capital. Although Becker has done pioneering work in this field,[192] there have been momentous contributions from other economists as well.[193] The idea here is that for societies to advance, particularly technologically, there must be substantial investments in education and training.[194] Families have always done this type of training; in fact, Blackstone called it the father's most important task.[195] It was not until the mid-nineteenth century that the importance of education, and the vocation of the mother-teacher, became part of the married woman's "separate sphere."[196] Fathers and mothers contribute directly and extensively to determining what type of citizens and wage earners their children will become.

A Legal Test of Marriage as Firm: Marital Privileges

In a paper on marital privileges,[197] Milton Regan addresses the interesting problem of the evidentiary privilege in terms of "interior" and "exterior" views of marriage. His position is that the communications privilege (disallowing revelation of communications privately made to a spouse) fosters the "external stance." The engaged couple enters into a bargain (thus external to the incident itself), each partner making the decision that the protection the privilege provides outweighs the disadvantages of not being able to testify even when he or she would like to do so. In contrast, the adverse testimony privilege, in those states where it is required, is inconsistent with the external stance, because it is the marriage per se, rather than the voluntary conduct of the spouses, that triggers the protection of the privilege. The disability from testimony fosters a kind of security and trust, and therefore freedom within the marriage.

In order to think more carefully about what Regan is saying, we need to know a bit more about the privileges. At common law, the spouse was unable to testify at all, since in law the spouses were one, and there was an inability to give evidence for or against oneself.[198] The more modern position has been that one spouse is competent to testify against the other without that spouse's permission. This is not a requirement of federal constitutional law,[199] but may be mandated by state codes more protective of individual rights than the federal Constitution requires them to be.[200] Each spouse is capable of testifying in favor of the other at any time, but spouses may testify without the other's permission in criminal actions only where the witness or the child of either of them was a victim,[201] in actions where one spouse is the accused and the other the accuser, or when the marriage has been dissolved by divorce. The status of the marriage at the time of trial determines the competency.[202] In addition to the incompetence to testify, there is also a marital privilege. If one has communicated a matter to one's spouse by virtue of the marital relationship,[203] it may not be disclosed without permission. This is true even if the parties are divorced at time of trial, so long as the privileged communication took place while they were married. The spousal privilege exists because of the public policy of encouraging free communication between husband and wife. As the Court found in *Hawkins* (1958), "that would render susceptible of an exposure to public observation and knowledge all confidential conduct, transactions and acts not consisting of spoken or written words, which the continued tranquility, integrity and confidence of their intimate relation demands to be shielded and protected by the inviolate veil of the marital sanctuary."[204]

The same problem of balancing other societal interests with the "inviolate veil" can be looked at from an economic perspective as well. Admitting confidential communications might increase convictions of guilty persons (or reduce false negative errors), but it causes an externality: in the next court case, the total amount of available evidence will decrease because spouses will be on guard against each other and will share less. The rule's impact on the family may also cause loss. This is the risk that concerns both the author of the nineteenth-century case quoted earlier and Milton Regan. Another way of approaching this concern is to note that one of the ramifications of a confidentiality rule is the lowering of transactions costs. This low-friction system is what makes the corporation model attractive, as opposed to spot contracting. By analogy, we marry and we trust in part because it relieves us of a huge burden, both tangible and psychological, of continually reevaluating the trustworthiness of our confidant. Marriage and family life shortcut the market, and "the inviolate veil" protects us as we dare to be intimate with one another.

Although the classical theory of the firm gives us some valuable insights into marriage, it falls short in part because of the special characteristics of marriages, primarily intimacy and privacy. It may tell us why a continual stream of contracts will not work in the context of marriage, and even why people marry, but not why in the most successful marriages each spouse will gladly contribute without "counting the cost." Here the new institutional economics does far better. Through stressing transaction costs, the new institutional economics approaches the idea of covenant and the broader community concerns about marriage.

In the next chapter we will get perhaps an even clearer picture of covenant as we explore the parent-child relationship. The idea of covenant, however, includes the concept of permanence. In Chapter 6 I will grapple with the question of how to reconcile the idea of permanent commitments with divorce and emancipation, completing the description of covenant in Chapter 7 with the theory of the family franchise.

Parent and Child

I continue my discussion of covenants by examining the relationship of parent and child. This is a more straightforward candidate for covenant because the relationship does not usually begin with a contract and because children are unable to perform like most contracting parties, particularly when they are very young. Parents therefore have the legal and moral obligation to love and provide for their children without the promise of recompense (and therefore "naturally" behave as people do when they make covenants).

Although the parent-child relationship theoretically looks like a covenant, the legal movement, with very few exceptions, has, as with marriage, moved some distance toward a contract view. I begin with a discussion of the covenant relationship between parent and child, and continue with a description of the various incursions made by state regulation and the concept of children's rights into what used to be the sole province of parental decision making. The strong presumption that parents act in their children's best interests became the prevailing legal standard before the underlying framework changed. As with the consideration of marital sharing and division of labor, which in the ideal are also entirely consistent with covenant, we need to question whether the parental decision-making presumption still fits the economic realities.

The parent-child relationship is covenant-like in that parents have duties of love and support even if the child does not love them back. Further, the state, which might be described as the silent third party to the adults' hypothetical parenting contract, will enforce the obligations if the parents falter, assuming them only if they fail completely. Yet despite all I have said about the inapplicability of contract law to the relationship of parent and child, there are useful insights to be gained by examining the parents' traditional obligations as if they were contracts, and considering what the parents can hope to gain from the child in return for all they do.

Except in very unusual circumstances (such as adoption of an adult or the "tough love" contract sometimes made between troubled adolescents and their parents), any contracts that bind the generations together are implicit rather than express. Although frankly contractual contexts, such as apprenticeship, used to be widely recognized, contracts made directly between father and child or mother and child have never been legally, as opposed to morally, enforceable. The current trends toward thinking of the family in more explicitly contractual terms and recognizing more and more children's independent rights tempt some to question whether assumptions about the "traditional" family still hold. My own position is that the parent-child exchange ought to remain unenforceable because far more than contract binds the members of a family together. Covenant thinking thus acknowledges certain limits to the ability of traditional economics to describe family behavior.

Even aside from the erotic bond between spouses, the relationship between parents and young children is not the same as that between the parents, and for good reason. Children are not merely "little adults." Although the vast majority possess the potential to make meaningful adult contributions, their needs during childhood and even adolescence are quite different from their parents' or other emancipated people's. Children do not make decisions like adults, and should not be asked to. They therefore need legal protection to ensure satisfaction of their primary needs. They need to be free just to be children, and to do so they must rely on adults, usually their parents, to make adult decisions. The parents thus act as fiduciaries,[1] that is, trustees or stewards of their offspring.

Treating children as independent legal actors in any but the narrowest range of circumstances limits not only their ability to be children but also their parents' ability to be good parents. This is not to say that children should never be considered independently of the adults who act in their name, to repeat a point made in Chapter 2 during the discussion of surrogacy and adoption. Sometimes the interests of parents and child conflict, and sometimes the presumption that parents should always hold the trump card is simply misapplied. But "divorces" by children or damage actions for parents' less dramatic failures destroy families.[2] Recently discovered children's "rights" to sexual activity, contraception, abortion, medical care, and search and seizure privacy weaken parents' traditional legal authority as well as the opportunity for true family intimacy. They are inconsistent with the idea of covenant in many ways.

It is appropriate to begin this discussion of child rearing by considering once again, as with marriage, what the parties are trying to achieve (maximize). This time there clearly are more parties involved, whether we consider the effects on children and society directly or as externalities of the parents' activities. One possible way of looking at the parent-child relationship is to consider only what the parents want—that is, to say that the parents have the right to rear their children in whatever way they decide is appropriate. This strong form of parental rights holds that the state should never intervene in parental decisions, that children are like property possessed by their parents.[3] Although few today would advocate so absolute a position, a number of state legislatures have been considering the not too dissimilar prescription that, absent abuse, parents should have complete freedom to direct their children's upbringing without state interference.[4]

Another interest that might be maximized is the state's. The state is independently interested, on the one hand, in raising good future citizens and workers and, on the other hand, in minimizing the cost of crime, delinquency, and unemployment. During what lawyers refer to as the heyday of substantive due process, the Supreme Court considered various state attempts to create such model citizens. In the famous cases of *Meyer v. Nebraska*[5] and *Pierce v. Society of Sisters*,[6] the Court struck down statutes aimed at standardizing education in the name of protecting the citizenry and improving society. Fifty years later, Wisconsin tried unsuccessfully to insist that Amish students between ages fourteen and sixteen fell under its compulsory education statute. Again, the state's reasoning was that the additional years of schooling were necessary to create informed and capable citizens.[7] An effort (also by Wisconsin) to make marriage licenses contingent on showing that children from prior relationships were adequately supported met with a similar fate.[8] The statute was designed to encourage two-parent families, reduce welfare dependency, and strengthen the public fisc—all goals consistent with rearing responsible citizens.

A third interest that might be maximized is that of the child. The child might thus be said to have the right to adequate parents, the necessities of life, and stability, the right to be loved or to have a happy childhood. United Nations conventions[9] guarantee the first several of these rights. The others are implied by that ubiquitous formulation of the child custody and welfare laws, "the best interests of the child."[10] Perhaps the most extreme of this position's advocates are those who would allow children to "divorce" their parents or to possess an independent (and determinative) voice in questions of medical care and religious freedom.[11]

Rules for Resolving Conflicts: The "Best Interests" Presumption

Determining the possible interests that might be maximized serves more than an academic value. When two of the three—parent, state, and child—conflict, as they all too frequently do, there should be some rules for deciding which right triumphs. This problem of selecting the most important right recurs in parent-child interactions more than in any other area of family law. Though neglected in the lawmaking process and the academic literature,[12] the problem has been addressed fairly frequently in the general economic literature. Further, whether recognized or not, the Supreme Court's family law caseload has been dominated almost completely by this problem of identifying the most important interest. Some writers call it the rules-versus-discretion problem, some the choice of Type I versus Type II error. Type I error is whichever case lawmakers most want to avoid (an error of overinclusion or a "false positive"), even though they realize that their choice makes some Type II (underinclusion or "false negative") errors inevitable. Assume, for example, that the shaded area in Figure 5.1 represents a group of child abusers. There are two choices (A and B) about whether or not the state should intervene by taking the child out of the home or arresting the parents:

Choice A: Intervene on the basis of social science evidence about the patterns of abuse victims or abusers.
Choice B: Do not act on such evidence, but wait for intervention until it becomes clear that the victim actually has been abused.

In both situations A and B some abuse will occur, and some portion of that abuse (the shaded area that is also within a circle) will be appropriately identified and dealt with. And in both regimes there will also be errors. In case A, which should be thought of as a much bigger circle and much greater intervention, quite a few errors of overinclusion will be made. Some situations will apparently fit the stereotype of abuse, but the family will not in fact be appropriate for intervention. In case B, quite a few errors of underinclusion will be made. Some abusers will never be prosecuted or otherwise dealt with. The judge or lawmaker must choose which type of error is worse and identify it as Type I. If allowing some abuse to continue is the greater harm (that is, if the Type I error is failing to stop the abuse and protect the child, while the Type II or less critical error is to interfere with parental rights by misclassifying some non-abusive parents as abusers), the decision maker will make Choice A. If society decides that unnecessarily interfering with parents and their decision making is the greater harm (or that Type I error is misidentifying non-abusive parents as abusers while Type II is failing to stop abuse), it will opt for choice B. Historically, and in the vast majority of modern cases, courts and legislatures have classified interfering with parental rights as the Type I error.

Case law formulates this choice not to intervene—inconsistent with contract but consistent with the covenant ideal for families—as the rule that parents are presumed to act in their children's best interests.[13] I will argue later in this chapter that as the cases and statutes move closer and closer toward thinking about families in terms of contracts, the choice of nonintervention becomes less and less appropriate. The greater harm to modern families frequently occurs when interests conflict and children are not protected from their parents. I will suggest how these cases may be

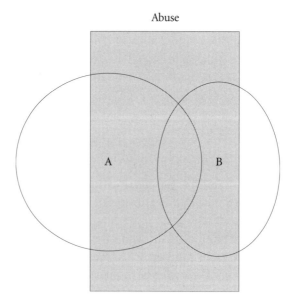

Figure 5.1 Types of error in child abuse cases

identified in advance so that children at risk can be protected without de-molishing all the social changes that have led to contract thinking. A re-turn to a more covenant-friendly system would also assuage the situation, but perhaps too many irreversible changes have taken place to make this option viable. In modern society it is hard to trust some parents even if the majority are doing their best. When parents are inclined to think of them-selves and overlook their responsibilities, and when children indignantly proclaim that they can make important choices for themselves, the hands-off treatment may be doomed.

What Makes a Parent? Nature and Nurture

One more theme of a universal type, more than a little inconsistent with the parental presumption, needs to be mentioned at least briefly at this point. The presumption that parents in most cases act in their children's best interests begins with the biological tie between parent and child,[14] which of course is missing from the bond between husband and wife. The blood (or, more accurately, genetic) relationship between parent and child is what creates the duty of parental support and the rights and privileges accompanying custody. To the extent that contract applies—and I will dis-cuss a related arrangement of a fiduciary nature—it runs between parent and child.

Some sociological research, however, disputes the accuracy of assum-ing a genetic source of parental affection. The idea is that affection and therefore felt responsibility come not from biology but from relationship. At least for men, the *felt* as opposed to the *legal* obligations of parent-hood come from the man's ongoing relationship with the child's mother.[15] Noncustodial fathers may thus prefer their stepchildren to children from a failed former relationship if they interact with the stepchildren more fre-quently and more positively. Not only are the new feelings stronger, but also the fathers may act on these impulses and support the new family to the detriment of the old.

This theory would imply that the parent-child relationship arises, at least in part, from some kind of a contract between the child's parents: a contract that could be amended as circumstances changed. But it is also consistent with a sense that for men, proximity and frequent contact with their children (with or without their children's mothers) is what counts.[16] If the necessarily close and frequent contact with his children persists beyond divorce—through joint custody and frequent visitation, for example—the original relationship or something very much like it might be better preserved, obviously with some losses in freedom to the children's parents.

The Duties of Parent and Child: Implicit Contracts

With some general idea of the ways courts interpret cases involving parents and minor children, we can turn to the implicit contract between parent and child that forms the basis of a covenantal or traditional family. This bargain was detailed by William Blackstone, writing between 1765 and 1769. At that time the language of contract was quite appropriate, for Western families then had quite different structures and functions.[17] In Blackstone's time the family contract looked something like this:

Parent's Duty	Child's Duty
Support[18]	Wages during minority;[19] support in parents' old age
Protection[20]	Protection in parent's old age
Education	Honor and reverence[21]
Discipline[22]	Subjection
Religious instruction[23]	Obedience

The fact that this contract is between members of different generations may at first glance seem problematic. Yet, as the Bible says, the sins of fathers may devolve upon their children.[24] Accepted wisdom dictates that societies receive the customs and institutions of their ancestors.[25] There will also be a "passing down" of attitudes about parenting. For example, the authors of one paper claim that in single-earner families, the father's attitude toward the fathering he received as a youngster will be the most consistent predictor of the amount of time he spends with his children.[26] As we saw in Chapter 3 on family formation, scholars have debated whether illegitimacy and welfare dependence are transmitted as well.[27] Economists have built important models assuming implicit ties between parent and child. For example, altruistic behavior within the family is said to occur in part because of the expectation of future inheritance from a parent.[28]

The change from the more static view of family duties and responsibilities to what we are now tempted to think of as a much more contingent parent-child relationship requires a short explanation. Legal historians have already examined the difference in laws relating to child custody and support as the role of children has changed. They have concluded that many of the current perceptions of childhood postdate the change from an agricultural to an industrial economy.[29] In the older agrarian economy, children over the age of five were assets, since they could work around the farm or household.[30] As cottage industry and then factory production developed, the feeding, clothing, and educating of children became more of a consumption activity than a financial investment.[31] The only positive input children could provide for the total family financial picture was their income,[32] which theoretically belonged to their parents.[33] And when child labor laws and compulsory education statutes were enacted,[34] even the relatively small income that most children could provide evaporated.[35] In the agrarian society, parents' interests, because they were economic as well as emotional and genetic, were very likely to coincide with the child's. It is not surprising that parents were left with almost complete control over the family domain.

The power of the implicit contract (or, more properly, covenant) analogy in Blackstone's time becomes more questionable when we analyze the contemporary family as an economic unit. This lack of fit is particularly evident when we consider the incentive structure within the family. Currently the incentive provided for investment in children is almost entirely subjective.[36] Parents may "spend" time or money on their children because they are altruistic.[37] They may invest in their children because they feel some sort of duty to do so.[38] They may act as they do because they take pride in their children's achievements, which enhance either the family reputation or their own immortality.[39] They may be hoping for some eventual reciprocity, at least in terms of a meaningful relationship with their children as adults.[40] Unlike eighteenth-century parents, they are unreasonable if they expect any sort of monetary reward. Yet we continue to have children, although as the economist Joseph Schumpeter put it: "As soon as men and women learn the utilitarian lesson and refuse to take for granted the traditional arrangement that their social environment makes for them . . . they cannot fail to become aware of the heavy personal sacrifices that family ties and especially parenthood entail under modern conditions. . . . The question that is so clearly in many potential parents' minds [is]: 'Why should we stunt our ambitions and impoverish our lives in order to be insulted and looked down upon in our old age?'"[41]

The law still presumes that some sort of a formal and fairly permanent relationship exists in the family setting. Parents clearly enjoy enormous discretion and privacy as they raise their children, although Blackstone's implicitly contractual family, with its covenantal overtones, seems to have nibbled at this concept from the direction of both the state and the child. The state now plays a far greater role in family life than in the past, and children have been given independent rights. But there are still limits on what children can do legally, in part because the law recognizes that they cannot make adult decisions. Consequently, the fully contractual or market-like family will never emerge.

Limits of Contract Caused by Differences in Children's Decision Making

As the Supreme Court noted in the abortion case of *Bellotti v. Baird*,[42] the constitutional rights of minors cannot be equated with those of adults because of the "peculiar vulnerability of children; their inability to make critical decisions in an informed, mature manner; and the importance of the parental role in child rearing."

Children do not make choices in the same way as their parents. They are deemed legally incompetent for some years after they can reason abstractly. These limitations may be placed on their decision making because children are at first more, then less, risk-averse than adults. Moreover, they are far more selfish than adults and demand immediate gratification. In this section I explore why these differences may have evolved as well as some new evidence that they exist. I am, in effect, exploring the peculiar makeup of the child's utility function.

Most of the sociobiological research to date focuses on behavior directly connected to reproduction, such as mate selection or infidelity, issues I explored earlier. This combination of biological and social sciences, however, maintains that all areas of social activity are related in some way to the transmission of genes. For example, sociobiology predicts that adult males will be more risk-taking than females because too much caution inhibits their financial and ultimately reproductive success. Younger males and females have not yet differentiated in all respects, and young people of both sexes exhibit the traits needed to survive to puberty—including risk aversion. In fact, the limited studies of risk taking in children have confirmed this behavior, although they have not explained it using sociobiology.[43] One study observed children at different locations in a zoo, such as on the elephant rides and at a riverbank, to see which age and sex groups would be most willing to take risks at those sites.[44] Boys, but particularly older boys, tended to take more risks. In empirical work of my own, I have confirmed the prediction that young children are far more risk-averse than adults or adolescents.[45]

Sociobiology also predicts that men will be less altruistic than women after puberty, because women must continuously make sacrifices for their children during the child-rearing period.[46] Children of both sexes should be relatively more selfish than adults in order to ensure their chances of survival until they reach reproductive age, and again, my studies have confirmed the selfishness found by others.[47] Finally, sociobiology would predict that children have much higher discount rates (that is, they need to be paid more to "save") than adults. They do not particularly need to plan, but do need immediate satisfaction of their material needs, in part because they do not have the physical reserves of adults. Common experience shows that young children have quite a different sense of time and seek immediate gratification.[48]

As John Locke wrote:

> The power, then, that parents have over their children arises from that duty which is incumbent on them, to take care of their offspring during the imperfect state of childhood. To inform the mind, and govern the actions of their yet ignorant nonage, till reason shall take its place and ease them of that trouble, is what the children want, and the parents are bound to do. For God, having given man an understanding to direct his actions, has allowed him a freedom of will and liberty of acting as properly belonging thereunto, within the bounds of that law he is under. But whilst he is in an estate wherein he has not understanding of his own to direct his will, he is not to have any will of his own to follow.[49]

Because of their biologically driven preferences, children need the protection and care of adults. They require the interventions of parents precisely because, as we have seen, they do not function like adults.[50] Adult preferences interpose reasonable amounts of risk taking, long-term planning, and altruism in order to ensure that children are provided for and to keep them from making irreversibly bad experiments.[51]

Mapping the Expanse of the Contractual View

Recently children have been given some autonomy in areas of personal privacy, such as contraception and abortion,[52] though the Supreme Court has upheld statutes giving parents of immature pregnant minors the right to be informed of their daughter's pregnancy in most cases.[53] As the child approaches majority, he or she may also acquire decision-making power in terms of elective medical care[54] and child custody placement when parents divorce.[55] Children over age seven are able to testify in most cases, and where criminal behavior directed at them is involved, even younger children may be witnesses if they understand the difference between right and wrong.[56]

Despite this growing legal independence, children are usually incapable of enforcing their parents' contracts, in suits with the parents or otherwise. The first reason why this is so, and why courts will not interfere in most families, involves an unwillingness to disturb family privacy. This reluctance was discussed earlier in connection with the Type I/Type II error problem. The doctrine is similar to the marital privacy concerns discussed in Chapter 4. *Kilgrow v. Kilgrow,*[57] for example, is a classic case involving an intact family. Mr. Kilgrow sued his wife for failing to abide by her agreement prior to marriage to educate the children in parochial school. The court reasoned:

> [I]f we should hold that equity has jurisdiction in this case, such holding will open wide the gates for settlement in equity of all sorts and varieties of intimate family disputes concerning the upbringing of children. It does not take much imagination to envision the extent to which explosive differences of opinion between parents as to the proper upbringing of their children could be brought into court for attempted solution. . . . Never has the court put itself in the place of the parents and interposed its judgment as to the course which otherwise amicable parents should pursue in discharging their parental duty.[58]

Thus, the first concern is that courts would have to deal with a flood of "intimate family disputes." Second, the court does not wish to "interpose its judgment" about proper child rearing.[59] Taking an extreme position even for a legal academic, Wendy Fitzgerald has argued that if children could enforce their parents' obligation to support them, they might evolve legally from what she calls a status of chattel to a higher form of personhood. She states that "children will remain excluded" from personhood under current law because "[t]heir experiences and perspectives of dependency find no recognition in any legal model positing an exchange between autonomous individuals."[60]

Courts do not usually allow the type of intervention Fitzgerald suggests, even when family privacy (a value separate from children's autonomy) has already been breached by the parents' divorce. Even contemporary courts therefore do not fully extend contract thinking to include the parent-child relationship. For example, children cannot sue to recover unpaid child support under a parental agreement or divorce decree, although courts may permit suits based on promises made solely for the child's benefit.[61] Nor will courts entertain the child's action for parental support if the child refuses to submit to parental authority or to live with either parent.

Although the outcome is nearly always against contractual enforcement, the reasoning takes several distinct paths. The court may reason that the child lacks standing to sue,[62] or, similarly, that the child was not a party to the parents' contract.[63] A second group of cases parallels the tort doctrine of intrafamilial immunity[64]: a child should not be free to sue a parent for support because such a suit would be disruptive to familial harmony or to the disposal of the "parental exchequer." As one court put it:

> The members of a family work together and contribute to the common good and welfare. They, through mutual effort and cooperation, make the determinations that contribute to that end. During minority the parents, because of their usual greater knowledge and experience, make the final determinations. Contributions during such period made by the child to his own support, maintenance and education out of his own earnings must be regarded as voluntarily made, either with the express or implied consent of the parents. It is the rule, as it ought to be, that no member shall idle away any portion of his time and when not engaged in the acquisition of education he will be otherwise employed and earn and contribute to his own welfare and that of the family. It is well established, based on sound reason and principles, that a child may not maintain an independent suit to recover against his parents for support and maintenance.[65]

As the cases make clear, to some extent the duty to pay child support rests on parents' reciprocal obligations of custody and support.[66] There is also an important relationship, arguably tied to the Judith Seltzer findings discussed in the "nature and nurture" section of this chapter, between the duty of support and the ability of the parent to exercise control over the child. For example, in *Oehler v. Gross*,[67] a seventeen-year-old girl refused to live with her father, who was willing to have her reside with him. She sought reimbursement for apartment rent, and the court denied that he had an obligation, stating: "It is quite clear from reviewing this record that the father is not refusing to support his daughter. Rather, he is refusing to allow his daughter to dictate the proper allocation of support monies." She somehow was not living up to her part in the family scheme.

Even the parents may not be able to enforce the implicit family contracts. As *Kilgrow* shows, courts are reluctant to invade the privacy of the intact family even when basic parental decision making is involved. If one spouse goes so far as to abuse the child, the other has the duty to protect the child,[68] but there is no way to compel affirmatively good behavior.[69] The only remedy seems to be breaking up the family by filing for divorce.[70] If the spouses divorce, there are still limits to enforcement. Decades of federal intervention have not ameliorated the child support enforcement problem: only 63 percent of the amount ordered is collected.[71] Visitation cannot be tied to child support.[72] Nor may the noncustodial parent force the other to spend the child support money for the child's benefit rather than her own.[73] Children must rely on other institutions, such as the informal pressure of the obligor's employer or the more formal pressure of child welfare authorities, to ensure parental cooperation in their upbringing. Because they cannot enforce contracts, the rationale for something like covenant becomes clear.

Finally, analysis of many of the third-party enforcement cases under the principal-agent framework of Robert Cooter and Bradley Freedman[74] reveals a ratification problem. Usually the child ratifies the parents' contract for support by providing what might be called "childhood services." Although many of these "childhood services" have been attenuated today by state involvement with the family,[75] parent and child still operate on a reciprocal basis, and the child's function at a minimum involves accepting parental support and advice. Rescission of ratification occurs when the child refuses to abide by the parent's wishes. The child may refuse to go to the college of the parent's choice, or to live at home while unmarried. In the extreme, the parent may be "abandoned" by the child. In such a case, the child will not be entitled to support.[76]

Measuring Changes through Investments in Children

In the brief discussion of family history that began this chapter, we saw that although commentators such as Locke and Blackstone used the language of contract to describe the family, in fact the relationship was one of covenant. But many family functions have changed with time. One observable change is that as recently as when our parents were children, elderly people frequently lived with their children's families. In the days before Social Security, when no one had heard of pension plans, IRAs, or TIAA-CREF, children provided the security when their parents could no longer work. Granted, there were fewer octogenarians and nonagenarians,[77] and most families had more children to share the expense of housing and caring for an aged parent.[78] But the change since then affects more than how children deal with their parents. In some industrialized nations, even though aged parents, like children, are no longer gainfully employed, they remain far more integrated into the economy and their families' lives than in the United States.[79] In North America and western Europe, we expect our elderly parents to support themselves out of some combination of accumulated savings, pension plans, and Social Security.[80] Unlike the elderly in non-Western industrialized nations,[81] our "seniors" largely live alone or in nursing homes. In this section of the chapter I explore the question of whether there is a connection between treatment of elderly parents and investment in minor children. As we will see in Chapter 6, this is one link between the covenant (involving children) and the franchise (involving parents).

Reduced to its simplest nonmathematical terms, the argument is that positive investments in children will depend in part on the parents' expectations of reciprocal care, or at least of substantial interaction with their children, when they reach an advanced age. Since families tend to mirror patterns of care through the generations,[82] an adult's current involvement with his or her own parents reflects these expectations. Of course, the family expectations will not be the only force influencing investment, so the empirical work must control for other factors as well. How can we measure investment in children, and what are some of the other factors that influence investments? Beginning with Gary Becker, researchers have examined the investment in children based on the number of children in the family (fertility rates).[83] Economists have related the number of children to factors such as parental income, years of education, and the divorce rate.[84] Another way of measuring investment in children is to calculate the time spent on their care. Studies have modeled time spent on children as a function of their age and gender, and parents' income and employment status.[85]

Other measures of investment in children may be quantifiable. One obvious additional measure of parental investment is the financial outlay.[86] One data source measuring this outlay is the payment of agreed-upon or court-ordered child support by noncustodial parents.[87] Another is the investment by the state in education for children; studies reveal, however, that this is not a successful predictor of performance on tests such as the Scholastic Aptitude Test.[88] A closer proxy might be state investment in gifted secondary school students by enrolling them in college-level courses. A data measure of the output of this investment is success on the Advanced Placement examination. Another data source measuring successful parenting is the child's performance on standardized tests given to all children in the school system.[89] Unfortunately, in addition to these positive contributions, families also make negative "investments," akin to dissipation or wasting of assets.[90] The data source that relates most directly to negative investment in children is parental child abuse.

If it is correct that there at least used to be an intergenerational pact to care for elderly as well as minor dependents,[91] investment in children will be greater where more elderly people are cared for by their adult children. Conversely, where many elderly people live alone, their children will not invest as much in minor children. In order to explore these predictions (as well as the alternative that parents will invest more in children if they do not have a responsibility to care for the elderly), I collected both national and international data.[92] I looked for evidence of both positive and negative contributions by parents. In each case I examined whether I could isolate provision for the elderly as an important contributing factor to the investment. The independent variables included general demographic information as well as the percentage of elderly people living alone. In all cases I found that the percentage of elderly living alone was statistically significant, and was in the direction I expected: more positive investment (reflected in test performance) occurred where a lower percentage of elderly lived alone, more negative investment (abuse or nonsupport) where there were more elderly on their own.

There are at least two possible explanations for the observed relationship between treatment of the elderly and treatment of children. One possibility is the strictly contractual or economic one: parents who expect to be supported by their children in their declining years are likely to make greater investments in them. The other, not inconsistent explanation is that some cultures revere elderly family members more than others. Data within the United States tend to support this second possibility only to the extent that American states are heterogeneous. A better test would be to examine very similar countries that differ only in the percentage of elderly living alone. For example, if one could examine data from North and South Korea, Croatia and Slovenia, or former West and East Germany, in a series of pairwise comparisons, the observations would be interesting. Another study that could be done would involve a negative relationship with elderly people. Is there more elder abuse in places where people detach themselves from their adult children, all other things being equal?

Of course, both explanations are related. If the culture supports reverence for one's ancestors for a non-economic reason such as religion, the economic result may hold true as well: the aged will be supported by their adult children.[93] A deeper regard for all family members will increase benefits for both the children and the elderly. Thus, one would expect the investment in children that is reflected in my analysis.

There are therefore two recommendations, besides the suggestion for further study, that might be made. One assumes that the economic motivation is dominant: if public provision for the elderly results in less investment in children, some thought might be given to discontinuing or limiting public support.[94] The other assumes that the cultural motivation dominates, although the economic effect might follow.[95] Under this alternative view, the Western nations, which are the ones with the least significant connection between adults and their parents, might try to strengthen these ties. We could begin the process by making heavy investments of time and money in our own children,[96] or by setting the example for our children by offering a home for our elderly parents.[97]

Finally, to some extent, strengthening connections by marriage, adoption, and joint custody, especially for men, who tend to be removed from direct participation in the care of both children and the elderly,[98] may require a change in emphasis in legal interpretation.[99] This, of course, is exactly the opposite position from that adopted by writers such as Martha Fineman,[100] who, though she acknowledges dependency on the part of the very young, the very old, and their caregivers, advocates a secondary role for both marriage and fathering, and stresses public support.

Does Efficiency Work as a Goal of the Law of Parent and Child?

The fledgling lawyer-economist asks the family practitioner what is efficient, not what is best. Perhaps this is because newcomers to law and economics seem at once attracted to and confused by various concepts of efficiency. They understand that many of the more venerable thought in the movement has concentrated on maximizing efficiency as the goal to which society, and therefore law, should strive. The confusion sets in when they try to differentiate between the theoretical concepts of Pareto efficiency[101] and what is called Kaldor-Hicks efficiency.[102]

Pareto efficiency results when an agreement or action leaves *none* of the parties worse off than before, and perhaps benefits both. Kaldor-Hicks efficiency promotes conduct in which the sum of the benefits exceeds the sum of the costs. A third party may in fact not be compensated under the Kaldor-Hicks criterion so long as theoretically he or she could be made whole from the benefit to the transacting parties.

The question of whether Kaldor-Hicks efficiency is welfare-maximizing comes up in family situations because parents often make decisions that may be optimal for themselves but perhaps harmful for their children. For both a mother and father to work outside the home may not be the best situation for the children,[103] though it may give each of the parents greater satisfaction. Two working parents may be necessary for financial survival of the family, and may provide the additional funds needed to purchase goods such as private schooling or sleep-away camp. Entering the labor force may be necessary for the psychological well-being of the parent who had stayed home to care for the children when they were very young.[104] He or she may be better equipped to deal with the children's needs after a day spent in some sort of meaningful activity with adults. In any event, if the well-being of the entire family, including the disadvantages to any children, is considered in making this type of decision, it will be Pareto as well as Kaldor-Hicks efficient.

In the family setting, the two efficiency criteria are likely to produce different results when the parents separate or divorce. Then mother and father may well be making an agreement that is efficient for the two of them, considered separately.[105] The decision to dissolve the family, however, almost always disadvantages the children, sometimes very substantially.[106] Because the divorce process is usually painful for the adults, even if they could, they do not always think about compensating the children for the losses they will suffer: the absence of the noncustodial parent and the financial losses that are inevitable in most divorcing families. Perhaps for this reason, state legislatures and courts provide some remedies for children of divorcing families that are not available in intact families. Good examples of these are the provision of support beyond the child's minority,[107] or the requirement that the noncustodial parent supply medical insurance[108] or college tuition.[109] Such compensation is not perfect, and may be inadequate in most cases, but it may be enough to deter couples on the margin from separating and causing the children harm. Nothing yet convinces child advocates of the wisdom of these developments toward Pareto efficiency (in which everyone involved is actually, as opposed to theoretically, made at least as well off).[110] It may be true that the separating parents could not even meet the Kaldor-Hicks criteria—that the surplus they gain from divorcing is not even hypothetically enough to compensate the children for their loss. In this case the divorce is truly inefficient for the family as a whole.[111]

To understand this problem of mixed loyalties fully, we must spend a little time on the doctrines of parental tort immunity as we did on the limitations on children's ability to sue their parents in contract. We also need to reflect briefly about parents who are not considering their children at all. Increasing the rights of parents and further immunizing them from scrutiny makes little sense where parents are not behaving appropriately under any test of efficiency.

The common law handles torts involving family members as part of a system forged during a much simpler time. The father used to control all his children's property, and owed them support, protection, discipline, and education; they owed him obedience and respect. Children were conclusively presumed incapable of making decisions and of defending themselves from enemies in armed combat. In consequence, the tort system presumed that the parent would be responsible for the child's actions, and thus there could be no suit between parent and child.

The case that set the pace for the accompanying doctrine of parental immunity in this country was *Hewellette v. George*.[112] In *Hewellette*, a mother had her child committed to an insane asylum without just reason to do so. The child later brought a claim against this parent for false imprisonment, and the Mississippi Supreme Court barred the claim under parental tort immunity. In this and succeeding cases, the Mississippi court delineated rationales for the doctrine (somewhat similar to those in *Kilgrow*, which

involved parents' disagreement over whether to send their daughter to parochial school), including (1) the maintenance of peace and harmony
within the family unit;[113] (2) the parent's need for broad discretion when
disciplining and controlling the child;[114] (3) the fact that, through inheritance, a parent would ultimately procure the damages paid to the child after the child's death; and (4) the fear that the child would ultimately suffer
from the exhaustion of the family's financial resources because of the parent's litigation expenses.[115]

As some of the strictly financial concerns of *Hewelette* have been alleviated through insurance, the parental immunity doctrine has been abrogated or limited in a number of jurisdictions. For example, Illinois now allows a child recovery for any parental breach of a duty owed by the general
public.[116] The court in question, however, expressly provided that the parent has no legal duty to supervise the child. Thus, any injuries to the child
which result from a failure to supervise do not constitute a breach of duty,
so the child cannot sue in tort.

The concerns about interference with appropriate parental decision
making have not been so quick to disappear.[117] For instance, in *Holodook v.
Spencer*,[118] the New York Court of Appeals gave careful consideration to
such possible objections as it abolished the doctrine. First, the court high-
lighted the concern that a negligence action brought by the child might
place an undue burden on a parent by restricting the parent's necessary
discretion in raising the child. Second, the opinion expressed concern that
a parent might not properly segregate the child's tort recovery but might
use the money paid by a third party (such as an insurer) as a refund for
whatever sum the court ordered the parent to pay the child. The result in
such a case would be that the parent would not have to bear any consequences of wrongdoing. The court recognized, however, that children may
wait until they are adults to bring suit, since the statute of limitations does
not begin to run until the child reaches the age of majority. Even if the
child chooses not to wait and sues as a minor, the court can place the
money award from the parent in a trust, thus eliminating the threat of mis-
appropriation of the child's funds.

Like New York, California abolished parental tort immunity. But California replaced the doctrine with the "reasonable parent" principle.[119] In
an effort to define a duty owed to a child by a parent, in *Gibson v. Gibson*
the California Supreme Court created the "reasonable prudent parent"
standard,[120] holding that "[t]he standard to be applied is the traditional

one of reasonableness, but viewed in light of the parental role." In the California case, a father ordered a child to get out of an automobile and onto a highway at night. A passing vehicle struck the child and the child sustained injuries, for which he was held able to recover from the parent.

Yet, in most states, some qualifications to unlimited tort suits against parents prevail. First, there are the cases in which the parent is merely trying to exercise a parental role, such as supervision of a child. An example is *Wright v. Wright*,[121] where a daughter was injured after her contractor father permitted her to play in his backyard shed, in which he had stored dangerously sharp awnings. In these cases, if the parent is to be allowed the necessary freedom to bring up the child, second-guessing parental decisions violates the covenant concept. Carried to an extreme, the child would sue for what was in essence bad parenting. The most famous of these cases is *Burnette v. Wahl*,[122] involving a group of institutionalized children who unsuccessfully litigated against their parents for neglecting them. Related to this idea is the holding of *Kilgrow v. Kilgrow*,[123] which forbade judicial interference with an intact couple's decision making about where to send their daughter to school. Allowing such suits, and interfering with parental judgment calls, might eventually lead to suits for failure to allow the child to see certain movies or to have the latest model of tennis shoes. Allowing litigation (where there is no insurance coverage) promotes contractualization, making the home more like the market. Disallowing damage actions in all but the "outrageous" cases promotes family harmony and unity, more consistent with covenant, where no one considers suing another or requires precise accountings either of money or of behavior.

Another way of looking at these cases involves reconsideration of the doctrine of family privacy, discussed at some length in Chapter 3. The outside community does not have the right to interfere in the functions that parents have never ceded to it: those involving the upbringing of their children.[124] But neither the common law view nor the constitutional one provides an easy application of law and economics principles. For this we must once again return to the difference between individual autonomy and family decision making, the market and the firm. In this view, courts do not (and should not) interfere with the types of decisions that are necessary to the internal functioning of the "family firm."[125] These, of course, include parental choices about the upbringing of the children (unless these violate some criminal prohibition), which choices may include some delegation to government as an *ex ante* contract.[126] The noninterference (firm or covenant) position would also allow parents unfettered discretion in carrying out the everyday tasks of family life.[127]

Not just because they love their children but also because, as members of the family, they work toward common goals, parents will presumably act in the next generation's best interests and seek to maximize their children's value as future friends and citizens. They will therefore act efficiently in the broadest, non-financial sense, supervising them as much as is worthwhile (without "coddling" or detracting from the other functions the parents must perform). Only if parental behavior is clearly at odds with family goals—directly harming the children, or indirectly keeping them from thriving[128]—should the state interfere by allowing suit. Interfering with parental prerogatives is thus the Type I error in an ongoing covenantal family.

The Parental Covenant

As parents we presumptively act in our children's best interests. We are bound by some sort of unenforceable contract to do so. As with the married couple, the covenant is an analogy for parent-child relations that holds more promise than the contract. The parties to a covenant may enjoy horizontal equality, although parents and children are typically in a more vertical relationship.[129] Unlike their contract-bound counterparts, however, they are not generally seeking "fairness," but rather are willing to give beyond what is fair.[130] The biblical parallel to family covenants is God's generosity even when what we are given—or what we accomplish in return—may not be equal. The family under the rubric of covenant extends beyond the nuclear arrangement. It includes close relatives such as grandparents and, at least in some senses, the whole community.[131] And, as we will see, the reciprocal relationships continue even after children reach majority.

Covenant, much better than contract, explains why some aspects of parenthood cannot be altered even if both parents agree.[132] For example, parents cannot avoid the duty of child support entirely.[133] Even when the minor child marries or moves in with a boyfriend or girlfriend, the duty to support may revive if the child becomes indigent.[134]

The strict law and economics view is that noncontractual obligations are default or off-the-rack provisions,[135] or that they substitute for what parties wanted *ex ante*.[136] But since both the parties in question may not want these obligations, even beforehand, the law and economics view of prior agreement does not explain all the obligations that bind family members.[137] Some aspects of family life, which I attribute to covenant, are invariable because they are necessary for the family to meet both its historical and its present-day societal obligations. They make the family what it is. They are beyond economics, and therefore beyond contract. Covenant thus explains, at least in part, why even well-intentioned attempts to move family law too much toward individuality or contract, like the "children's rights" movement described earlier in this chapter, have very significant negative consequences.[138]

Covenant, to repeat some of the ideas from the previous chapter, describes a relationship characterized by a special kind of love: one that is boundless and unearned. The person in a covenant relationship expects, with justification, that it will go on forever. The emphasis is on giving, not receiving; on enjoying the gifts given to others rather than reveling in the gifts one receives from them. Covenant, then, describes altruism in the framework of relationship. It is the essence of the "firm-ness" described throughout this section of the book, although, of course, the family is not a traditional market firm. Covenantal love also differs in some respects from Becker's description of altruism,[139] which he derives from a single parent's caring. In addition to requiring only one active party rather than the two or more needed for covenant, Becker's definition of altruism also implies that the altruist must have the means to withdraw or withhold support from the rest of the family,[140] and does not imply sacrifice without expectation of reward.

Legally, a covenant frequently is an especially solemn type of contract, one that cannot be broken without significant penalties.[141] A covenant, or promise under seal, will support a gift to a third party where a simple contract would not.[142] Covenant implies donative intent, conferring a benefit upon another. Since the other will act (for our good) regardless of our own behavior, it implies that once we give our initial assent, much of our behavior is constrained by the covenant. As a theologian notes: "[P]arenthood is a participation in the covenant with God, who presides over the generations of our history on the land. Both parents participate in the covenant as parents, not as spouses. . . . Upon the failure of the marriage this covenant cannot be dissolved summarily and reconstructed by the courts."[143]

When the covenant is made, therefore, more than the two people are involved. The imprimatur of the state (or God) is placed on the solemn promise.[144] The covenant concept also allows us to make some judgments about the unwed father.[145] He is increasingly litigating his plight in the language of lost parental rights.[146] Although there are undoubtedly many exceptions to the rule, most unwed fathers are unwilling to make the commitment necessary for fatherhood.[147] They want the rights but not the covenantal imprint of parenthood. This may be simply because of their lack of connection to the children's mother. Particularly if we look in terms of what is best for the children in such situations,[148] the two-parent alternative is usually more attractive for a host of reasons, including the health of the child.[149]

An example drawn from Milton Regan's book *Family Law and the Pursuit of Intimacy*[150] illustrates the difference between contract, status, and covenant. Regan's conclusion features a hypothetical married man who has gradually become more involved with his work and less involved with his wife and daughter and is contemplating divorce. Regan notes that modern society promotes the message that "ultimately Dad's involvement with his family is a matter of personal choice."[151] The modern marriage, even fatherhood, becomes a matter of contract, to be honored only if there is no better alternative. Regan's suggestion is that family law should provide an alternative—a vision of a person in context or relationship.[152] In his terminology this is "status," which in this case would at a minimum cause the hypothetical man "to think very carefully about the ramification of what he does" for his wife and daughter.[153] Yet however hard he has thought about his family relationships, the man can still extricate himself in Regan's relational or status-based family. But a covenant, even more than a diamond,[154] is forever.[155] Even if the couple divorce, vestiges of their relationship remain, particularly if there are children. A family covenant, much like a promise "running with the land," cannot ever completely dissolve. The parent still remains a parent even when his own hair is graying.

Earlier I implied that men and women are complementary factors in child rearing.[156] Women may be more likely to perform their role as parents without prodding (or channeling) than men. But, as Judith Seltzer[157] puts it: "For women, marriage and parenthood are distinct institutions. Women provide for children's needs, whether or not the women are married to their children's fathers. For men, marriage defines responsibilities to children. At divorce, men typically disengage from their biological children. When men remarry they may acquire new children whom they help to support."[158] Men are most likely to contribute in cash or in kind when they are certain of fatherhood, and when they can interact with the child. They are most likely to invest when they have the ability to monitor how their money or energy is spent and how their child is doing, either through frequent contact with the child or through trust of the maternal "agent." They are also most likely to keep their support commitments when they do not have new families to distract them or drain financial resources. All of these reasons suggest why marriage, as opposed to some alternative family arrangement, is necessary for "first best" child rearing.[159] Children are not just secondary factors to be ignored or non-actors whose preferences should be lumped in with their parents'.[160]

Conflicts between Parents and Children: Veering toward Contract

More and more frequently courts must decide cases involving parents' competing interests.[161] The language of these opinions emphasizes parental rights, not the obligations owed to children. For another example of conflicts between parents' and children's interests, let us revisit the surrogacy problem we saw in Chapter 2. The parents on both sides of the recent wave of surrogacy contracts seem to be acting largely for their own benefit rather than that of the children concerned. The infertile couple contracting does so to relieve marital stress or to continue the father's genetic line.[162] Obviously the particular child benefits from an existence he or she would not otherwise know, but at a large potential cost: publicity as opposed to privacy is still the order of the day in such families, and conflict between the biological parents (surrogate and married father) may result.[163] As we saw earlier, the surrogate acts from a mixture of motives.[164] She may need the additional money to make her life more comfortable, may act out of sympathy for the father and his wife, or may wish to bear more genetic children than she can afford to raise herself. Since most contracts require the surrogate to have borne at least one child of her own to overcome questions of lack of informed consent, surrogacy may therefore pose problems for her existing children. Is the surrogate acting in their best interests?[165]

A number of other custody cases also place the parents and child in potential conflict. For example, the Supreme Court case of *May v. Anderson*[166] held that a father could not be awarded custody of his children, then living with their mother out of state, when the mother did not appear in court, because "a parent's right to custody is a personal right more precious than alimony." In the much-publicized "Baby Jessica" case, *Schmidt v. DeBoer*,[167] the parents' litigation over rights in the context of a jurisdictional dispute resulted in custody being transferred after more than two years' placement in a suitable adoptive home, at a tremendous cost to the child involved. This case illustrates the expansive power of biological parents, particularly unwed fathers, to withhold consent for adoption. Despite the child's long placement away from her birth parents and the fact that it was the birth mother's deception that created the loophole voiding adoption,[168] custody was returned to them because of the procedural irregularity of nonconsent by the father.

Thus, courts as well as legislators and economists tend to place greater emphasis on parental rights than on those of the children they purport to help.[169] I have discussed this problem in the context of divorce cases, where parents are pitted against each other. In part because courts recognize this problem, they place limitations on the parents. For example, they cannot entirely bargain away the child's right to receive support.[170]

A few custody cases speak in terms of the child's right to parental custody, thus moving toward covenant by minimizing the parents' rights and emphasizing their obligations.[171] Yet in many adoption and termination cases courts have extended the power of natural parents, presumably because interference with the parent is deemed a Type I error.[172] It has become extremely difficult procedurally and substantively to prove permanent parental unfitness,[173] with the result that the number of children in foster care whose parents still have enough "rights" to prevent adoption has expanded geometrically.[174]

The presumption that parents act to best benefit their children works in many cases. That, no doubt, accounts for its longevity and ubiquity. There are identifiable occasions, however, when the parents cannot be presumed to be putting their children's needs above their own, when neither Kaldor-Hicks not Pareto efficiency describes their decision making. In these cases the strong presumption that parents know best seems tragically misplaced.

Child Abuse: Where Parents and Children's Interests Conflict

If a child is "different" whether ugly, or disabled, or in a parent's way, or even because she is a girl—she may suffer many of the torments of the Ugly Duckling in the Hans Christian Andersen fairy tale. But "The Ugly Duckling" is make-believe. In reality, the abused child will usually *not* emerge a beautiful swan, but will become permanently scarred emotionally, if not physically. Abused children do not fare as well as others in school, as adults, and particularly as parents. They make up a tragically large proportion of criminals and others who never seem to be able to adjust. The victims of abuse are seen as different from other children. They may simply be unattractive. They frequently do not seem useful to the adults who care for them, perhaps because they are disabled and will require ongoing care, or because their problems interfere with the abusing parent's other adult relationships.

Children may be considered ugly because their faces or bodies are not perfectly symmetrical.[175] Thus the premature child who must spend many days in intensive care is harmed not only because he is separated from the contact and love of his parents,[176] but also because his skull may be malformed or because he may not act like a cute, cuddly baby when he is first released to his parents.[177] Beautiful people, throughout their lives, are revered by a society that rewards vigor and youth.[178] They are popular as dates and chosen early as mates, and the most beautiful of all may grace magazine covers or feature films. Ugly people, by contrast, are discriminated against in the marriage market and find it difficult to be successful on the job market as well.[179] Most troubling of all, ugly or even "plain" children are more apt to be abused by their families than those with a more pleasing appearance. The tendency for these children to be abused increases if family resources are scarce.

Ugliness, then, has some connection with lack of fitness for breeding purposes.[180] Physical ugliness may be overlooked if the person is "useful" enough: if he or she can contribute in other ways to society to make up for the lack of comeliness. This consideration may have a genetic basis, too, for the natural inclination is to wish to pass on one's helpful genetic endowments. Ugliness thus relates to one's ability to be a successful producer as well as a successful breeder. This is why disabled children are more apt to be abused by their parents, which only adds to their tragedy. They are not likely to be able to support their parents in old age,[181] and frequently they will not be able to support themselves. They also tax their parents' patience, thereby "costing" more. They are therefore seen as a burden to their parents and society.[182] A child may also be seen as ugly, regardless of physical appearance, when the parent perceives that the child is troublesome, such as a child who has mild learning disabilities.[183] Although the child will have just as many chances as the average person to reproduce, and may well enjoy a productive life as an adult, once past the pressures of having to conform to the conventional learning style, the parents of a learning disabled child, especially a bright one, will find the school years much more difficult than if the child were a normal learner. The parent must "run interference" with school authorities and continually set limits for the child. There may well be special education expenses or visits to a counselor or medication, all of which stretches the parents' capacities and patience and limits their leisure time.[184] Further, the child with hyperactivity or attention deficit disorder will frequently be emotionally taxing for the parent. He or she may be unable to "read" the parent's emotions to see when the parent has reached the point of exasperation. Also, the learning disabled child, regardless of physical appearance, may be emotionally dull and therefore "ugly."

Another form of ugliness having nothing to do with the child's physical or mental beauty is ugliness by interference, as when a child lives with a parent involved in a new romantic interest.[185] Having a child lessens the custodial parent's chances for remarriage, and second marriages involving children of prior relationships stand a much greater chance of dissolving.[186] This child's unattractiveness also emanates from a biological concern. The parent or stepparent may consciously or unconsciously feel that the child competes for the other adult's affection,[187] thus threatening the chances for producing offspring from the new relationship.

Applying the sociobiological tools I have discussed,[188] we can see that a child who is disabled, unattractive,[189] or interfering[190] (all from the point of view of the caregiver) would be less successful at, or would at least create barriers to, passing along a parent's "good" genes and therefore would "naturally" be the target for abuse. Even if the parent did not directly harm the child, he or she might not prevent harm, or might be guilty of neglect.

Using data obtained by researchers at Cornell University,[191] drawn from a national sample of abused children[192] and consisting of 2,305 adults and 2,662 children under eighteen in families where abuse was confirmed,[193] Frank Buckley and I[194] have isolated characteristics of the abused child that differentiated him or her from the siblings. Because all the families in the sample included at least one abused child, there was no obvious "normal" group to act as a control. We therefore concentrated on families with at least two children.[195] We selected those families in which one child was abused and at least one other was not (140 families). The foregoing discussion would predict that, where abuse occurred in a family with a disabled child and other children, the disabled child would be the one most likely to be abused. We therefore were most interested in the factor of "disability," though we also looked at the child's age, birth order, and racial background (compared to the parents), and alcohol or drug use by the parents.

In all equations, the child's disability was significantly related to increased abuse. This finding strongly supports the hypothesis that disabled children are more apt to be abused. Not surprisingly, the incidence of abuse increases with age and decreases with birth order. Thus, children who are expected to succeed and then disappoint parental expectations, such as older or mildly disabled children, are most likely to be victims of parental abuse. On the margin, parents who have more than one child will abuse only the child who is "ugly." The parents in our study did became abusive, but only selectively so. The coefficient for stepparents was positive where it was tested, consistent with the hypothesis that children who are "ugly" because they are in the way are also abused more often.

From this study of parents who demonstrably did not take their children's interests seriously enough, we can draw some tentative conclusions. When parents' and children's interests partially or totally conflict, the presumption that parents are acting in the child's best interests may not be the best rule, particularly when the child is "ugly." Legislators should consider changing the burden of proof so that such children are not returned over and over to abusive parents.[196] As the popular media have pointed out, the foster care system does not adequately protect these children. Frequent moving is the worst thing for them: they cannot bind with any adult and may never be able to trust even if they are not physically destroyed.[197]

The current practice of continually reuniting child and parent and keeping the relationship extant despite years of foster care should yield to a different presumption the first time a disabled child is abused. The presumption should be that the child would be better off elsewhere, despite the strains of such a move. This would prevent such tragic cases as those of Pauline Zile, who let her new husband torture and abuse her daughter,[198] or Joshua DeShaney,[199] beaten into a permanent vegetative state by his father despite frequent prior hospitalizations for what was obviously abuse. Such a change would also require permanent separation (placement for adoption) in many of the cases of termination of parental rights that have been landmarks for procedural due process: *Santosky v. Kramer*,[200] *Lassiter v. Department of Social Services*,[201] and *M. L. B. v. S. L. J.*[202] In all of these, parental rights were terminated without proper procedural protections, according to the Supreme Court. But in each instance the parents had already been found responsible for very serious prior abuse.

Toward Covenant

In this chapter we have seen the full gamut of the contractualization and individualization of the family. We have noted the growing tendency toward recognition of children's independent rights and the concomitant movement toward more state usurpation of parental decision making. We have seen that incentives for parents to invest optimally in their children diminish in the world of the family contract just as they flourished in the heyday of the family covenant. My own conclusion is that contract and tort suits may not be the most successful path toward ensuring that children are brought up to become "productive citizens." Legal recognition of the family covenant simultaneously protects against infringements by the state and supports beneficial investments by parents on their children's behalf.

Parents are presumed to act in their children's best interests. When interference by the state is involved, this is usually an appropriate presumption. but when parents' and children's interests partially or totally conflict, as in cases where marriages break up, new romantic interests are involved, or children are disabled, this may not be the best rule, even for fit parents. Courts must then continue to ensure that the child's best interests are served by parental decision making.

Families are more like firms than they are like markets, but the commercial analogies still break down because families do not simply maximize financial wealth. They are full of unconditional love, and they last, in at least some senses, forever. Unlike commercial contracts, they consistently must take their external effects into account. These differences from the standard world of firm and contract make economic analysis difficult and cause us to look beyond economics for some explanations.

Because families have tremendous social importance, and because their strength lies precisely in the lack of current contractual enforcement that characterizes covenant, the state for the most part does not intervene unless the family demonstrates that it is simply not up to the task at hand.[203] Parents must have tremendous freedom and privacy in order to raise their children. A couple's division of labor must take advantage of the strengths of each spouse. The most successful marriages will not be driven primarily by outside concerns for labor force participation or some sort of equality of results.[204]

Despite the increase in independence of both spouses and children and the growing legal tendency to allow family relationships to end prematurely, the problems of the increasingly transitory modern family illustrate other limitations of the contract and firm analogies. These I have characterized as limitations of law rather than of economics. I will explore these contrasts between firm and family still further in the final chapters.

Families in Disequilibrium
and the Family Franchise

Families in Transition:
Between Firm and Franchise

In this portion of the book I complete my model of the family. I begin this chapter by discussing the dissolution of two kinds of family relationships: husband and wife (by divorce) and parent and child (through emancipation). A third, the termination of parental rights, was discussed in Chapter 3 in the context of adoption. In the dissolution of the family, we will see that the contractual model returns with a vengeance as people rend the legal ties that once held them together.

In Chapter 7 we will look again at the covenant, or what remains of it after the legal family ties have been dissolved. I will spend some time on divorcing couples, particularly parents, devote a good deal of time to a discussion of adult children and elderly parents, and look again briefly at birth parents and adopted children. These, of course, are the same relationships that form the basis for the discussion in Chapter 5. Here I develop a model of franchise, a new family equilibrium—contrasting it with a sovereign nation model characterized by lack of legal accountability—and discuss how legal rules can affect which of the two possible results will emerge.

The Relationship between Divorce and Marriage

Before I begin my study of divorce, I want to pause and reexamine the question why couples decide to divorce as well as the role of divorce as it is understood today. This is necessary because, once again, we must ask what is being maximized by the couples in question. Instead of taking into account the utility of the other spouse, the person seriously considering divorce is trying to maximize individual happiness and wealth in choosing between the single as opposed to the married state. (In fact, the spouse considering divorce may be interested in *minimizing* the other's happiness.) The "goods" involved here involve tangible property (houses, cars, or securities), intangible assets (earning capacity and the established household routine), as well as personal wealth (time with the children and influence over their upbringing, sexual pleasure, or freedom from bodily harm). Sometimes husbands and wives will have gender-specific differences in preferences over these several types of goods, as I discussed in Chapter 4. My inquiries into the etiology of divorce will require another brief excursion into sociobiology, and a more lengthy one into family history. Once we understand what couples are attempting to do when they divorce, it becomes appropriate to discuss whether limits should be placed on their private decisions as states regulate the divorce process or oversee divorce contracting. Again I will review rationales for state intervention: contracting difficulties, externalities, and intractable holdup problems.

In their 1977 article,[1] Gary Becker, Elisabeth Landes and Robert Michael demonstrated that in many instances the divorcing couples they studied left their marriages when they were unpleasantly surprised, that is, when it turned out they had not searched long enough in the marriage market to find a compatible lifetime companion. Thus, mismatched couples might include those of very different religions or socioeconomic status; those including previously married women, particularly women with children from their first unions; those suffering from unemployment; or very young couples. These observations about mismating should withstand the tests of time, for in addition to being theoretically sound, they conform to common experience. Figure 6.1 shows that a large number of divorces do occur within the first several years of marriage, as Becker, Landes, and Michael predicted. Their model does not explain very well, however, why marriages of longer standing deteriorate.[2]

If we try to figure out what motivates people to be fickle or disloyal or cruel, it is easy to overlook economic reasons and dwell on the psychological or sociological. Thus, people sometimes cheat on their spouses because they genuinely fall in love with others. They abuse their spouses because they saw their parents abused (or were hurt themselves as children). They leave because they have "drifted apart."

But economics, imperialistic as it is, may offer some reasons why this behavior occurs—why, for example, there is a "seven-year itch."[3] Seven years is the national average length of relationships ending in divorce, and in the

1980s and 1990s was also the modal (half above and half below) length of dissolving marriages. Adultery may be rational (and rationality is the central claim of economics), as may cruelty or desertion, but it may also have something to do with biology as well as "falling in love."

Robert Wright's book *The Moral Animal*[4] postulates that the prominence of infidelity in human relationships is due to "infidelity genes" which have proliferated because the people who were unfaithful had the greatest number of healthy offspring (who also carried the propensity to be unfaithful). Similarly, in *The Red Queen: Sex and the Evolution of Human Nature*,[5] Matt Ridley documents studies that have shown that men place great emphasis on youth and beauty in their mates, while women look for financial stability. This difference is logical, according to Ridley, because men simply want to ensure that their mate is healthy and able to care for a child, while women must often depend on their mates for financial support during the child-rearing years. Also, the common perception that men are less discriminating in choosing sexual partners can be explained by the fact that a man has a virtually limitless supply of sperm compared to the small number of ova a woman produces, so the man's investment in intercourse is much smaller.[6] Therefore, men can afford to have more partners than women and are more concerned with quantity

Figure 6.1 Length of marriage before divorce, Virginia, 1991 (source: Margaret F. Brinig and Douglas W. Allen, "These Boots Are Made for Walking: Why Mostly Women File for Divorce," *American Economics and Law Review*, forthcoming)

than quality, whereas women must choose a limited number of good partners to gain the greatest possible chance of passing on their genes to healthy offspring with each sexual encounter.

Biology also helps explains another phenomenon that I discussed in Chapter 4 in the context of bargaining during marriage: the ability of spouses to "trade" interest in sexual intercourse for concessions in other areas of the marriage.[7] When, because men and women age differently, a spouse loses a relative property right—the ability to acquiesce graciously to intercourse—there should be more marital instability and more mates who become "tired" of their lawful sexual partners, since consensual sexual intercourse can no longer make up for other problems in the marriage. We should therefore see more couples divorcing and more adultery occurring. In a study reported elsewhere,[8] I observed both effects: at the point when their biologically based relative willingness to pay for (or supply) sexual activity changed, the spouses were more likely to be adulterous and to divorce.

Abuse, as we will see shortly, also may be a rational (economic) response as well as a random action spurred by intoxication or frustrations on the job. It is at least rational to the extent that for the undecided person (or the spouse "on the margin"), some potential abusers will hold back if they know they will be substantially punished for abusing. Desertion—the third typical "fault" ground for divorce—also seems to be related (historically as well as at present) to a rational decision: the desire to start one's life anew.

In Europe until about 1600, marriages were viewed as indissoluble[9] as well as central to the preservation of land within particular families.[10] Although affection might grow out of long and close association between spouses, it was by no means considered necessary for the practical purposes of marriage. This oldest and nearly universal model of marriage became obsolete in England and its colonies as first the church and then land ceased being necessarily central to the relationship.[11] Marriage for romantic reasons became the ideal, and since human emotions need not remain eternally constant, and because marriage was no longer absolutely necessary for maintaining wealth, divorce became practically possible.[12]

The consolidated remedy of divorce and alimony became an exclusive remedy during the nineteenth century, largely because of the development of the doctrine of interspousal immunity. Although a spouse could sue for breach of contract or for ejectment from solely owned property, there could be no action for torts to person or property. In part this was because of a reluctance on the part of courts to become involved in the intimacies of the marital relationship, although the doctrine expressed a fear of disrupting marital stability that probably was not warranted, given the severity of some of the harm alleged. As I noted in Chapter 4, one court went so far as to write, "We will not inflict upon society the greater evil of raising the curtain upon domestic privacy to punish the lesser evil of trifling violence."[13]

This, then, was the "old marriage," a relational contract[14] designed for the most part to be permanent, which encouraged values of altruism, sharing, and investment in the marriage—a covenant, if one with flaws.[15] The idea of fault, and of alimony as damages for breach of the terms of the marriage contract, was central to the stability of this scheme. "Damages" is used here in its broader sense to include the remedy of specific performance of some of the marital obligations,[16] consistent with the covenant obligation. The threat of an action for damages would encourage women to invest specifically in the marriage while encouraging their husbands to adhere to their portion of the marriage bargain[17]: "It is still less desirable that an adulterous husband should have pecuniary interest in adding cruelty and desertion to his adultery and thus evading the permanent alimony awarded on judicial separation [because the wife obtained an absolute divorce], and this he would have if the amount of the maintenance to be accorded to his wife varied not with his misconduct, but with the form of her remedy."[18] The wife's specific investment in the household freed her husband to invest in market skills, easily transferable to a new relationship, and encouraged more efficient production of market and household goods because of her comparative advantage in "household production."[19]

The "old marriage," which might have existed at any time prior to the 1960s and seems the model for Gary Becker's treatment of marriage, was legally characterized in terms of an entity or a union rather than as the arrangement for gain between two players that an economist might expect.[20] There was a clear understanding of what conduct was acceptable and what the terms of the contract were.[21] And there were clear consequences for breaching those standards: for women, the loss of their status and support;[22] for men, the loss of wealth through property division or alimony.[23]

The "old marriage" began to be threatened as an institution during the Progressive era. The mortal blow came in the 1940s, when, because of World War II, large numbers of women entered the marketplace.[24] Soon, numerous unhappy spouses were traveling to states where divorces were relatively easy or less costly to obtain and procured "quickie" ends to their marriages. Another means to evade a strict divorce law was the collusive or fraudulent divorce, in which the complaining spouse would commit perjury or actually manufacture incidents (most often of adultery) with the collaboration of the other spouse.[25]

"No-fault" divorce was first introduced in 1969 in California, which until then had retained adultery as its only ground for divorce. Before this, several states had allowed divorce on the "no-fault" ground of "living separate and apart" for some period of time. This usually required both spouses to agree to divorce, however, since otherwise the departure of one spouse would be desertion (a ground for divorce both then and now in many states). This separation ground remains the only "no-fault" ground in a number of states. (New York added cruelty and separation for two years as grounds in 1966.)[26] After 1969, California divorces could be granted on a finding of "irretrievable breakdown of the marriage," which eliminated not only the necessity for a showing of fault but also the need for both spouses to agree to divorce.[27] Its proponents heralded the California statute as the opportunity for release from a moribund marriage. Some feminists argued that with increasing professional opportunities available to women outside marriage and no barriers to exit from wedlock, women ought to be free to reach their true potential. In addition, the threat of fault-based divorce, with its disastrous economic consequences, would no longer be available to penalize a wife who left a bad marriage.[28]

But there is some evidence that women were correct in being hesitant to embrace no-fault divorce. My own research indicates that it was the wife who filed in more than 67 percent of the cases of legislative divorce from 1792 to 1890.[29] This pattern continued throughout the early twentieth century.[30] Before no-fault divorce, men filed for divorce in only 29 percent of cases,[31] but immediately thereafter, men filed in 68 percent of cases.[32] More recently, the number of women filing has begun to increase again, despite the economic and other problems of divorce.[33]

Freedom from the restrictions of fault divorces (i.e., a no-fault liability rule that made exit easier) has proved troublesome for the institution of alimony. Fault (breach), which had previously been the trigger for alimony (damages), was no longer necessary (or, in some cases, available) for divorce. Alimony consequently was to serve the function of providing for the needy spouse who could not support himself or herself because of lack of job training or education or the competing burdens of child care. Alimony was thus to be only a temporary measure, for once the dependent spouse was rehabilitated or was no longer in need, it was now believed that alimony payments should not bind the other spouse financially.

By the reformers' design, the marriage relationship thus ended in a "clean break,"[34] a concept I will reexamine in the next chapter. The primary method of securing economic equality was to be through property distribution (non-human capital), which could be made without regard to fault and with a recognition that each spouse contributed to the marriage as a partner, whether working in the home or in the labor market.[35] This would also have the advantage of being backward-looking, dividing the wealth that had already been accumulated by the couple, but not restricting the ability of the divorcing spouses to begin their lives anew.

The changes to equitable distribution of property and the provision of alimony in cases of real need have not been complete solutions, however. Since many women do not earn as much as their husbands,[36] their opportunity costs of remaining out of the labor force are lower, and so they remain primary caretakers for their children.[37] Despite the gender neutrality of custody laws, if the couple breaks up, mothers still usually get child custody. In those marriages that do not last long enough to accumulate significant tangible property, many women upon divorce have found themselves with less wealth than they would have had before no-fault divorce. Many marriages end at a point where the couple own only their automobiles and perhaps a small amount of equity in a home. If the house must be sold and the proceeds divided, and the woman must find alternative housing for herself and the children, the small cash award of the property division will be quickly spent. Many writers have noted these presumably unintended consequences of no-fault divorce.[38]

There is yet another repercussion of no-fault divorce that is less prominent in the literature: its effect on the marriage contract itself.[39] The marriage obligations have been themselves rendered illusory (unenforceable) because no penalties can be exacted for breach of any marital promises. There are therefore few incentives other than a moral obligation or a feeling of affection to prevent either party from engaging in bad marital behavior, or what economists call postcontractual opportunism.[40] Some state legislatures have tried to meet this objection to no-fault divorce by compensating spouses who make sacrifices during marriage, in addition to splitting marital property.[41] Courts, struggling with this problem, have modified existing legal doctrines to recognize additional assets as "property."[42] Privately, more and more couples have written antenuptial (and postnuptial) contracts that can be the basis for actions for breach.[43] Nevertheless, there has been little recognition of the cost of the change in economic incentives.

Although the divorce rate itself has leveled off after its steady growth since the Second World War[44] and its upward shift following the introduction of no-fault statutes, there has been no apparent decrease in advantage-taking behavior (what economists call opportunistic behavior). For one thing, more and more cases of spousal and child abuse are being reported.[45] Of course, this may be due either to increased facilities for reporting or to the increasing consciousness of women who believe, for the first time, that something may be done if they complain about abuse. If this were true, we would expect this increase in reporting to occur uniformly across all states (or at least to be equal, controlling for the tendency to report). A second change is that more and more decisions chronicle sacrifices made to advance the career of an ungrateful spouse.[46] This behavior lags, in the sense that the investments in human capital characteristic of the reported "degree division" cases occur prior to a realization by the disadvantaged spouse that such investments might not be recouped. Predictably, there will be fewer such marriage-specific investments in the future as women become less likely to specialize in household production or in their husbands' careers, and more likely to continue working to advance their own careers during the marriage. Some writers suggest that this preventive behavior may itself undermine the marriage. It certainly is inconsistent with the unconditional and unselfish loving and giving typical of covenant.

These observations are consistent with the change from a paradigm that recognized that marriage, like any other relational contract, provides occasions for opportunism.[47] In the older system, the rule of fault-based divorce was designed to limit such behavior through its delineation of implied or express covenants, violation of which would lead to breach of the marital contract, with its concomitant (alimony) damage remedy. Where the marriage contract can no longer be enforced, the "divorce revolution" has rendered the bargain itself illusory.[48] Outside the marriage context, the principles of breach and remedy for breach remain even for dischargeable contracts so long as these agreements remain in effect. What currently happens in marriages in many states,[49] though, is that they are never effective contracts, so the parties to them are free to act strategically at minimal cost: "Because the obligations in relational contracts are not specified with particularity, it is often difficult to determine whether or not behavior by the relational promisor falls within the parameters of the contract as contemplated by the parties. Thus, relational promisees are often victimized by what is now called opportunistic behavior."[50]

Hundreds of years ago, before the possibility of divorce, a wife had little power over her husband: she could plausibly impose a minimal financial burden on him if he "abandoned" her, or she could make his life miserable with continual nagging during marriage. The husband, however, had a great deal of power over his wife because he could threaten to "cast her out," leaving her with only very limited sources of income and social standing and no opportunity to remarry: "If the breaching partner must continue to work or live with the other party and abide by the terms of a cooperative arrangement he now regrets, he will almost certainly find it more difficult to distance himself from his original values."[51] One would expect to find—and did find during this period—many "marriages of convenience," in which marital fidelity was not important, particularly for husbands,[52] and women were thought of in some ways as little more than servants.[53]

There were all sorts of problems with this older characterization of marriage, including the fact that husbands would frequently desert their wives, leaving them remediless and without any property or other means of support.[54] The law gradually evolved, in consequence, to a new typical form of marriage, in which there was a state-imposed set of contractual obligations, a remedy for breach (specific performance through alimony, a continuation of the duty of support),[55] and a clear understanding of what was and was not permissible behavior. Thus, alimony "is the allowance of such a sum of money in gross or in installments as will fairly and reasonably compensate [the wife] . . . for the loss of her support by the annulment of the marriage contract. In this limited sense at least it may be deeded an assessment of damages in her favor for breach of the contract by the husband."[56]

During this period (lasting some two hundred years in this country), marriage, though begun with hortatory expressions of covenant, was at least legally an enforceable contract. Because of its complexity and indeterminate length, the marriage agreement was necessarily incomplete and flexible. As Charles Goetz and Robert Scott note, "definitive obligations may be impractical because of the inability to identify certain future conditions or because of inability to characterize complex adaptations adequately even when the contingencies can be identified in advance."[57] Elizabeth and Robert Scott describe marriage as a relational contract.

North Dakota in 1985 became the last state to adopt no-fault divorce.[58] What no-fault means is that fault on the part of the spouse need not be *proved* by the plaintiff in order to obtain a divorce. Some states—those I call no-fault here and elsewhere—go a step further.[59] In these, fault cannot be *considered* either in obtaining the divorce or in obtaining alimony.[60] Consequently, there is no breach and no remedy, so the contract has become completely illusory. The wife may have even less power in these states where fault is irrelevant than she did in the divorceless form of marriage, since the only threat she can make is that it may take the husband some time to replace her "household services" after their divorce (either by purchase from others—usually women—or remarriage). It is more difficult for the woman to remarry,[61] and she usually earns far less than the husband in the job market, for a variety of reasons.[62] Divorce, therefore, will cost her more than it does him, giving him more bargaining power within the marriage.[63] Even the cost of very deviant behavior has decreased, so that predictably there will be more divorces and more opportunistic (strategic) behavior between spouses.[64] In other words, no-fault divorce comes with the dual prices of substantial negative externalities (some of which are popularly called "the feminization of poverty") and problems for the marriage itself (called rent-extraction or holdup in the economic literature). First I will examine the offshoots of this latter price, which affects the marriage itself.

Strategic behavior should occur primarily in lengthy marriages begun under the old rules, when marriage was closer to covenant. Spousal abuse is one way to measure the effect of the change in regimes on existing marriages entered into under the older system, or at least those begun without sufficient understanding of what the new system might mean in terms of compensation upon divorce. In states where fault imposes no costs, significantly more abuse is reported, other things held equal.[65] For couples entering into marriages more recently, the effect is different and more complex. With marriages contemplated when no-fault divorce has been in place for some years, we would expect other effects, such as a decrease in the number of marriages contracted and the number of children. No-fault states do in fact show a decline in marriages and births since the 1970s.

The Impact of Divorce Law on Divorce Rates

It has become progressively easier for couples to divorce as states have moved to no-fault regimes. With lower divorce costs, one would expect an increase in divorce levels. Yet the bulk of the scholarly literature describes only a temporary growth in the divorce rate. As we shall see, what might be called divorce law irrelevance has been analyzed, in which differences in the legal regime affect property settlements on divorce but do not prevent efficient divorces or threaten efficient marriages.[66]

In work done with Frank Buckley on the determinants of divorce,[67] I found that divorce rates by state from 1980 to 1991 were significantly and positively correlated with liberalization of the divorce law. States that took fault into account in granting a divorce or in dividing up matrimonial assets had lower divorce rates than no-fault states. Although people divorce for all sorts of reasons, highly idiosyncratic and highly personal, aggregate divorce levels respond to broad legal and socioeconomic conditions. For this reason, we thought it important to identify the determinants of divorce.

THE RELEVANCE OF DIVORCE LAW.   The divorce law relevance proposition which Buckley and I defended might sound self-evident. In a well-known paper,[68] however, the economist Elizabeth Peters has argued for divorce law irrelevance as an application of the Coase Theorem, which, it will be recalled, maintains that in a world of minimal or no transaction costs, parties will bargain to an efficient result no matter what the legal rule. Whatever the legal regime, Peters maintained, couples will bargain for efficient divorces and reject inefficient divorces. Divorce levels would thus be independent of the legal regime.

The divorce irrelevance proposition has been criticized for failing to take the transaction costs of divorce into account.[69] In a bilateral regime (one where both parties must agree to divorce), transaction costs, including legal fees, court costs, and other costs of bargaining, might prevent the husband who seeks a divorce from securing his wife's consent, with the result that divorce rates would be lower. And in a unilateral regime (where divorce may be obtained at the instigation of one spouse), transaction costs within the marriage might prevent the wife who seeks to preserve her marriage from persuading her husband to abandon his divorce petition, with the result that divorce rates would be higher. Because of the emotionalism and spite that a divorce might engender, the parties might fail to exploit all value-increasing opportunities, including preserving the marriage and refraining from the disturbing behavior.[70] There is, however, little evidence that such problems are more pressing in the context of divorce than in other bargains. Even under fault-only regimes, the great majority of divorcing couples resolved their differences before litigation through a separation agreement.[71]

Finally, the divorce law irrelevance proposition might not hold as a consequence of the incentive or moral hazard effects of a change in legal regime. In a unilateral regime, the party who initiates divorce proceedings need not pay the spouse to waive veto rights. Divorce will therefore be cheaper, and the matrimonial faults which might cause divorce will become less costly. Because adultery or abuse is less costly, there will be more such behavior,[72] and more straying or outraged spouses who seek divorce. With a greater probability of divorce, the parties will also invest less in marriage-specific assets, such as children, and this will further increase divorce levels. (Children of the marriage, though present in most divorcing families, tend to reduce divorce levels. Children from former relationships have the opposite effect; they increase the probability of divorce.)

Less obviously, a shift in the legal regime might result in a change in divorce levels if the choice of legal regime shapes personal preferences. In the past, social penalties for divorce were stronger, and probably deterred at least some couples from divorcing. When these norms were internalized, a couple might simply have regarded divorce as not an option, quite apart from the external social sanction. But these norms are weaker today.[73] In part, the change in social norms may have resulted from the change in legal rules, since social stigmas are easier to maintain when they dovetail with the legal regime.[74]

In sum, the move from a bilateral to a unilateral divorce regime might plausibly be expected to result in increased divorce levels. A unilateral regime, however, is not precisely the same as a no-fault regime (where fault will be irrelevant, even in the property distribution context). We will next consider whether a similar increase would have been expected on the adoption of no-fault divorce laws.

NO-FAULT LAWS.   It is unsurprising that divorce rates increased when states moved from fault to no-fault laws. In the nineteenth century, most couples seeking a divorce were required to prove fault, such as adultery, desertion, or physical abuse. The passage from fault to no-fault divorce regimes progressed slowly, but the pace of change greatly accelerated in the 1960s and 1970s.[75] Not surprisingly, American divorce rates doubled during that period, as may be seen in Figure 6.2.[76] Since 1985, an at-fault party can obtain a divorce in every state on no-fault grounds, such as irreconcilable differences, an irretrievable breakdown of the marriage, or a short-term separation. When a new equilibrium was reached in the 1980s, the leveling-off of divorce rates was also to be expected.

My study with Frank Buckley focused on post-1980 divorce rates, by which time most of the legal change had already occurred. While an innocent party has everywhere lost the right to veto the divorce, some thirty-two states still permit him or her to raise the question of the spouse's fault to alter the split of matrimonial assets. The innocent party might commence divorce proceedings on fault grounds, or counterclaim on fault grounds when the guilty party has sought a divorce on no-fault grounds. Bargaining in the shadow of fault,[77] the parties may decide not to divorce at all, or they may agree to seek a divorce on no-fault grounds but with a more one-sided division of assets than they would have agreed to in the absence of fault.

EMPIRICAL STUDIES OF DIVORCE RATES. Empirical studies prior to our own had failed to detect strong evidence that the move to no-fault increased divorce rates. Elizabeth Peters's study looked at panel (or individual sample) data for a three-year period in the late 1970s when divorce rates peaked, and reported that they were uncorrelated with no-fault divorce laws.[78] From this she concluded that no one who seeks a divorce will be kept in a marriage, and where fault is required the parties will produce it.[79] This was just as her theory predicted. Yet when another economist omitted data from three fault states where Peters had overestimated divorce levels, he found a significant positive no-fault coefficient.[80] Apart from a religious predictor used by Peters, no other state-based predictor was employed in either study. It is difficult, therefore, to draw strong conclusions from either study about the effect of a change in divorce regimes.

A panel study by Martin Zelder of pre-1982 divorces also reported that a no-fault dummy variable was not correlated with increased divorce levels.[81] Where the dummy variable was multiplied by a measure of expenditures on children, though, there was a significant relationship with increased di-

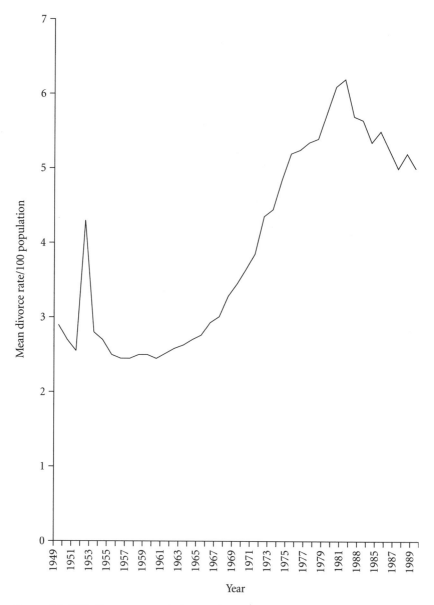

Figure 6.2 U.S. divorce rates, 1949–1989 (source: Department of Health and Human Services, National Center for Health Statistics, Vital Statistics, 1949–91: Divorces)

vorce levels. From this Zelder concluded that transaction cost barriers do not prevent the parties from bargaining around the divorce regime, but that divorce law irrelevance does not hold when the parties have children.

More recently, Paul Nakonezny, Robert Shull, and Joseph Lee Rodgers reported that states which enacted no-fault laws saw a significant increase in divorce rates over the following three years.[82] The authors did not attempt to demonstrate a long-term effect however. The short-term effect is easy to imagine. Some couples who seek a divorce around the time of the legal change will delay proceedings until the new law is enacted in order to reduce the costs of the divorce. We would thus expect to see a fall in divorce rates immediately prior to enactment, a subsequent increase, and finally a return to preenactment trends. By contrast, my study with Buckley is largely free of short-term overhang effects, since we examined a twelve-year period during which only two states changed from fault to no-fault regimes, and we controlled for these two with dummy variables.[83]

A related puzzle concerns the division of property on divorce. In a fault regime, as defined here, the at-fault party is penalized for the fault in the property settlement. There is little evidence, however, that the move to no-fault affected the bargaining over matrimonial assets. An early article used panel data to show that alimony awards were indeed lower in states that had adopted no-fault divorce laws.[84] Similarly, Lenore Weitzman's famous study of property settlements before and after passage of a no-fault divorce law in California concluded that women's standard of living diminished dramatically following divorce, while men's improved.[85] More recently, however, several writers have dissented from the property settlement relevance thesis, reporting that property settlements did not change much when no-fault laws were passed. Weitzman's study of the economic impact of no-fault divorce has met with a barrage of criticism, to the point where she herself has admitted serious problems with the data or its analysis.[86] An empirical study of New York divorces found that no-fault settlements differed little from those of the earlier fault-based divorce era,[87] and a national study of panel data found little difference in divorce settlements between fault and no-fault states.[88] My paper with Michael Alexeev compared 1987 divorce settlements in Virginia (a fault state) and Wisconsin (a no-fault state), and found nearly identical payouts.[89]

A final puzzle is that most divorce petitions are brought by women, even after the move to no-fault.[90] There is at least one explanation for this, even if we assume that husbands are more likely to have committed a matrimonial fault. A husband who wishes to terminate a marriage will often leave his wife and children without initiating divorce proceedings, since he usually takes his investments in human capital with him on divorce.[91] The abandoned wife must then begin divorce proceedings in order to enforce the husband's support duties and formalize custody arrangements. This was clearly the historical reason for judicial as opposed to legislative divorce, as well as the invention of alimony. Men did not need legal assistance to start over elsewhere, but women needed the judicial relief for support, particularly since the property they brought to the marriage became the husband's "under coverture."[92] Since the disparity in filing rates continues to the present, there are likely more factors at work than this. Empirical research to date indicates that which spouse files varies directly with which spouse ends up with custody of the children, with the wife's relative educational achievement, and even with race (white women file more often than black women).[93]

The principal finding of my work with Buckley was that the change to a no-fault legal regime is significantly correlated with increased divorce levels, where we looked at a relatively lengthy time period and employed social as well as legal and economic variables. We found that in a state with an average divorce rate of 5 percent, passage of a no-fault law increased the rate by about 1 percent. We concluded that no-fault laws reduced the transaction costs and alimony penalties of divorce and made it a more appealing option for many couples. At the same time, the change in divorce laws may have contributed to a weakening of social sanctions against divorce. With a broader exit option, couples will also invest less heavily in their marriages.[94] They might marry less wisely (though also, as we have seen, less frequently), and repent more hastily of their questionable decision.[95]

Bargaining at Divorce

As we have seen, couples resolve the vast majority of family law disputes without litigating. Most of these conflicts, like most other legal disputes, end when the lawyers for the opposing parties reach agreement.[96] The tendency to rely on private agreements has been hailed as one of the real achievements of no-fault divorce, and has undoubtedly lowered the costs of divorce for many couples.[97] Although not everyone believes that these lower transaction costs (and thus lower exit costs from marriage) are a good thing, the relaxed proof requirements clearly mean that lawyers do not necessarily have to be involved in divorce proceedings. The vast majority of marriages dissolve on the basis of written agreements between the parties. No-fault divorce has also energized the divorce mediation movement.[98]

Mediation is the least intrusive form of third-party involvement in a dispute. Whereas a judge or arbitrator imposes an outcome on the disputants, the mediator assists the parties to reach a mutually satisfactory agreement,[99] helping to "identify the issues, reduce misunderstandings, vent emotions, clarify priorities, find points of agreement, and explore new areas of compromise and possible solutions."[100]

Family mediation was seen as a way to provide "divorcing couples with an opportunity to nurture" their necessarily continuing relationships.[101] No longer would the unhappy spouses have to engage in legal combat. A group of non-lawyer divorce mediators proclaimed that mediation was "more expeditious, less expensive, procedurally reasonable, and amenable to truth-finding and the open airing of differences."[102] Feminists heralded mediation because it promised to consider disputes in the language of relationships rather than individual rights.[103]

Initially the organized bar considered divorce mediation inconsistent with professional ethics on two sets of grounds. First, the use of non-attorney mediators would violate rules forbidding "unauthorized practice of law."[104] Second, attorneys would be unable to represent both (necessarily adversarial) spouses without creating a conflict of interest. They would thus end up favoring one or the other, either through their handling of the mediation process, their providing legal information, or the drafting of the resulting agreement. Because of their extensive training in legal rules as opposed to counseling, lawyer-mediators would be unable to resist giving legal advice. Because divorce in most cases does not raise difficult legal issues, some non-lawyers suspected that the protests of the organized bar were little more than a smoke screen to deny them entry into what had been the lawyer's exclusive domain.[105]

There was also concern that no-fault divorce would merely remove conflict to areas other than the divorce itself.[106] As one author wrote: "Disputes over property and custody are often battlegrounds on which spouses indirectly work through their feelings about the end of marriage. We must ask whether the provision of an explicit mechanism for dealing with marital misconduct in certain instances might better channel and control these impulses."[107]

Now that the bar seems to have adjusted to mediation, certain feminists in both the United States and Canada have attacked the process. Their objection seems to be twofold. Some argue that because women more than men seek connection through relationships,[108] women might systematically fare worse in mediation. Others argue that women might trade money for custody to avoid litigation because, at least where custody is concerned, they are more risk-averse than their husbands.[109] There is also a more generalized fear that husbands will take advantage of their wives' lack of power within the marital relationship.[110] Studies to date, however, have not shown that women systematically fared worse in mediation, in terms of either financial or custodial outcomes or their satisfaction with the process.[111] Trina Grillo writes: "The fundamental premise that must be understood in order to analyze the impact of the use of mediation in family law is that women are less powerful than men in this society. Generally women are economically dependent on the men in their families, both during childbearing years and when they are in the work force earning only three-fifths of what their male counterparts can."[112]

The most influential article on the divorce negotiation process (and one of the most frequently cited works in the dispute resolution literature generally) is the paper by Robert Mnookin and Lewis Kornhauser, a law professor and an economist.[113] Mnookin and Kornhauser write that parties bargain from "endowment points." In the divorce context, they begin bargaining knowing that if they do not reach an agreement, they will go to court, and the court will make their settlement for them. The divorce and custody regimes, set by statute and court interpretation, provide the background (and endowment points) for the divorcing parties. If rational, they should not settle for less than the expected court outcome (minus the costs of litigating).

Further, Mnookin and Kornhauser classify the subjects of bargaining into two categories: custodial time and money. They find that "over some range of alternatives, each parent may be willing to exchange custodial rights and obligations for income or wealth, and parents may tie support duties to custodial prerogatives with a minimal level of resources." Mnookin and Kornhauser's *Bargaining in the Shadow of the Law,* also suggests that women might be more risk-averse then men when it comes to litigating custody. That is, they might trade assets they could expect to receive from a court outcome in order to avoid even the relatively small chance that they would lose custody if they went to court. In particular, risk-neutral men might exploit their risk-averse wives by threatening custody actions.[114]

Mnookin and Kornhauser's gloomiest prediction therefore was that when divorce laws changed from fault to no-fault, women would be injured in terms of custody time and property distribution. Their warnings echoed loudly in the academic literature.[115] The common wisdom is that mediation is particularly harmful to women. As we have seen, however, a number of articles (including one of my own) have looked empirically at no-fault divorce and its consequences, and have found that, regardless of regime (mediation versus litigation), wives receive between 45 and 55 percent of total marital assets, while receiving a custody share of between 71 and 75 percent.[116] It is entirely possible, as we will see in a moment, that the controlling factor is not differences in risk taking but the fact that women and men have different preferences about custody.

In addition to these questions about the legal background of negotiation, some literature addresses the role of lawyers in divorce negotiation. For example, Marygold S. Melli, Howard Erlanger, and Elizabeth Chambliss[117] warn that lawyers frequently withhold legal information from clients and bias outcomes by substituting their own views about the litigation process. Lawyers' use of problem-solving methods in negotiation is explored in Carrie Menkel-Meadow, "Toward Another View of Legal Negotiation: The Structure of Problem Solving."[118] The particular problems that negotiation poses for women are the subject of a number of works including John Ilich and Barbara S. Jones's *Successful Negotiating Skills for Women*[119] and many feminist articles on divorce mediation.[120]

To summarize, legal rules provide the framework within which couples bargain at divorce. Their expectations about the likely result if a judge intervenes provides the alternative (or, in the bargaining literature jargon, the BATNA, or Best Alternative to a Negotiated Agreement) to continuing to bargain for a better outcome.[121] Further, this legal alternative, defined by state statutes and less precise information about local judicial practices, serves as a benchmark (the same as the endowment point discussed earlier) that each spouse uses to determine the extent of his or her concessions to the other.[122]

For these reasons, the outcome of the bargaining between the spouses depends on the divorce laws of the particular state as well as what the spouses want, or what their partners think they want.[123] For settlement purposes, there are four very significant legal variables. The first is the statutory preference for child custody arrangements. Most states currently provide for joint custody (legal or physical),[124] or else have a presumption that the primary caretaker before separation, usually the mother, is the best custodian following divorce.[125] The second involves grounds for divorce. As we saw earlier in this chapter, states use either a combination of fault and no-fault or no-fault alone. The third is the prevailing rationale for alimony (support of a dependent former spouse or temporary payments for rehabilitative purposes). Finally, but no less significant, is the property regime, which at divorce may be equitable distribution or the division of community property.

Regardless of the legal rule, the outcomes in terms of ultimate child custody arrangements and marital wealth distribution are very similar across all regimes. There is a difference, however, in terms of the number of divorces, and also in terms of the amount of litigation initiated by the divorcing parties.[126]

The substantially similar settlement results across states seem most peculiar in the case of spouses who settle for less than they might have obtained by going to court.[127] This occurs with some frequency in the case of wives, who apparently "trade" property shares for the relatively constant amount of custodial time we observed. If this behavior operates according to accepted economic principles of rationality, either there must be something about the bargaining process itself that disadvantages women, a concept I have addressed in terms of risk aversion, or else women must have a greater preference for custody than their husbands.

Let us consider first the preferences of the noncustodial parent (usually the father). The utility he derives from visiting his children depends not only on the amount of time he is allowed to spend with them but also on the quality of the children.[128] This quality is, presumably, positively related to the quality of their living conditions in the ex-wife's home. These living conditions depend to some extent on the share of marital property received by the wife. The husband's desire to spend time with the children is also affected by the opportunity cost of his time. The net outcome of all these interdependent factors may be such that his ideal divorce arrangement assigns large shares of both custody and the marital property to the wife. The data suggest that, if anything, husbands are often willing to accept both reduced time with their children and a lesser share of marital property than would have been awarded to them had they gone to trial.

This is a rather curious result, for usually the less something costs, the more one wants of it. Here, however, husbands are apparently less willing to give up property after a certain point in order to get more time with their children, thus showing a positive relation between quantity and price. This behavior is typical in family law situations but is inconsistent with neoclassical economic theory. This pattern may occur because of interdependencies among preferences, as Lewis Kornhauser postulates,[129] or because economists are concerned only with behavior over the relevant trading space. For wives, or for men in the days when the only feasible option would have been "reasonable visitation," the preferences would also have been convex over the relevant space.

By reaching settlement, the wife's share of child custody might be increased from the already high percentage the court would normally award her, but a woman usually would want to ensure some participation of her former husband in the upbringing of their child. This may be because she feels that the more participation, the better for the child. It may also be for the less child-centered reason that she wants some time for herself: to get tasks done that cannot be completed with children around, to enjoy recreation, pursue hobbies, enhance her earning capability, or begin a new relationship.[130] The corollary of this is that the husband may not experience a "downside risk" that deviates substantially from the expected outcome were he to go to court, since the probability of catastrophic financial loss or loss of all visitation with the child is very low.[131]

Liquidating the Marriage: Dividing Marital Wealth

Division of assets upon dissolution of a marriage, like allocation on dissolution of a business, may be usefully thought of in terms of separating stocks and flows.[132] In such a system, marital "stocks" would take the form of what we usually think of as property: houses, securities, and, less obviously, partnership interests, goodwill, pensions, and human capital. As with other stocks, over time these will produce income "flows": capital gains or rents, dividends or interest, increased book value, annuities, or salary.

Alimony (the "flow" concept) deals with claims on future earnings streams,[133] while property division (at least as seen by divorce lawyers and perhaps law reformers)[134] deals with past acquisition of tangible property.[135] The legal distinctions seem to be quite clear:

> "Earning capacity" has no meaning or existence independent of the method used to measure it. It is generally measured by finding a present value for all or some part of the individual's future earnings, and is thus no more than a shorthand term for that present value. A rule characterizing earning capacity as marital property is a rule treating future earnings as marital property, which in operation requires that those earnings be estimated at divorce so that their present value can then be fixed and allocated between the spouses.[136]

Economists see no real distinction between stocks and flows even when they consider future earnings. Marital homes, automobiles, and other assets that do not generate income flows in a conventional sense are conceptually the easiest property for courts to divide. They do not involve the difficult characterization problems posed by earning capacity. The bridging concept is that of human capital, which Joan Krauskopf first articulated in the family law context.[137]

As the economist sees it, alimony "frozen" in time (the present) is simply another form of property. Thus, finance models depict stock prices as reflecting the market's anticipation of all future dividends.[138] If a divorcing spouse has any claim to joint property, it is worth thinking about why it can only be a claim to the fixed share (or "stock") rather than the ongoing stream (or "flow").[139] The problem becomes particularly acute in cases such as *Mahoney v. Mahoney*,[140] where the couple divorced shortly after the husband acquired his M.B.A. degree. The wife had worked throughout the marriage and provided the husband with support while he was in school. As with most modern marriages, at the time of divorce the most valuable things the Mahoneys owned were not their house or car but their future earning capacities.[141] Economist Allen Parkman's answer, found (among other places) in his *No Fault Divorce: What Went Wrong?*[142] is that the portion of this human capital acquired during marriage is in fact a small one: the business, medical, or law degree could not be earned without substantial pre-marriage preparation and investment (in grade school through college).[143]

One real question, therefore, is how much of the value of Melvin Mahoney's degree came from investments prior to marriage. My own students feel that there really is a special investment made by spouses as well as oneself in professional degrees.[144] The hours of preparation, the pressures of being called on repeatedly in class, and the lack of any outside-school "life" push the rigors of law school far beyond those of undergraduate or high school studies. These add to the law student's stress, and are part of his or her unique investment. This would suggest that the increment made during graduate education, at least if measured by its total cost, is quite substantial.

The cases involving division of professional degrees have dwelt on the fact that the degree-earning spouse will be handicapped in future years if his degree (or professional license) is called property and divided in the present. He may not take chances with his employment that he would take if still married, simply because of the inevitable payments he would have to make to his former spouse.

Courts have also been preoccupied with the idea that the student spouse may, for a variety of reasons, never realize his expected income. Expected value (used to award the present value of Melvin Mahoney's degree) takes into account, by definition, the prognosis for the *average* degree holder.[145] But is that what we ought to be doing in a divorce case, or should we be concerned with this *particular* obligor when we bind him or her in this way? If we should be concerned with each particular obligor as an individual, how do we obtain the information necessary to calculate his or her individual degree's expected value? If the projected earnings are way off the mark, the disappointed spouse should be able to modify the remaining amounts to be paid.

The reasoning in *Mahoney* and similar cases might cover other kinds of investments in a spouse. These include, for example, sacrifices made for an officer in the armed forces, or by an IBM executive's wife who has had to move every few years,[146] or the many years of investment by a scholar's wife before he wins the Nobel Prize.[147] On the one hand, all spouses sacrifice and invest in each other, so that confining compensation only to cases like *Mahoney* seems less than fair. On the other hand, New York, which, since the case of *O'Brien v. O'Brien*,[148] does allow degrees to be treated as divisible property, has had serious problems dealing with the commercialization of marriage that has set in. The reported cases reveal a tendency to work through a very detailed accounting of exactly what each spouse did and provided during the marriage.[149] There is a cost here to the covenant idea of performing services without either toting up a balance sheet or expecting an eventual compensation.

INCENTIVE-BASED RATIONALES FOR AWARDS.   One reason we might give the supporting spouse a share in the other's enhanced earning capacity is to change the spouses' incentives. Given no-fault divorce and the ability to leave marriage at will, a shared future interest in a degree might encourage spouses to make the sacrifice (in terms of their own career or current standard of living) that will pay off only in the future, perhaps only after the marriage has ended. It is also possible that, in jurisdictions where property division is affected by fault, an incentive to avoid being at fault will be created or strengthened. In the absence of any compensation, we can expect this efficient way of encouraging higher education to dry up or at least decrease.[150] But this incentive-based theory suffers from the same problem as an incentive rationale for alimony[151]: it does not present a reason *why* the interest in the degree ought to be awarded, as opposed to suggesting an equitable basis for such an award, a subject I will take up presently. This comparison is not an idle one, for as we have seen already, alimony and marital property division can properly be viewed as species of the same thing.[152]

There also might be an effect on the incentive to marry in the first place. Since the introduction of no-fault divorce, the marriage rate has decreased. Saying that there is a relationship between no-fault and the marriage rate on its face poses a *post hoc ergo proper hoc* problem. But if other factors such as rising wages for women and the trend toward completion of graduate as well as undergraduate education are factored out, there is still a marked decrease. Women are less happy, men more happy, in marriages today.[153] Women are harmed by divorce (at least financially) more than their former husbands. Who currently has the most incentive not to marry? Taking these factors only into account, it would appear that no-fault makes marriage more attractive for men and less so for women. Since both must agree to marry, the decline in the marriage rate seems most likely to be caused by an increasing reluctance of women to marry. Allowing spouses claims against earning capacity (especially when the marriage has lasted for many years) would seem to make marriage more attractive to women, thus evening out the incentives that no-fault skewed. One would therefore predict an increase in the marriage rate (at least to the pre–no-fault level).

EQUITABLE REASONS FOR AWARDS.   When a couple marries, as we saw in Chapter 4, they share.[154] They take advantage not only of their mutual affection and shared good times but also of savings that are accrued because of time-based economies of scale.[155] But this time it is not the lowered costs of living in one location, one household, that are at issue but the fact that only one spouse must stay at home to let in the appliance repair person or the exterminator. Time unites these two concepts of the exchange of alimony and property and the type of investment that is made when a couple marries.

In finance theory, there is an accepted way in which time relates "stocks," or capital assets, to "flows," or future earning streams. According to at least one widely accepted theory, investors price shares of stock according to the corporation's expected future return, or the average of all possible returns,[156] discounted for nondiversifiable risk.[157] Many factors, both systemic and company-specific, are considered in this equation, and differences in opinion among market participants about the correct price of stock are resolved through trading.[158] Simply put, those investors who think the price is too low buy, while those who think the price is too high sell. In this way the market reaches a consensus about a corporation's future prospects, and the trading price of the company's stock reflects this consensus.

The allocation of time, and its relation to marriage, is in fact the subject of one of Gary Becker's pathbreaking articles.[159] Becker sees workers as dividing their time between labor and leisure. They have only twenty-four hours to divide, and wish to maximize the amount of leisure they have and also the enjoyment they may have when resting (access to cruises or cable television, for example). When one stays out of the job market to raise children or manage the household, the opportunity cost of the time is what is given up. Presumably the use of this time in the household is more valuable than whatever would be gained (financially or otherwise) by the spouse's remaining in the labor force.[160] This is also the reason why married men do better in the business world (as well as in terms of health) than do single men with similar qualifications: someone else is supplying them with the time (and freedom from distractions) that allows them to perform at their best. A good example from the student world is the resident student, for in college, at least, most housekeeping functions in a dormitory are assumed by the university (the stay-at-home spouse surrogate).

I have already acknowledged that marriage is obviously a complex human activity. Among its other benefits, it gives spouses a chance to create a family in an atmosphere of trust and intimacy.[161] Less obviously, perhaps, it furnishes security. The married person enjoys security against the vagaries of the marriage market.[162] Further, a committed partner who can work if one loses a job, or who can perform physical tasks if one becomes ill or disabled, supplies a kind of insurance against illness and unemployment.[163]

Marriage also provides some obvious financial benefits. Having one household instead of two means there is only one rent or mortgage check, one set of utility bills, and food is purchased in larger (less expensive per unit) quantities. If, as Becker urges, one spouse specializes in managing the household's finances, car maintenance, or grocery shopping,[164] there are obvious gains (which, of course, may be outweighed by the fun of sharing a joint activity). If the specialization goes further, so one spouse has primary responsibility for paid employment and the other for household management, both married people are making a substantial investment in their relationship. If, like most couples, they marry when they are relatively young and beginning their careers in the workplace, there will probably be substantial investments in one or both careers.[165]

These investments may be of the obvious kind—one spouse may finance the other's advanced degree—or may be more subtle. One may take the more flexible job in order to accommodate child rearing or the repair people who need access to the home. One spouse may follow the successful upwardly mobile executive through a series of moves across the country or through foreign tours of duty in the armed forces. The corporate, diplomatic, or military career may require substantial entertaining or relationship building by the other spouse. Frequently, all these domestic investments take many years to bear fruit.

Marriage also signals to the outside world that the person is more stable than a single one of comparable age.[166] Married people in their twenties, for example, are typically more conscientious (as well as better drivers and health risks)[167] than their single contemporaries. They are therefore more apt to be lent money or given positions of responsibility. The outsider looking at a married person can be more confident (because of the pattern observed with other couples and singles) that he or she can afford a nice car or a large home or a trustworthy position as a manager.

Since the early 1970s, academics have pictured marriage as a kind of partnership,[168] one in which contributions are difficult to measure but both spouses clearly gain so long as the marital unit remains intact. But, as with many joint enterprises, how best and most fairly to compensate the spouses' efforts has proven intractable.[169] One obvious choice that works in the commercial but not in the domestic context is to "pay by the piece," allowing recompense based on the result produced.[170] But a salary arrangement seems completely distasteful in the context of marriage.[171] Economists suggest that allowing entrepreneurs (again, in the business context) a share in the profits of a firm gives them the appropriate incentives.[172] So long as the marital unit remains intact, and so long as spouses care for each other, the deep hurts caused, for example, by belittling the homemaker's efforts are unlikely to occur.[173] But in a world where not all marriages last until death parts husband and wife, judges and attorneys often must value the claim.

If undertaking marriage entitles one to a residual claim, several questions remain. The first is whether the claim is against the other or the mutual enterprise. Clearly the marriage begins one's life anew, at least in certain important respects. Yet the spouses promise to "take each other" in the marriage ceremony,[174] complete with individual attributes (attractive and unattractive)[175] and education and training.

The spouse is worth more[176] if highly educated and properly employed. But, as with the corporation the share of stock represents, the greatest financial value of such a marital partner lies in the expectation that he or she will do well.[177] The spouse who weds the young graduate of Harvard Business School pays more—invests more by giving up the other potential attractive spouses that she "merits" through her own worth on the marriage market—than the one whose best alternative is marrying the high school dropout pumping gas.

Marriage (and even more the conduct following the promise), then, is investment, not just sacrifice.[178] As investment, the spouses should be rewarded not only with current purchases and living standards (the dividends) but also the promise of future income (the capital gains). Divorce lawyers deal with another vexing feature of the marital investment (troubling because it cannot be predicted with certainty)[179] when they divide pensions upon divorce.[180] The spouse may not continue to work for the same employer until retirement age (through change of job, illness, or early retirement).[181] The employer's pension fund may not do as well as expected at the time of divorce. What some states do in pension cases is estimate the present value of the pension[182] and award the non-employed spouse some share in it—a share that will be paid whenever the employed spouse begins to receive the annuity. The divorce court thus assesses the present value, awards a percentage of it, and delays payment until a future time. This should be possible with earning capacity as well.

The primary objection seems to be that to the extent that the spouse must wait for payment, the marriage does not end in the "clean break" envisioned by no-fault supporters.[183] We cannot predict future employment with any accuracy, so we must make adjustments (modifications) in the future.[184] But, as noted, we do this anyway with pensions (for contingencies controllable or not by the employee). Besides, divorce is *not* a clean break.[185]

WHY NO CLEAN BREAK?   When stock is sold, the present value (of current capital and future dividends) is reflected in the stock's price. But divorce does not mark reentry into something like the stock market. There may be no intent or ability to remarry,[186] and the success or failure of the business part of the enterprise is necessarily enmeshed with other personal characteristics of the working spouse (tendencies toward substance abuse, physical violence, or infidelity, for example). There is no immediate and accurate valuation of the spouse's worth.

THE TROUBLE WITH DIVIDING ASSETS.   As others have written,[187] developing the atmosphere in which the joint enterprise can flourish most often requires an unequal sharing of the unpaid work.[188] The lack of protection for the homemaker, in particular, has led to a spate of articles recommending pension protection,[189] equal division of assets,[190] or changes in the tax code.[191] None of these ideas necessarily conflicts with the premises of this book, and perhaps a combination of them will prove most satisfactory for eventual legislative activity.

If we see marriage as, at least in part, a couple's investment in each other's earning capacity and a joint investment in children, the decision maker on divorce has to answer several questions. The first is exactly what sort of investment was made: How much of a spouse's career stems from pre-marriage training and experience, how much from growth during the marriage?[192] One way to approach this problem is to look at the wage rates of people generally. In most occupations a person is hired at a relatively low wage, works for some number of years acquiring the skills necessary to be most productive for the employer, and then works at peak nearly until retirement. The increase in wages over this life of employment derives from at least two factors: the need to keep pace with inflation (and thus to make employment continue to be more attractive than unemployment)[193] and the need to pay the worker his or her marginal product of labor, which increases during the work cycle. In other words, as the human capital the employed person brings to the task increases, the wage rises. The difference between the wage increase and the rate of inflation is presumably due to the increase in human capital.

Second, recompense for investing in a spouse's human capital resembles the award of future earnings as part of a worker's compensation[194] or wrongful death claim[195] because it requires calculation of the expected value of the spouse's future career. The increment made during the marriage will be a fraction of this total expected value.[196] What proportion should go to the supporting spouse depends on the state's general property division laws. Is there a presumption or requirement of equal division?[197] Does the fact that one spouse studied or went to endless meetings while the other worked or provided relief from household chores[198] entitle the student or manager to a greater share? Are there other assets that can be offset against the earning capacity?[199] Finally, as with pensions, payout need not occur until the time when the income is actually realized, so that it can be adjusted in case of illness, injury, or involuntary unemployment.[200] Since an earning capacity is just like any other asset, the investor-spouse should be compensated for contributions to the other's career.

The distinction between alimony and property does not seem to make much sense, given no-fault divorce. If earning capacity is most couples' greatest asset, and alimony ceases to be a private welfare system (based on need), then doctrinally there is little difference. As a result, states may have to stop prohibiting modification of property distribution. They may also have to rethink the distinction between alimony (not dischargeable) and property (dischargeable) treatment of post-divorce bankruptcy,[201] if earning capacity awards are put under the current "property" rubric rather than becoming, as the American Law Institute has suggested, part of "compensatory spousal payments."[202] For example, if future earnings are the "property" being distributed, conceptually they are exempt from Chapter 7, the wage earner's bankruptcy. Current property distribution is not exempt from discharge in bankruptcy, though spousal support cannot be discharged. Property distribution cannot now be modified but might be in these earning capacity cases.

Reimbursement for lost career opportunities plus a share in the couple's tangible property will usually be fair compensation.[203] But this will be true only when one spouse's lost career opportunities approximately equal the gain to the other's enhanced career, plus interest (the ordinary rate of return).[204] Sometimes the "investing" spouse may not have lost much, if anything, in terms of career potential.[205] Should such a fortunate person nonetheless be given no reimbursement for an investment to the other's career? Sometimes the amount sacrificed will exceed the amount gained.[206] Unless there are large sums in other assets to spread around, in these cases the presumptive amount (the expected value of the career enhancement) may be modified if the income that eventually comes in is, through no fault of the benefited spouse, lower than expected.[207]

This new way of looking at dividing property will undoubtedly prolong ties between people who are legally free to pursue separate lives. Some future contact will be necessary unless they can agree that the expected value of the enhancement, like property, cannot be modified in the future,[208] discount this amount to present value,[209] and transfer the sum at the time of divorce. To get around the contact, some states might decide to have payments made directly from the employer. Perhaps more controversially, the idea that the relationship can be neither easily nor cheaply discarded—that it is a covenant—will cause some spouses to work a bit harder on their marriages.[210] Elizabeth and Robert Scott propose a two-year "notice" requirement before a spouse can obtain a unilateral divorce.[211]

These suggestions do not account for all cases in which compensatory payments ought to be made. There may well be investments in children that do no more than hold both spouses' earnings even.[212] Marriage, after all, is not just about, or even mainly about, creating wealth.[213] There may also be career moves for lifestyle purposes (to a teaching career from practice, or to a climate more suitable to an allergy sufferer), changes that make the marriage better off but do not make sense from a money-in-the-pocket standpoint.[214] In any case, the resulting gains in fairness among divorcing couples (middle class versus those who are not) and between the spouses themselves (between career enhancer and career-enhanced) certainly seem worth the valuation efforts.

While the justifications advanced for the current covenant model are conventional ones, the symbolic consequences are quite different from those of the other models. Covenant—and partnership—theories will not satisfy the traditionalists who fully embrace what Becker calls "the sharp sexual division of labor in all societies between the market and the household sectors" or the lifetime marriage necessary, in Becker's view, to make that division possible.[215] At the same time, the partnership and the covenant approaches eschew the liberals' insistence that women be encouraged to look to their own careers rather than to their husbands as the primary source of financial security.[216] These models reserve their greatest benefits for marriages with the greatest income disparity, and do so independently of any actual contribution made. The proposals validate decisions to value not just raising children over individual advancement but marriage over career and the search for a financially attractive mate over investment in one's own earning capacity.[217] In other words, partnership models, in their effort to maximize the number of choices for women, also make the role of the housewife more comfortable. None of these goals is particularly acceptable to liberal feminists.

In his *No-Fault Divorce: What Went Wrong?*[218] Allen Parkman notes that much of what makes modern economic divisions at divorce unfair to women is a failure by courts and legislatures to take the concept of human capital into account.[219] Gary Becker and others wrote about human capital in the family and labor markets in the early 1970s.[220] Subsequent changes in the modern family take note of the fact that we invest more in earning capacity than in land.[221] In 1980 Joan Krauskopf suggested that degrees earned during marriage ought to be divided upon divorce because they constitute investments in human capital.[222] Parkman goes to some lengths to explain that he does not believe the entire value of a new degree earned during marriage ought to be considered marital property, since "in normal circumstances the investments in human capital that occur before marriage will be so large and essential compared with the investments after marriage that an individual's human capital is best treated as separate property. When the investments after the marriage are substantial, it may be appropriate to treat the additional human capital as marital property."[223] Parkman goes on to state that what the courts have treated as goodwill is just the return to reputation. He notes that the "timing of the acquisition of the professional goodwill is usually ignored, with the courts tending to assume that it was acquired during marriage."[224] Allowing recovery only for spouses of professionals is unjust, since reputation is no more important to a professional practice than it is to, say, a car dealership. Further, recoupment of human capital investments should also be allowed for nonprofessional career advancements if these occurred during marriage.[225]

THE PROBLEM OF DIVIDING CHILDREN: EXTERNAL EFFECTS OF DIVORCE. The stock purchase example with which this discussion began is the quintessential contract at will. Marriage cannot be one of these at-will contracts because of its external effects.[226] The state makes it relatively difficult to exit marriage because the institution itself has value (as the basic building block of society[227] or as a signal of the spouses' characteristics, physical and mental)[228] and because of its important child rearing functions.

Most divorces involve minor children.[229] Whether or not we characterize them as unwilling victims of their parents' decision to separate, they are immediately affected, whether because of the emotional or relocation costs of divorce,[230] the probable lowered standard of living, or the loss of a familiar parental presence. They also suffer over the very long term according to a number of studies.[231]

Children may lose out for a number of reasons. They tend to be poorer than those from intact families,[232] and will in all probability suffer a variety of psychological and social problems. The least controversial explanation for the way divorce hurts children involves its financial consequences. Children of divorce make up a very large proportion of those below poverty level[233] and historically have received the majority of public assistance payments.[234] Because they are relatively poor, children of divorce disproportionately suffer the consequences of poverty: poor schools, less medical care (in the United States, at any rate), less appealing and less permanent living conditions, more crime, fewer amenities.

When parents divorce, children suffer lower academic achievement, more behavioral problems, poorer psychological adjustment, more negative self-concepts, more social difficulties, and more problematic relationships with both mothers and fathers than children from intact homes.[235] These psychological effects run counter to the optimism expressed early in the no-fault era that divorce would give children "greater insight and freedom as adults in deciding whether and when to marry," that they would learn from stepparents to "break away from excessive dependency on their biological parents,"[236] and that divorce would increase "[parental] personal autonomy, a new sense of competence and control, development of better relationships with children, and the freedom and time to develop . . . interests."[237] Children, it was hoped, would learn "more cooperation and respect, more regard for differences as well as similarities," and "grow into the unique individuals they are capable of becoming."[238] Recent research demonstrates quite convincingly that the rosy picture painted by divorce reformers was inaccurate. In the first few years following divorce, children show more antisocial, impulsive acting-out disorders, more aggression and noncompliance, more dependency, anxiety, and depression, more difficulties in social relationships, and more problem behavior in school than children in intact families.[239] The American Academy of Pediatrics found that up to half of all children of divorced parents were likely to manifest symptoms in the first year after the divorce, with aggression in school-age boys and depression in early and mid-adolescent girls the most troublesome. These problems persist well beyond this time, for the children's "sense of loss is ongoing and may reemerge especially on holidays, birthdays, special school events, and when attempting to integrate multiple new family relationships."[240]

Even after some years have passed, the differences between children of divorced and those of intact families persist. In a study in *Child Trends* taken from the National Survey of Family Growth in the United States, Kristin Moore and Alma Driscoll found that teenage girls who grew up with both biological parents are less likely to have sex than other teenagers and are less likely to give birth in their teens.[241] Mavis Hetherington and her co-authors[242] found that six years after divorce, boys who lived with their mothers still showed more acting-out behavior and less social competence than sons in nondivorced families.

Adolescent girls whose fathers were absent because of divorce showed more dependence on female adults than did their peers who lived with their fathers.[243] They were also more likely to seek praise, encouragement, and attention from male adults, and tended to initiate physical contact and nearness with male peers. Hetherington suggests that the lack of opportunity for constructive interaction with a loving, attentive father resulted in apprehension and inadequate skills in relating to males. (This may also be the reason for Moore and Driscoll's findings about increased teen sexuality and pregnancy.) Judith Wallerstein and Joan Kelly have found that children visited infrequently by their fathers suffered severely diminished self-esteem during the first five years after the separation of their parents.[244] Frequent contact with largely noncustodial fathers was found to be more important for self-esteem for children from nine to twelve than for other age groups.[245]

Fatherless boys have been found to show increased delinquent and anti-social behavior, which is much more pronounced when the father is absent because of separation or divorce rather than death.[246] Both genders, when grown, exhibit less psychological well-being, more behavioral problems, less education, lower job status, a lower standard of living, lower marital satisfaction, a heightened risk of divorce, a heightened risk of becoming a single parent, and poorer physical health than adults from intact families.[247]

In short, the children of divorce fare worse in school, have problems in their peer relationships, and are more apt to "act out." M. Anne Hill and June O'Neill[248] found that growing up with a divorced parent has a significant negative effect on children's scores on standardized tests. This disappears when family income is taken into account (and therefore may occur simply because the children of divorce are poorer). Over the longer term, researchers report that the children of divorce are more likely to drop out of school. Men raised in single-parent households had almost a year less education than those raised in intact families.[249]

Clearly there can be no clean break in divorce when children are involved. The presence of children makes divorce "sticky" for one other reason as well. (This is a term economists use for an inability to move smoothly and costlessly from one state to another, such as with "sticky wages" or "sticky prices.") The presence of children implies in nearly all cases a caretaker who must sacrifice both leisure time and employment time for them.[250] Losses to the caretaker's career, whether the children are born early or late in the marriage, are permanent (and estimated at 1.5 percent of total future earnings per year out of the job market).[251] If the custodial parent must accept flexible employment after divorce because, for example, there is not enough money to hire a full-time nanny, the loss accepted during the marriage (at the time the child is conceived or born) continues after divorce.[252]

This argument, of course, completely ignores the need for ongoing contact between divorcing parents to accommodate child support and visitation. These necessary (and, from the child's perspective, overwhelmingly desirable) connections[253] also preclude any clean break. The more involved both parents remain, the better for the child.[254]

One of the issues arguing both for investment in marriage and against making a clean break is the kind of role the parents' relationship plays in their child's upbringing. Ira Lupu refers to this in the constitutional language of balancing, or separating, powers.[255] In a two-parent family, one parent restrains the other who might act too hastily or too much out of self-interest and therefore harm the child. A different analogy that may explain parents' roles is to think of them as complements like tennis balls and tennis racquets, both needed to play the game, or as the right shoe and the left.[256] As we have seen, I like to think in these economic terms of complementarity.[257] Complementary goods are those that are both necessary for some productive activity. Both are necessary, but they do different things. The same-sex parent may act as role model plus disciplinarian or provider or chauffeur. The opposite-sex parent may educate the child in how best to deal with the other sex in future relationships and may also instill morality or secure medical care or coach the soccer team. Child rearing thus is a joint productive activity of the marriage.[258]

To sum up, the phenomenon of no-fault divorce, accompanied by modern alimony and property distribution laws, facilitates easy exit from marriage and envisions a "clean break" from the terminated relationship. These aspects of contemporary family law typify a contractual approach to the family, and, taken together, make it more difficult for the intact marriage to resemble a community, or covenantal relationship, in which intimacy is shared. The reason why this is so is that the emphasis on marriage as a less-than-permanent phenomenon from which one must emerge independent and self-sufficient if the marriage ends in divorce encourages investment in one's self and one's career while discouraging investment in the other spouse or in the marriage itself.

The malaise that numerous divorced people and commentators feel stems at least in part from a sort of cognitive dissonance: the judge says that the marriage is over and that one must begin life anew, but the couple's lives may still be hopelessly entangled. The difficulty of splitting marital assets arises from their being connected to the future as well as the past. Explicitly recognizing investments in marital assets such as earning capacity pushes us toward a less contractual, more covenantal notion of marriage. I will continue my discussion of these issues in Chapter 7.

Leaving the Family Firm: Emancipation of Minors

In many societies the transition from child to adult is marked with great ceremonies or tests of readiness to accept adult responsibilities.[259] In modern-day America, reaching age eighteen is signaled by two events: graduating from high school and, for middle-class young people at least, receiving major credit card applications. Despite the lack of fanfare, eighteen-year-olds are usually able to marry without permission, sue and be sued in their own names, join the armed forces, see X-rated movies, and enter into virtually any contract. Since 1971 they have also been allowed to vote in presidential elections.[260]

The age of majority used to be determined by one's ability to function as an adult.[261] For a man in medieval times, this might mean being a knight in service to his liege lord. For a woman, emancipated at a younger age, this meant being transferred from the custody of her father to the custody of her husband, to bear his children and maintain his household. More recently, adulthood has been associated with the ability to make mature decisions on one's own.[262]

We no longer ask our eighteen-year-olds to do the same. In fact, because education is so important in acquiring wealth, we postpone many adult responsibilities while young adults go to college (and, to a lesser extent, graduate school).[263] The transitional time is thus spread over a longer period, extended still further because of the additional decision-making ability legally granted to youth even before eighteen.

Parents do not usually ask for "child services,"[264] as I called them in Chapter 5, once children leave the home, but they may require obedience and some deference if they are continuing to support a child.[265] Before age eighteen, in order to become emancipated, a child must usually receive parental permission,[266] and parent-like responsibilities are transferred to some other agency. For example, marriage (with appropriate permission from parents and sometimes a court) will emancipate, with responsibility going to the spouse.[267] So will entry into the military, again with parental permission, with responsibility going to the government.[268] Finally, some parents will give minors who are close to majority age permission to live outside the family home, earning and keeping their own income.[269] Because of the variety of conditions of emancipation, several statutes have enacted legislation detailing ways in which children may become emancipated from their parents.[270] In addition, some recent cases have illustrated ways in which children can free themselves from parental ties while they are still minors.

Despite the enormous publicity when a lower court apparently allowed him to "divorce" his parents, the Florida youth Gregory Kingsley, as a minor, was ultimately found incapable of bringing a termination of parental rights proceeding in his own right.[271] The court terminated his mother's parental rights, however, because Gregory's attorney (who was also his adoptive father) had filed a petition on his behalf as his next friend.[272] In another notorious case,[273] fourteen-year-old Kimberly Mays, who had been switched at birth with another baby, was significantly more successful in her suit to terminate her relationship with her birth parents, the Twiggs, when the court found that it would be detrimental to her to enforce the stipulation making her have contact with them.[274] The court specifically considered the interests of the child to be its most important concern, and criticized the Twiggs for their position "that their interests, whatever they might be, are paramount."[275]

Emancipation, like divorce, frees parents and children from legal bonds.[276] But even more than in the case of divorce, emancipation does not terminate the relationship. Some examples of retention of the bond include cases in which parents remain responsible for children's support after emancipation, whether by marriage or age, occurs. For example, if a child becomes[277] or remains disabled,[278] the parents may be liable for the child's support. As I have mentioned several times, couples who divorce may be required by the court to pay for their (adult) child's college education.[279] And, as we will see shortly, the children may reacquire responsibility for their parents.

As Carol Sanger and Eleanor Willemsen point out,[280] the transition to adulthood in our society is marked by ambivalence:

Leaving home in America, like other rites of passage such as graduating from high school, going to college, getting one's first real job, and getting married, most often occurs between eighteen and twenty-two years of age. From a developmental perspective, leaving home usually is associated with such markers as a consolidation of ego identity, increased responsibility, and a more mature relationship with parents. Feelings of insecurity and even abandonment that result from the transition into adulthood are offset by the freedom of the new status, the new address.

They note that the end of any intimate relationship, even one desired or planned by both parties, may result in intense feelings of loss, but they contrast emancipation with romantic break-ups in several respects. "[P]arents and adolescents do not each enter the relationship voluntarily; the relationship is almost always one of asymmetrical dependence; and parents and child are at different stages of emotional development in ways that are quite different from whatever emotional imbalances may exist in relationships between adults."[281] Emancipation is also different from adoption and termination because of the procedural protections in place in those cases.

Whether in cases of divorce or emancipation, the break is never clean. The covenant relationship does not end even though the legal one does. The result is legal uncertainty and considerable psychological turmoil: a state of disequilibrium. Several centuries ago the transitions would at least have been more gradual. A young man might have continued to work the family farm owned by his father.[282] The woman who had obtained a bed and board divorce from her husband would not have remarried, but would have secured a living from her absent husband's estate.

Times have changed, as has technology. It is now possible to divorce and to marry again, and for children to take up careers different from their father's. Law now frequently severs marital and parental relations. I have argued that the legal rending of family bonds may not end them in fact. We turn in the next chapter to a discussion of how these loose ends may be secured.

Winding Up the Firm:
The Family Franchise

The plan for this chapter is to launch an exploration into what the family means in a peculiar context in which there are few legal obligations but some of the strongest and most important personal relationships in life. Perhaps the reader shares relationships with some of these people: elderly and increasingly idiosyncratic parents, siblings with families of their own, former spouses and co-parents, children now beginning their own independent lives, or even birth parents or children now seemingly "lost." What I call the family franchise encompasses the relationships that are still present even after the strongest legal bonds are broken by divorce, emancipation, or adoption.

To tie these in to my earlier observations, I hope to show how this largely untraversed area of family law relates to the concerns treated in preceding chapters as more central—in particular, the laws relating to provision for minor children and to marital property. On a more general level, I will argue in this chapter that the current preoccupation with "rights"[1] has forced us into the less attractive model described here.

Before sketching two contrasting models of what we might call post-family relationships, I want to describe again briefly the two different ways I have pictured families throughout this book. I have argued that many of the workings of a family can be described in terms of the market or contract model[2] and the firm or covenant paradigm.[3] We have seen that the idea of contract is particularly useful for describing the law and relations that govern parties about to enter into family relationships, for example, people engaged in courtship and adoption.[4] To some extent, contract may also be appropriate for framing the context of dissolving families, those disrupted by separation, divorce,[5] or termination of parental rights.[6] Yet contract law dragged out of its usual commercial context and into family law has serious drawbacks. The most obvious of these is that it is virtually useless for treating love, trust, faithfulness, and sympathy, which more than any other terms describe the essential elements of family.[7] The second problem is that contract law implies the possibility of breach. When a better deal comes along, it may be most appropriate to breach, pay damages, and recontract with the inviting third party. But when other people are involved, particularly if some of them are children, paying damages does not compensate. One's affections are not—and, normatively speaking, should not be—readily transferable. Moreover, the idea of continually being on the lookout for better family "deals"—better spouses, children, or parents—itself destroys family life.[8]

The concept of covenant, by contrast, better describes families that are well under way: it illuminates the relationship between husband and wife or parent and child.[9] As explained earlier, covenant implies a particularly serious commitment that has characteristics of permanence and unconditional love. The parties are bound not only to each other but also to some third party (God or the state or both).[10] The discussion in Chapter 6 involved families that are legally dissolving, noting that there are features of the relationship, such as child custody or interests in earning capacity or the ability to enforce promises of future support made during the child's minority, for which legal resolution seems incomplete. When children reach adulthood and leave their parents, or when couples divorce, or when parents give up their children for adoption, the law no longer binds them together as families. What happens then to the covenant—the forever and unconditional part of the family relationship?

Families as Sovereign Nations: The State of Nature

First, consider what is perhaps an obvious model of the family after dissolution, and one that is suggested by the contractual approach to family law. In this model, called the "sovereign nation," the dissolved family is made up of discrete individuals no longer legally bound to one another. According to political scientists who study warfare, many of the problems existing between nations arise when their dealings can be characterized as revealing miscalculation and betrayal rather than credibility and trust.[11] Groups who have committed terrible crimes, as the Russians under Stalin did in the Ukraine, are seen as being more difficult to deal with in bargaining not only because they are dangerous but also because they are untrustworthy. The choice whether or not to trust depends at least to some extent on whether the countries retell their joint histories in similar ways.[12] As Henry Kissinger and others have pointed out, even allies should never be fully trusted, for a nation is not a "philanthropic" institution charged with absorbing the losses caused by another country's change of heart or mind.[13] For any given country, if it will afford an excuse for building up the military or some other bureaucracy, a characterization of another regime as "evil" may cause the revising of history itself. Thus the Germans rewrote interpretations of their prior dealings with the British during the military expansion before World War II.[14] And once a country takes a stand by revising history, the protagonists believe in their new "truth" because of a process described as "blowback dynamics." The nation's credibility is therefore engaged with the winning historical interpretation as much as with one's allies. Further, once an issue passes into public debate, truth may be compromised, for then the citizenry continues to hear its own government's version.[15] In the game theory terminology popular for describing international negotiation,[16] the equilibrium model becomes one of tit-for-tat, or, as it is sometimes called, reciprocity.[17]

With the family, the paradigm developed under this model sounds almost pathological. Parents and siblings would attempt to look out for their own interests rather than the family's as a whole. They would think in short- rather than long-range terms, and solidify their positions by airing family disputes in public. Thankfully, this is not the prevalent pattern, except perhaps after divorce.

How does this unhappy confrontational situation with its frequent escalation and conflict improve, if at all? In the ordinary sense of a contract that cannot be enforced, Thomas Hobbes sees a hopeless situation: "For he that performeth first, has no assurance the other will perform after: because the bonds of words are too weak to bridle man's ambition, avarice, anger, and other passions, without the fear of some coercive power; which in the condition of mere nature, where all men are equal, and judges of the justness of their own fears, cannot possibly be supposed, and therefore he which performeth first, does but betray himself to his enemy: contrary to the right, he can never abandon, of defending his life, and means of living."[18]

Beginning his essay "Contract Law and the State of Nature" with this quotation from Hobbes, Anthony Kronman has written that informal mechanisms[19]—hostage taking, collateral, union, and hands-tying—might be used to channel conduct in situations in which individuals and groups must "arrange their transactions . . . without the aid of an independent enforcement mechanism whose powers are significantly greater than their own."[20] Hostage taking has attracted international attention not only when criminals take prisoners but also when international provocateurs detain innocent citizens of another nation. The idea is that the other side will be willing to deal, or at least refrain from attacking, if people (or goods) that they value are held by the hostage takers, for whom they have little value except as negotiating devices.[21] Kronman defines collateral as something that has value on the open market held by one side (or a third party) as a guarantee or pledge of performance by the other (or both).[22] In the international setting, an example is the International Monetary Fund, in which many nations invest. In the family, an instance is the diamond engagement ring that bonds the affianced and belongs to the non-breaching party if the marriage promise is broken.[23] Union is described by Kronman as the building of a shared affection[24] or, as political scientists would put it, a shared history. This building can be done, as with nations, through emphasis on common characteristics ("Aryanism," fear of another nation) or for members of other unrelated groups through "cheerleading," such as school songs or bumper stickers. A related idea is hands-tying behavior,[25] the most famous (and literal) example of which is Ulysses' binding himself to the mast.[26] More formally, economists describe such precommitment as investing in transaction-specific capital, as, for example, when the railroad invests in a spur that can lead only to the mine and the mining company invests heavily in equipment useful only at that particular site.[27] The parties' hands are tied so they cannot rationally act uncooperatively.

This set of binding devices in the state of nature helps explain family institutions such as reunions, Christmas giving to—and by—aunts and uncles, visiting cousins when one is "in town," and even the custom of retaining the family name when one becomes an adult, all of which are "union building" devices, in Kronman's terminology. Family names, of course, also make sense from the outside world's perspective: it is easy to recognize who is the landowner and who the blacksmith from one's surname, and therefore names establish one's reputation.[28] We have, of course, weakened this kind of identification in the modern concept of retaining maiden names or adopting new surnames when we marry or have children.[29] Hostage taking is more difficult to see in the family context, since usually siblings and even former spouses value the same things, whereas hostage taking presumes that the hostage is valued by one side but not the other.[30] As Kronman notes, "The process [of spouses'] identification is consummated in the procreation and rearing of children who . . . strengthen their parents' union, by giving it an 'objective' or 'external' form."[31] Collateral pledging may lie behind some of the phenomena described in writings about the rent seeking attached to the giving and receiving of bequests, which we will examine in the following pages.[32]

The Alternative View: The Family Franchise

We can also think of post-dissolution or emancipation families as a kind of franchise or reorganization. These analogies are meant to be not exact, however, but metaphorical. For example, the commercial franchise can be terminated without ongoing relationships between franchisor and franchisee. The corporate reorganization is virtually always precipitated by creditor action, while in divorce both spouses may be simultaneously debtor and creditor. Nevertheless, each commercial arrangement carries on in some capacity after the original relationship has legally dissolved.

The law and economics view of franchising is that it exists as an alternative to company-owned businesses to save on transaction costs, which are the economist's equivalent of friction.[33] The franchisor wishes to continue the firm's reputation for quality and price, and therefore will allow the franchisee the benefit of any of the firm's innovations or trade secrets, as well as the necessary tools and supplies (usually given at a substantial discount), and, most valuable, use of the firm name.[34] In return, the franchisee is expected to keep the establishment at least in the condition necessary to maintain the unsullied name of the franchisor. This agreement is necessary, writes Gillian Hadfield, because the franchisee "is inclined to make decisions about how much effort to put into the business based on the profits that will accrue directly to her in her own outlet. She is not inclined to take into account that, because customers will make judgments about the quality of the entire franchise system based on their experience at an outlet, cost-saving reductions in quality at her outlet will affect the overall value of the trademark and thus the profits of other franchisees and the franchisor."[35] In order to enforce such promises, franchises typically run for a determinate period of time, provide opportunities for interim monitoring, and specify the quality of goods sold as well as inputs for the concern.[36] While the franchisor is concerned that the franchisee will be tempted to "free-ride" on the chain's reputation while offering goods of sub-par quality, the franchisee typically is concerned about opportunism on the part of the franchisor, who may increase input prices or impose additional costs on the franchisee once the contract term begins.[37]

The family metaphor has not been lost on industry commentators, who stress the human relationships involved in franchising. Harry Kursch writes: "Being a franchisor is pretty much like being a parent. If there's a squabble amongst the kids you try to get in there and solve it. You have to handle it with diplomacy."[38] Their writing also illustrates the inequality that is the hallmark of the franchise business relationship, as well as the parent-child relationship. John Hooker writes: "The function of the franchisee is to follow the wisdom and system of the franchisor. . . . [T]ell him, 'Look, partner, we are both playing a role, and the role I've got is the Daddy, and the role you've got is the son, and I'm going to tell you how to do it. If you do it right we're going to do it better.'"[39]

The corporate reorganization begins with a bankruptcy,[40] that is, the liabilities of the firm exceed its assets. The bankruptcy court may allow the debtor to continue to operate the business rather than go through liquidation because there is a larger social (employee or farmer or consumer) value to continued production of goods or services.[41] The creditors may prefer liquidation, since they would receive some share of their investment.[42] Under reorganization, they may get nothing at all if the business continues to suffer.

Divorcing childless couples, and perhaps parents whose custody is terminated for cause, also reorganize their lives because, to a very real extent, their liabilities exceed their assets. The existing marriage is worse than the option of leaving marriage via divorce, even with its problems and uncertainties. For a parent placing a child in foster care, or whose rights have been terminated for neglect, the bleak option of giving up the child seems nonetheless better than the family's current suffering.

In both reorganized family forms, the social, or external, value of the relationship continues. The vestige may be the continued obligation to pay spousal or child support (which is due even while a child is in foster care).[43] Thus there are characteristics of both the old situation and the new—the same players, perhaps, but with a greater freedom to reorganize their lives.

As I noted in Chapter 1, these family situations in which reorganization is the appropriate motif are atypical: most children enter a franchise-like relationship with their parents without ever going through a "bankruptcy" phase. Divorcing couples with children (about 65 percent of all divorcing couples) exhibit some characteristics of each analogy. The new relationship begins with marital failure and certainly differs from the intact family in that neither parent typically has all possible parent time with the children as before. But it is franchise-like because both parents retain the same general interest in the child's well-being.

With these metaphorical models in mind—sovereign nation or corporate reorganization or closely knit franchise—let us look at several kinds of family relationships after the law has declared them ended. We begin with the most obvious candidate for examination, the divorcing couple.

Couples at War: Sovereign Nations at Divorce

Although it is probably obvious from the discussion in the last chapter, it may be worth noting again that the movement toward the abolition of permanent alimony signals at once a return to a contractual approach to marriage and a change from an enforceable contract to a state of nature. Even though this may seem a contradiction in terms, permanent alimony, because it continues at least the support obligations of the marriage beyond the legal termination of the relationship, is covenant-like.[44] At the same time, to the extent that alimony serves as a type of damage remedy for enforcing marital obligations, it secures legal recognition of the marriage contract.[45] If no-fault divorce is seen as a termination of a marriage contract "at will," why should either party be able to claim a contractual interest in a continuing marriage that would justify support after divorce? If the less wealthy spouse cannot make such a claim on the other, the push must be toward independence after divorce. Divorce should, according to this contractual theory, be a "clean break." I have shown how this analysis has some defects, even for childless couples, if investment in earning capacity is a candidate for recognition on divorce.

Whatever attraction the clean break philosophy holds for childless couples who have been married for a short time, it runs afoul of reality when there are minor children. The idea of cleanly breaking off a lengthy marriage presents problems as well. The vast majority of these marriages, too, have produced children who are now grown, and the remainder still involve lives that are commingled. As we saw at the end of Chapter 6, the dissolution of a family results in a long-term malaise or disequilibrium felt by children and parents alike.[46] We will look at some tangible evidences of this malaise shortly.

I have discussed (in Chapter 6) some of the theoretical problems created by the current alimony and marital property systems, but have not yet looked at the corresponding approach to child support and custody. It is worth turning to these problems now, for the solutions to them make more sense in terms of franchise theory.

Post-divorce Responsibilities to Children: A Contractual Approach

When parents divorce and the family breaks up, one parent gets custody according to the usual practice in most states.[47] (Even in the relatively progressive state of Montana, where there is a presumption of joint custody, it is actually awarded less than half the time. And the custody situation in practice may be even more traditional than the divorce decree provides.) This physical separation has several effects on financial support, despite the fact that the noncustodial parent still loves the child. First, the parties must now maintain two households, eliminating economies of scale that were present during the marriage.[48] Thus, given the same incomes, the parties are effectively poorer because of increased costs. The second and perhaps even more intractable problem (since it affects all couples, even the most wealthy) involves monitoring, a version of the principal and agent problem we first saw in Chapter 3 in the context of foster parents.[49] Yoram Weiss and Robert Willis argue that as long as the family remains intact, parents view the upbringing of the children as a joint enterprise or "collective good."[50] Each dollar allocated for a child benefits both parents because as the child thrives, the parents' happiness or satisfaction increases.

Once the couple separates, only part of each payment sent to the custodian will be spent on the child. Part will go to benefit both custodial parent and child, and perhaps part will benefit only the custodian. Because he is no longer physically living in the marital home, the noncustodial parent cannot monitor how the custodian allocates support payments.[51] In addition, the implicit trust that is central to the marriage relationship often disintegrates as the couple separates and divorces,[52] particularly if one party has found a new partner. Finally, because he lives away from the children and sees them less frequently, the noncustodial father, even if not embittered by the divorce or disputes regarding visitation rights, may lose interest in the child or become preoccupied with his new life.[53] (In this context, remember the earlier discussion of Judith Seltzer's studies of the tendency of men to feel responsible to the children of their current relationship.)[54] From the divorced father's perspective, the only way to make sure that the money is being spent appropriately would involve conditioning support payments on expenditures for the child.[55] But because the noncustodial parent cannot verify actual expenditures, this proves unworkable.

Divorce also produces substantial differences in the allocation of responsibility between parents. Not only each dollar but also each hour allocated for a child benefits both cohabiting parents because as the child thrives, their happiness or satisfaction increases. Once the couple no longer live together, the noncustodial parent (and perhaps the custodial parent as well, if she is working outside the home for the first time) cannot spend long periods of time with the child on a day-to-day basis. In other words, the custodial arrangement typically cannot mirror the pre-divorce sharing of rewards and responsibilities.

To complicate matters, the child and the custodial parent do not have precisely the same interests. Perhaps this is obvious, since the child is concerned only about his or her own well-being, while the custodial parent thinks both about her own consumption and the welfare of the child.[56] Further, because divorce usually benefits the adults far more than the children, there may be hard feelings between parent and child. Only the parents have ended a relationship when they divorce; the child's a connection with the noncustodial parent continues.[57] In the extreme, because the divorce may have been acrimonious, the custodian may want emotional distance from, may desire to control, or may even want to hurt the noncustodial parent. The natural desire for personal autonomy following divorce can also be a problem if either parent decides to move out of the jurisdiction.[58] These needs for independence and "space" in turn may lead to the custodian's lowering her request for child support in order to minimize interference by the divorced spouse. The custodial parent may even compensate the other in exchange for reduced demands for visitation, thus "purchasing" more time with the child (or less contact with the noncustodial parent) at the child's expense.[59] If there is less visitation by a fit parent, both the noncustodial parent and the child lose.[60]

The tragic result is that from the child's perspective, the situation may be far worse than before. Guidance, confidence, and tangible support frequently are not forthcoming from the noncustodial parent. Decades of federal intervention have not ameliorated the child support enforcement problem.[61] Courts provide that visitation cannot be tied to child support, since this would cause the child to suffer loss not only of the financial benefits but also of the relationship with the parent.[62] Nor may the noncustodial parent force the other to spend the child support money solely for the child's benefit rather than her own.[63] For children, whatever right they might have had before divorce to enforce any family contract (such as one for support and guidance in exchange for "child services") has now vanished.[64]

In child support cases, children are unable to bring independent actions. The courts may reason that the child lacks standing to sue,[65] or similarly, that the child was not a party to the parents' contract.[66] A second group of enforcement cases parallels the tort doctrine of intrafamilial immunity.[67] The tort cases reason that a child should not be free to sue a parent because, especially if the family is intact, such a suit would be disruptive to familial harmony, or to the disposal of the "parental exchequer." As one court put it:

> The members of a family work together and contribute to the common good and welfare. They, through mutual effort and cooperation, make the determinations that contribute to that end. During minority the parents, because of their usual greater knowledge and experience, make the final determinations. Contributions during such period made by the child to his own support, maintenance and education out of his own earnings must be regarded as voluntarily made, either with the express or implied consent of the parents. It is the rule, as it ought to be, that no member shall idle away any portion of his time and when not engaged in the acquisition of education he will be otherwise employed and earn and contribute to his own welfare and that of the family. It is well established, based on sound reason and principles, a child may not maintain an independent suit to recover against his parents for support and maintenance.[68]

Nor does this rationale disappear once the parents have divorced, since, at least theoretically, the parent-child relationship continues even if the former spouses are free to begin or pursue other romantic relationships.[69] In a slightly different context but for similar reasons, courts are reluctant to allow custodial mothers who have reverted to their maiden names or adopted a new husband's surname to change their children's names. Short of adoption by a stepfather, a name change would weaken the bond with the child's noncustodial father without substituting another responsible person.[70]

As the cases make clear, to some extent the duty to pay child support rests on parents' reciprocal obligations of custody and support.[71] There is also an important relationship between the duty of support and the ability of the parent to exercise control over the child. When parents live apart, particularly if they no longer get along even minimally well, they may undermine each other's ability to provide guidance and discipline.[72] When the child refuses to accept any advice from the noncustodial parent (or even to visit him), enforcing the child support obligation seems particularly unfair from the parent's perspective.[73] Thus, since the child is legally unable to enforce the support obligation and the custodial parent frequently is practically unable to do so, it becomes relatively easy for a noncustodial parent to escape responsibility and become a deadbeat.

Why Do Some Parents Become Deadbeats?

Family deadbeats seek to avoid legal obligations, abandoning their former spouse and children to public welfare or private charity.[74] They are the stuff of Dickensian novels and of Grimm's fairy tales. They are the immigrants who never sent for their wives, and the pioneers who cast off their families to move West. They live lives without accountability, and, because they have always been with us, we have the laws of support, alimony, and divorce.[75] For them, the American West, in particular offered freedom from family responsibilities as well as political freedom.

Deserted wives historically could assert a variety of remedies against their spouses. Desertion was a ground for divorce,[76] and states mandated child support obligations.[77] There is, however, a wide variation among states in family support obligations, so deadbeat spouses have an incentive to move to low-payout and low-collection states.

The deserted spouse could still sue for support in her home jurisdiction, and seek to enforce the order in the state to which her spouse had moved. This was never an entirely effective remedy, however. In the past, many states were unwilling to enforce support decrees from a foreign jurisdiction, particularly since this required the application of criminal extradition laws.[78] Under the prodding of the federal government, states enacted Uniform Reciprocal Enforcement of Support legislation in the 1950s.[79] Where the child support obligor can be located, these statutes provide an expeditious remedy for the deserted spouse, without court filings and attorney costs. The social service agency in the home state simply sends a copy of the decree mandating the obligation to the social service officials in the state where the defendant lives (the responding state). He is permitted to present a defense: he never owed the money, he has already paid, or he has no money. The defendant may also argue that the award should be reduced because the plaintiff needs less money than she requested. Not all states enforce foreign awards to the same degree. In some states they are frequently reduced, particularly when the defendant has remarried and has a new family in the responding state.[80] Even with reciprocal enforcement of support laws, then, a state might compete for divorced spouses through the promise of reduced support obligations.

Nearly a quarter of family support cases involve deadbeat dads who have crossed a state line. In 1997 the total number of cases in which support orders were enforced or modified was 9.93 million.[81] Of these, more than a million involved interstate collections.[82] Deadbeat migrants are apparently attracted to jurisdictions that permit them to scale back family obligations, such as Florida, which did not collect 85 percent of the child support due in 1992.

In "The Market for Deadbeats,"[83] Frank Buckley and I conducted an empirical examination of migration trends within the United States for the period 1985–90, looking for, among other things, the indices of nonpayment of child support. Since our use of 1990 data introduced endogeneity concerns (that is, migration might cause as well as be caused by a lax child support enforcement system), we separately estimated nonpayment of child support. The temptation to default on personal support obligations is presumably stronger when temporary family support payments (formerly AFDC) are relatively high, and there is a greater incentive to share support duties with the state.[84] We also expected to see a greater prevalence of family deadbeats in states where the incidence of divorce is high, on the assumption that those who breach marriage vows are more likely to shortchange their families in other ways. Similarly, we anticipated a positive correlation between family deadbeat variables and the unwed birthrate, assuming that a man who is unwilling to marry the mother of his children is less likely to support the mother and children financially than a man who is willing to marry the mother.[85] On the positive side, we expected to see fewer deadbeats in states which prescribe joint custody orders for children on divorce. Noncustodial parents are less likely to pay child support since, as we have seen, it is harder for them to monitor the way their payments are spent.[86] In addition, the more time one spends with a child, the stronger the attachment and the greater the willingness to pay child support.[87]

Other predictors of family deadbeats were more ambiguous. A high percentage of unsupported children in the under-eighteen population might actually indicate a good collection mechanisms, assuming economies of scale, since in states where only a few children are left unsupported compared to the number of taxpayers, the burden on the state fisc may not be great enough to spur collection of the debt. We also expected a positive correlation between the infant mortality rate and family deadbeats, for many studies have reported a relationship between a parent's attachment to his or her children and the likelihood that they will survive to adulthood.[88] Nevertheless, with this variable we might be measuring the behavior of the wrong parent, since infant mortality is more closely related to maternal behavior, while deadbeat variables generally measure behavior by fathers. We might expect more family deadbeats, too, given a higher percentage of women in the labor force,[89] since women will have a stronger incentive to work when their husbands fail to support them, though working women are also less likely to need spousal support. They have more power within individual marriages, however, and are more apt to share child rearing responsibilities with their spouse. These characteristics suggest a negative relationship between the percentage of deadbeats and the percentage of women in the labor force.

There were few surprises among predictors of noncustodial parents who did not pay child support. The most interesting finding for purposes of this book involves joint custody.[90] I will explore the connections between custody and child support payment at greater length in the section on child rearing franchises, but it is worthwhile to note that the joint custody dummy was negative and significant. Parents appear more likely to support their children when they maintain close contact with them through joint custody orders.

Part of the reason why joint custody is associated with higher payment rates may be that mediated and otherwise party-generated settlements encourage both practices. Better enforcement has always been touted as an advantage by proponents of mediation.[91] At the same time, it is quite clear that mediators frequently advocate joint custody following divorce.[92] Both high payment rates and cooperative custody outcomes are more likely to be found in less hotly contested divorce because of a selection bias: the cases in which couples cannot agree on much of anything are the ones most likely to need court action,[93] whereas if the spouses can agree to co-operate in raising their children, they probably will not have to go to court to resolve their disputes. States do not collect data on the relative frequency of divorce litigation, so this variable was not considered in our deadbeats research.

The Marriage Franchise

June Carbone and I in an article written in 1991[94] noted that feminist agendas "call for uncoupling marriage and childrearing." Obviously this "uncoupling" is reflected in the suggestion that marriage should be abolished entirely, discussed in Chapter 3 in connection with the work of Martha Fineman. But once someone is "married, with children," one cannot completely sever the ties with one's spouse.

The franchise approach to marriage and divorce suggests that even though the legal relationship ends, common interests, this time in the common good of marriage, the children, will encourage parents to remain involved at least until these children are grown. Of course, there is no real franchisor in the business sense, though the state assumes some of the franchisor's roles, allocating resources and enforcing deviations from the divorce court–ordered standard. The dual problems of overcoming spite and hostility over whatever went wrong with the marriage and taking on the other practical difficulties I have discussed present hurdles that may be exacerbated by a conflict-ridden divorce process itself.[95]

We have seen that payment of child support is apparently linked to joint custody, legal or physical. In other empirical work, Frank Buckley and I found a similar negative relationship between the divorce rate and the presence of a joint custody regime or awards of joint custody the preceding year.[96] The data used in both studies was from the state level. But they are very suggestive, at least, of the idea that close involvement between divorced parents and their children encourages more responsive (and responsible) behavior. This idea contradicts not only the writings of some feminists,[97] who worry about the increased power joint custody gives to divorcing men, but also the important work of Joseph Goldstein, Anna Freud, and Albert Solnit,[98] which suggests that one parent should have control over visitation by the other (or anyone else) to satisfy the child's need for stability. It reaches the same end result, though, as the essay by Ira Lupu discussed in Chapter 5,[99] and the American Law Institute's Project,[100] as well as the older articles by John Murray and Elizabeth Scott,[101] all of which suggest that continued involvement of the father is tremendously important to children. Scott's and Murray's (and the American Law Institute's) suggestion is that the custody regime chosen at divorce ought to mirror as closely as possible the actual sharing of responsibilities during the marriage.

Covenantal marriage may exist without the tie of children, too, although probably only in marriages that last for many years, and then under the reorganization rather than the franchise framework.[102] The "displaced homemaker" has proven one of the most difficult problems for courts and scholars discussing the role of alimony. Many times she (for at this time it is almost always the wife) married and raised children under the type of system described in Chapter 4, where she was expected to invest in human capital that would aid her in "household production," remaining in the home rather than the labor market. When no-fault divorce made it possible for her marriage to end without fault, she was left with few market skills, no reasonable prospect of "rehabilitation," and a life in shambles.[103]

In many cases such women present a good vehicle for looking at marriage as a more permanent commitment where there are children who have now grown. Income sharing,[104] which is the likely remedy for such women, ties husband and wife together unless she remarries,[105] and is clearly a reorganization-like result: a continuation of some obligations despite the change in the underlying relationship. The obligations continue because of the social value of homemaking. (Note the connection to the idea of community established in Chapter 2.)

Older women from long marriages also constitute the most troublesome category for feminists who want to discourage dependence by eliminating alimony. As a transitional humane matter, they must be protected.[106] The real question is whether the large investment discussed in connection with the covenant marriage, one that necessarily creates dependence, should be encouraged. Perhaps this is where the two categories of marriage, the "lite" version (without children and of short duration) and the "standard" or "covenant" version (with children or having lasted many years), might diverge upon divorce, with different rules[107] and different compensation schemes envisioned for each.[108] The "lite" marriage might entail a simple division of property with possible short-term alimony, and might terminate through unilateral action after a very short waiting period. (This is in fact the current regime in many states.) The "standard" or "covenant" divorce could free the couple to marry again, but would envision more substantial continuing relations, such as shared parenting, long-term alimony, or the degree sharing discussed in Chapter 4. Divorce would be possible only after a more lengthy separation period, with the consent of both spouses, or after some showing of fault, such as family violence.

Adult Children and Elderly Parents: The Mature Family Franchise

In this section I describe another aspect of what might be called the vestiges of covenant. After the legal ties of infancy and parental responsibility disappear, something remains. As we shall see, what that something is may change. Some of the bond between parent and adult child undoubtedly is primordial and emotional, and therefore unlikely to alter with years and fortunes. Whether siblings maintain that sort of relationship with one another and, together, vis-à-vis their parents depends to some extent on whether the parents are viewed as a net good, in which case what I have described as the franchise model operates, or a net neutral or bad, in which case the "state of nature" governs.

The institution of franchise itself may be seen, from the perspective of the franchisees, as a tamer sort of sovereign nation model. Although other franchises may be competitors (there are two Exxon stations and two 7-Eleven stores within six blocks of each other on the commercial street nearest my home), their rivalry is more friendly than that with competing brands. What they have in common outweighs the competitive instinct. By protecting the transactions with the franchisor, the law encourages referrals and other sharing among the franchisees.

Law makes a critical difference in what form is chosen: the franchise or the largely unenforceable agreements of the state of nature. And law will certainly be involved where family governance—of whatever sort—fails. There may be elder abuse, estate problems, suits to enforce statutory duties of support, quarrels over competency, and the increasingly common disputes over grandparent visitation, in which grandparents who wish to visit grandchildren are prevented from doing so by the parent.

From the point of view of the parent, when the child becomes an adult there may still be hope of enforcing the implicit contract made when the child was young: I will take care of you, love you, invest in you, and in return be cared for by you when I am enfeebled.[109] But the younger person, at least one without the expectation of inheritance, has the opportunity for gaining what economists call quasi-rents, for the greatest parental investment was made in that person's youth, and without his or her explicit concurrence. A quasi-rent is income that is not earned but extracted from the contracting partner's "consumer surplus," the amount of satisfaction gained from the transaction in excess of the price paid or opportunity forgone.[110] The idea here is that the child may comfortably rely on the fact that the parent is extremely committed to him or her, and may therefore misbehave for quite a long time or quite substantially before the parent will complain or seek to disinherit or end contact. "I never agreed to have you live with me, and I have a life of my own," may be the child's response to the parent's growing ill health or incapacity.

Thus there are again two possible models for describing the behavior of what might be called mature families (or related adults): one is the sovereign nation international law model or the state of nature; the other is the franchise. Although I begin by applying the state of nature model to mature families, I should note again that, apart from legal challenges, the cues to the appropriate model include in part the parent's health, cheerfulness, and mental youthfulness, and whether the parent's estate is seen as large, small, or negative. There may thus be a shift in paradigms as the parent ages or his or her fortunes change. On the one hand, siblings may act as franchisees during their forties and their parents' late sixties, and as sovereign nations (perhaps warring ones) during their own late fifties and their parents' seventies and eighties, as the parents become less pleasant to deal with or the bond market crashes. On the other hand, the siblings may begin as "independent nations" and end up as franchisees if their parent wins the lottery or recovers from alcoholism. Both models are therefore worth considering, and, to repeat, we can influence which one dominates by our choice of legal regime.

The Sovereign Nature Model in Mature Families

Students of human nature, at least since the time of John Locke, have seen the obvious parallels between the associations of adult children and their elderly parents and those of unrelated citizens and communities.[111] Locke, in his *Second Treatise on Government,* describes extended families residing together under the father's guidance or "rule" through their own consent, that is, through their new and voluntary contract: "In commercial countries, where the authority of law is always perfectly sufficient to protect the meanest man in the state, the descendants of the same family, having no such motive for keeping together, naturally separate and disperse, as interest or inclination may direct. They soon cease to be of importance to one another."[112] Without such an agreement, the former infants are at liberty to govern themselves, or to unite at will with other societies or communities.[113] The relationship with their extended family is in many ways similar to the relationship between sovereign nations.

If, however, elderly parents have property the younger generation wants, the estate then acts like collateral to induce the young to do what pleases the older people.[114] Perhaps the absence of any such collateralizing bond[115] between adult siblings is the reason why these relationships tend to be weaker, becoming intensely competitive as the elderly parents near death. At the same time the competition for the inheritance is growing, other ties that would bind the siblings together are fading.[116] Memories of a childhood spent happily playing together may be faint, especially in the reality of dealing with a cantankerous and sickly senior.[117] The siblings may now see in one another the traits they most disliked in their parents, such as indecisiveness, greed, or intolerance, especially if they are reminded of these characteristics by the presence of the old people themselves.[118]

In families without a great deal of wealth to pass on, or where the elderly person is senile, the model also may explain certain types of hands-tying behavior: on the one extreme moving far away from the family home so as to avoid frequent visits with the aged parent or uncomfortable decisions such as the question of moving the parent to a nursing home;[119] or, on the other extreme, building the in-law apartment that will be useful only for the parent to occupy.

Franchise: The Ties of Shared Investment

As we saw previously, there is an alternative metaphor for looking at the same relationships, which may also be fruitful. At least some elements of these extended families are like franchise arrangements: the older person is the franchisor, with reputational stakes[120] as well as "up-front" investment in the middle-aged generation.[121] The adult children are franchisees, who have reaped the benefit of their parents' educational and other investments in them, and who now actively operate their own family units with the name, possibly the fortune, and the reputation of their parents at risk.

Decisions to have children and how to behave toward them in infancy and early childhood are unilateral but are probably affected by expectations concerning future mutual relationships. Yoram Ben-Porath mentions that "large outstanding balances are tolerated," and "enforcement is mostly internal." The investments are specific because "embedded in the identity of the partners," without which they lose their meaning, and thus "specific and nonnegotiable or nontransferable.[122]

Like the commercial franchisor, the elderly parent has a heavy specific investment in the family name as well as in the children he or she has raised. The parent almost never terminates the parental relationship: although there may be threats of disinheritance, these usually will not be credible. (Think of the Prodigal Son in Luke 15:11–32). The parent, however, may well prefer, or even insist on, frequent monitoring. This serves two functions. First, as Marshall Kapp suggests, the parent may actually desire the contact with the child: "[P]eople live their lives embedded within various relationships, among which the family for most of us is paramount. Since these relationships tend to grow stronger over time, they take on added significance for most older persons. These relationships have an empowering quality contributing to the older person's potential for positive, affirmative autonomy to think and act, as opposed to the simple, negative autonomy to be left alone."[123]

In addition to feeling maternal or paternal affection, the parent may genuinely value the child as a friend. He or she may also be lonely, and one's children may be better company than other old people, especially when one's friends begin to die off. Finally (and this is related to the franchise analogy), the parent may be monitoring the child's activities to make sure that the family tradition, whatever it is, is being carried on. Of course, keeping in touch with one's children was simple in the era when many parents did not live long, and those who did were likely to own the land their children worked or the home the children lived in.[124] As we have moved away from our ancestral homes (if, indeed, any are left) and off to faraway parts of the world, we of course distance ourselves from our parents and make monitoring more difficult. We are also less likely to support them, given Social Security, Medicare, and pensions.[125]

For the children who are franchisees, the relationships are complex. Children sometimes vie not to support their parents. They compete in rivalries about which of their own children are most successful, about who has enjoyed the most successful career, sometimes about who has best been able to keep up the family traditions. (Note, for example, the jealousy of the elder son in the biblical story of the Prodigal Son.)[126] Yet they still care about their siblings.[127] And they have a common interest in maintaining the family name, and perhaps in keeping the family property intact,[128] though this would be more apparent in rural communities, as it was under Continental feudalism. What may be more important now, as John Langbein argues, is human capital. Our parents' investments in our human capital occurred when we were young. Whether we choose to repay the parents for their investment will depend in part upon non-financial considerations: love, guilt, and generalized emotional intermeshings.[129] It will depend also on state requirements, for example, for support of the elderly, although legislation against elder abuse (which I will discuss shortly) involves a coercive type of state intervention.[130] Finally, it will depend on whether the unpleasant short-term burdens of caring for the older person outweigh the longer-term benefits, either in memory or inheritance.

The child may also be concerned that, like the franchisor, the elderly parent may "up the ante" by requiring increasingly onerous performance. Such opportunism could take the form of whining, complaints about physical ailments, or demands for attention that point up the competition among siblings. To some extent the escalation is inevitable, given the deteriorating health of the parent. The franchisee-child has the problem, like the parent of an infant faced with an onslaught of crying, of differentiating selfish behavior from grounds for genuine concern. And, as Adam Smith maintained, "[I]t is only to the virtuous and humane that the infirmities of old age are not the objects of contempt and aversion."[131]

One of the immediate puzzles is the question why elderly parents are more concerned with the long-term benefit of the family's reputation than are their adult children. The answer lies in the concept of wasting assets.[132] If an adult is conceived of as having two goals, lifetime consumption and the preservation of "trademark capital" for the future, the first goal will predominate during most of his or her life. As there becomes less and less time to enjoy present consumption, however, the second goal will ascend, until, shortly before death is anticipated, it will occupy a preeminent position in the elderly person's utility function.

DISPUTES ABOUT THE FRANCHISE.   Sometimes, of course, elderly people attempt to interfere in the decisions made by their children, violating the terms of the franchise agreement that allows independent operation by the franchisee. Of course, the continued contact may also be seen as an attempt by the grandparent-franchisor to monitor the upbringing and well-being of the genetic franchise. In recent years the courts have witnessed a rash of grandparent visitation cases.[133] The decisions have fairly uniformly allowed visitation if the family has been disrupted by divorce or death of an adult child.[134] They have not been as receptive where the child's parents live together,[135] or when a new family has been formed by adoption.[136] For example, in the Tennessee Supreme Court case of *Hawk v. Hawk*,[137] the grandfather and his adult son had operated a bowling alley together for many years before and after the son's marriage. When the business relationship began to deteriorate, so did the emotional relationship between the generations, until the son and his wife refused to allow the grandparents to visit their grandchildren. For constitutional reasons the court allowed the parents the freedom to make this choice, characterizing the family as full of "entrenched animosity."[138] In an infamous example of another type of interference,[139] after allegations of unfitness on both sides, a Virginia woman named Pamela Bottoms successfully wrested custody of her grandson from her daughter Sharon, a lesbian.

Of course, sometimes continued parental control over adult offsprings' lives is most welcome. In some divorce cases husbands have been able to protect their assets in large family holdings precisely because they were controlled by their own fathers.[140] In other instances parents have established family firms eventually run by their children.[141]

DISPUTES ABOUT PROPERTY. As parents approach old age, the competition motive among their children frequently prevails. Shakespeare's *King Lear* provides a classic depiction of this kind of infighting. The old king's strength is failing. He loves each of his three daughters exceedingly, and though he loves the youngest more than the others, he strives to be fair: he will divide his substantial kingdom in three shares, giving one third to each.[142] This is the presumptive amount, for he gives each daughter an opportunity to demonstrate why she should be given a larger share. We recall that the first says, at some length, that she loves him more than life itself.[143] The second says she loves him as much or more: more than anything else in the world[144] (including her intended husband).[145] The youngest refuses to engage in this game of flattery.[146] She points out that she knows how much her father loves her, and that she loves him as much in return, exactly as a daughter ought.[147] Of course, the rest of the tragedy involves the competition for greater shares that takes place between the two eldest, Regan and Goneril. Lear fails to see the truth in what his favorite child has told him and succumbs to the flattery of the others. (The play is complicated by a parallel dispute between the illegitimate and legitimate sons of the Duke of Gloucester, showing, among other things, that this problem is not confined to female offspring.)

What can be learned from *Lear?* First, the problems of competition between the "franchisees" of the family firm increase as the patriarch nears death. Apparently Lear's two elder daughters have let their jealousy smolder until his death—and the settling of the estate—draws near. The second interesting lesson concerns the turf over which the children dispute: the father's estate, which none of them has "earned" other than as their birthright.[148] (Obviously, because the play was set in pre-Christian England, had there been sons, they would have inherited. The daughters' shares could therefore not be fixed until their father either died or made the sort of *inter vivos* disposition that occurs in the play.) The third, and perhaps most important, insight for our purposes has to do with the process by which the conflict evolves.

Students of economics, political science, and game theory who have read Kenneth Arrow know about the phenomenon of cycling.[149] The classic example is not too far distant from the problem posed in *Lear:* three thieves seek to divide their booty, and may decide how to divide it by majority rule. The problem is that any two may form alliances to defeat the interests of the third.[150] Game theorists call the result the "empty core": there is no determinate solution short of violence among the thieves of approximately the sort that transpires in *Lear.*[151] As with Kronman's contracts and the state of nature,[152] the solution to the cycling problem is to require unanimity: the building of consensus as to the appropriate division.[153]

James Buchanan has proposed that there be a rigidly defined succession rule such as primogeniture to prevent rent seeking, cycling, or other strategic behavior.[154] If all understand from the beginning that only one child can inherit and which child that one is, the cycling will not occur.[155] Of course, this analysis is challenged by hundreds of years of English history in which younger sons killed off their older siblings or sent them off to fight in the Crusades, which might amount to the same thing. Examples of this phenomenon that come to mind include Richard III, as well as modern portrayals of the phenomenon in Disney's *The Lion King* and the Peter Sellers film *The Wrong Box.* The biblical story of Jacob and Esau also fits the pattern of maneuvering to obtain greater inheritance shares, though with less violence. It also is complicated by the maneuvering for Isaac's blessing and a form of "blackmail" or "holdup" associated with Jacob's provision of "insurance" in the form of a stew for Esau.[156]

Modern America has, of course, emphatically rejected the customs of primogeniture, and has made it unprofitable to use violence to end the cycling phenomenon.[157] Laws have been enacted that allow parents to disinherit their offspring, and that allow challenges to testamentary gifts on the grounds of unfairness. Courts generally do not allow the challengers to recover unless the unfairness shows lack of testamentary capacity on the part of the testator.[158]

How do lawmakers "fix" this problem? In one sense it has been fixed already. Not only have we abolished primogeniture and prohibited property gains through murder, but also we have done much as a society to ensure that there will not be too much left in most people's estates to squabble over. As we saw previously, most elderly people live on their own.[159] Most of them support themselves through some combination of Social Security and Medicare, pension plans, and private savings. Many elderly live long enough at this turn of the century to use up most of the resources they have saved, and perhaps more, leaving nothing but debts to nursing facilities and hospitals. Life expectancy increased from 54.1 years in 1920 to 75.4 in 1990.[160] Medical technology can prolong the physical body past the point where mental activity has reached diminishing returns: a point, in fact, where the old person may actively dislike his or her existence.[161] Also, estates are taxed at such a high rate that the wealthy are deterred from doing anything besides investing in their children's education and spending the balance on their own comfort.

The franchise paradigm suggests that this is a factor or the relationship between elderly parents and their children. The nature of the relationship depends on whether the elderly person has, or is expected to have, property left to devise at the end of his or her life. If there is property, competition for it will prevail.[162] If there is no property (as may be the case with many elderly women who have outlived their husbands and any resources put aside for old age), a different kind of competition prevails. The siblings may engage in a "hot potato" avoidance game, which may hurt the elderly person directly (particularly a woman, since most victims of elder abuse are women), or indirectly as she sees that she is no longer valued, or even wanted, by the children for whom she sacrificed so much. If the commercial franchise has no value, the franchisees may well breach the franchise agreement and start out on their own, abandoning the franchise.[163] The franchisor will go out of business.[164] With human relationships, adjustment for the failing franchise is not so simple. Rejection of elderly people has always been a concern, but not a common law concern. States have fairly recently enacted requirements that adult children provide for their "aged and necessitous" parents,[165] and still more recently have drafted legislation to deal with the increasingly visible phenomenon of elder abuse.

The fact that reports of elder abuse are on the rise suggests that this application of the franchise model may also be testable. Positive contacts with our parents may be signals to our own children about how we wish to be treated someday.[166] They may also be evidence of Buchanan's rent seeking,[167] or angling for parental affection in expectation of a larger testamentary gift. All other things being equal, adults are more likely to abuse their parents when the "franchise" fails—as the size of the parent's expected estate decreases. In order to verify the franchise story empirically, reliable statistics on elder abuse would be needed. On an individual level, other factors to be held constant would include whether the parent lives with the child, the size of the parent's estate, the number of siblings, the income of the child's family, and the life expectancy of the parent.[168]

Toward a Few Conclusions: Choosing the Model through Law

To the extent that we have chosen public support or self-support of the elderly over the historical mode of family protection, we have closed off a vital link in the intergenerational structure of society. Gary Becker makes this argument in his Nobel Prize address when he states: "Parents who do not need support when they become old do not try as hard to make children more loyal, guiltier, or otherwise feel as well-disposed toward their parents. This means that programs like social security that significantly help the elderly would encourage family members to drift apart emotionally, not by accident but as maximizing responses to those policies."[169]

Any abolition of pensions and other old age benefits may have an unfortunate effect that goes beyond causing hardship to a current generation left without financial support.[170] Without the cultural or community motivation, there might still be little investment in children but only a greater investment in one's own human capital by the middle generation.[171] The expectation under this alternative would be that one must provide for one's own old age and prepare to live it in isolation from one's kin—a lonely future indeed. As we think about the family in this time when we perennially rethink the federal budget and reorder various social welfare programs, we need to remember these connections between the generations and the importance of the family. We need to regain some of the closeness of the famous Middletown study, where adults maintained regular contact with their parents, and "a high level of understanding, appreciation, obligation and love [was] apparent between the generations."[172] In fact, we need to invest in these relationships more than ever since our lives will overlap with our parents' to a considerably greater extent today than in earlier generations.

As I mentioned at the beginning of this chapter, the idea that family relationships continue even after legal ties dissolve or become less important is one with implications beyond the problems we have looked at here. We have already seen that the franchise model has implications for divorcing couples, especially those with children, and we can imagine applying it to children just "leaving the nest" to go to college or otherwise start out on their own. (I will shortly discuss another context, the family whose ties are broken by adoption.) The fact that the compacts we undertake in the family are not simple contracts with end points means that family policy is critically important.

In this chapter I have presented two family models: the sovereign nation and the franchise. We have some choice about which we as a society prefer. The sovereign nation model is obviously independent and market-like, implying all the fragmentation characteristic of individualism carried to an extreme.[173] As should be obvious by this time, my personal choice, and the one I believe better fits family reality and family law, is the franchise. Franchise also unifies us as a community—with our siblings as well as with our parents and children.[174]

Obviously, to encourage this behavior we theoretically could repeal some of the twentieth-century laws that have shaped the family so as to reapproach the idea of franchise. But, like the "right to choose," no-fault divorce is something that we have gotten used to. The lobby of people over sixty-five (understandably, since the safe harbor of family is no longer there) would probably prevent any retrospective changes in Social Security or other transfer programs for the elderly. Our college-age children are likewise going to be hard-pressed to relinquish the emancipation that entitles them to vote and to possess their own Visa cards (though they might relish the idea of giving up paying back the debt that ensues). Without social change, however, we are right to be concerned about elder abuse and neglect.

A Short Look at One Final Problem: Open Adoption

In her celebrated novel *The Joy Luck Club,* Amy Tan describes a fictional mother[175] who left her infant twin daughters beside the road in despair that she was dying and in the hope that they would be found and raised in a better life.[176] She spends the rest of her life looking for them, and it is only after her death many years later that they are found. In a case law parallel, a Vietnamese woman placed her children in a Saigon orphanage after a harrowing journey through the wartime Central Highlands.[177] Both she and they ended up in the United States, where, by the time she found them, several of the children had been placed for adoption in an American home.

Someone who acted in good faith will clearly be unhappy with any adverse outcome in a court case where custody has been ceded for a legitimate interest and many years have passed.[178] But when a family has been disrupted by war or hardship or death, need the ties be cut as cleanly as we sever them in adoption? From the perspective of such mothers as these, placement of the child was clearly the appropriate action at the time.[179] From the perspective of the child, however, he or she will certainly benefit from knowing about the heritage and how much love the parent felt.[180]

The quest by birth parents and children for each other defies easy characterization. The law protects birth parents by hiding their identities from all who would seek them,[181] except in some clear cases of emergency. This is clearly what adoptive parents want, for the protection allows them to determine when their children should be told of their adoptive status. But increasingly states are responding to lobbying efforts on the part of both birth parents and adoptive children and enacting statutes permitting birth parents to leave identifying information with adoption agencies.[182] Although the provisions differ, they usually allow the adopted child, at his or her option, to discover the birth parent's identity at majority.

Does this appropriately satisfy the longing felt on both sides of what seems to be a genetically-based or deeply culturally ingrained franchise?[183] Or should we, as a society, move toward a more open adoptive process in which the parties know one another beforehand and maintain a relationship, as some are urging?[184] One commentator has suggested that this might be a "middle ground" for cases in which the father's rights have been cut off without proper notice, but which would still allow children to remain with their adoptive family.[185] Of course, it might also give more "market" power to birth parents, who already seem to have the upper hand in this time of relative scarcity of adoptable children. My own view, consistent with the franchise theme I have been developing in this chapter, is that on balance, permitting continued contact between birth parents and children (so long as the parents wish it) is a good thing.

A Brief Conclusion about Franchises

The family relationship enriches us most obviously as helpless infants completely dependent on adults, or as growing children flourishing under parental care and affection, or as loving spouses sharing a common life. To the extent that we stop thinking about other members of our family as special people, we become poor indeed, relative to other times and other places. The nuclear family may be the central image, but what has happened to all the animating forces that surround it? In the end we have to remember that above all, one's family provides a psychological home, and that "[h]ome is the place where, when you have to go there/They have to take you in."[186]

The system of family law I have proposed here in some ways reflects a "difference" feminist approach.[187] I have mentioned that men, more than women, think bimodally and in terms of absolutes: right and wrong, victor and vanquished, self versus other. To these dualities I would add married versus unmarried, child versus adult, parent versus stranger. I maintain that family, and therefore family law, is continuous, not discrete. One does not just turn a family off and on like an electric switch. To the extent that we have built laws that deny the oceanic expanse and eternity of family life, we create regret and hurt, malaise and longing. We encourage pathological behavior: elder abuse, disputes over inheritance, deadbeat attitudes, surrogacy contests, and other ugly custody battles. As we legislatively choose the franchise-type solution, we can encourage more positive family outcomes.

8

The Role of Law Reform

Domestic relations is an unusual field because, except where constitutional questions are involved, federal courts have been quick to proclaim that they will not entertain diversity jurisdiction. This is not a matter of constitutional limitation but a self-proclaimed unwillingness to tamper with the "special proficiency developed by state tribunals."[1] Thus, particularly in divorce, alimony, and child custody cases, state law prevails. The result is, predictably, a kind of competition among the states,[2] and, since financial efficiency is not a primary goal, one not always leading to the best legal rules.[3] (The debate about whether jurisdictional competition produces the most efficient laws continues in the fields of corporate, environmental, and state government law.)[4] For example, the differences in state family law regimes induce migration of people who seek a jurisdiction permitting easier adoption or divorce, more favorable custody rules, or more lax child support enforcement. If state laws seek primarily to protect children, this forum-shopping may not be desirable. In fact, an examination of divorce rates and the success of child support enforcement reveals dramatic differences among states despite the ubiquity of no-fault rules and federal-induced child support guidelines and enforcement measures.[5]

American divorce law developed on the frontier. The absolute divorce became primarily a wife's remedy for financial support and remarriage.[6] Frequently, the husband would have obtained an informal or shadow divorce by moving West and perhaps acquiring a second (or third) family.[7] His desires would be accommodated, for "[w]ith the westward march of settlement, divorce proneness and governmental willingness to accommodate a settler's desire to free himself from old bonds and start life anew moved westward, too."[8] Although most divorces were at first granted by state legislatures, during the nineteenth century this practice was phased out in favor of judicial divorces[9] since legislatures could not keep up with the demand.[10] Under fault-based statutes, petitioners pressed the bounds of divorce and gradually extended states' definitions of offenses such as cruelty.[11]

Much of the pressure to relax divorce laws came from these migration markets.[12] Unhappy spouses migrated from eastern states, with their more conservative divorce laws, to laxer divorce regimes, found first in Indiana,[13] then in the Dakotas.[14] Horace Greeley, editor of the *New York Tribune,* attacked Indiana for divorce policies that, he concluded, caused social disintegration. Greeley characterized the state as "the paradise of free-lovers," where men and women could "get unmarried nearly at pleasure."[15] A wife unhappy with her husband's Indiana divorce wrote that nullification of the decree would "deter that large class of discontented or lecherous pilgrims seeking the Mecca of divorce, who turn their faces towards Indiana."[16] Nevada, the most famous divorce mill of all,[17] competed legislatively with New York as that state relaxed its very strict divorce laws in the 1960s.[18] Previously, when New York had required proof of adultery, Nevada permitted divorce on proof of cruelty. By the late 1960s, when New York allowed divorce for cruelty, desertion, and separation for two years under a judicial order, Nevada amended its statute to permit divorce after a one-year separation.

Aiding the push toward migratory divorces, *Williams v. North Carolina*[19] held that domicile of one of the parties in a jurisdiction was sufficient for divorce, so long as actual or constructive notice was given the defendant. In the short run, this added to Nevada's attractiveness as a divorce mill; in the long run, the rule promoted relaxation of strict divorce statutes as other states competed with Nevada to aid their own residents.Unlike divorce, child custody, child support, and alimony require *in personam* jurisdiction (personal service by someone having power within the state); incidental contacts with the forum state are not sufficient.[20] This requirement results in spouses and parents leaving the state where they lived when married and moving to another where it may be harder to establish their obligation to pay. In turn, this migration has led to a spate of federal and state uniform legislation, such as the Uniform Child Custody Jurisdiction Act and the Uniform Interstate Family Support Act. Recently, some states have been allowing a "status adjudication" in child custody cases when one parent and the child are domiciled in the state,[21] instead of following the older rule requiring *in personam* jurisdiction.[22] Even where there is personal jurisdiction, the appropriate forum is the child's home state, usually the place where the child has lawfully resided for the previous six months.[23] Because even orders that were valid under the Uniform Child Custody Jurisdiction Act were being ignored, Congress enacted the federal Parental Kidnapping Prevention Act,[24] requiring that full faith and credit be given to a valid foreign decree. The problems have not evaporated, however, as can be seen from the celebrated adoption cases of *In re Baby Girl Clausen* (Schmidt v. DeBoer)[25] and *In re Baby Richard*,[26] turned down for review by the United States Supreme Court. In each of these cases, interstate adoptive placement (and actual decrees of adoption) were ultimately vacated because the biological father had not been notified to give his consent to the adoption, and in each there were conflicting decisions between the two states concerned.

Migration flows motivated by differences in family laws are of some interest to the public choice theorist. Migration changes life for natives as well as for migrants, for a state might enact general policies to attract a favored class of migrants or repel a disfavored one. The result might be either a race to the top or a race to the bottom. The race is to the top if states try to attract migrants through value-increasing laws, and to the bottom if states compete for migrants through inefficient laws whose costs are exported to parties outside the jurisdiction or to other state governments. Whatever the direction of the race, however, state laws might be very different under the competition for migrants than they would be in a world of closed borders.[27]

Americans are relatively mobile, and migration trends are well reported in American newspapers. More than a hundred years ago, one of America's most celebrated historians concluded that westward migration flows were the touchstone of American history. According to Frederick Jackson Turner's "Frontier Theory,"[28] states adopted liberal laws and democratic values to attract migrants. In this way the competition for migrants was seen to shape the most basic legal institutions.

Under the Frontier Theory, the competition for migrants is wholly benign. States offer efficient laws to attract valuable migrants, who confer gains on natives. The result is a race for the top, won by the state with the best set of laws and institutions. But the competition for migrants might also be value-decreasing if states adopted inefficient laws to attract migrants. Thus a state might compete for migrants on the basis of their expected political sympathies rather than their ability to benefit natives. For example, a pro-welfare political party might attract welfare-seeking migrants through wealth transfers from wealthy natives.[29] In this way an unpopular politician might seek to circumvent the electorate and create one more to his liking. The kind of migration that laws of this sort produce is unlikely to result in efficiency gains, and results only in transferring costs.

There is a reason why the competition for migrants through family laws might be value-decreasing: states might compete for those parents who cross state lines to avoid repayment of obligations of spousal or child support. Given collection costs, moving increases the probability that the custodial parent will write off the arrearages as a lost cause. The obligor parent might also reduce the probability of repayment by moving to a state with pro-debtor insolvency laws. The prospect of deadbeat migration might indeed lead a state to adopt pro-obligor laws. Deadbeats, whether parents or not, are often entrepreneurs or professionals with high expected earnings, and the cost of their default is borne primarily by out-of-state former spouses.

In another interesting form of family law competition, Hawaii became the first state whose courts allowed gay and lesbian couples to marry. One of the most widely discussed cases dealing with marriage in years was *Baehr v. Lewin*,[30] which involved a suit by homosexual couples seeking relief against Hawaii's marriage requirement statute permitting only heterosexual marriages.[31] The trial court upheld the requirement as a matter of law. The Hawaii Supreme Court vacated and remanded, finding unresolved factual questions. The legislature enacted a statute reaffirming the traditional limitation to heterosexuals,[32] which the Hawaii Supreme Court found was outside the legislature's prerogative, remanding to the trial court to apply "strict judicial scrutiny." The district court found that the statute did not withstand constitutional challenge,[33] and that therefore same-sex marriages should be allowed. Although the litigation involving Hawaii's statutes will undoubtedly continue for some time,[34] it has provoked widespread enthusiasm among gays and lesbians, and considerable comment in general.

Baehr provoked federal legislation, the Defense of Marriage Act, which allows states to decide whether or not to recognize same-sex marriage[35] and defines marriage for federal purposes as between a man and a woman only.[36] By early 1999, thirty states had enacted laws prohibiting same-sex marriage,[37] with another two giving the matter consideration in current legislative sessions. Meanwhile, suits similar to *Baehr* were filed in Alaska and Vermont. On the other end of the spectrum, the Eleventh Circuit allowed the Georgia attorney general's office to withdraw an employment offer made to a woman who publicly married her lesbian lover in a Reconstructionist Jewish ceremony,[38] while the state of Colorado unsuccessfully attempted to invalidate local domestic partnership and antidiscrimination ordinances protecting gays and lesbians.[39]

There will undoubtedly be an eventual constitutional challenge to the federal statute, which seeks to circumvent the Constitution's full faith and credit clause.[40] There is precedent, however, for states' ignoring the marriage laws of jurisdictions that violate their own public policy, at least when the couple has traveled to the friendly jurisdiction to avoid the requirements of the state where they are domiciled.[41]

Jennifer Gerardo Brown[42] points out the financial benefits that may inure to Hawaii by having been the first to allow same-sex couples to marry. Her argument is that talented upper-middle-class people will marry in Hawaii in order to make their lives more fulfilling. They may need to relocate there permanently, because other states will refuse to recognize the marriage as valid if a couple migrated to Hawaii simply to take advantage of the new statute. In the process of marrying and honeymooning in Hawaii, nontraditional couples will, according to Brown, spend substantial sums as tourists, and, if they decide to remain, will greatly add to that state's pool of human capital. This, of course, is an interesting public choice argument that takes no position on the desirability of allowing permanent committed relationships for such couples.[43] One concern with Brown's view (at least as applied to those couples who remain in the state because of uncertain status elsewhere) might be that because of the prevalence of AIDS among male homosexuals and the cost of AIDS treatment, insurers may not wish to write new policies in the state.[44] The burden of caring for AIDS patients may then be borne by Hawaii taxpayers, erasing the benefits caused by healthy same-sex couples' productivity. If the couples merely married and honeymooned in the state, the AIDS costs would be minimal. Another question would be whether other tourists, including heterosexual newlyweds, would find the state as attractive as they currently do.

A similar kind of jurisdictional competition may develop over the covenant marriage legislation discussed in Chapter 2, or over the various state efforts to return to a fault-based regime.[45] Although the laws in many states may change (and there was certainly legislative activity in that direction in the late 1990s), no matter where they live during their marriage, a couple may still "vote with their feet" when it comes to selecting a divorce jurisdiction, and many will likely, if they have the resources, travel to less restrictive environments. Legislative policies encouraging more stable and permanent marriages should affect the marriages themselves, however, even if most people continue to marry under the less rigorous regime. Although empirical work needs to be done, scholars expect a lower divorce rate (including among couples who move elsewhere when their marriage founders) for states such as Louisiana and Arizona that engage in post–no-fault reform.

Predicting Family Law Reform

One of the more interesting observations about family law reform, modern or ancient, is that it always seems to benefit attorneys. In fact, to the extent that one can predict the future of family law, paying attention to what will cement family practices will prove most successful. Normal economic and even public predictors do not tend to fare as well, as I have observed in the past. For example, in "Rings and Promises,"[46] I tried to predict which states would abolish the breach of promise action that allowed women to sue if a fiancé was unwilling to go through with the planned marriage. About all I could tell with accuracy was that these were states with a much higher than average marriage rate (some, such as Nevada, actively encouraged marriages within its borders), and some of them were centers for women's rights reform (New York and California were; Illinois and Alabama were not). In "Marriage and Opportunism,"[47] Steven Crafton and I attempted to model states' enactment of no-fault legislation as a function of Catholicism, women in the labor force, the divorce-to-marriage ratio, and political liberalism. We could identify only the extremes of early enactment of no-fault legislation and the lack of no-fault.[48] Allen Parkman speculated that divorce reform occurred in male-dominated legislatures "in a process of benign neglect" reinforced by the lobbying efforts of male interest groups.[49] (It is unclear why women could not also have organized.) The fact that there were very few women either on the committee that recommended reform of California's family law or in the legislature may have made the difference in the way the statutes were drafted.[50] Although I am not completely convinced by this analysis, I am more interested in Parkman's point that it was not merely the change in property and alimony laws that made the difference in people's attitudes about divorce,[51] but also the push that the no-fault movement made toward negotiated settlements.[52] Part of my 1995 paper on gender and divorce mediation[53] involved identification of opponents to alternative dispute resolution of family law matters and proponents of the tax reform efforts in 1984 and 1986. Some of the results are outlined in the discussion that follows.

At first, the organized bar considered divorce mediation inconsistent with professional ethics. In addition, because of their extensive training in legal rules as opposed to counseling, critics argued, lawyer mediators would be unable to resist giving legal advice.

In fact, lawyers ultimately capitulated to the inevitable, and most states now allow mediation by both attorney and non-lawyer mediators. But they have raised the stakes considerably for the non-lawyers. Since the advent of no-fault divorce, and contemporaneously with the rise of mediation, the practice of family law has shifted from being a rather disreputable one (only slightly above criminal defense work, and perhaps below "ambulance chasing" and loan collection in terms of public perception) to a practice that looks very much like a general business practice. The effective family law practitioner is not only counselor and strategist. He or she must also know a good deal about taxation,[54] finance,[55] and human capital theory, as we saw in Chapter 6. In fact, the work in some states has spawned a valuation industry in which the experts also testify in business dissolutions.

Just when the complexities of property distribution began to be understood, Congress changed the tax laws relating to divorce.[56] If we look carefully at this legislation, which disrupted the regime that had been in place since 1961, we see that there were no obvious gains by divorcing husbands or wives. A unitary payment of alimony and child support used to be taxable to the recipient and deductible by the payor under §71. Now, to be treated this way, payments need to be clearly for the benefit of the recipient, not the children. Further, property transferred from one spouse to the other incident to divorce used to be treated as taxable, with the capital gain payable by the original property holder. Now such a transfer is treated as a gift for income tax purposes: it is not taxable at the time of divorce, and the capital gain is realized only when the property is sold to a third party.[57] The first of these changes largely benefited wives, who now pay less in taxes on the amount received from former husbands. The second change largely benefited husbands, who not only had to part with property held in their name but also had to pay taxes on it. The legislation was promulgated by tax attorneys and the family law section of the American Bar Association, not by men's or women's groups. Attorneys were benefited by the revised tax provisions because the changes were complex and probably beyond the competence of non-lawyer mediators, who previously had profited by the relative stability of divorce taxation.

Nor are my suspicions of the motivations behind such changes limited to the modern era. Eileen Spring, in *Law, Land, and Family*,[58] has looked at a series of early laws ostensibly designed to benefit women. According to the legislative histories she discovered, the proponents were the solicitors who eventually drew up the marriage settlements that guaranteed fixed sums for women marrying with estates. This practice, according to Spring, disadvantaged many if not most women, since they were likely to have outlived their husbands and, absent the settlement, would have acquired the whole of the property rather than a certain small share in it.

Another instance of family law reform that supposedly helped women was the institution of judicial divorce, beginning in the United States around 1830. Until then, aggrieved spouses who sought an absolute divorce could obtain one only by legislative action after first gaining a judicial decree of separation.[59] Consistently since 1800, most divorce plaintiffs in this country have been women. The legislative divorce practice was expensive, since the local legislator who would sponsor the bill of divorce would undoubtedly have to be paid. But unless she wished to remarry, the wife did not need an absolute divorce. Even earlier, if she could convince a judge that she had been deserted or abused, or that her husband was otherwise at fault, a wife could be awarded what today would be called a legal separation, which gave her an allowance out of the husband's estate. Because of the serious stigma associated with divorce (and remarriage), this was probably the most attractive alternative for all but the most desperate wives.

Why would lawyers, more than wives, prefer judicial divorces? First, because of volume. Since the transaction costs of divorce were lowered substantially, there presumably would be more of them. In fact, Lawrence Friedman and Robert Percival show a gradually rising divorce rate during this period, which lasted from colonization until about 1880.[60] The second pragmatic reason is that there was probably little an attorney could do for a wife beyond what was necessary for the legal separation when the task was to secure passage of a simple piece of legislation. (Sometimes the bills consisted of one-sentence paragraphs allowing divorces for as many as ten couples, without even stating reasons for the divorce.) Once a suit was necessary, a new form of practice emerged, one that remained lucrative for attorneys for decades.

Some Candidates for Law Reform

I have already discussed the changes wrought by no-fault divorce, in terms of both their effects and the interest groups who lobbied for them. By now it should be obvious that I am concerned about the effects of no-fault divorce on marriages as well as on divorced women and children. My partial solutions, discussed in Chapters 2 and 6, involve allowing couples to choose their divorce regime through a covenant marriage option, retaining or returning to fault in the granting of alimony or in the division of property, or explicitly recognizing investment in earning capacity.

There are other candidates for law reform that are worth mentioning. The first is the change in custody laws, in particular joint custody. In empirical work discussed in Chapters 6 and 7, I have found that joint custody laws discourage divorce and encourage payment of court-ordered child support. From the child's perspective, therefore, the data suggest that they are a desirable innovation in many cases, even apart from the obvious fact that children prosper most when they have contact with two parents. Feminists criticize these laws from the wife and mother's perspective, claiming that they enhance the power of husbands. They argue that divorcing husbands may ask for joint custody they do not plan to exercise in order to extract a favorable financial settlement. This would be a futile strategy under a standard such as the American Law Institute's, in which custodial time mirrors pre-divorce participation. Further, men might use their increased power as decision makers to continue to control or harass their former wives. Empirical work is equivocal on the subject of the first concern. Maccoby and Mnookin[61] found very little evidence of strategic bargaining through the threat of seeking custody, although in "Lurking in the Shadow,"[62] Scott Altman found that among the California lawyers he surveyed, about 20 percent reported that they had seen this technique used against their clients. To date, no one has tested the second contention: that men might use joint legal custody to maintain power over their wives. Ira Lupu[63] indicates a contrary benefit from the child's perspective: joint custody may act as a power balancer to ensure that the child receives the best possible care. The alternative primary caretaker presumption has largely been untested except in terms of its allocational result: more mothers are awarded custody than under a best interests or joint custody regime. Because the standard is indeterminate (it is difficult to know in all cases who the primary caretaker has been), there has been significantly more litigation in primary caretaker states. The more determinate American Law Institute "replication" test would avoid this concern as well.

Another possible reform is a statutory prohibition (or discouraging) of transracial adoption. This was briefly addressed in Chapter 3. While statutes like those in place in Minnesota[64] would have the desired effect of keeping minority children in their communities, because there is a shortage of minority prospective adoptive parents and a queue of non-minority would-be parents, banning transracial adoption means that some children who would otherwise be adopted must remain in foster care. If the problems of poverty leading to these children's placement with state agencies cannot be alleviated,[65] adoption seems the second-best choice from the individual child's perspective. Preference for same-race parents, like a religious preference, seems unobjectionable, but if a same-race adoptive parent cannot be found in a short time, adoption by a parent of a different race should be allowed.

Welfare reform, as of the time of this writing, remains a volatile subject (new federal legislation is discussed in Chapter 3).[66] My empirical work and reading suggest that the old system of AFDC deters men from being involved with their children either through paying court-ordered child support (Chapter 5), through marrying the mothers (Chapter 6), or remaining married rather than divorcing (Chapter 6). These are clearly bad results worth remedying. Nevertheless, the welfare caps that have been enacted in several states have not yet been shown to affect the unwed birthrate. (The "caps" put a ceiling on the amount that can be received even if additional children are born.) To the extent that women might go on having children even when there are caps in place, the people who are penalized are the children. Reducing child support subsidies (which would lower the amount available even for the first child and therefore reduce financial incentives for even the first pregnancy), or placing time limits on their receipt, as is required by the federal legislation, seems a more humane way of dealing with this important problem, and may in fact reduce unwed births.[67]

As for alimony, Virginia at the time of this writing was considering joining a number of other states in reforming alimony laws to make rehabilitative, as opposed to permanent, alimony the norm. The economic effects of alimony (even though at the time only about a third of Virginia divorcing couples included alimony as part of their decrees) have been noted in Chapter 6. Alimony laws seem to be associated with greater investment in marriage and in children, and with a lower incidence of spousal abuse.[68] "Rehabilitative alimony" is ineffective, as we saw in Chapter 7, for when a parent remains out of the job force or otherwise changes work to accommodate children, the loss is permanent (as Victor Fuchs suggests,[69] there is a lifetime loss of 1.5 percent for each year the parent remains out of the job market). The custodial parent can never be "rehabilitated." Rehabilitative alimony also seems inappropriate for many women who married, and made investments in their marriage or their spouse, based on the older system. While it might be perfectly appropriate for very short, childless marriages, the majority do not seem good candidates for rehabilitative alimony.

A final possible set of law reforms involves transfer payments made to the elderly through Social Security and Medicare. Unquestionably both systems need reforming. There is tremendous waste in the provision of medical care for the elderly, and underfunding will bankrupt Social Security in another generation unless something is done. Were neither system in place, there would probably be private provision for old people—arguably, as we saw in Chapter 5, a good thing for both the elderly and minor children. As with welfare reform and alimony, however, one cannot change the rules midstream without creating tremendous hardship for people who are already in the system. Other incentives for private care, like those discussed in Chapter 7, might work in a more just way than termination of the present system.

One of the rewards of a large project like this one is the learning that takes place as one writes. Although I had worked for several years on the application of contracts principles to family law, when I began this book in the spring of 1994, I had just completed my first work on the family covenant. At that point I was still unsure how the permanence of covenant could be explained in an era of no-fault divorce and early emancipation of children. The metaphor of franchise came to me in the late spring of 1995. Now it is much easier to see how all these ideas fit together, how a change in one area of family law affects many others, and even how economics can help predict the likely effects of proposed law reform efforts.

The more I teach and think about family law, the more I feel its inter-connectedness. Just as I am not a rock or an island,[70] no part of family law can ever be usefully "deconstructed" in isolation. For example, every time we change divorce law, there are obvious effects on support and custody.[71] Another ripple affects marriage—both when couples decide to marry and what they do once they are married.[72] Farther out lie the effects on children born out of wedlock,[73] juvenile delinquency,[74] and, arguably, child[75] and elder abuse.[76]

How have we made our choices as a nation? To the extent that the contract or market-like sovereign nation model dominates today, it is the product of several forces, some directly and some only indirectly legal. The first is no-fault divorce. Once it became easier for couples to separate and form new families, attachments to spouses and children became in many ways more contingent. Particularly for men, who seem to view attachment to children in terms of their current relationships, family life in many cases becomes discrete: rent-a-husband or rent-a-dad. The grand sweep of family life disappeared. The second legal intervention includes the whole set of laws that established Social Security and Medicare and made private pensions attractive for employers and workers. When we concentrate on saving for our own old age (voluntarily or through taxation), we spend less on our children and trust less in our continued relationships with them. A third legal change has been the lowering of the age of emancipation to eighteen. What this does (besides the obvious political changes of increasing the number of young voters) is to make paying for college more the child's responsibility than the parents' (except in cases of divorce), and remove any force from parental guidance about decisions such as youthful marriage. We have a shorter time when our children are primarily our responsibility, and we have less time during which we can learn from one another and strengthen family bonds. Finally, and perhaps in response to the social changes I would argue were inevitably wrought by all these other legal innovations, we have enacted a spate of child-protective, parental responsibility, and elder abuse prevention laws. These constrict the scope of family privacy but protect against the abandonment or mistreatment of our children or parents.

What, then, should we do? I read a story about a Scottish immigrant minister who built a house for his wife and children on an island in Lake Superior. Ninety years later, four generations of the family still come, each with fond memories of summer vacations spent there.[77] Home places are like that—they bring us back from our diaspora to a shared family experience. Even though most of us have lost the family farm, and certainly Lear's kingdom, we can still rediscover (or begin) family traditions, frequently centered on one place. Electronic mail can be a wonderful family unifier when physical closeness, though ideal, is impossible.[78]

Less concretely but more publicly, we can encourage investment in our families. Joint custody laws apparently motivate noncustodial parents (most of them fathers) to continue to support their children. A two-level divorce system, with divorce more difficult to obtain when there are children, or if a covenant form of marriage is selected at the beginning, also encourages healthier families. Virginia and Tennessee now require a longer waiting period for divorces involving minor children.[79] Louisiana and Arizona allow a no-fault divorce after a six-month separation only in standard marriages, while for covenant marriages the waiting period is two years. Another such family-reinforcing idea is the tuition deduction, particularly for college education. The federal government could also authorize tax deductions for payments made to support elderly parents. The state might encourage low-interest loan programs for people who wish to build "in-law" additions to their homes, or reduce inheritance taxes so that elderly people need not feel that a large part of what they have earned will be lost if they do not consume it during their lifetime.

As I pointed out in Chapter 7, the system of family law I have proposed in this book in some ways reflects a "difference" feminist approach.[80] It rejects bright line distinctions between married and unmarried, child and adult, parent and stranger. I maintain that family, and therefore family law, is continuous, not discrete. It is in fact a covenant that does not end, even if the law says it does. Law has limits and cannot always control the complex of human relationships we call families. In some senses, therefore, families are beyond law. To the extent that we must look elsewhere for satisfying explanations of love and the makeup of other utility functions, we have also ventured beyond economics.

NOTES

INDEX

Notes

1. Introduction

1. For my earlier writing dealing with contract, see, e.g., Margaret F. Brinig and Michael V. Alexeev, "Fraud in Courtship: Annulment and Divorce," 2 *European Journal of Law and Economics* 45 (1995); Margaret F. Brinig, "The Effect of Transactions Costs on the Market for Babies," 18 *Seton Hall Legislative Law Journal* 553 (1994); Margaret F. Brinig and Steven M. Crafton, "Marriage and Opportunism," 23 *Journal of Legal Studies* 869 (1994); and Margaret F. Brinig, "Rings and Promises," 6 *Journal of Law, Economics, and Organization* 203 (1990).

2. Margaret F. Brinig, "Status, Contract, and Covenant," 79 *Cornell Law Review* 1573 (1994); Margaret F. Brinig, "The Family Franchise: Elderly Parents and Adult Siblings," 1996 *Utah Law Review* 393.

3. Hal Varian, *Microeconomic Analysis* 5, 262–263 (2d ed. 1984); D. N. McCloskey, *The Applied Theory of Price* 103, 224 (1982).

4. Varian, supra note 3, at 50.

5. Id. at 35.

6. In addition to the articles cited in note 1, see Marjorie Maguire Shultz, "Contractual Ordering of Marriage: A New Model for State Policy," 70 *California Law Review* 204 (1982).

7. Margaret F. Brinig and June Carbone, "The Reliance Interest in Marriage and Divorce," 62 *Tulane Law Review* 855 (1988); June Carbone, "Economics, Feminism, and the Reinvention of Alimony: A Reply to Ira Ellman," 43 *Vanderbilt Law Review* 1463 (1990); Arthur Cornell, "When Two Become One, and Then Come Undone: An Organizational Approach to Marriage and Its Implications for Divorce Law," 26 *Family Law Quarterly* 103 (1992); Brinig and Crafton, supra note 1.

8. Margaret F. Brinig and F. H. Buckley, "The Ugly Duckling: The Law and Economics of Child Abuse," 1 *Journal of Law and Family Studies* 41 (1999).

9. Milton C. Regan, *Family Law and the Pursuit of Intimacy* 176–183 (1993); Brinig, "Status, Contract, and Covenant," supra note 2, at 1573; Carl E. Schneider, "Moral

Discourse and the Transformation of American Family Law," 83 *Michigan Law Review* 1803, 1832 (1985).

10. Brinig, "Status, Contract, and Covenant," supra note 2, at 1586 and n.79.

11. Rabbi Rami Shapiro, "A Rabbi's Manual," found at www.judaica.com.

12. See Governor John Winthrop's speech "A Modell of Christian Charity," in 2 *Winthrop Papers* 292, 294 (1931) (sermon titled "Christian Charity" preached aboard the *Arabela*, Massachusetts Bay, 1630); Brinig, "Status, Contract and Covenant," supra note 2, at 1598.

13. Armen Alchian and Harold Demsetz, "Production, Information Costs, and Economic Organization," 62 *American Economic Review* 777 (1972); Ronald Coase, "The Nature of the Firm," 4 *Economica* 386 (1973), reprinted in Ronald H. Coase, *The Firm, the Market, and the Law* (1988).

14. Alfred D. Chandler, *Scale and Scope: The Dynamics of Industrial Capitalism* (1990).

15. Adam Smith, *Wealth of Nations,* bk. 1, chap. 2 (reprint 1976); Coase, supra note 13, at 36–40.

16. Gary S. Becker, *A Treatise on the Family* 30–42 (2d. ed. 1991).

17. See Brinig, "Status, Contract, and Covenant," supra note 2; Regan, supra note 9 (using status rather than covenant terminology); see also William Everett, "Contract and Covenant in Human Community," 36 *Emory Law Journal* 557 (1987). For discussions of partnership in the context of dissolution, see Bea Ann Smith, "The Partnership Theory of Marriage: Borrowed Solution Fails," 68 *Texas Law Review* 689 (1990); Cynthia Starnes, "Divorce and the Displaced Homemaker: A Discourse on Playing with Paper Dolls, Partnership Buyouts, and Dissociation under No-Fault," 60 *University of Chicago Law Review* 67 (1993).

18. Brinig, "Status, Contract, and Covenant," supra note 2 at 1597–99.

19. Most of the law and economics literature criticizes this device. See, e.g., Barry E. Adler, "A Theory of Corporate Insolvency," 72 *New York University Law Review* 343 (1997); Theodore Eisenberg and Shoichi Tagashira, "Should We Abolish Chapter 11: The Evidence from Japan," 23 *Journal of Legal Studies* 111 (1994) (may be successful for some small firms with relatively greater assets, however); but see Karen Gross, "Taking Community Interests into Account in Bankruptcy: An Essay," 72 *Washington University Law Quarterly* 1031 (1994) (suggesting that the interests that would be adversely affected by liquidating the firm, such as dislocated employees, need to be balanced against the needs and interests of the corporate debtor); Eric A. Posner, "The Political Economy of the Bankruptcy Reform Act of 1978," 96 *Michigan Law Review* 47, 118 (1997) (the interests of large creditors, the lawyers, and managers prevailed in bankruptcy reform over those of the shareholders and the small creditors); Alan Schwartz, "A Contract Theory Approach to Business Bankruptcy," 107 *Yale Law Journal* 1807 (1998) (suggesting that post-insolvency bargaining will promote efficiency); Elizabeth Warren and Jay Lawrence Westbrook, "Searching for Reorganization Realities," 72 *Washington*

University Law Quarterly 1257 (1994) (suggesting empirical work be done before policy changes are made).

20. Gillian K. Hadfield, "Problematic Relations: Franchising and the Law of Incomplete Contracts," 42 *Stanford Law Review* 927 (1990); Paul H. Rubin, "The Theory of the Firm and the Structure of the Franchise Contract," 21 *Journal of Law and Economics* 223 (1978).

21. Varian, supra note 3 at 545–546; McCloskey, supra note 3, at 331.

22. Varian, supra note 3, at 348.

2. Courtship

1. George Stigler, "The Economics of Information," 69 *Journal of Political Economy* 216 (1961); see also Phillip Nelson, "Information and Consumer Behavior," 78 *Journal of Political Economy* 311 (1970). Stigler's theory is extended to the marriage market in Paula England and George Farkas, *Households, Employment, and Gender* 31–42 (1986); and Margaret F. Brinig and Michael V. Alexeev, "Fraud in Courtship: Annulment and Divorce," 2 *European Journal of Law and Economics* 45 (1995).

2. Lynn A. Baker and Robert Emery, "When Every Relationship Is above Average: Perceptions and Expectations of Divorce at the Time of Marriage," 17 *Law and Human Behavior* 439 (1993).

3. Id.

4. For a discussion of marriage as a case of "market failure," see Jana B. Singer, "Alimony and Efficiency: The Gendered Costs and Benefits of the Economic Justification for Alimony," 82 *Georgetown Law Journal* 2423, 2451–53 (1994); and for a reply, see Margaret F. Brinig, "Comment on Jana Singer's 'Alimony and Efficiency,'" 82 *Georgetown Law Journal* 2461–64 (1994).

5. Amy L. Wax argues in "Bargaining in the Shadow of the Market: Is There a Future for Egalitarian Marriage?" 84 *Virginia Law Review* 509 (1998) that this is the only time when the spouses will ever be able to bargain equally.

6. See, e.g., Williams v. Walker-Thomas Furniture, 350 F.2d 445 (D.C. Cir. 1965); see, generally, Anthony Kronman, "Paternalism and the Law of Contracts," 92 *Yale Law Journal* 763 (1983); Duncan Kennedy, "Distributive and Paternalist Motives in Contract and Tort Law with Special Reference to Compulsory Terms and Unequal Bargaining Power," 41 *Maryland Law Review* 563 (1982).

7. Samuel Taylor Coleridge, *Biographica Literaria,* chap. 12 (1817).

8. Baker and Emery, supra note 2.

9. Id.

10. Milton C. Regan, *Family Law and the Pursuit of Intimacy* 159–160 (1993); Janet L. Dolgin, "Status and Contract in Feminist Legal Theory of the Family: A Reply to Bartlett," 12 *Women's Rights Law Reporter* 103 (1990); Mary Joe Frug, "Re-reading Contracts: A Feminist Analysis of a Contracts Casebook," 34 *American University*

Law Review 1065 (1985); Mary Joe Frug, "Rescuing Impossibility Doctrine: A Postmodern Feminist Analysis of Contract Law," 140 *University of Pennsylvania Law Review* 1029 (1992); Robin West, "Jurisprudence and Gender," 55 *University of Chicago Law Review* 1 (1988).

11. But see Elizabeth S. Scott and Robert E. Scott, "Marriage as a Relational Contract," 84 *Virginia Law Review* 1225 (1998), arguing that marriage should be governed by "relational norms" of the individual couple and "social norms" of the community, and stressing that the balance-keeping of spot contracting is not what they refer to by using the language of contracts.

12. See, e.g., Martha Fineman, *The Illusion of Equality: The Rhetoric and Reality of Divorce Reform* 149 (1991); Regan, supra note 10, at 94–95, 188; Jeffrey E. Stake, "Mandatory Planning for Divorce," 45 *Vanderbilt Law Review* 397 (1992); Elizabeth Scott, "Rational Decisionmaking about Marriage and Divorce," 76 *Virginia Law Review* 9 (1990).

13. Compare Karen Czapanskiy, "Volunteers and Draftees: The Struggle for Parental Equality," 38 *UCLA Law Review* 1415 (1991); Trina Grillo, "The Mediation Alternative: Process Dangers for Women," 100 *Yale Law Journal* 1545 (1991); Beverly Horsbaugh, "Redefining the Family: Recognizing the Altruistic Caretaker and the Importance of Relational Needs," *University of Michigan Journal of Law Reform* 423 (1992); Joan Williams, "Gender Wars: Selfless Women in the Republic of Choice," 66 *New York University Law Review* 1559 (1991).

14. But see Scott and Scott, supra note 11, for a contrary argument.

15. Regan, supra note 10, at 116–117; see also Bruce Hafen, "The Family as an Entity," *University of California–Davis Law Review* 865, 892 (1989).

16. Margaret F. Brinig, "Status, Contract, and Covenant: A Review of *Family Law and the Pursuit of Intimacy*," 89 *Cornell Law Review* 1573 (1994).

17. Regan, supra note 10, at 2.

18. Id. at 148; Scott, supra note 12, at 36.

19. See, e.g., Gary S. Becker, *Treatise on the Family* 325–327 (2d ed. 1991); and "A Theory of Marriage," in *Economics of the Family: Marriage, Children, and Human Capital: A Conference Report of the National Bureau of Economic Research* (Theodore W. Schultz, ed., 1974). Becker is abstracting from George Stigler's more general search model, supra note 1; see also Nelson, supra note 1. A much more intuitive description of the marriage market appears in England and Farkas, supra note 1, at 31–42.

20. See, e.g., England and Farkas, supra note 1, at 31–42; Brinig and Alexeev, supra note 1. With some traits, such as educational achievement, social class background, physical attractiveness, and personality type, the individual will seek a positive match. With others, such as earning ability and "household production" skills (such as cooking), the person's interest may focus on one whose attributes are complementary. Becker, supra note 19, at 327; England and Farkas at 34–35. People signal each other about characteristics such as reliability through proffer-

ing and accepting the marriage proposal. William Bishop, "Is He Married? Marriage as Information," 34 *University of Toronto Law Journal* 245, 258–59 (1984).

21. Becker, supra note 19, at 325.

22. Matthew 2:25; see also William Brundage, *Law, Sex, and Christian Society in Medieval Europe* 453 (1987).

23. Edward Shorter, *The Making of the Modern Family* 55 (1987).

24. Brundage, supra note 22, at 183.

25. Shorter, supra note 23, at 21.

26. John Demos, "The American Family in Past Time," 43 *American Scholar* 422, 425 (1978).

27. Beth Bailey, *From Front Porch to Back Seat: Courtship in Twentieth-Century America* 17 (1988).

28. Id. at 21.

29. Willard Waller, "The Rating and Dating Complex," 2 *American Sociological Review* 726, 730 (1937).

30. Bailey, supra note 27, at 26–31.

31. Id. at 56–57.

32. Alfred C. Kinsey et al., *Sexual Behavior in the Human Male* 336 (1948).

33. K. A. Loudon, "Advance Data from Vital and Health Statistics," no. 194, Center for Health Statistics (1991). See also D'Vera Cohn, "Cohabiting Couples Are a Settled Bunch; Many Unwed Partners Own Homes, Have Children, Census Reveals," *Washington Post*, B1. (March 20, 1994).

34. Bishop, supra note 20, at 258–259; Ellen Rothman, *Hands and Hearts: A History of Courtship in America* 162–163 (1987).

35. Margaret Brinig, "Rings and Promises," 6 *Journal of Law, Economics, and Organization* 203 (1990); Margaret Brinig and June Carbone, "The Reliance Interest in Marriage and Divorce," 62 *Tulane Law Review* 855 (1988). See also Rothman, supra note 34, at 270–271.

36. Mary Ann Glendon, *The New Family and the New Property* 31–32 (1981); Elizabeth Craik, ed., *Marriage and Property* 166–67 (1984); Michael Grossberg, *Governing the Hearth: Law and the Family in Nineteenth-Century America* 36 (1985).

37. Rothman, supra note 34, at 163.

38. Kinsey, supra note 32; Paul Gebhard and Alan Johnson, *The Kinsey Data: Marginal Tabulations of the 1938–63 Interviews Conducted by the Institute for Sex Research* 20 (1979).

39. Theodore Cousens, "The Law of Damages as Applied to Breach of Promise of Marriage," 17 *Cornell Law Quarterly* 367, 372 (1932).

40. Nathan P. Feinsinger, "Legislative Attack on Heart Balm," 33 *Michigan Law Review* 979, 983 (1935).

41. W. J. Brockelbank, "The Nature of the Promise to Marry—A Study in Comparative Law," 41 *Illinois Law Review* 1, 8 (1946).

42. See, generally, Brinig and Alexeev, supra note 1.

43. Bailey, supra note 27.

44. England and Farkas, supra note 1, at 41. See also Michael Trebilcock, "Marriage as Signal," in *The Fall and Rise of Freedom of Contract* (F. H. Buckley, ed., 1999).

45. Id.; see also Cohn, supra note 33.

46. Larry L. Bumpass, James A. Sweet, and Andrew Cherlin, "The Role of Cohabitation in Declining Rates of Marriage," 53 *Journal of Marriage and the Family* 913 (1991).

47. Brundage, supra note 22, at 453.

48. Roderick Phillips, *Putting Asunder: A History of Divorce in Western Society* 134–135 (1988).

49. *Project of the Governor's Commission on the Family* (1966); Lynn D. Wardle, "No-Fault Divorce and the Divorce Conundrum," 1991 *BYU Law Review* 79, 107.

50. See, e.g., Gordon v. Pollard, 336 S.W.2d 25 (Tenn. 1960); Flaxman v. Flaxman, 273 A.2d 567 (N.J. 1971).

51. Brinig and Carbone, supra note 35.

52. In re Ladrach, 513 N.E.2d 828 (Ohio Misc. 1987).

53. *Project of the Governor's Commission,* supra note 49.

54. Nelson, supra note 1, at 312.

55. Id. at 327.

56. Michael Darby and Edi Karni, "Free Competition and the Optimal Amount of Fraud in Contracts," 16 *Journal of Law and Economics* 67 (1973).

57. See, e.g., Becker *(Treatise),* supra note 19, at 326.

58. Brinig and Alexeev, supra note 1.

59. See, e.g., Va. Code Ann. §20–89.1.

60. See, e.g., V. J. S. v. M. J. B., 592 A.2d 328 (N.J. Super. Ct. Ch. Div. 1991).

61. See, e.g., In re Marriage of Liu, 242 Cal. Rptr. 649 (Cal. 1987); Kshaiboon v. Kshaiboon, 652 S.W.2d 219 (Mo. Ct. App. 1983); and Sites v. Johns Manville Products, 503 A.2d 377 (N.J. Super. 1986).

62. See, e.g., Bilowit v. Dolitsky, 304 A.2d 774 (N.J. Super. Ct. App. Div. 1973); State Compensation Fund v. Foughty, 476 P.2d 902 (Ariz. Ct. App. 1970); and Wolfe v. Wolfe, 378 N.E.2d 1181 (Ill. Ct. App. 1979).

63. But see Scott and Scott, supra note 11.

64. W. Va. Code §48–1–12(b) prescribes a similar ritual for civil ceremonies taking place in that state.

65. This includes those of the Roman Catholic Church. Where the vows exchanged do not include this term, it will be implied because of the centrality of child rearing in the marriage function.

66. Avnery v. Avnery, 375 N.Y.S.2d 888 (N.Y. App. Div. 1975).

67. See Henry Butler, W. J. Lane, and Owen R. Phillips, "The Futility of Antitrust Attacks on Tie-In Sales: An Economics and Legal Analysis," 36 *Hastings Law Journal* 173 (1984); Robert G. Natelson, "Consent, Coercion, and 'Reasonableness' in Private Law: The Special Case of the Property Owners Association," 51 *Ohio State*

Law Journal 41 (1990); Gregory Alexander, "Freedom, Coercion, and the Law of Servitudes," 3 *Cornell Law Review* 883 (1988).

68. 172 N.W.2d 334 (Wis. 1969).

69. Judges are less familiar with annulments, so they require a higher quality of proof and legal argument from the plaintiff's lawyer.

70. See, e.g., Cohn, supra note 33; see also Bumpass, Sweet, and Cherlin, supra note 46, at 931.

71. These cohabitation relationships differ from common law marriage, in which there is also no ceremony, but there is a marriage agreement made by the cohabiting couple plus a "holding out," or representation, to the public that proves the agreement took place. A common law marriage made in a state that recognizes it is a true marriage. Cohabitation, by definition, is not. See, e.g., Grace Blumberg, "Cohabitation without Marriage: A Different Perspective," 28 *UCLA Law Review* 1125 (1981).

72. Regan, supra note 10, at 120–122. See also Claudia A. Lewis, "From This Day Forward: A Feminine Moral Discourse on Homosexual Marriage," 97 *Yale Law Journal* 1783 (1988).

73. For example, Virginia's sexual offense statute, Va. Code Ann. §18.344, prohibits fornication by unmarried persons. Another section forbids "lewd and lascivious cohabitation"; see Va. Code Ann. §18.2–345.

74. See Harry Krause, "Legal Position: Unmarried Couples," in "Law in the U.S.A. Faces Social and Scientific Change" (Supplement), 34 *American Journal of Comparative Law* 533 (J. Hazard and W. Wagner, eds., 1986).

75. See, e.g., Haw. Rev. Stat. §§87–25.5 et seq.; Madison, Wisconsin, General Ord. §3.36, 28.03; Rene Sanchez, "D.C. Council Approves Partners Bill," *Washington Post*, B1 (April 8, 1992).

76. Compare Carl Schneider, "The Channelling Function in Family Law," 20 *Hofstra Law Review* 495 (1992).

77. See, e.g., Ala. Code §13A-13–2; Ga. Code Ann. §16–6–18; Mass. Ann. Laws ch. 272, §18; N.C. Gen. Stat. §14–184; Va. Code Ann. §18.2–344.

78. Henry N. Butler, "General Incorporation in Nineteenth-Century England: Interaction of Common Law and Legislative Processes," 6 *International Review of Law and Economics* 169 (1986); Henry N. Butler, "Nineteenth-Century Jurisdictional Competition in the Granting of Corporate Privileges," 14 *Journal of Legal Studies* 129 (1985).

79. See Lawrence M. Friedman, "Rights of Passage: Divorce Law in Historical Perspective," 63 *Oregon Law Review* 649 (1984).

80. Reynolds v. United States, 98 U.S. (8 Otto) 145, 25 L.Ed 244 (1878); see generally Homer Clark, *The Law of Domestic Relations in the United States* §2.6 (2d ed. 1988).

81. Margaret F. Brinig and F. H. Buckley, "The Market for Deadbeats," 25 *Journal of Legal Studies* 201 (1996).

82. La. Civ. Code Art. 9, §102; Ariz. Rev. Stat. §§25–901 et seq. See, e.g., Margaret F. Brinig, "Economics, Law, and Covenant Marriage," 16 *Gender Issues* 4 (1998); Martha Minow, "All in the Family and in All Families: Membership, Loving, and Owing," 95 *West Virginia Law Review* 275 (1992); Stake, supra note 12. See generally Eric Rasmusen and Jeffrey Stake, "Lifting the Veil of Ignorance: Personalizing the Marriage Contract," 73 *Indiana Law Journal* 453 (1997); Scott, supra note 12.

83. La. Civ. Code Art. 9, §102; Ariz. Rev. Stat. §§25–316.

84. La. Civ. Code Art. 9, §229 and §272; Ariz. Rev. Stat. §25–903.

85. See Dorothy A. Brown, "The Marriage Bonus/Penalty in Black and White," 65 *University of Cincinnati Law Review* 787 (1997); Pamela B. Gann, "The Economic Recovery Tax Act of 1981: The Earned Income Deduction: Congress' 1981 Response to the 'Marriage Penalty' Tax," 68 *Cornell Law Review* 468 (1983).

86. See Brinig, supra note 16, at 1587 and n.82 (1994). The point is that within the more permanent relationship, the spouse is "freer" to invest in the other and in the relationship. Because the marriage functions as "insurance," at least on the labor market, a spouse may also be able to take greater personal risks. See also Christopher Wolfe, "The Marriage of Your Choice," *First Things,* 37, 38 (January 1995); Pope Paul VI, *Humanae Vitae* [On the Regulation of Birth] no. 9 (1968).

87. Scott and Scott, supra note 11.

88. Rasmusen and Stake, supra note 82. For another suggestion on how to increase marital investment through taxation and social security schemes for homemakers, see Nancy Staudt, "Taxing Housework," 84 *Georgetown Law Journal* 1571 (1996).

89. Katherine Silbaugh, in "Turning Labor into Love: Housework and the Law," 91 *Northwestern University Law Review* 1 (1995), argues that couples should be free to contract between themselves over household tasks and to compensate one another for household work. See Pyeatte v. Pyeatte, 661 P.2d 196 (Ariz. Ct. App. 1982). There cannot be a contract not to divorce, however (Dumais v. Dumais, 122 A.2d 322 [Me. 1956]), nor a contract not to support each other during marriage (Motley v. Motley, 120 S.E.2d 422 [N.C. 1961]; Hurley v. Hurley, 615 P.2d 256 [N.M. 1988]), nor to provide services to each other (Frame v. Frame, 36 S.W.2d 152 [Tex. 1931]).

90. Margaret F. Brinig and F. H. Buckley, "Joint Custody: Bonding and Monitoring Theories," 73 *Indiana Law Journal* 393 (1998). See, generally, Oliver Williamson, "Credible Commitments: Using Hostages to Support Exchange," 73 *American Economic Review* 519 (1983); Jon Elster, *Ulysses and the Sirens: Studies in Rationality and Irrationality* 37–47 (1984).

91. Baker and Emery, supra note 2.

92. See, e.g., Rasmusen and Stake, supra note 82; Judith T. Younger, "Perspectives on Antenuptial Agreements," 40 *Rutgers Law Review* 1059 (1988). For another useful discussion of marital contracting in general, see Wax, supra note 5.

93. Regret, particularly when another attractive alternative comes along, is one of the factors economists take into account in "gaming" most transactions. They, like

judges, are not sympathetic to arguments involving the opportunity costs of doing business or undertaking contracts generally, unless the other side breaches. See Margaret F. Brinig, "A Maternalistic Approach to Surrogacy," 81 *Virginia Law Review* 2377 (1995).

94. Gary S. Becker, Elisabeth M. Landes, and Robert T. Michael, "An Economic Analysis of Marital Instability," 85 *Journal of Political Economy* 85, 1141–87 (1977).

95. Francine Klagsbrun, *Married People: Staying Together in the Age of Divorce* (1985).

96. A number of religious groups currently require such counseling before their adherents can be married in a religious ceremony. See, e.g., Sara Shipley, "Making Vows Last Longer in Louisiana," *Christian Science Monitor* 1 (July 1, 1997); Hanna Rosin, "Separation Anxiety: The Movement to Save Marriage," *New Republic,* 14 (May 6, 1996); but see Glenda Winters, "Don't Put a Headlock on Those Entering Wedlock," Copley News Service (July 11, 1997).

97. See especially Bishop, supra note 20, at 262. The signaling issue is also discussed in Rasmusen and Stake, supra note 82; and Trebilcock, supra note 44.

98. Margaret F. Brinig, Randy Holcombe, and Linda Ann Schwartzstein, "Public Choice and Lobbying Regulation," 74 *Public Choice* 371 (1993).

99. Compare Schneider, supra note 76.

100. Blaise Pascal, *Pensées* 944 (1976). See also David Hume, "Of Polygamy and Divorces," in *Essays: Moral, Political, and Literary* 181–190 (Eugene Miller, ed., 1987).

101. Some feminists believe that marriage is inevitably hierarchical and dominated by the man involved, and that this would be true of virtually all heterosexual relationships. See, e.g., Catharine MacKinnon, *Feminism Unmodified: Discourses on Life and Law* (1987); Martha Fineman; *The Neutered Mother, the Sexual Family, and Other Twentieth-Century Tragedies* (1995); Paula England and Martin Kilborne, "Markets, Marriage, and Other Mates: The Problem of Power," in *Theory on Gender, Feminism on Theory* (Paula England, ed., 1993).

102. See Wax, supra note 5.

103. Id. at 4–12, and sources cited therein.

104. Wax, supra note 5, at 21–34.

105. See, e.g., Cote v. Cote, 404 S.W.2d 139 (Tex. App. 1966). For other examples, see Reed v. Reed, 329 P.2d 633 (Colo. 1958), and generally Max Rheinstein, *Marriage Stability, Divorce, and the Law* 247–260 (1972); Legislation Notes, Domestic Relations, "A Survey of Mental Cruelty as a Ground for Divorce," 15 *De Paul Law Review* 159, 163 (1965).

106. Margaret F. Brinig and Steven M. Crafton, "Marriage and Opportunism," 23 *Journal of Legal Studies* 869 (1994). But see Ira Ellman and Sharon Lohr, "Marriage as Contract, Opportunistic Violence, and Other Bad Arguments for Fault Divorce," 1997 *University of Illinois Law Review* 719.

107. Some feminist writers are opposed to covenant marriage because, they note, women file the majority of divorce petitions. But as Frank Buckley and I noted, supra note 90, women have always filed the substantial majority of petitions for

reasons of convention and because court action was necessary for them to secure temporary support and custody from their higher-earning husbands. As Rasmusen and Stake have pointed out, supra note 82, no-fault divorce in some ways benefited men. But see Steven L. Nock, *Marriage in Men's Lives* (1998), showing the many ways in which marriage benefits men.

108. See, e.g., Ephesians 5:22–30. The husband in return is to "love his wife" just "as Christ loves the Church."

109. See, e.g., Book of Common Prayer, "Solemnization of Matrimony," reprinted in Carl E. Schneider and Margaret F. Brinig, *An Invitation to Family Law* 4, 5 (1996).

110. See, e.g., Irene Hanson Frieze and Angela Browne, "Violence in Marriage," in *Family Violence* 163, 201 (Lloyd Ohlin and Michael Tonry, eds., 1989).

111. Elizabeth Scott and Andre Derdeyn, "Rethinking Joint Custody," 45 *Ohio State Law Journal* 455, 478 (1984); Scott, supra note 12; Sara McLanahan and Gary D. Sandefer, *Growing Up with a Single Parent: What Hurts, What Helps* (1994); Jean Harin, "Patterns of Childhood Residence and the Relationship to Young Adult Outcomes," 54 *Journal of Marriage and the Family* 846 (1992). See also Brinig and Buckley, supra note 90; Mary Ann Glendon, "Family Law Reform in the 1980s," 44 *Louisiana Law Review* 1553 (1984).

112. La. Civ. Code Art. 9, §§307(4) and 308(4).

113. W. Va. Code §48–2–4(9).

114. Matter of Alyne E., 448 N.Y.S.2d 984 (N.Y. Fam. Ct. 1982).

115. Brinig and Crafton, Supra note 106; Regan, supra note 10; Elisabeth M. Landes, "The Economics of Alimony," 7 *Journal of Legal Studies* 35 (1978).

116. The birthrate in the United States among married couples has been decreasing dramatically since 1960, while the percentage attributable to unwed births has increased threefold for whites and twofold for African Americans.

117. Brinig and Crafton, supra note 106; see also Scott and Scott, supra note 11.

118. Margaret F. Brinig, "Property Distribution Physics: The Talisman of Time and Middle-Class Law," 31 *Family Law Quarterly* 93 (1997); see also Gary S. Becker, *Human Capital: A Theoretical and Empirical Analysis with Special Reference to Education* (3d ed. 1993); Allen Parkman, *No-Fault Divorce: What Went Wrong?* (1992): Allen M. Parkman, "Human Capital as Property in Celebrity Divorces," 29 *Family Law Quarterly* 141 (1995); Joan Krauskopf, "Recompense for Financing Spouse's Education: Legal Protection for the Marital Investor in Human Capital," 28 *Kansas Law Review* 379 (1980).

119. Landes, supra note 115.

120. Marsha Garrison, "Good Intentions Gone Awry: The Impact of New York's Equitable Distribution Law on Divorce Outcomes," 57 *Brooklyn Law Review* 621 (1991).

121. Yoram Weiss and Robert Willis, "Transfers among Divorced Couples: Evidence and Interpretation," 11 *Journal of Labor Economics* 629 (1993).

122. Margaret F. Brinig and Michael V. Alexeev, "Trading at Divorce: Preferences, Legal Rules, and Transaction Costs," 8 *Ohio State Journal on Dispute Resolution* 279 (1993).

123. See, e.g., Richard A. Peterson, "A Reevaluation of the Economic Consequences of Divorce," 61 *American Sociological Review* 528 (1996); and Ross Finnie, "Women, Men, and the Economic Consequences of Divorce: Evidence from Canadian Longitudinal Data," 30 *Canadian Review of Sociology and Anthropology* 205 (1993).

124. See Brinig, supra note 118.

125. See Margaret F. Brinig, "The Family Franchise: Elderly Parents and Adult Siblings," 1996 *Utah Law Review* 393.

126. Becker, supra note 19.

127. See, e.g., Don McLeese, "Louisiana Legislating Levels of Love," *Austin American-Statesman*, B1 (July 29, 1997); Nadine Strossen and Geraldine Ferrara on *Crossfire*, August 7, 1997; "Call It the Covenant Adultery Act," *The Advocate* (Baton Rouge), B7 (July 26, 1997); Judy Markey, "'Marriage Lite' Is Good Enough for Most of Us," *Chattanooga Times*, B9 (July 18, 1997); Katha Pollit, "What's Right about Divorce," *New York Times*, A29 (June 27, 1997); "Two Kinds of Marriage, One Bad Idea," *Dayton Daily News*, 10A (June 30, 1997).

128. Shipley, supra note 96.

129. See Brinig, supra note 118, at 114.

130. Alan P. Herbert, *Holy Deadlock* (1934); see also Amitai Etzioni, "How to Make Marriage Matter," *Time*, 76 (September 6, 1993).

131. American Law Institute, *Principles of the Law of Family Dissolution: Analysis and Recommendations*, Proposed Final Draft, pt. 1, at 14 (Reporter's Comments on Topic 2), and also the Family Law Reporter's discussion of the 1996 meeting, June 1996.

132. Census Bureau statistics show that 20 percent of all Americans move at least out of county during each two-year period.

133. For example, Louisiana Civil Code, Art. 112, provides: A. (1) When a spouse has not been at fault and has not sufficient means for support, the court may allow that spouse, out of the property and earnings of the other spouse, permanent periodic alimony, which shall not exceed one-third of his or her income. Alimony shall not be denied on the ground that one spouse obtained a valid divorce from the other spouse in a court of another state or country which had no jurisdiction over the person of the claimant spouse.

134. See Strossen and Ferrara, supra note 127.

135. See, e.g., Wendy Williams, "The Equality Crisis: Some Reflections on Culture, Courts, and Feminism," in *Feminist Legal Theory: Readings in Law and Gender* 15, 22–25 (Katharine Bartlett and Roseanne Kennedy, eds., 1991); and Herma Hill Kay, "An Appraisal of California's No-Fault Divorce Law," 70 *California Law Review* 291 (1987). For a suggestion that covenant marriage will encourage specialization within the marriage, see Rasmusen and Stake, supra note 82.

136. See, generally, Patricia A. Cain, "Imagine There's No Marriage," 16 *Quinnipiac Law Review* 27 (1997).

137. See, e.g., Andrew Sullivan, *Virtually Normal* (1995); Regan, supra note 10.

138. Examples include Baehr v. Lewin, 852 P.2d 44 (Haw. 1993); Dean v. District of Columbia, 653 A.2d 307 (D.C. App. 1995). On December 3, 1996, the district court in Hawaii, on remand, decided that the statute disallowing same-sex marriage unconstitutionally violated the state's equal rights law; see 1996 WL 694235 (Hawaii Cir. Ct.); aff'd. Baehr v. Miike, 80 Haw. 341, 910 P.2d 112, injunction granted, Baehr v. Miike, 96 Daily Journal D.A.R. (Haw. Ct. App. 1996). For an account of the case, see Lyle Denniston, "Judge OKs Same-Sex Marriages," *Baltimore Sun*, 1A (December 4, 1996). A ballot to call for a constitutional convention to amend the Hawaii State Constitution passed in November 1996 with a bare majority. Meanwhile, to avoid problems with the full faith and credit obligations of other states to accept Hawaii-granted same-sex marriages, Congress enacted the so-called Defense of Marriage Act, 28 U.S.C. §1738C. Section 3 of the act defines marriage as "only a legal union between one man and one woman as husband and wife."

139. See Ellen Lewin, *Recognizing Ourselves: Ceremonies of Lesbian and Gay Commitment* (1998).

140. See, e.g., Butcher v. Superior Court, 188 Cal. Rptr. 503 (Cal. Ct. App. 1983).

141. See, e.g., Marjorie Maguire Shultz, "Contractual Ordering of Marriage: A New Model for State Policy," 70 *California Law Review* 204 (1982); and Lenore J. Weitzman, *The Marriage Contract: Spouses, Lovers, and the Law* (1981).

142. See Lewin, supra note 139, at 35.

143. The usual rule is that such agreements will be enforced to the extent that they did not involve explicit payment for sexual services. See, e.g., Morone v. Morone, 50 N.Y.2d 481, 429 N.Y.S.2d 592, 413 N.E.2d 1154 (1980); Kozlowski v. Kozlowski, 80 N.J. 378, 403 A.2d 902 (1979); Trutalli v. Meraviglia, 215 Cal. 698, 12 P.2d 430 (Cal. 1932).

144. See, e.g., Turner v. Safley, 482 U.S. 78, 107 S.Ct. 2254, 96 L.Ed.2d 54 (1987); Lockhart v. Faulkner, 574 F. Supp. 606 (N.D. Ind. 1983).

145. Some states prohibit adultery. See, e.g., Ala. Code §13A-13–2 (1996); Ariz Rev. Stat. §13–1408 (1996); Ark. Code §5–15–102 (1995).

146. See, e.g., Bowers v. Hardwick, 478 U.S. 186, 106 S.Ct. 2841, 92 L.Ed.2d 140 (1986) (twenty-four states as of 1986).

147. Hewitt v. Hewitt, 77 Ill. 2d 49, 394 N.E.2d 1204 (1979).

148. Restatement of Contracts §589 (1932).

149. See, e.g., Sun Lumber v. Thompson Land Co., 138 W. Va. 68, 76 S.E.2d 65 (1953). For a discussion of why specific performance might not work in the marriage contract, see Lloyd Cohen, "Marriage, Divorce, and Quasi-Rents; or, 'I Gave Him the Best Years of My Life,'" 16 *Journal of Legal Studies* 267, 300–302 (1987).

150. See Lake River Corp. v. Carborundum Co., 769 F.2d 1284 (7th Cir. 1985).

151. Compare Avitzur v. Avitzur, 58 N.Y.2d 108, 459 N.Y.S.2d 572, 446 N.E.2d 136 (N.Y. 1983).

152. Use of a pledge or bonding device is described at length in Anthony Kronman, "Contract Law and the State of Nature," 1 *Journal of Law, Economics, and Organization* 5, 15–18 (1985). See also Scott and Scott, supra note 11.

153. See Jennifer Gerarda Brown, "Competitive Federalism and the Legislative Incentives to Recognize Same-Sex Marriage," 68 *Southern California Law Review* 745, 773 (1995). But see M. V. Lee Badgett, "The Wage Effects of Sexual Orientation Discrimination," 48 *Industrial and Labor Relations Review* 726 (1995).

154. See Brown, supra note 153, at 781.

155. Becker, supra note 19, at 39.

156. But see Mary Louise Fellows et al., "Committed Partners and Inheritance: An Empirical Study," 16 *Law and Inequality* 1 (1998).

157. Gomez v. Perez, 409 U.S. 535, 35 L.Ed.2d 56, 93 S.Ct. 872 (1973).

158. See, e.g., Bottoms v. Bottoms, 249 Va. 410, 457 S.E.2d 102 (1995).

159. Becker, supra note 19, at 34–35.

160. See Carol Bruch, "Property Rights of De Facto Spouses, Including Thoughts on the Value of Homemakers' Services," 10 *Family Law Quarterly* 101, 102 (1976).

161. See Lenore Weitzman, "Legal Regulation of Marriage: Tradition and Change," 62 *California Law Review* 1169, 1281 (1974).

162. Becker, Landes, and Michael, supra note 94; H. Elizabeth Peters, "Marriage and Divorce: Informational Constraints and Private Contracting," 76 *American Economic Review* 437 (1986).

163. Cohen, supra note 149.

164. See Shultz, supra note 141.

165. In re Higgason's Marriage, 516 P.2d 289 (Cal. 1973).

166. See, e.g., Favrot v. Burns, 332 So.2d 873 (La. Ct. App. 1976).

167. See, e.g., Matthews v. Matthews, 162 S.E.2d 697 (N.C. Ct. App. 1968); Cummings v. Cummings, 102 S.E. 572, 574 (Va. 1920).

168. Scott and Scott, supra note 11.

169. Oliver Williamson, *The Economic Institution of Capitalism* 5 (1985).

170. The actual figure for marriages ending in divorce is about 50 percent, according to Arthur J. Norton and Jeanne E. Moorman, "Current Trends in Marriage and Divorce among American Women," 49 *Journal of Marriage and the Family* 3 (1987).

171. Baker and Emery, supra note 2, at 443.

172. See, e.g., Stees v. Leonard, 20 Minn. 494 (1874); Charles Goetz and Robert Scott, "Principles of Relational Contracts," 67 *Virginia Law Review* 1089, 1149 (1981); and generally Robert Scott, "Error and Rationality in Individual Decision-Making: An Essay on the Relationship between Cognitive Illusions and the Management of Choices," 59 *Southern California Law Review* 329 (1986); Alan Schwartz and Louis L. Wilde, "Intervening in Markets on the Basis of Imperfect

Information: A Legal and Economic Analysis," 127 *University of Pennsylvania Law Review* 630 (1979).

173. Brinig, supra note 4, at 2461–63.

174. Id. See also Stake, supra note 12, at 427 and n.126.

175. Alexander v. Kuykendall, 63 S.E.2d 746, 747–748 (Va. 1951).

176. Joel P. Bishop, 1 *Commentaries on the Law of Marriage and Divorce* 2, §3 (6th ed. 1881).

177. Maynard v. Hill, 125 U.S. 190, 8 S.Ct. 723 (1888)(Field, J.). See also Adams v. Palmer, 51 Me. 481, 483.

178. See generally Brinig, supra note 35; Comment, "Twelve Years with the Heart Balm Acts," 33 *Virginia Law Review* 314 (1947).

179. Grossberg, supra note 36, at 46–47.

180. Id. at 62–63.

181. These states, with the year of legislation, are North Dakota (1877); Illinois (1935); Indiana (1935); New Jersey (1935); Pennsylvania (1935); Alabama (1935); New York (1935); Michigan (1935); Colorado (1937); Massachusetts (1938); California (1939); Maine (1941); Wyoming (1941); New Hampshire (1941); Nevada (1943); and Florida (1945).

182. See, e.g., Miller v. Ratner, 688 A.2d 976, cert. denied, 693 A.2d 355 (Md. 1997).

183. Feinsinger, supra note 40, at 979.

184. Kronman, supra note 152, at 15–18.

185. Brinig, supra note 35.

186. Id. at 209–211.

187. David Koskoff, *The Diamond World* 273–274, 277 (1981).

188. Lindh v. Surman, 702 A.2d 560 (Pa. Super. 1997); Aronow v. Silver, 538 A.2d 851 (N.J. Super. Chan. 1987).

189. 557 P.2d 106 (Cal. 1976).

190. Larry L. Bumpass and James A. Sweet, "National Estimates of Cohabitation," 26 *Demography* 615, 620–621 (1989).

191. See, e.g., Philip Blumstein and Pepper Schwartz, *American Couples: Money, Work, Sex* 594 (1983), table 3.

192. Bumpass, Sweet, and Cherlin, supra note 46 (higher by a third).

193. Robert J. Willis and Robert T. Michael, "Innovation in Family Formation: Evidence on Cohabitation in the United States," presented at the International Union for the Scientific Study of Population seminar, Sendai City, Japan, 1988.

194. Brinig and Buckley, supra note 90.

195. Scott and Scott, supra note 11.

3. Becoming Parents

1. Bureau of the Census, Current Population Survey, June 1997, P70–9 and table 1. Stephanie J. Ventura et al., "Advance Report of Final Natality Statistics, 1994,"

Monthly Vital Statistics Report, vol. 44. no. 11, supp. p. 28. National Center for Health Statistics, 1996; U.S. Bureau of the Census, "Percent Childless and Births per 1,000 Women in the Last Year: Selected Years, June 1976 to Present," Table H1, internet release date November 25, 1997.

2. R. Robin Baker and Mark A. Bellis, "Human Sperm Competition: Ejaculate Manipulation by Females and a Function for the Female Orgasm," 46 *Animal Behavior* 887, 903 (1993).

3. John J. Billings, *Natural Family Planning: The Ovulation Method* (3rd ed. 1975).

4. Gary Anderson and Robert Tollison, "A Theory of Rational Childhood," 7 *European Journal of Political Economy* 199 (1991).

5. Gary S. Becker, *A Treatise on the Family* (2d ed. 1991); Gary S. Becker and H. Gregg Lewis, "On the Interaction between the Quantity and Quality of Children," 81 *Journal of Political Economy* S279 (1973); Gary S. Becker and Nigel Tomes, "Child Endowments and the Quantity and Quality of Children," 84 *Journal of Political Economy* S143 (1988).

6. See, e.g., Griswold v. Connecticut, 381 U.S. 479 (1965); and Eisenstadt v. Baird, 405 U.S. 438 (1972).

7. Roe v. Wade, 410 U.S. 113 (1973). See also Planned Parenthood of S.E. Pennsylvania v. Casey, 505 U.S. 833 (1992).

8. See Paul Rubin, James B. Kau, and Edward F. Meeker, "Forms of Wealth and Parent-Offspring Conflict," 2 *Journal of Social and Biological Structures* 53 (1972).

9. See Becker and Lewis, supra note 5.

10. See, e.g., Tan Tarn How, "Family Planning a Necessity," *Straits Times* (Singapore) (September 13, 1995); "How to Handle a Little Emperor," *South China Morning Post,* 21 (February 28, 1995).

11. Margaret F. Brinig and Steven M. Crafton, "Marriage and Opportunism," 23 *Journal of Legal Studies* 869, 885–886 (1994).

12. See, e.g., Heup v. Heup, 172 N.W. 2d 334 (Wis. 1969).

13. Gary S. Becker, Elisabeth M. Landes, and Robert Michael, "An Economic Analysis of Marital Instability," 85 *Journal of Political Economy* 1141 (1977).

14. Victor Fuchs, *Women's Quest for Economic Equality* 44–45 (1988).

15. Roe v. Wade, 410 U.S. 113 (1973); National Committee for Adoption, *Adoption Factbook* 175 (1991).

16. See Margaret F. Brinig and F. H. Buckley, "The Price of Virtue," 98 *Public Choice* 111 (1999).

17. Santosky v. Kramer, 455 U.S. 745 (1982); Lassiter v. Dep't. Soc. Servs., 452 U.S. 18 (1981).

18. This increased caseload has resulted in part because of the increase in drug usage by parents, and in part because of new abuse reporting requirements. See, e.g., Va. Code Ann. §63.1–248.6, mandating investigation of any abuse complaint.

19. See, e.g., Elizabeth S. Scott and Robert E. Scott, "Parents as Fiduciaries," 81 *Virginia Law Review* 2401, 1406 (1995); Barbara Bennett Woodhouse, "Hatching the

Egg: A Child-Centered Perspective on Parents' Rights," 14 *Cardozo Law Review* 1747, 1784–95 (1993).

20. Richard A. Posner, "The Regulation of the Market in Adoptions," 65 *Boston University Law Review* 59, 65 (1987). See also J. Robert S. Prichard, "A Market for Babies?" 34 *University of Toronto Law Journal* 341, 343 (1984). Janet Hopkins Dickson reports that between twenty and forty couples may compete for every infant placed for adoption; see Comment, "The Emerging Rights of Adoptive Parents: Substance or Specter?" 38 *UCLA Law Review* 917 and n.7 (1991). She discusses the popular interest in adoption, id. at 918 and n.10. The wait before placement can take from two to ten years; see *Adoption Factbook,* supra note 15, at 175. See also Comment, "Independent Adoption: Regulating the Middleman," 24 *Washburn Law Journal* 327 (1985)(waiting period of three to five years).

21. See generally Comment, "Black-Market Adoptions," 22 *Catholic Lawyer* 48 (1976); Peter Reuter, *The Organization of Illegal Markets: An Economic Analysis* (1985); Prichard, supra note 20, at 343 (prices as high as $40,000 for newborns).

22. Elisabeth Landes and Richard Posner, "The Economics of the Baby Shortage," 7 *Journal of Legal Studies* 323 (1978). See also Posner, supra note 20; and the various editions of his *Economic Analysis of Law.* See, e.g., §5.3, at 139–144 (3d ed. 1986); §5.4, at 149–154 (4th ed. 1992).

23. See, e.g., John J. Donohue III and Ian Ayres, "Posner's Symphony No. 3: Thinking about the Unthinkable," 39 *Stanford University Law Review* 791 (1987); Ronald A. Cass, "Coping with Life, Law, and Markets: A Comment on Posner and the Law-and-Economics Debate," 67 *Boston University Law Review* 73 (1987); Jane Maslow Cohen, "Posnerism, Pluralism, Pessimism," 67 *Boston University Law Review* 105 (1987); Tamar Frankel and Francis H. Miller, "The Inapplicability of Market Theory to Adoptions," 67 *Boston University Law Review* 99 (1987); Mark Kelman, "Consumption Theory, Production Theory, and Ideology in the Coase Theorem," 52 *Southern California Law Review* 669, 688 n.51 (1979); Prichard, supra note 20; Robin West, "Submission, Choice, and Ethics: A Rejoinder to Judge Posner," 99 *Harvard Law Review* 1449 (1986); Paul M. Barrett, "Influential Ideas: A Movement Called 'Law and Economics' Sways Legal Circles," *Wall Street Journal,* 1, 16 (August 4, 1986); Anne McDaniel, "Free-Market Jurist," *Newsweek,* 93–94 (June 10, 1985); Lincoln Caplan, "Meet Richard Posner, the Judge Who Would Sell Homeless Babies," *Washington Post* (National Weekly Edition), 23, (October 29, 1984).

24. Cohen, supra note 23, at 154–155; Frankel and Miller, supra note 23, at 100–101; Margaret Jane Radin, "Market Inalienability," 100 *Harvard Law Review* 1849, 1853 (1987).

25. This argument was anticipated, and dismissed, by Landes and Posner, supra note 22, at 343.

26. See, e.g., Caplan, supra note 23, at 23. Donohue and Ayres, supra note 23, at 791.

27. Posner, *Economic Analysis of Law,* supra note 22, at 152–153 (4th ed.); Prichard, supra note 20, at 345.

28. Prichard, supra note 20, at 346; see also Cass, supra note 23, at 79–80 and n.23. Surrendering a child causes great and prolonged grief to the birth parent. See Eva Y. Deykin, Lee Campbell, and Patricia Patti, "The Postadoption Experience of Surrendering Parents," 54 *American Journal of Orthopsychiatry* 271, 278–80 (1984).

29. Landes and Posner, supra note 22, at 329–330; Prichard, supra note 20, at 345–346.

30. Landes and Posner, supra note 22, at 329; Cass, supra note 23, at 79.

31. See, e.g., Alaska Code §25.24.150(c); Ariz. Rev. Stat. §25–403; Ark. Stat. §9–13–101; Cal. Civ. Code §3011(d); Joseph Goldstein, Anna Freud, and Albert Solnit, *Beyond the Best Interests of the Child* (1973); Robert F. Cochran, Jr., "The Search for Guidance in Determining the Best Interests of the Child at Divorce: Reconciling the Primary Caretaker and Joint Custody Preferences," 20 *University of Richmond Law Review* 1 (1985); Elizabeth S. Scott, "Pluralism, Parental Preference, and Child Custody," 80 *California Law Review* 615 (1992); Woodhouse, supra note 19; Michael H. v. Gerald G., 491 U.S. 110 (1989); Garska v. McCoy, 278 S.E.2d 357 (W. Va. 1981).

32. Michael H. v. Gerald D., 491 U.S. 110 (1989); In re Baby M, 537 A.2d 1227 (N.J. 1988). See generally Scott and Scott, supra note 19.

33. See, e.g., Michael H. v. Gerald D., 491 U.S. 110 (1989); Parham v. J. R., 442 U.S. 584 (1979); Santosky v. Kramer, 455 U.S. 745 (1982); Gary Crippen, "Stumbling beyond the Best Interests of the Child: Reexamining Child Custody Standard-Setting in the Wake of Minnesota's Four-Year Experiment with the Primary Caretaker Preference," 75 *Minnesota Law Review* 427 (1990).

34. May v. Anderson, 345 U.S. 528 (1953).

35. Scarpetta v. Spence-Chapin Adoption Serv., 269 N.E.2d 787 (N.Y.), cert denied, 404 U.S. 805 (1971); Matter of Baby M, 537 A.2d 1227 (N.J. 1988).

36. Landes and Posner, supra note 22, at 343.

37. Posner, supra note 20; Posner, *Economic Analysis of Law,* supra note 22, at 152 (4th ed.). Cass, supra note 23, at 75, 82; Cohen, supra note 23, at 169–171, and Prichard, supra note 20, at 352, 354, do discuss the problem briefly from the children's viewpoint.

38. Posner, supra note 20, at 66; Prichard, supra note 20, at 353–354.

39. Prichard, supra note 20, at 346.

40. See, e.g., Richard A. Posner, "Theories of Economic Regulation," 5 *Bell Journal of Economics and Management Science* 335 (1974); see also George J. Stigler, *The Citizen and the State: Essays on Regulation* (1975).

41. Agencies therefore prefer mature two-parent couples who have relatively high incomes, heterosexual preferences, and conventional religious practices.

42. *Adoption Factbook,* supra note 15, 22–33.

43. See generally Margaret F. Brinig, "The Effect of Transactions Costs on the Market for Babies," 18 *Seton Hall Legislative Law Journal* 553 (1994).

44. *Adoption Factbook,* supra note 15, at 22–33.

45. There are *ex post* checks if parents are unfit, and occasionally newborns are removed from homes where parents have abused older siblings.

46. For a discussion of the history of foster care, see Tim Hacsi, "From Indenture to Family Foster Care: A Brief History of Child Placing," 74 *Child Welfare* 162 (1995).

47. See, e.g., Jamil Zainaldin, "The Emergence of a Modern American Family Law: Child Custody, Adoption, and the Courts, 1796–1851," 73 *Northwestern University Law Review* 1038, 1083 (1979), for a description of the history of foster care.

48. See, e.g., Robert H. Mnookin, "Foster Care: In Whose Best Interests?" 43 *Harvard Education Review* 599 (1973).

49. See, e.g., Mnookin, supra note 48; see also Katherine T. Bartlett, "Rethinking Parenthood as an Exclusive Status: The Need for Legal Alternatives When the Premise of the Nuclear Family Has Failed," 70 *Virginia Law Review* 879 (1984); Marsha Garrison, "Child Welfare Decisionmaking: In Search of the Least Drastic Alternative," 75 *Georgetown Law Journal* 1745, 1798–99 (1987).

50. See, e.g., Mnookin, supra note 48, stating, for example, that according to one study, 62 percent of foster children in San Francisco could be expected to remain in foster care until they reached majority.

51. Rebecca Hager and Maria Scannapieco, "From Family Duty to Family Policy: The Evolution of Kinship Care," 74 *Child Welfare* 200 (1995).

52. This was a major concern for plaintiff's counsel in Smith v. OFFER, 431 U.S. 816 (1977). She stated that "the book was the case," that is, the foster mother had become the children's "psychological parent," the critical person according to Goldstein, Freud, and Solnit, supra note 31.

53. See, e.g., Toni Locy, "Receiver Takes Over City Agency; Official to Revamp Child Welfare System," *Washington Post,* B1 (August 12, 1995) (five thousand at-risk children).

54. Stephen Ross, "The Economic Theory of Agency: The Principal's Problem," *American Economic Review* 134 (1973). See also Joseph Stiglitz, "Principal and Agent," 3 *New Palgrave Encyclopedia* 966 (1987).

55. Ross, supra note 54.

56. Id. The classic lawyer's counterpart can be found in Warren Seavey, "The Rationale of Agency," 29 *Yale Law Journal* 859 (1920).

57. For more, see e.g., Ross, supra note 54; Kenneth Arrow, "Economics of Agency: An Overview," in *Principals and Agents: The Structure of Business* 37 (John Pratt and Richard Zeckhauser, eds., 1985). See also Bengt Holmström, "Moral Hazard and Observability," 10 *Bell Journal of Economics* 74 (1979); Steven Shavell, "Risk Sharing and Incentives in the Principal and Agent Relationships," 10 *Bell Journal of Economics* 55 (1979); Sanford Grossman and Oliver Hart, "An Analysis of the Principal-Agent Problem," 51 *Econometrica* 7 (1983).

58. Ross, supra note 54, at 138; Holmström, supra note 57.

59. See Michael Darby and Eli Karni, "Free Competition and the Optimal Amount of Fraud in Contracts," 16 *Journal of Law and Economics* 67 (1973); and George Akerlof, "The Market for 'Lemons': Quality Uncertainty and the Market Mechanism," 84 *Quarterly Journal of Economics* 488 (1970). It is applied to principals and agents in Holmström, supra note 57, at 76.

60. Robert Cooter and Bradley J. Freedman, "The Fiduciary Relationship: Its Economic Character and Legal Consequences," 66 *New York University Law Review* 1045 (1991); see also Arrow, supra note 57, at 43–45.

61. See, e.g., Frank Knight, *Risk, Uncertainty, and Profit* (1933); Armen Alchian and Harold Demsetz, "Production, Information Costs, and Economic Organization," 62 *American Economic Review* 777 (1972); Michael Jensen and William Meckling, "Theory of the Firm: Managerial Behavior, Agency Costs, and Ownership Structure," 3 *Journal of Financial Economics* 305 (1976); Oliver Hart, "An Economist's Perspective on the Theory of the Firm," 89 *Columbia Law Review* 1757 (1989); Bengt Holmström and Robert Tirole, "The Theory of the Firm," 1 Yale School of Organization and Management Working Paper no. 35 (1987); Stiglitz, supra note 54.

62. The workers usually need capital as well, but that complicates this analysis.

63. The concept dates from Adam Smith's *Wealth of Nations* (bk. 1, chap. 2, 1776) and was explained by Ronald Coase in *The Firm, the Market, and the Law* 36–40 (1988).

64. Ronald Coase, "The Nature of the Firm," 4 *Economica* 386 (1937); reprinted in Coase, supra note 63, at 33.

65. See, e.g., Jensen and Meckling, supra note 61; Alan Bromberg and Larry Ribstein, *Bromberg and Ribstein on Partnership* (1988); Larry Ribstein and Henry Butler, "Free at Last? The Contractual Theory of the Corporation and the New Maryland Officer-Director Liability Provisions," 18 *University of Baltimore Law Review* 352 (1989); Henry Butler, "The Contractual Theory of the Corporation," 11 *George Mason University Law Review* 99 (1989).

66. See Alchian and Demsetz, supra note 61.

67. George Akerloff and Janet Yellin, *Efficiency Wage Models of the Labor Market* (1986); Stiglitz, supra note 54, at 970; Joseph Stiglitz and Andrew Weiss, "Incentive Effects of Terminations: Applications to the Credit and Labor Markets," 73 *American Economic Review* 912 (1983).

68. Cooter and Freedman, supra note 60, at 1065.

69. Id. at 1069.

70. 20 N.Y. 268 (Ct. App. 1859). This insight may be less obvious in the third-party beneficiary case of Seaver v. Ransom, 120 N.E. 639 (N.Y. 1918) (helpful niece recovered when uncle refused to execute dying aunt's intentions), than in Lawrence v. Fox, in which the defendant quite clearly was seeing what he could get away with.

71. Ratification is in some senses like the reliance implied in §302 of the *Restatement*

of Contracts (Second), Illustration 3(d): "[I]f the beneficiary would be reasonable in relying on the promise as manifesting an intention to confer a right on him, he is an intended beneficiary."

72. See Institute of Judicial Administration and American Bar Association, *Juvenile Justice Standards Project: Standards Relating to Abuse and Neglect* §6.6 (D)(1976). See also John T. Pardeck, *The Forgotten Children: A Study of the Stability and Continuity of Foster Care* (1982).

73. Compare Yoram Weiss and Robert Willis, "Children as Collective Goods and Divorce Settlements," 3 *Journal of Labor Economics* 268 (1985).

74. See Smith v. OFFER, 431 U.S. 816 (1977), and DeShaney v. Winnebago Co. Dept. Soc. Servs., 489 U.S. 189 (1989); Madeleine L. Kurtz, "The Purchase of Families into Foster Care: Two Case Studies and the Lessons they Teach," 26 *Connecticut Law Review* 1453 (1994); Betty R. Mandell, *Where Are the Children? A Class Analysis of Foster Care and Adoption* (1973); Richard Kagan and Shirley Schlosberg, *Families in Perpetual Crisis* (1989).

75. For example, the Court rejected a similar argument made by amicus in Doe v. Kirchner, 115 S.Ct. 2599 (1995). See also In the Interest of G.C., 735 A.2d 1226 (Pa. 1999), in which foster parents were not allowed to intervene in a custody case.

76. See, e.g., Matter of J. C., 417 S.2d 529 (Miss. 1982).

77. Weiss and Willis, supra note 73, at 270 (citing Paul Samuelson, "Diagrammatic Exposition of the Theory of Public Expenditures," 37 *Review of Economics and Statistics* 350 [1955]). See also Martin Zelder, "Inefficient Dissolutions as a Consequence of Public Goods: The Case of No-Fault Divorce," 22 *Journal of Legal Studies* 503 (1994).

78. On the connection between visitation and attachment to children, see Judith A. Seltzer, "Father by Law: Effects of Joint Legal Custody on Nonresident Fathers' Involvement with Children," NSFH Working Paper no. 75, University of Wisconsin, Center for Demography and Ecology (1997).

79. See Mnookin, supra note 48.

80. Weiss and Willis, supra note 73, at 269. See, e.g., Lenore Weitzman, "Economics of Divorce: Social and Economic Consequences of Property, Alimony, and Child Support Awards," 28 *UCLA Law Review* 1181 (1981).

81. Weiss and Willis, supra note 73, at 270.

82. Jessica Pearson and Nancy Thoennes, *Child Custody and Child Support: A Literature Review and Preliminary Data Analysis* (1984).

83. Weiss and Willis, supra note 73, at 288; David Chambers, "Rethinking the Substantive Rules for Custody Disputes in Divorce," 83 *Michigan Law Review* 477 (1984); Jerry W. McCant, "The Cultural Contradiction of Fathers as Nonparents," 21 *Family Law Quarterly* 127 (1987).

84. See J. M. A. v. State, 542 P.2d 170 (Alaska 1975).

85. For examples, see Matter of J. C., 417 So.2d 529 (Miss. 1982); In re Haun, 286 N.2d 478 (Ohio Ct. App. 1972).

86. Cooter and Freedman, supra note 60.

87. See, e.g., Maureen P. Kieffer, "Child Abuse in Foster Homes: A Rationale for Pursuing Causes of Action against the Placement Agency," 28 *St. Louis University Law Journal* 975 (1984). Compare Rosenblatt v. Birnbaum, 212 N.E.2d 37 (N.Y. 1965).

88. See Watson v. Shepard, 229 S.E.2d 897 (Va. 1976); and see generally Goldstein, Freud, and Solnit, supra note 31.

89. See, e.g., In Interest of Kingsley., no. JU90–5245 (Fla. Cir. Ct. 1992); see George H. Russ, "Through the Eyes of a Child, 'Gregory K.': A Child's Right to Be Heard," 27 *Family Law Quarterly* 365 (1993). See generally Richard J. Delaney and Frank R. Kunstal, *Troubled Transplants: Unconventional Strategies for Helping Disturbed Foster and Adoptive Children* 7–8, 14 (1993).

90. See Karen Czapanskiy, "Child Support and Visitation: Rethinking the Connections," 20 *Rutgers Law Journal* 619 (1989). The court, however, may provide noncontractual sanctions for parental misbehavior, such as incarceration for contempt and occasionally a change in the custody order. See, e.g., Va. Code Ann. §20–108.

91. See, e.g., Va. Code Ann. §16.1–290.

92. In re Gregory K. is the exception. See Christina Dugger Sommer, Note, "Empowering Children: Granting Foster Children the Right to Initiate Parental Rights Termination Proceedings," 79 *Cornell Law Review* 1200 (1994). For a limitation on children's rights to sue their abusive parents after they had been removed and placed in foster care, see Burnette v. Wahl, 588 P.2d 1005 (Ore. 1978).

93. An unemancipated minor cannot sue on his own behalf, but someone else could always file for the child.

94. See DeShaney v. Winnebago Co. Dep't. of Soc. Servs., 489 U.S. 189 (1989).

95. Douglas Bernheim, Andre Shleifer, and Lawrence Summers, "The Strategic Bequest Motive," 93 *Journal of Political Economy* 1045, 1049 (1985). See also Gary Becker, "A Theory of Social Interactions," 82 *Journal of Political Economy* 1063 (1974).

96. See, e.g., Commonwealth ex rel Mickey v. Mickey, 280 A.2d 417 (Pa. Super. Ct. 1971); Fritschler v. Fritschler, 208 N.W.2d 336 (Wis. 1973); Thomas v. Thomas, 335 S.W.2d 827 (Tenn. 1960).

97. See, e.g., Bloch v. Bloch, 112 N.W.2d 923, 927 (Wis. 1961); Radford v. Matczuk, 164 A.2d 904 (Md. 1960); Judith Wallerstein and Sandra Blakeslee, *Second Chances: Men, Women, and Children: A Decade after Divorce* 233–235, 237–239 (1989); Mavis Hetherington, Martha Cox, and Roger Cox, "Effects of Divorce on Parents and Children," in *Nontraditional Families: Parenting and Child Development* (M. Lamb, ed., 1982); Czapanskiy, supra note 90, at 636–637; Carolyn E. Taylor, Note, "Making Parents Behave: The Conditioning of Child Support and Visitation Rights," 84 *Columbia Law Review* 1059 (1984); Dee Wagner Phelps, "Child Support v. Rights to Visitation: Equity, Economics, and the Rights of the Child," 16 *Stetson Law Review* 139 (1986).

98. For two such examples, see Carter v. Dinwiddie Co. Dep't. of Soc. Servs., 1993 Va. App. LEXIS 149; and Matter of Adoption of Francisco A., 866 P.2d 1175 (N.M. Ct. App. 1993).

99. Doe v. Kirchner, 515 U.S. 1152 (1995). See Woodhouse, supra note 19.

100. For concerns about unfairness, see, e.g., Leroy H. Pelton, *For Reasons of Poverty: A Critical Analysis of the Public Child Welfare System in the United States* (1989).

101. See also Bartlett, supra note 49; and Stacy Robinson, "Remedying Our Foster Care System: Recognizing Children's Voices," 27 *Family Law Quarterly* 395 (1993).

102. The studies cited in Mnookin, supra note 48, suggest the right idea but are too old.

103. Thus the observations of Cooter and Freedman, supra note 60, are particular useful, as are those of Scott and Scott, supra note 19.

104. One exception is the removal case of Rivera v. Marcus, 696 F.2d 1016 (2d Cir. 1982), where the foster mother was also the children's blood relative.

105. Judith A. Seltzer, "Consequences of Marital Dissolution for Children," 1994 *Annual Review of Sociology* 235.

106. See also June Carbone and Margaret F. Brinig, "Rethinking Marriage: Feminist Ideology, Economic Change, and Divorce Reform," 65 *Tulane Law Review* 953, 1007 (1991); June Carbone, "Income Sharing: Redefining the Family in Terms of Community," 31 *Houston Law Review* 359 (1994).

107. This may be when they identify their own traits in their child, whether mathematical ability or nervous habits. Also, children after a certain age are more fun, and being with them has its own entertainment value. From an evolutionary standpoint, these children have lived past the danger age and will likely survive to adulthood.

108. Compare Martha A. Fineman, *The Neutered Mother, the Sexual Family, and Other Twentieth-Century Disasters* (1994).

109. See Anderson and Tollison, supra note 4. The "lumping together" phenomenon is my characterization of Gary Becker's treatment of children in his *Treatise on the Family,* supra note 5. See especially chap. 8, the "Rotten Kid Syndrome."

110. Ira Lupu, "The Separation of Powers and the Protection of Children," 61 *University of Chicago Law Review* 1317 (1994).

111. Margaret F. Brinig and F. H. Buckley, "The Price of Virtue," 98 *Public Choice* 111 (1999).

112. Fineman, supra note 108.

113. Stephen D. Sugarman, "Financial Support of Children and the End of Welfare as We Know It," 81 *Virginia Law Review* 2523 (1995); Sara Ruddick, "Procreative Choice for Adolescent Women," 126, and Diana M. Pearce, "'Children Having Children': Teenage Pregnancy and Public Policy from the Woman's Perspective," 46, both in *The Politics of Pregnancy: Adolescent Sexuality and Public Policy* (Annette Lawson and Deborah Rhode, eds., 1993).

114. Daniel P. Moynihan, *The Negro Family: The Case for National Action,* Department of Labor, Office of Policy Planning and Research (1965).

115. Judith Havemann and Helen Dewar, "Dole Courts Consensus on Welfare; Reform Plan Carries Tough Work Mandates," *Washington Post,* (August 8, 1995).

116. Anne M. Hill and June O'Neill, *Underclass Behaviors in the United States: Measurement and Analysis of Determinants* (rev. 1993); Roger A. Wojtkiewicz, Sara McLanahan, and Irwin Garfinkel, "The Growth of Families Headed by Women, 1950–80," 27 *Demography* 19 (1990).

117. Panel on High-Risk Youth, Commission on Behavior and Social Sciences Education, National Resource Council, *Adolescents in High-Risk Settings* (1993).

118. Andrew Peyton Thomas, *Crime and the Sacking of America: The Roots of Chaos* (1994).

119. E. Mavis Hetherington, Martha Cox, and Roger Cox, "Effects of Divorce on Parents and Children," in *Non-traditional Families: Parenting and Child Development* 233 (Michael Lamb, ed., 1982).

120. J. J. Card, "Long-Term Consequences of Divorce for Children of Teenage Parents," 18 *Demography* 137 (1981); compare Hill and O'Neill, supra note 116.

121. Lisabeth Dilalla et al., "Aggression and Delinquency: Family and Environmental Factors," 17 *Journal of Youth and Adolescence* 233 (1988); Judith Wallerstein and Joan B. Kelly, "Fathers and Children," in *Anthology on Fatherhood* (S. Cath et al., eds., 1982); Judith Wallerstein and Joan B. Kelly, *Surviving the Breakup: How Children and Parents Cope with Divorce* (1980).

122. Douglas Smith and Roger G. Jarjoura, "Social Structure and Criminal Victimization," 25 *Journal of Research in Crime and Delinquency* 27 (1988).

123. See, e.g., Chong-Bum An, Robert Haveman, and Barbara Wolfe, "Teen Out-of-Wedlock Births and Welfare Receipt: The Role of Childhood Events and Economic Circumstances," 75 *Review of Economics and Statistics* 195 (1993); Robert Moffitt, "Incentive Effects of the U.S. Welfare System: A Review," 30 *Journal of Economic Literature* 1 (1992); Sara S. McLanahan and Irwin Garfinkel, "Single Mothers, the Underclass, and Social Policy," 501 *Annals,* AAPSS 92 (1989); Peter Gottschalk, "AFDC Participation across Generations," 80 *American Economic Review* 367 (1990).

124. Becker, Landes, and Michael, supra note 13.

125. Selwyn M. Smith, Ruth Hanson, and Shiela Nobel, "Social Aspects of the Battered Baby Syndrome," in *Child Abuse: Commission and Omission* 217 (Joanne V. Cook and Roy T. Bowles, eds., 1980).

126. Lawrence Ganong and Marilyn Coleman, "An Exploratory Study of Step-sibling Subsystems," 19 *Journal of Divorce and Remarriage* 125 (1993); Kay Peeley, Mary G. Koch, and Marilyn Ihinger-Tallman, "Problems in Remarriage: An Exploratory Study of Intact and Terminated Remarriages," 20 *Journal of Divorce and Remaerriage* 63 (1993).

127. Under the Personal Responsibility and Work Opportunity Reconciliation Act of 1996, 42 U.S.C. §§603 et seq., this is termed a cash grant.

128. Robert O'Harrow and Patricia Davis, "Faces of Welfare; Single Women, Fatherless Children," *Washington Post,* A14 (June 29, 1995).

129. Margaret F. Brinig, "Rings and Promises," 6 *Journal of Law, Economics, and Organization* 203, 205 (1990); George A. Akerlof, Janet L. Yellin, and Michael L. Katz, "An Analysis of Out-of-Wedlock Childbearing in the United States," 111 *Quarterly Journal of Economics* 277 (1996).

130. Walter Wadlington, "Shotgun Marriage by Operation of Law," 1 *Georgia Law Review* 183 (1967).

131. Robert Moffitt, "Has State Redistribution Policy Grown More Conservative? AFDC, Food Stamps, and Medicaid, 1960–84," Discussion Paper 851–88, University of Wisconsin, Institute for Research on Poverty, 1988.

132. See J. Mark Ramseyer, "The Market for Children: Evidence from Early Modern Japan," 11 *Journal of Law, Economics, and Organization* 127 (1995).

133. 434 U.S. 374 (1978).

134. Roe v. Wade, 410 U.S. 113 (1973); Skinner v. Oklahoma, 316 U.S. 535, 541–542 (1942).

135. Com. ex rel. Holland-Moritz v. Holschuh, 292 A.2d 380 (Pa. 1972), State v. Meyers, 183 S.E.2d 42 (Ga. Ct. App. 1971); Mullen v. Mullen, 49 S.E.2d 349 (Va. 1948); Comment, "Emerging Rights," supra note 20, at 982: "Our system enshrines the biological tie and assumes that children belong with their biological parents at almost any cost."

136. See, e.g., Va. Ann. Code §63.1–204C(1). See generally Susan Yates Ely, "Natural Parents' Right to Withdraw Consent to Adoption: How Far Should the Right Extend?" 1992–93 *University of Louisville Journal of Family Law* 685.

137. Johnson v. Cupp, 274 N.E.2d 411 (Ind. App. 1971). See Scott and Scott, supra note 19, at 2433–34.

138. Deykin, Campbell, and Patti, supra note 28.

139. See, e.g., Engstrom v. State, 461 N.W.2d 309, 319 (Iowa 1990); see generally Comment, "Emerging Rights," supra note 20.

140. The exact frequency is unknown. See, e.g., *Adoption Factbook*, supra note 15, at 170 (up to 10 percent of cases); see also David K. Leavitt, "The Model Adoption Act: Return to a Balanced View of Adoption," 19 *Family Law Quarterly* 141, 153 (1985)(less than 2 percent of California cases); Comment, supra note 21, at 967 and n.258 (4 percent of California cases).

141. Goldstein, Freud, and Solnit, supra note 31, at 32–33, 36; Comment, supra note 21, at 977.

142. See Milton Friedman and L. R. Savage, "A Utility Analysis of Choices Involving Risk," *Journal of Political Economy* 279, 290 (1948); Robert Jerry, *Understanding Insurance Law* 11–15 (1987); Ejan Mackaay, *Economics of Information and Law*

173–174 (1982). For nuclear power, consider Duke Power Co. v. Carolina Environmental Study Group, 438 U.S. 59, 85–86 (1978).

143. Transracial adoption is discussed briefly in the law reform section of Chapter 7. See also Carl E. Schneider and Margaret F. Brinig, *An Invitation to Family Law* 1073–75 (1996).

144. See, e.g., Cal. Civ. Code §221.63; Iowa Code §600.1; Tenn. Code Ann. §36–1–101; Michael H. v. Gerald D., 491 U.S. 110 (1989); Uniform Marriage and Divorce Act, 9A U.L.A. 197 (1979); Robert Mnookin, "Child Custody Adjudication: Judicial Functions in the Face of Indeterminacy," 39 *Law and Contemporary Problems* 226, 236 (1975).

145. See Note, "Lawyering for the Child: Principles of Representation in Custody and Visitation Disputes Arising from Divorce," 87 *Yale Law Journal* 1126 (1978).

146. Parham v. J. R., 442 U.S. 584 (1979). See also Matter of Spence Chapin Adoption Service v. Polk, 274 N.E.2d 431, 436 (N.Y. 1971).

147. Goldstein, Freud, and Solnit, supra note 31, at 53.

148. See, e.g., Malpass v. Morgan, 192 S.E.2d 794 (Va. 1972).

149. Stanley v. Illinois, 405 U.S. 645 (1972).

150. 502 N.W.2d 649 (Mich. 1993). This case is analyzed at length in Scott and Scott, supra note 19, at 2407–11.

151. 502 N.W.2d at 697–698, 670–671 (Levin, J., dissenting). The court ruled, "While a child has a constitutionally protected interest in family life, that interest is not independent of its parents' in the absence of a showing that the parents are unfit." Id. at 665–666.

152. As the New York Court of Appeals stated in Bennett v. Jeffreys, 356 N.E.2d 277, 281 (N.Y. 1976).

153. *Adoption Factbook,* supra note 15, at 34.

154. Ankenbrandt v. Richards, 504 U.S. 689 (1992).

155. See Swift and Co. v. United States, 196 U.S. 375, 398 (1905)(Holmes, J.).

156. See, e.g., Clarkson v. Bliley, 38 S.E.2d 22, 26 (Va. 1946); see generally Zainaldin, supra note 47, at 1083.

157. Mass. Gen. Laws ch. 210, §2; Miss. Code Ann. §93–17–9; C. C. I. v. Natural Parents, 398 So. 2d 220 (Miss. 1981); and Utah Code Ann. §78–30–4.14.

158. 398 So. 2d 220 (Miss. 1981).

159. Id. at 225. See also Golz v. Children's Bureau of New Orleans, Inc., 326 So.2d 865 (La. 1976).

160. See Alaska Stat. §25.23.070; Ark. Stat. Ann. §9–9–209; 13 Del. Code tit. 13 §909; Ga. Code Ann. §19–8–26; Treiber v. Stong, 617 P.2d 114 (Kan. Ct. App. 1980); Md. Family Code Ann. §5–311; Mich. Comp. Laws §710.29; In re Blankenship, 418 N.W.2d 919 (Mich. Ct. App. 1988); and 10 Okla. Stat. §7503–2.7.

161. These changes of heart, or at least feelings of regret, are nearly inevitable for parents who relinquish their children. Johnson v. Cupp, 274 N.E.2d 411 (Ind. Ct.

App. 1971). Regret occurs even when the parent knows before conception that the child will be placed for adoption, as can be seen from surrogate cases. Matter of Baby M., 537 A.2d 1227 (N.J. 1988); Johnson v. Calvert, 851 P.2d 776 (Cal. 1993).

162. Matter of Blankenship, 418 N.W.2d 919, 922 (Mich. Ct. App. 1988).

163. See Ala. Code §26–10A-13; Conn. Gen. Stat. §17a–112; Bailey v. Mars, 87 A.2d 388 (Conn. 1952); Fla. Stat. §63.082; Idaho Code §16–1504; De Bernardi v. State Bd., 723 P.2d 829 (Idaho 1986); 750 Ill. Rev. Stat. art. 50/11; In re David, 256 A.2d 583 (Me. 1969); Minn. Stat. §259.24(6)(a); Mo. Rev. Stat. §453.030; In re Mayernick, 292 S.W.2d 562 (Mo. 1956); Neb. Rev. Stat. §43–104; Kellie v. Lutheran Fam. Serv., 305 N.W.2d 874 (Neb. 1981); Nev. Rev. Stat. §127.080; Blanchard v. Nevada State Welfare Dep't., 542 P.2d 737 (Nev. 1975); N.J. Rev. Stat. Ann. §9:2–16, N.M. Stat. Ann. §32A-5-21(F); Kira M. v. New Mexico, 864 P.2d 803 (N.M. Ct. App. 1993); R.I. Gen. Laws §15–7–6; In re Julie, 334 A.2d 212 (R.I. 1975); S.C. Code Ann. §20–7–1720; Vt. Stat. Ann. tit. 15, §2–408(b); In re M and G, 321 A.2d 19 (Vt. 1974); Va. Code Ann. §63.1–225; Wash. Rev. Code §20–7–1720; W. Va. Code §48–4–5; Wis. Stat. §48.46; In re D. L. S., 332 N.W.2d 293 (Wis. 1983); Wyo. Stat. §1–22–109(d); In re Parental Rights of T. R., 772 P.2d 1106 (Wyo. 1982).

164. Laidlow v. Oregon, 15 U.S. (2 Wheat.) 128 (1817); see generally Anthony Kronman, "Mistake, Disclosure, Information, and the Law of Contracts," 7 *Journal of Legal Studies* 1 (1978); Darby and Karni, supra note 59.

165. Ariz. Rev. Stat. Ann. §8–53l; Webb. v. Charles, 611 P.2d 562 (Ariz. Ct. App. 1980); Ind. Code §31–3–1–6(f); Thodes v. Shirley, 129 N.E.2d 60, 64 (Ind. 1955); Iowa Code §600.7; Ky. Rev. Stat. Ann. §199.540; Mont. Code Ann. §40–6–125(7); Matter of Male Child Born July 15, 718 P.2d 660 (Mont. 1968); N.H. Rev. Stat. Ann. §170-B:1; In re Adoption of Baby C., 480 A.2d 101 (N.H. 1984); N.Y. Dom. Rel. Law §111; Dickson v. Lascaris, 423 N.E.2d 361 (N.Y. 1981); N.C. Gen. Stat. §48–3–608; In re Kasim, 293 S.E.2d 247 (N.C. Ct. App. 1982); N.D. Cent. Code §14–15–08; Oregon, Ore. Rev. Stat. §109.312(2); Small v. Andrews, 530 P.2d 540 (Ore. Ct. App. 1975); 23 Pa. Cons. Stat. Ann. §2711; Tex. Fam. Code Ann. §162.011.

166. See, e.g., Scarpetta v. Spence-Chapin Adoption Serv., 269 N.E.2d 787 (N.Y.), cert denied, 404 U.S. 805 (1971). See also Bennett v. Jeffreys, 356 N.E.2d 277, 281 (1976). As Lewis Kornhauser put it in a slightly different context, utility functions become interdependent, so that the usual assumption of convex indifference curves no longer holds; see Lewis Kornhauser, "The Great Image of Authority," *Stanford Law Review* 349, 361 and n.38 (1984).

167. See, e.g., Wartz v. Fleichman, 278 N.W.2d 266, 270–272 (Wis. Ct. App. 1978); Posner, "Economic Analysis of Law," supra note 22, at §4.7; Restatement (Second) Contracts §175.

168. 398 So. 2d 220 (Miss. 1981).

169. Id. at 223.

170. See, e.g., In re Adoption of Susko, 69 A.2d 132 (Pa. 1949); cf. Meyers v. State, 183 S.E. 2d 42 (Ga. Ct. App. 1971).

171. See Cal. Fam. Code §8814.5; Colo. Rev. Stat. §19–5–203; Custody of C. C. R. S., 872 P.2d 1337 (Colo. App. 1993); Haw. Rev. Stat. §578–2(b); Iowa Code §660.3; La. Children's Code §1123; Ohio Rev. Code Ann. §3107.081 (Baldwin); Morrow v. Catholic Charities, 504 N.E.2d 2 (Ohio 1986); Tenn. Code Ann. §37–1–117.
172. In many states, potential birth and adoptive parents can both advertise. See *Adoption Factbook,* supra note 15, at 22–33. Question 7 lists thirty-two states; pp. 121–122 contain examples of such advertisements.
173. Matter of Adoption of a Child by T. W. C., 636 A.2d 1083 (N.J. Super. Ct. App. Div. 1994).
174. 636 A.2d at 1089.
175. N.J. Stat. Ann. §9:3–46(a).
176. The number of adoptable children is very small. If the mother does not place her child with one set of parents, it will be easy to secure another set to adopt her baby. The adoptive couple, by contrast, must start their search for a baby anew. Prichard, supra note 20, at 343, reports that in metropolitan Vancouver, thirty newborn children were available for adoption at a time when one thousand couples had been approved and were ready to receive an adopted child.
177. See, e.g., Timothy J. Muris, "Opportunistic Behavior and the Law of Contracts," 1981 *Minnesota Law Review* 521; Brinig and Crafton, supra note 11; Lloyd Cohen, "Marriage, Divorce, and Quasi-rents, Or 'I Gave Him the Best Years of My Life,'" 16 *Journal of Legal Studies* 267 (1987).
178. See, e.g., Matter of Gregory B., 542 N.E.2d 1052 (N.Y. 1989); Curt Suplee, "The Ties That Bind: The Case for 'Open' Adoption," *Washington Post,* B4 (July 17, 1990).
179. This would permit contact with the child upon its reaching adulthood. See, e.g., John M. Stoxen, "The Best of Both 'Open' and 'Closed' Adoption Worlds: A Call for the Reform of State Statutes," 13 *Journal of Legislation* 292 (1986).
180. See, e.g., Comment, supra note 21, at 917.
181. Brinig, supra note 43.
182. States explicitly disallowing revocation received the score of 0. The list appears at note 160 supra. States with explicit revocation periods were given the value of the length of the period. The lists are at note 163 supra (short periods) and note 165 supra (longer periods). If withdrawal of consent is allowed before placement with the adoptive family, or the statute allows withdrawal only if there was fraud and coercion, the state was awarded a 50, as in the states listed in note 165, supra. If withdrawal is allowed before the final decree in the best interests of the child, the value was 75; see states in note 171 supra. If a parent could withdraw consent at any time before the final adoption decree, the value was 360; the list appears at note 165 supra. If the parent may withdraw consent at any time, I awarded a score of 500; see note 165 supra.
183. The number of adoptions came from *Adoption Factbook,* supra note 15, at 80–81 (table 1).

184. The number of households appears in U.S. Department of Commerce, Bureau of the Census, *Statistical Abstract* (1990).

185. See, e.g., "A World without Fathers: The Struggle to Save the Black Family," *Newsweek,* 16 (August 30, 1993), suggesting that for the Afro-American segment of the population, single parenthood is becoming the norm rather than the exception. See also Comment, supra note 21, at 919 and n.17.

186. This number is reported in *Adoption Factbook,* supra note 15, at 96–97 (table 9).

187. This number was obtained from *Statistical Abstract,* supra note 184.

188. These numbers came from the United States Department of Labor, Bureau of Labor Statistics, *Monthly Labor Reports* (1987). The number of infertile couples in the United States "rose from about one in ten in the 1950s to about one in six in the mid-1970's." Lincoln Caplan, *An Open Adoption* 40 (1990). The relationship between infertility and age in women is discussed in Resolve, Inc., *When You're Wishing for a Baby: Myths and Facts* (1989); and *Infertility: Medical, Emotional, and Social Considerations* 3 (M. Mazor and H. Simons, eds., 1984). See also Comment, supra note 20, at 931–932; Landes and Posner, supra note 22.

189. Akerlof, supra note 59. The lemons problem is briefly discussed by Prichard, supra note 20, at 349.

190. See, e.g., Darby and Karni, supra note 59, at 165; Phillip Nelson, "Information and Consumer Behavior," 78 *Journal of Political Economy* 311 (1970).

191. Placement of handicapped children because of the baby shortage is acknowledged by Cass, supra note 23, and is one of the primary reasons given by Cohen, supra note 23, for not allowing a free market.

192. See, e.g., Kevin Johnson, "Family Sues over Adoption," *USA Today,* 3A (March 8, 1990); Richard Barth and Marianne Berry, *Adoption and Disruption: Rates, Risks, and Responses* 112–113, 169 (1988); Trudy Festinger, *Necessary Risk: A Study of Adoptions and Disrupted Adoption Placements* 40 (1986). The category also includes siblings who need to be placed together and older children who have been removed from their parents' custody because of abuse or neglect. *Adoption Factbook,* supra note 15, at 184. Public agencies place about 50 percent of these children. *Adoption Factbook* at 175. Since there are too few homes available for them, they frequently remain unadopted. See, e.g., "The Baby Chase," *Time,* 86 (October 9, 1989). *Adoption Factbook* at 184 reports that in 1989, approximately 21,600 special needs children were awaiting adoption.

193. These are discussed in Cass, Cohen, and Frankel and Miller, all cited supra, note 23.

194. There are also the usual public choice reasons of maximizing the agency's budget and power for placing a large number of children. See, e.g., Dianne Klein, "'Special' Children; Dark Past Can Haunt Adoptions," *L.A. Times,* 1, 32 (May 29, 1988) (numbers are an indication of a social worker's efficiency, and statistics justify staff); compare William A. Niskanen, *Bureaucracy and Representative* (1971). See generally Sharon F. Gustafson, "Regulating Adoption Intermediaries: Ensuring

That the Solutions Are No Worse Than the Problem," 3 *Georgetown Journal of Legal Ethics* 837 (1990).

195. See, e.g., Stigler, supra note 40; In re Baby Girl D, 517 A.2d 925 (Pa. 1986).

196. Annette Baran and Reuben Pannor, "Open Adoption," in *The Psychology of Adoption* 316, 318 (David Brodzinsky and Marshall D. Schechter, eds., 1990). At least the parties can meet and discuss family and health histories and aspirations. Because the relationship may continue after relinquishment, there are greater incentives to be truthful. See generally Caplan, supra note 188; Ruth G. McRoy, Harold D. Grotevant, and Kerry L. White, *Openness in Adoption: New Practices, New Issues* (1988); Carol M. Amadio and Stuart L. Deutsch, "Open Adoption: Allowing Adopted Children to 'Stay in Touch' with Blood Relatives," 22 *Journal of Family Law* 59 (1983–84). Compare Benjamin Klein and Keith Leffler, "The Role of Market Forces in Assuring Contractual Performance," 89 *Journal of Political Economy* 615 (1981).

197. See, e.g., Daniel Golden, "When Adoption Doesn't Work," *Boston Globe Magazine*, 16, 78–82 (June 11, 1989); Klein supra note 194, at 1.

198. See, e.g., Janet L. Dickson, "The Emerging Rights of Adoptive Parents: Substance or Specter," 38 *UCLA Law Review* 917, 951 and n.175 (1991).

199. See, e.g., Betty Reid Mandell, *Where Are the Children? A Class Analysis of Foster Care and Adoption* 78–79 (1973). Compare Robert Springer and J. E. Frech III, "Deterring Fraud: The Role of Resale Price Maintenance," 59 *Journal of Business* 433 (1986).

200. See, e.g., Klein, supra note 194 (sixty-nine failed adoptions in California between 1983 and 1987).

201. Burr v. Board of Co. Comm'rs., 491 N.E.2d 1101 (Ohio 1986); Meracle v. Children's Service Soc., 437 N.W.2d 532 (Wis. 1989); Michael J. v. County of Los Angeles Dep't. Adoptions, 247 Cal. Rptr. 504 (Cal. Ct. App. 1988); M. H. v. Caritas Family Services, 488 N.W.2d 282 (Minn. 1992); Gibbs v. Ernst, 150 Pa. Com. 154, 615 A.2d 851 (Pa. 1992); Mohr v. Commonwealth, 653 N.E.2d 1104 (Mass. 1995); Mallette v. Children's Friend and Service, 661 A.2d 67 (R.I. 1995); Jackson v. State. 1998 Mt. 46, 956 P.2d 35 (1998).

202. Burr v. Board of Co. Comm'rs., 491 N.E.2d 1101 (Ohio 1986); Meracle v. Children's Service Soc., 437 N.2d 532 (Wis. 1989); Michael J. v. County of Los Angeles Dep't. Adoptions, 247 Cal. Rptr. 504 (Cal. App. 1988).

203. 247 Cal. Rptr. at 513.

204. Engstrom v. State, 461 N.W.2d 309 (Iowa 1990); Allen v. Children's Services, 567 N.E.2d 1346 (Ohio Ct. App. 1990); Matter of Adoption of Baby Boy C., 596 N.Y.S.2d 56 (A.D. 1993); April v. Associated Catholic Charities, 629 S.2d 1295 (La. Ct. App. 1993); Foster v. Bass, 575 So. 2d 967 (Miss. 1990). In other cases, though the facts might have suggested recovery, the parents' claims were barred because of sovereign immunity (see Zernhelt v. Lehigh Co. Office of Children and Youth Servs., 659 A.2d 89 [Pa. Commw. 1995]; Hren v. Board of Co. Commr's., 1995

Ohio App. LEXIS 4012) or expiration of the statute of limitations (Henning v. Tuscarawas Co. Dep't. of Human Servs., 1996 Ohio. App. LEXIS 733).

205. Allen v. Children's Services, 567 N.E.2d 1346 (Ohio App. 1990).

206. Engstrom v. State, 461 N.W.2d 309 (Iowa 1990).

207. Foster v. Bass, 575 So. 2d 967 (Miss. 1990).

208. Id. at 984.

209. As we saw, this was a particular concern of Cass, supra note 23, and Cohen, supra note 23.

210. 537 A.2d 1227 (N.J. 1988).

211. 851 P.2d 776 (Cal. 1993).

212. The issue of surrogacy has spawned a wealth of scholarly articles. See Richard A. Epstein, "Surrogacy: The Case for Full Contractual Enforcement," 81 *Virginia Law Review* 2305 (1995); Margaret F. Brinig, "A Maternalistic Approach to Surrogacy: Comment on Richard Epstein's 'Surrogacy: The Case for Full Contractual Enforcement,'" 81 *Virginia Law Review* 2377 (1995); Anne Goodwin, "Determination of Legal Parentage in Egg Donation, Embryo Transplantation, and Gestational Surrogacy Arrangements," 26 *Family Law Quarterly* 275 (1992); Alexander M. Capron and Margaret Radin, "Choosing Family Law over Contract Law as a Paradigm for Surrogate Motherhood," in *Surrogate Motherhood: Politics and Privacy* (Larry Gostin, ed., 1990); Marjorie Maguire Shultz, "Reproductive Technology and Intent-Based Parenthood: An Opportunity for Gender Neutrality," 1990 *Wisconsin Law Review* 298; Herbert T. Krimmel, "Can Surrogate Parenting Be Stopped? An Inspection of the Constitutional and Pragmatic Aspects of Outlawing Surrogate Mother Arrangements," 1992 *Valparaiso University Law Review* 1.

213. See, e.g., Ariz. Rev. Stat. §25–218(A); Ala. Code §26–10A-34; Ark. Stat. §9–10–201; Cal. Rev. Code §§200, 8794; Ind. Stat. Ann. §31–20–1–1 and 31–20–1–2 (Burns); N.J. Rev. Stat. Ann. §168-B:-25.V (allowing so long as not for financial gain); N.Y. Dom. Rel. Law §§122 (prohibiting); Va. Code Ann. §§20–160.B.4 (regulating); Wash. Rev. Code §26.26.230 (not for financial gain). See generally Walter Wadlington, "Contracts to Bear a Child: The Mixed Legislative Signals," 29 *Idaho Law Review* 383 (1992–1993).

214. George Priest and Benjamin Klein, "The Selection of Disputes for Litigation," 13 *Journal of Legal Studies* 1 (1984).

215. Anthony T. Kronman, "Contract Law and the State of Nature," 1 *Journal of Law, Economics, and Organization* 5 (1985).

216. See Richard A. Epstein, "The Varieties of Self-Interest," 8 *Philosophy and Policy* 102 (1991); see also Matt Ridley, *The Red Queen: Sex and the Evolution of Human Nature* (1994); Robert Wright, *The Moral Animal: The New Science of Evolutionary Psychology* 35–36 (1994); Michael J. Trebilcock and Rosemin Keshvani, "The Role of Private Ordering in Family Law: A Law and Economics Perspective," 41 *University of Toronto Law Journal* 533, 572 (1992). Couples who use surrogacy and in vi-

tro techniques because of infertility problems may pass these problems on to their offspring, according to Doris Lambauch and David Page in *Human Reproduction* (July 1999); reported in Tina Hesman, "Parents Can Pass on Infertility, Study Shows," *Dallas Morning News*, 2for (July 5, 1999).

217. William Stern, the father in the Baby M case, wanted to have a child that was biologically his because the other members of his family had been killed in the Holocaust. Matter of Baby M, 537 A.2d 1235 (N.J. 1986). See also Richard A. Posner, "The Ethics and Economics, of Enforcing Contracts of Surrogate Motherhood," 5 *Journal of Contemporary Health Law and Policy* 22 (1989).

218. See Lori B. Andrews and Lisa Douglass, "Alternative Reproduction," 65 *Southern California Law Review* 623, 674 (1991); Jane Maslow Cohen, "Legal Claims of Coercive and Exploitative Agreement: Introducing Coercion-Feel," 94 *American Philosophical Association Newsletter* 99 (1994). Epstein, supra note 212, at 2319.

219. These are explored at some length in Brinig, supra note 212.

220. See, e.g., Matter of Baby M, 537 A.2d App. 1227, 1267 (N.J. 1988); see generally Judith Areen, "Baby M. Reconsidered," 76 *Georgetown Law Journal* 1741, 1754 (1988). Surrogacy statutes in New Hampshire and Virginia make people inducing any party to enter into a surrogacy contract guilty of a misdemeanor. N.H. Rev. Stat. Ann §§168-B:16(IV), 168-B:30(II); Va. Code. Ann. §20–165. Virginia also makes the broker civilly liable to the surrogate and intended parents for up to three times the amount charged by the broker. Va. Code Ann. §20–165(B).

221. See, e.g., Posner, supra note 217, at 21, 24–25.

222. Cohen, supra note 177, at 300. See also Trebilcock and Keshvani, supra note 216, at 584–585, who recommend a cooling-off period of seventy-two hours after childbirth in order to make "the two sides of the exchange more simultaneous" and confront the birth mother "with a more reasoned and informed choice." But see Note, "Rumpelstiltskin Revisited: The Inalienable Rights of Surrogate Mothers," 99 *Harvard Law Review* 1936, 1948–54 (1986).

223. Carl E. Schneider, "Surrogate Motherhood from the Perspective of Family Law," 13 *Harvard Journal of Law and Public Policy* 125, 138 (1990); Maurice Suh, "Surrogate Motherhood: An Argument for Denial of Specific Performance," 22 *Columbia Journal of Law and Social Problems* 357, 360–361 and n.17 (1989).

224. Posner argues that there may be "extortion" by the surrogate where the contracts cannot be specifically enforced. Richard A. Posner, *Sex and Reason* 422 (1992).

225. Va. Code Ann. §20–162(a)(3) provides for a twenty-five–day period in cases where there is a surrogacy arrangement that is not judicially approved.

226. Epstein, supra note 212, at 2337.

227. See Richard A. Epstein, "Why Restrain Alienation?" 85 *Columbia Law Review* 970, 990 (1985). See also June Carbone, "The Role of Contract Principles in Determining the Validity of Surrogacy Contracts," 28 *Santa Clara Law Review* 581, 582 (1988).

228. For discussions of Pareto optimality, see Jack Hirschleifer, *Price Theory and Appli-*

cations 496–497 (4th ed. 1988); Hal Varian, *Microeconomic Analysis* 5, 262–263 (2d ed. 1984).

229. At least the compensation occurs theoretically, according to Kaldor-Hicks optimality. See, e.g., P. R. G. Layard and A. A. Walters, *Microeconomic Theory* 32 (1978); Varian, supra note 228, at 218. The original articles are Nicholas Kaldor, "Welfare Properties of Economics and Interpersonal Comparisons of Utility," 49 *Economics Journal* 549–551 (1939); J. R. Hicks, "The Valuation of Social Income," 7 *Economica* 105–124 (1940).

230. This would include such conduct as drag racing, popularly called "chicken." See, e.g, In re Fox, Alleged Delinquent Child, 395 N.E.2d 918 (Ohio Ct. Com. Pleas 1979). For a game theoretic explanation, see Charles Goetz, *Cases and Materials on Law and Economics* 15–17 (1984).

231. This is the case in nuisance situations. See, e.g., Hart v. Wagner, 40 A.2d 47 (Md. Ct. App. 1944).

232. Cole v. Cole, 409 A.2d 734 (Md. Ct. Spec. App. 1979); Conway v. Conway, 395 S.E.2d 464 (Va. Ct. App. 1990).

233. See, e.g., Rohn v. Thuma, 408 N.E.2d 578 (Ind. Ct. App. 1980).

234. For example, adoption and custody matters are always conducted in the "best interests of the child." Parents cannot contract out of their duty to pay child support (Hogge v. Hogge, 16 Va. App. 520, 431 S.E.2d 656 [1993]; Richardson v. Moore, 217 Va. 422, 229 S.E.2d 864 [Va. 1976]), nor can they fail to provide medical care in life-threatening situations even if their own religion forbids it (Custody of a Minor, 375 Mass. 733, 379 N.E.2d 1053 [1978]; Hermanson v. State, 604 So. 2d 775 [Fla. 1992]; People in Interest of D. L. E, 645 P.2d 271 [Colo. 1982]). They are expected to protect their children because "natural bonds of affection lead parents to act in the best interests of their children." Parham v. J. R., 442 U.S. 584 (1979). They usually cannot make binding custody determinations either. Schneider, supra note 223, at 127; Trebilcock and Keshvani, supra note 216, at 577.

235. See also Posner, supra note 224, at 423 and n.31 (1992); Michelle Harrison, "Psychological Ramifications of 'Surrogate' Motherhood," in *Psychiatric Aspects of Reproductive Technology* 97, 103–105 (Nada L. Stotland, ed., 1990).

236. See, e.g., Armen A. Alchian and William R. Allen, *Exchange and Production: Competition, Coordination, and Control* 48–50 (3d ed. 1983). See also Posner, supra note 224, at 427, and Posner, supra note 217, at 30.

237. For example, in the debate over British surrogacy legislation, which ultimately prohibited commercial surrogate contracts, one speaker noted that "the distress . . . of infertile couples who are anxious to have a child should not be exploited [by commercial agencies] for financial gain." 464 Parl. Deb., H.L. (5th ser.) Col. 1521 (1985)(Eng.)(remarks of Lord Prys-Davies). For a discussion of the agency costs problems, see Trebilcock and Keshvani, supra note 216, at 587. For a discussion of "rent extraction" in the marriage context, see Cohen, supra note 23, at 285–289;

see also Marsha Garrison, "Surrogate Parenting: What Should Legislatures Do?" 22 *Family Law Quarterly* 149, 154–155 (1988).

238. Many couples have spent up to $100,000 in an attempt to achieve pregnancy through in vitro fertilization.

239. For a list of the state statutes, see Barbara L. Atwell, Note, "Surrogacy and Adoption: A Case of Incompatibility," 20 *Columbia Human Rights Law Review* 1, 29–39 and nn. 109, 110 (1988).

240. Va. Code Ann. §63.1–220.4.

241. See, e.g., Garrison, supra note 237; Prichard, supra note 20, at 343 (reporting increasing black market activity characterized by very high prices for newborns—as much as $40,000—but continued interest on the part of childless couples); Landes and Posner, supra note 22, at 338. See also Reuter, supra note 21. New York is one state that has completely outlawed commercial surrogacy contracts. N.Y. Dom. Rel. Law §§122; see also Mich. Stat. Ann. §722.855 (Callaghan 1992); Utah Code Ann. §76–7–204(1) to (3).

242. Andrews and Douglass, supra note 218, at 634.

243. Radin, supra note 24, at 853, 1905. See also Cass R. Sunstein, "Incommensurability and Valuation in Law," 1994 *Michigan Law Review* 779, 850; Joan Mahoney, "An Essay on Surrogacy and Feminist Thought," 16 *Law, Medicine, and Health Care* 81, 82 (1988).

244. Stein v. Stein, 831 S.W.2d 684 (Mo. Ct. App. 1992); and Fenn v. Fenn, 174 Ariz. 84, 847 P.2d 129 (Ariz. Ct. App. 1993).

245. Matter of Adoption of Baby Boy C., 596 N.Y.S.2d 56 (N.Y. A.D. 1993).

246. See, e.g., T. v. T., 224 S.E.2d 148 (Va. 1976); In re Adoption of Young, 364 A.2d 1307 (Pa. 1976); Atkinson v. Atkinson, 408 N.W.2d 516 (Mich. Ct. App. 1987). But see Simmons v. Comer, 438 S.E.2d 530 (W. Va. 1993); In re A. K., 620 N.E.2d 572 (Ill. Ct. App. 1993).

247. Whitlock v. Iowa District Court, 497 N.W.2d 891, 892 (Iowa 1993).

248. See In re Paternity of J. W. L., Ind. Ct. App., 1996, 23 Fam. L. Rptr. 1044.

249. See, e.g., Monahan v. Monahan, 153 N.E.2d 1 (Ill. 1958); Williams v. Murray, 236 S.E.2d 624 (Ga. 1977).

250. See, e.g., In re McConnell's Estate, 268 F. Supp. 346 (D.D.C. 1967). The states most likely to recognize equitable adoption will be those where common law marriage can be contracted. Clarkson v. Bliley, 38 S.E.2d 22 (Va. 1946).

251. Kupec v. Cooper, 593 So.2d 1176 (Fla. Dist. Ct. App. 1992).

252. Melvin Eisenberg, "Third-Party Beneficiaries," 92 *Columbia Law Review* 1358 (1992).

253. See, e.g., Carl E. Schneider and Robert Mnookin, "In the Interest of Children," 84 *Michigan Law Review* 919 (1986).

254. See Matter of Baby M., 537 A.2d 1227 (N.J. 1988); Johnson v. Calvert, 851 P.2d 776 (Cal. 1993).

255. Here is where I think my view is both similar to and unlike that of Elizabeth and Robert Scott, supra note 19. They believe that no legal actions between members of an ongoing family should be allowed. They use language such as "best efforts" and "utmost loyalty" to characterize the duties of parents.

4. Husband and Wife

1. See Saul Levmore, "Unconditional Relationships," 76 *Boston University Law Review* 807, 825 et seq. (1996); and Elizabeth S. Scott and Robert E. Scott, "Marriage as Relational Contract," 84 *Virginia Law Review* 1225 (1998).
2. For an example, see Amy Tan, "Rice Husband," in *The Joy Luck Club* (1992).
3. Cooper v. Cooper, 17 N.E. 892 (Mass. 1888).
4. Gary Becker, *Treatise on the Family*, chap. 2 (2d ed. enl. 1991). Compare Mary Ann Glendon, *The New Family and the New Property* (1980).
5. Milton C. Regan, *Family Law and the Pursuit of Intimacy* (1993).
6. Margaret F. Brinig, "Status, Contract, and Covenant: A Review of *Family Law and the Pursuit of Intimacy*," 79 *Cornell Law Review* 1573 (1994). See also Frances Olsen, "The Family and the Market: A Study of Ideology and Legal Reform," 96 *Harvard Law Review* 1497 (1983).
7. See June Carbone, *From Partners to Parents* (1999). Compare Martha Fineman, *The Neutered Mother, the Sexual Family, and Other Twentieth-Century Tragedies* (1995).
8. Carl E. Schneider, "Moral Discourse and the Transformation of American Family Law," 83 *Michigan Law Review* 1803, 1848 (1985).
9. See Becker, supra note 4. See also sources cited infra note 32. Compare Allen M. Parkman, *No-Fault Divorce: What Went Wrong?* 29–32 (1992) [hereinafter Parkman, *No-Fault*]; and "Why Are Married Women Working So Hard?" 18 *International Review of Law and Economics* 41 (1998) [hereinafter Parkman, "Married Women"].
10. John Demos, *A Little Commonwealth: Family Life in Plymouth Colony,* preface (1981)(quoting William Gouge, *Of Domesticall Duties* [1622]).
11. Quoting de Toqueville in her *Treatise on Domestic Economy* 5 (1841), Catharine Beecher writes: "The Americans have applied to the sexes the great principle of political economy, which governs the manufactories of our age, by carefully dividing the duties of man from those of woman, in order that the great work of society may be the better carried on."
12. Yoram Ben-Porath, "The F-Connection: Families, Friends, Firms, and the Organization of Exchange," 6 *Population and Development* 1, 3 (1980).
13. See, e.g., Hal R. Varian, *Intermediate Microeconomics: A Modern Approach* 323 (1987); Jack Hirshleifer, *Price Theory and Applications* 265 (2d ed. 1980).
14. See, e.g., Bea Ann Smith, "The Partnership Theory of Marriage: A Borrowed Solu-

tion Fails," 68 *Texas Law Review* 689 (1990). I will consider some of these different outcomes in Chapters 6 and 7.

15. See Regan, supra note 5, at 159–160. See also Janet L. Dolgin, "Status and Contract in Feminist Legal Theory of the Family: A Reply to Bartlett," 12 *Women's Rights Law Reporter* 103 (1990); Mary Joe Frug , "Re-reading Contracts: A Feminist Analysis of a Contracts Casebook," 34 *American University Law Review* 1065 (1985); Mary Joe Frug, "Rescuing Impossibility Doctrine: A Postmodern Feminist Analysis of Contract Law," 140 *University of Pennsylvania Law Review* 1029 (1992); Robin West, "Jurisprudence and Gender," 55 *University of Chicago Law Review* 1 (1988).

16. Alexander v. Kuykendall, 63 S.E.2d 746, 747–748 (Va. 1948).

17. See, e.g., Virginia Held, "Mothering versus Contract," in *Beyond Self-Interest* 287 (Jane Mansbridge, ed., 1990); Martha Fineman, *The Illusion of Equality: The Rhetoric and Reality of Divorce Reform* 149 (1991); Regan, supra note 5, at 94–95, 188.

18. Janet Moore, "Covenant and Feminist Reconstructions of Subjectivity within Theories of Justice," 55 *Law and Contemporary Problems* 159, 168 (1992). Compare Marion Crane, "Feminism, Labor, and Power," 65 *Southern California Law Review* 1819, 1857 (1992). An alternative to the term "feminine view" may be "relational ethic." Regan, supra note 5, at 164.

19. For a review of the literature, see Linda J. Waite, "Does Marriage Matter?" 32 *Demography* 483 (1995).

20. Compare Ian Macneil, "Efficient Breach of Contract: Circles in the Sky," 68 *Virginia Law Review* 94 (1982); and "The Many Futures of Contracts," 47 *Southern California Law Review* 691 (1974); Richard Posner, *Economic Analysis of Law* 89–90 (2d ed. 1977); and, in the marriage context, Ira Ellman, "The Theory of Alimony," 77 *California Law Review* 1, 66 and n.166 (1987).

21. Regan, supra note 5, at 116–117; see also Bruce Hafen, "The Family as an Entity," 22 *University of California–Davis Law Review* 865, 892 (1989).

22. Brinig, supra note 6.

23. Regan, supra note 5, at 2.

24. Id. at 148; Elizabeth Scott, "Rational Decisionmaking about Marriage and Divorce," 76 *Virginia Law Review* 9 (1990).

25. Ronald Coase, "The Theory of the Firm," 4 *Economica* 386 (1937); Benjamin Klein, Robert Crawford, and Armen Alchian, "Vertical Integration, Appropriable Rents, and Competitive Contracting Process," 21 *Journal of Law and Economics* 297 (1978).

26. Oliver Williamson, *The Economic Institutions of Capitalism: Firms, Markets, and Relational Contracting* (1985).

27. Alfred Chandler, *The Visible Hand: Managerial Revolution in American Business* (1977).

28. Becker, supra note 4, chap. 2. See also Shoshana Grossbard-Shechtman, *On the*

Economics of Marriage: A Theory of Marriage, Labor, and Divorce 25 (1992). But see Olsen, supra note 6.

29. See also Posner, supra note 20; Reuben Gronau, "Home Production—A Forgotten Industry," 62 *Review of Economics and Statistics* 408 (1980).

30. Even with a small difference in skills, specialization may eventually become complete. Ben Yu and Yoram Barzel, "The Effect of the Utilization Rate on the Division of Labor," 22 *Economic Inquiry* 18 (1984).

31. See, e.g., Gary Becker, "Human Capital, Effort, and the Sexual Division of Labor," 3 *Journal of Labor Economics* S33 (1985); Parkman, *No-Fault,* supra note 9; Margaret F. Brinig, "Comment on Jana Singer's 'Alimony and Efficiency,'" 82 *Georgetown Law Journal* 2461 (1994).

32. Gary Becker, *Human Capital: A Theoretical and Empirical Analysis, with Specific Reference to Education* (2d ed. 1975); and "A Theory of Marriage," 81 *Journal of Political Economy* 813 (1973) (hereinafter "Theory of Marriage"). See also Paula England and Gary Farkas, *Households, Employment, and Gender: Part I* (1987).

33. Gillian K. Hadfield, "Households at Work: Beyond Labor Market Policies to Remedy the Gender Gap," 82 *Georgetown Law Journal* 89 (1993).

34. Gary Becker, "A Theory of Marriage: Part II," 82 *Journal of Political Economy* 1063 (1974); Gary Becker, Elisabeth M. Landes, and Robert T. Michael, "An Economic Analysis of Marital Instability," 85 *Journal of Political Economy* 1141 (1977); Beverly Duncan and Otis D. Duncan, *Sex Typing and Social Roles: A Research Report* (1978).

35. There will be some loss in bargaining power for the spouse, usually the woman, who enjoys lower earnings in the labor market. Amy L. Wax, "Bargaining in the Shadow of the Market," 84 *Virginia Law Review* 509 (1998).

36. Margaret F. Brinig and Steven M. Crafton, "Marriage and Opportunism," 23 *Journal of Legal Studies* 869 (1994).

37. See Parkman, "Married Women," supra note 9.

38. Becker, supra note 4; Gary Becker, "A Theory of the Allocation of Time," *Economic Journal* 493 (1965); Becker, "Theory of Marriage," supra note 32; Becker, Landes, and Michael, supra note 34. See also Elisabeth Landes, "Economics of Alimony," 7 *Journal of Legal Studies* 35 (1978); Gronau, supra note 29; Ellman, supra note 20; Parkman, *No-Fault,* supra note 9.

39. See Becker, supra note 4, at 49.

40. Landes, supra note 38, at 46.

41. See Reva Siegel, "Home as Work: The First Woman's Rights Claims Concerning Wives' Household Labor, 1850–80," 103 *Yale Law Journal* 1073 (1994).

42. See, e.g., Victor Fuchs, *Women's Quest for Economic Equality* 42–74 (1988).

43. See, e.g., Parkman, *No-Fault,* supra note 9, at 26–27.

44. See, e.g., id. at 29–33; Becker, Landes, and Michael, supra note 34, at 1146.

45. I am using Parkman's simplification that married women earn only 60 percent of their husbands' income. Parkman, *No-Fault,* supra note 9, at 28 and n.7. See also

Francine D. Blau and Lawrence M. Kahn, "The Gender Earnings Gap: Some International Evidence," 82 *American Economic Review* 533, 534 and table 1 (59.44 percent for married women, 1985–86). More recent data place women's earnings at about 75 percent of men's. Bureau of Labor Statistics, *Current Population Survey* (1997), table 2; see John M. Berry, "Gap between Pay of Men, Women May Have Expanded since 1993: Data Called Too Imprecise to Be Sure Narrowing Trend Has Reversed," *Washington Post*, C3 (September 16, 1997). If the rest of the economic assumptions held true, "efficiency" would still dictate complete specialization, although the result would not be as strong. See Yu and Barzel, supra note 30.

46. Becker, supra note 4, at 56; see also Ellman, supra note 20, at 4 and n.2.

47. For a more lengthy discussion of this proposition, see Margaret F. Brinig, "The Law and Economics of No-Fault Divorce," 26 *Family Law Quarterly* 453, 456–457 and nn. 20–22 (1993). See, e.g., Parkman, *No-Fault*, supra note 9; Mary O'Connell, "On the Fringe: Rethinking the Link between Wages and Benefits," 67 *Tulane Law Review* 1421, 1478–88 (1993); see generally Deborah Rhode and Martha Minow, "Reforming the Questions, Questioning the Reforms: Feminist Perspectives on Divorce Law," in *Divorce Reform at the Crossroads* 192 (Stephen Sugarman and Herma Hill Kay, eds., 1990); Nancy Dowd, "Family Values and Valuing Family: A Blueprint for Family Leave," 30 *Harvard Journal on Education* 335 (1933).

48. Parkman, *No-Fault*, supra note 9, at 102–103; Ellman, supra note 20, at 54–55; Landes, supra note 38, at 35, 40. I have discussed this assumption in Brinig, supra note 47, at 457.

49. See, e.g., Ellman, supra note 20; Parkman, *No-Fault*, supra note 9, at 102. A brief discussion of this problem appears in Brinig, supra note 47, at 457–458.

50. Women and men seem to have quite different preferences for time with children. See Fuchs, supra note 42, at 68.

51. I know I personally went far beyond the point where diminishing marginal returns from caring for children set in one "snow day," when I had a lot to do at work, no child care, and five children marooned at home fighting with one another.

52. See Brinig, supra note 31, at 2474 for calculations.

53. See, e.g., Becker, supra note 4, at 44–45.

54. See, e.g., Brinig, supra note 47, at 456 and n.20.

55. See, e.g., Becker, supra note 4, at 30–31; see generally Lloyd Cohen, "Marriage, Divorce, and Quasi-Rents; Or, 'I Gave Him the Best Years My Life,'" 16 *Journal of Legal Studies* 267 (1987).

56. Becker, supra note 4, at 55 (noting that the need for prolonged child care is declining, so there is more incentive to invest in market-oriented human capital).

57. Becker, supra note 4, at 56.

58. See, e.g., Becker, Landes, and Michael, supra note 34, at 1145–47; but cf. Landes, supra note 38, at 41.

59. See, e.g., Smith, supra note 14 and sources cited therein.

60. Parkman, *No-Fault*, supra note 9, at 72; Douglas Allen, "What's at Fault with No-Fault?" paper presented at the Canadian Law and Economics Association, September 25, 1992.

61. See H. Elizabeth Peters, "Marriage and Divorce: Informational Constraints and Private Contracting," 76 *American Economic Review* 437, 449 (1986).

62. See, e.g., Cohen, supra note 55, at 297; Ellman, supra note 20, at 10 and n.18; Jeffrey E. Stake, "Mandatory Planning for Divorce," 45 *Vanderbilt Law Review* 397, 415–25 (1992); see generally Marjorie Maguire Shultz, "Contractual Ordering of Marriage: A New Model for State Policy," 70 *California Law Review* 204 (1982).

63. Martha Minow, "All in the Family and in All Families: Membership, Loving, and Owing," 95 *West Virginia Law Review* 275 (1993).

64. Parkman, *No-Fault*, supra note 9, at 94; Brinig and Crafton, supra note 36; Ellman, supra note 20, at 45.

65. Brinig and Crafton, supra note 36.

66. Becker, Landes, and Michael, supra note 34, at 1142; Cohen, supra note 55, at 287, 295; Brinig and Crafton, supra note 36; Ellman, supra note 20, at 25; Parkman *No-Fault*, supra note 9, at 94.

67. See Marsha Garrison, "The Marriage Contract," 131 *University of Pennsylvania Law Review* 1039, 1058 (1983); Cohen, supra note 55, at 295.

68. Brinig and Crafton, supra note 36; Becker, supra note 4, at 349; Becker, Landes, and Michael, supra note 34, at 1172.

69. See Parkman, *No-Fault*, supra note 9, at 94–96; Peters, supra note 61, at 443–444; Cohen, supra note 55, at 296; Brinig and Crafton, supra note 36.

70. Margaret F. Brinig and Steven L. Nock, "Weak Men and Disorderly Women: Divorce and the Division of Labor," Working Paper, Department of Sociology, University of Virginia, March 1999.

71. A paper documenting the NSFH is James Sweet, Larry Bumpass, and Vaughn Call, "The Design and Content of the National Survey of Families and Households," Working Paper NSFH-1, University of Wisconsin, Department of Demography and Ecology, 1988.

72. Until the nineteenth century, though, American women were frequently disabled from making contracts or holding property individually. These disabilities were removed in the Married Women's Property Acts between 1848 and 1900. See Siegel, supra note 41; Richard H. Chused, "Married Women's Property Law, 1800–1850," 71 *Georgetown Law Journal* 1359 (1983).

73. Becker, Landes, and Michael, supra note 34; Martin Zelder, "Inefficient Dissolutions as a Consequence of Public Goods: The Cost of No-Fault Divorce," 22 *Journal of Legal Studies* 503 (1993); Parkman, *No-Fault*, supra note 9, at 35; Peters, supra note 61; see also anthropologist Laura Bettzig, "Causes of Conjugal Dissolution: A Cross-cultural Study," 30 *Current Anthropology* 654 (1989).

74. For a valuable discussion of marital bargaining in general, see Wax, supra note 35.

75. Zelder, supra note 73, at 505.

76. Cohen, supra note 55. See also Brinig and Crafton, supra note 36.

77. Margaret F. Brinig and Douglas W. Allen, "'These Boots Are Made for Walking:' Why Wives File for Divorce," *American Economics and Law Review* (forthcoming).

78. For a thoughtful discussion of recontracting in marriage, see Scott and Scott, supra note 1.

79. Zelder, supra note 73, at 505.

80. See generally Wax, supra note 35; Katharine Silbaugh, "Turning Labor into Love: Housework and the Law," 91 *Northwestern University Law Review* 1 (1996).

81. Becker, supra note 4, at 278–285.

82. See also Paul A. Samuelson, "Social Indifference Curves," 70 *Quarterly Journal of Economics* 1 (1956) (establishing consumer demand units as families, who behave as if they were a single unit maximizing utility).

83. Ephesians 5:28–29: "So husbands ought also to love their own wives as their own bodies. He who loves his own wife loves himself; for no one ever hated his own flesh, but nourishes and cherishes it, just as Christ also does the church, because we are members of His body."

84. See, e.g., Marilyn Manser and Murray Brown, "Marriage and Household Decision-Making: A Bargaining Analysis," 21 *International Economic Review* 31 (1980); Marjorie B. McElroy and Mary Jean Horney, "Nash-Bargained Household Decisions: Toward a Generalization of the Theory of Demand," 22 *International Economic Review* 333 (1981); and Ellen B. Zweibel and Richard Shillington, "Child Support Policy: Income Tax Treatment and Child Support Guidelines," Policy Research Centre on Children, Youth and Families, Centre for Social Welfare Studies, Faculty of Social Work, Wilfrid Laurier University, Waterloo, Ontario (1994).

85. Douglas Allen, "What Does She See in Him? The Effect of Sharing on the Choice of Spouse," 30 *Economic Inquiry* 57 (1992). Even under such a "cooperative game," spouses may sometimes have difficulty reaching agreement, as the "Battle of the Sexes" game shows. See Jack Hirshleifer, *Price Theory and Applications* 518–519 (1988).

86. Roger Fisher and William Ury, *Getting to Yes: Negotiating Agreement without Giving In* 104–106 (2d ed. 1991).

87. See also Margaret F. Brinig and F. H. Buckley, "Joint Custody: Bonding and Monitoring Theories," 73 *Indiana Law Journal* 393 (1998).

88. Shelly Lundberg and Robert A. Pollack, "Separate Spheres Bargaining and the Marriage Market," 101 *Journal of Political Economy* 988 (1993).

89. Id. at 994.

90. Id. at 997.

91. Margaret F. Brinig and F. H. Buckley, "No-Fault Laws and At-Fault People," 16 *International Review of Law and Economics* 325 (1998).

92. See also Manser and Brown, supra note 84; Stake, supra note 62; Eric Rasmusen

and Jeffrey Stake, "Lifting the Veil of Ignorance: Personalizing the Marriage Contract," 73 *Indiana Law Journal* 453 (1998).

93. The results are rather striking. In three different empirical tests, women's labor force participation was negatively and significantly related to the divorce rates in surveyed states from 1979 to 1991.

94. See also Parkman, "Married Women," supra note 9; Wax, supra note 35.

95. This is greatly simplified, of course. She also might be receiving a psychic outlet when she is able to leave the household and perhaps her children for at least part of the day. Brinig, supra note 47.

96. June M. Reinisch and Ruth Beasley, *The Kinsey Institute New Report on Sex* 79 (1991); Cathy Perlmutter, "31 Facts and Tips on Sex after 30," 41 *Prevention* 3 (July 1989).

97. Reinisch and Beasley, supra note 96, at 80; E. R. Mahoney, *Human Sexuality* 46 (1983).

98. For a more complete explanation, see Douglas W. Allen and Margaret Brinig, "Sex, Property Rights, and Divorce," 5 *European Journal of Law and Economics* 211 (1998). See also Waite, supra note 19.

99. This is obviously factually inaccurate, as is evidenced by the many state statutes prohibiting marital rape and several convictions reported since 1970. See, e.g., Cal. Penal Code §262; Neb. Rev. Stat. §28–319; Ore. Rev. Stat. §153.375; Commonwealth v. Chretien, 417 N.E.2d 1203 (Mass. 1981); State v. Smith, 426 A.2d 38 (N.J. 1981); People v. Liberta, 474 N.E.2d 567 (N.Y. 1984).

100. See Wax, supra note 35.

101. For other results, see Brinig and Crafton, supra note 36. For another discussion of this topic, in game theoretic framework, see Linda R. Hirshman, *Material Girls: A Game Theoretic Revision of the Social Contract with Women Present* 101–109 (1995).

102. Allen and Brinig, supra note 98. See also Helen Fisher, "The Four-Year Itch: Do Divorce Patterns Reflect Our Evolutionary Heritage?" 96 *Natural History* 20, 22 (1987).

103. Cohen, supra note 55.

104. This lovely expression came from my aunt, Jean Friedlander.

105. See Anthony Kronman, "Contract Law and the State of Nature," 1 *Journal of Law, Economics, and Organization* 5 (1985); Michael Mann, "Discussing 'Credible Commitments,'" 29 *Antitrust Bulletin* 856 (1983); and Oliver Williamson, "Credible Commitments: Using Hostages to Support Exchange," 73 *American Economic Review* 519 (1983).

106. See, e.g., Cohen, supra note 55; Scott and Scott, supra note 1.

107. Joan C. Williams, "Gender Wars: Selfless Women in the Republic of Choice," 66 *New York University Law Review* 1559 (1991).

108. Armen A. Alchian and William R. Allen, *Exchange and Production; Competition, Coordination, and Control* 163–170 (3d ed. 1983); see also Armen A. Alchian and

Harold Demsetz, "Production, Information Costs, and Economic Organization," 62 *American Economic Review* 777 (1972).

109. Alchian and Allen, supra note 108, at 170.

110. See, e.g., Stephen Ross, "The Economic Theory of Agency: The Principal's Problem," 63 *American Economic Review* 134 (1973); also Joseph Stiglitz, "Principal and Agent," 3 *New Palgrave Encyclopedia* 966 (1987).

111. Hirshleifer, supra note 85, at 518–519. The idea is that two prisoners accused of a common crime are separated and questioned separately. Each is told that if he confesses, he will get a reduced punishment. If neither confesses, both will go free because there will not be enough evidence. The theory is that they will both confess if they cannot communicate, because for each that is the lowest-risk strategy.

112. Alchian and Demsetz, supra note 108.

113. Williams, supra note 107; see also Silbaugh, supra note 80.

114. Steven L. Nock, *Marriage in Men's Lives* (1998).

115. See, e.g., Shelley Coverman and Joseph Sheley, "Change in Men's Housework and Child-Care Time, 1965–75," 48 *Journal of Marriage and the Family* 413, 320 (1986); Suzanne M. Bianchi and Daphne Spain, "Women, Work, and Family in America," 51 *Population Bulletin* 2 (December 1996). Women are apparently both more committed and more dependent than are men. Steven L. Nock, "Commitment and Dependency in Marriage," 57 *Journal of Marriage and the Family* 503 (1995).

116. See, e.g., Jana Singer, "The Privatization of Family Law," 1992 *Wisconsin Law Review* 1443 (hereinafter "Privatization"); and "Divorce Reform and Gender Justice," 67 *North Carolina Law Review* 1103 (1989); Regan, supra note 5, at 146–147.

117. See Brinig, supra note 6.

118. See Margaret F. Brinig and Michael V. Alexeev, "Trading at Divorce: Preferences, Legal Rules, and Transaction Costs," 8 *Ohio State Journal of Dispute Resolution* 279 (1993).

119. Steven Cheung, "The Contractual Nature of the Firm," 26 *Journal of Law and Economics* 1, 3 (1983).

120. Id. at 8.

121. Id. at 9–10.

122. Compare Kronman, supra note 105.

123. For a discussion of marriage vows as hortatory, see Scott and Scott, supra note 1.

124. Brinig and Crafton, supra note 36. See also Posner, supra note 20, at 148.

125. See, e.g., Joan Krauskopf, "Recompense for Financing Spouse's Education: Legal Protection of the Marital Investor in Human Capital," 28 *Kansas Law Review* 379 (1980).

126. One very angry father who apparently feels this way is Robert E. Fay, M.D., "The Disenfranchised Father," 36 *Advances in Pediatrics* 407 (1989).

127. Brinig and Buckley, supra note 87.

128. Allen, supra note 85.

129. Garrison, supra note 67, at 1060; Herma Hill Kay, "An Appraisal of California's No-Fault Divorce Law," 75 *California Law Review* 291, 309 (1987)

130. See Margaret F. Brinig, "Equality and Sharing: Views of Households across the Iron Curtain," 7 *European Journal of Law and Economics* 55 (1999).

131. This is a somewhat circular proposition since wives rationally choose household production because of their lower opportunity costs of remaining out of the job market. See Wax, supra note 35; Silbaugh, supra note 80.

132. Cynthia Starnes, "Divorce and the Displaced Homemaker: A Discourse on Playing with Dolls, Partnership Buyouts, and Dissociation under No-Fault," 60 *University of Chicago Law Review* 67 (1993).

133. Fuchs, supra note 42, at 73–74; and see sources cited in Brinig, supra note 31, at 2477 and n.90; Bianchi and Spain, supra note 115.

134. Joan C. Williams, *Unbending Gender* (1999).

135. See Scott and Scott, supra note 1.

136. There is an extensive discussion of this line of reasoning in the Supreme Court case of United States v. Trammel, 445 U.S. 40 (1980) (immunity from adverse testimony by a spouse). See generally Milton C. Regan, *Alone Together: Law and the Meanings of Marriage,* chap. 5 (1999). More appears in Sundin v. Klein, 269 S.E.2d 787 (Va. 1980), where a murdered wife's estate tried to recover property held by the spouses as "tenants by the entireties."

137. See, e.g., Keister's Adm'r. v. Keister's Ex'r., 96 S.E. 315, 322 (Va. 1918) (Burke, J., concurring) (the duties of marriage "forbid the idea that this 'one flesh' may so divide itself that either spouse may sue the other"). See also William Blackstone, 1 *Commentaries on the Law of England* *442 (15th ed. 1809).

138. Although the tenancy by the entireties still exists in a few states (for example, Virginia permits this holding if the intent to create it explicitly appears in the deed [Va. Code Ann. §55–20]), and the marital community flourishes in others, customs such as dower and curtesy (giving wives and husbands, respectively, shares in the property acquired by the other during the marriage) have largely vanished. For one of the last holdouts, see Va. Code Ann. §64.1–19.2.

139. 61 N.C. 453 (1868).

140. Wait v. Pierce, 209 N.W.475, 482 (Wis. 1926)(Eschweiler, J., dissenting).

141. See e.g., Lewis v. Lewis, 351 N.E.2d 526 (Mass. 1976); Merenoff v. Merenoff, 388 S.E.314, 322 (N.J. 1978).

142. See, e.g., Surratt v. Thompson, 183 S.E.2d 200 (Va. 1971).

143. See, e.g., Eagan v. Calhoun, 347 Md. 72; 698 A.2d 1097 (1997). See generally Note, "Litigation between Husband and Wife," 79 *Harvard Law Review* 1650, 1659–63 (1966), for an old version of the doctrine, and Singer, "Privatization," supra note 116, for a modern feminist approach.

144. Planned Parenthood v. Casey, 505 U.S. 833 (1992).

145. Favrot v. Burns, 332 So. 2d 873 (La. Ct. App. 1976).

146. Ephesians 5:28.

147. See Chused, supra note 72; Siegel, supra note 41; Peggy Rabkin, *Fathers to Daughters: The Legal Foundations of Female Emancipation* 154–155 (1980).

148. Frederick Pollack and Frederic Maitland, *A History of the English Law* (1895).

149. Matthew Hale, 1 *The History of the Pleas of the Crown* 629 (1736).

150. See, e.g., State v. Smith, 436 A.2d 38, 42–43 (N.J. 1981). Further, no-fault divorce gave the wife the right to withdraw voluntarily from the marital relationship, terminating any such marital contract. See Weishaupt v. Commonwealth, 315 S.E.2d 847 (Va. 1984).

151. See, e.g., Kizer v. Commonwealth, 321 S.E.2d 291 (Va. 1984).

152. See Oliver Williamson, "Transaction Cost Economics: The Governance of Contractual Relations," 22 *Journal of Law and Economics* 233 (1979); see also Scott and Scott, supra note 1.

153. Robert Scott and Charles Goetz, "Principles of Relational Contracts," 67 *Virginia Law Review* 1089 (1981).

154. Scott, supra note 24.

155. Shultz, supra note 62; Scott, supra note 24. One other reason is that couples during engagement are convinced that their own marriage will not end in divorce, although they are aware that half of all marriages will. Lynn Baker and Robert Emery, "When Every Relationship Is Above Average: Perceptions and Expectations of Divorce at the Time of Marriage," 17 *Journal of Law and Human Behavior* 439 (1993).

156. See Milton C. Regan, "Spousal Privilege and the Meanings of Marriage," 81 *Virginia Law Review* 2045 (1995). Regan, supra note 136, discusses the tensions between marital community and autonomy.

157. Cass R. Sunstein, "Incommensurability and Valuation in Law," 92 *Michigan Law Review* 779, 850 (1994).

158. Coase, supra note 25, at 390; see also Armen Alchian, Benjamin Klein, and Robert Crawford, "Vertical Integration, Appropriable Rents, and the Corporate Contracting Process," 21 *Journal of Law and Economics* 297 (1978); Frank Easterbrook and Daniel Fischel, *The Economic Structure of Corporate Law* 8 (1991); and Michael Jensen and William Meckling, "Theory of the Firm: Managerial Behavior, Agency Costs, and Ownership Structure," 3 *Journal of Financial Economics* 305, 308–311 (1976).

159. Walter Wadlington, *Cases and Materials on Domestic Relations* 218 (2d ed. 1990).

160. See Singer, "Privatization," supra note 116. Singer argues that while privatization may well have some benefits, there are substantial problems as well, particularly for women and children.

161. For one account that questions whether marital privacy is worth retaining, see id.

162. Regan, supra note 5; Brinig, supra note 6.

163. Smith, supra note 14.

164. Gary Becker, "The Economic Way of Looking at Behavior," 101 *Journal of Political Economy* 385 (1993).

165. Ben-Porath, supra note 12.

166. Compare Lisa Bernstein, "Merchant Law in a Merchant Court: Rethinking the Code's Search for Immanent Business Norms," 144 *University of Pennsylvania Law Review* 1765 (1996); and "Opting Out of the Legal System: Extralegal Contractual Relations in the Diamond Industry," 21 *Journal of Legal Studies* 115 (1992).

167. Brinig and Crafton, supra note 36.

168. See, e.g., In re Marriage of Graham, 574 P.2d 75, 77 (Colo. 1978); In re Marriage of Weinstein, 470 N.E.2d 551, 560 (Ill. App. Ct. 1984); Mahoney v. Mahoney, 453 A.2d 527 (N.J. 1982). New York is the exception to this rule. O'Brien v. O'Brien, 66 N.Y.2d 576, 498 N.Y.S.2d 743, 489 N.E.2d 712 (1985).

169. Margaret F. Brinig and June Carbone, "The Reliance Interest in Marriage and Divorce," 62 *Tulane Law Review* 855 (1988).

170. Becker, supra note 4, at 24.

171. Margaret F. Brinig, "Finite Horizons: The American Family," 2 *International Journal of Children's Rights* 293 (1994).

172. See, e.g., Judith Wallerstein, "The Long-Term Effects of Divorce on Children: A Review," 30 *Journal of the American Academy of Child and Adolescent Psychiatry* 349 (1991); Mavis Hetherington, Martha Cox, and Roger Cox, "Long-Term Effects of Divorce and Remarriage on the Adjustment of Children," 24 *American Academy of Child Psychiatry* 518 (1985); Judith A. Seltzer, "Consequences of Marital Dissolution for Children," 1994 *American Review of Sociology* 235; see also Margaret F. Brinig and F. H. Buckley, "The Market for Deadbeats," 25 *Journal of Legal Studies* 201 (1996).

173. Zelder, supra note 73.

174. Cohen, supra note 55, at 300.

175. Brinig and Crafton, supra note 36. See Richard Morin and Megan Rosenfeld, "With More Equity, More Sweat; Poll Shows Sexes Agree on Pros and Cons of New Roles," *Washington Post*, A1 (March 22, 1998).

176. See Schneider, supra note 8, at 1848 (noting the phenomenon but calling it the doctrine of "nonbinding commitments").

177. Regan, supra note 4, at 67. See also Nock, supra note 115.

178. Regan, supra note 4, at 67. The family then becomes little more than a long-term contract subject to the threat of "efficient breach" should one's emotional life not seem satisfactory. See generally Macneil, supra note 20; Alan Schwartz, "The Case for Specific Performance," 89 *Yale Law Journal* 271 (1979).

179. Olmstead v. United States, 277 U.S. 438, 478 (1928) (Brandeis, J., dissenting).

180. Singer, supra note 116 ("Divorce Reform").

181. Brinig and Crafton, supra note 36.

182. Brinig, supra note 47.

183. Brinig, supra note 6, at 1587 and n.82. See also Margaret F. Brinig, "The Econom-

ics and Law of Covenant Marriage," 18 *Gender Issues* 4 (1998); Regan, supra note 85.

184. Brinig and Crafton, supra note 36. Scott and Scott, supra note 1, argue only for the first device.

185. Alfred E. Chandler, *Scale and Scope: The Dynamics of Industrial Capitalism* (1990).

186. Gary Becker, supra note 4, chap. 2 ("Household Production").

187. Nancy Staudt, "Taxing Housework," 84 *Georgetown Law Journal* 1571 (1996); Silbaugh, supra note 80.

188. Lloyd Cohen, "Rhetoric, the Unnatural Family, and Women's Work," 81 *Virginia Law Review* 2275 (1995).

189. In fact, John Stuart Mill wrote that working outside the home "seldom relieves her from [her ordinary duty as a wife], but only prevents her from performing it properly. . . . In an otherwise just state of things, it is not, therefore, I think, a desirable custom, that the wife should contribute by her labour to the income of the family." *The Subjugation of Women* [1869] 483 (1975).

190. For a discussion of this point and how it relates to choice of spouses, see Allen, supra note 60.

191. Thomas B. Edsall, "Understanding Oklahoma; Masculinity on the Run: From Workplace to Bedroom—to Timothy McVeigh," *Washington Post Outlook,* C1 (April 30, 1995). For a thoughtful theoretical discussion of this phenomenon, see Williams, supra note 134.

192. Becker, supra note 32 *(Human Capital);* see also Theodore Schultz, *The Economic Value of Education* (1963); Jacob Mincer and Solomon Polacheck, "Family Investments in Human Capital: Earnings of Women," in *Economics of the Family: Marriage, Children, and Human Capital: A Conference Report of "The Nation"* 397 (Theodore W. Schultz, ed., 1974).

193. Joseph Schumpeter, *Innovation in Technology, Industries and Institutions: Studies in Schumpeterian Perspectives* (Yuichi Shionoya and Mark Perlman, trans., 1994).

194. Paul M. Romer, "Increasing Returns and Long-Run Growth," 94 *Journal of Political Economy* 1002 (1986).

195. Blackstone, supra note 136, at 447–454 (written between 1765 and 1769).

196. Beecher, supra note 11, at 13; see also Nancy F. Cott, *The Bonds of Womanhood: Women's Sphere in New England, 1780–1835* (1977).

197. Regan, supra note 5. See also Regan, supra note 136.

198. Trammel v. United States, 445 U.S. 40, 44 (1980).

199. Id.

200. See, e.g., Va. Code Ann. §19.2–271.2.

201. Osborne v. Commonwealth, 204 S.E.2d 289 (Va. 1974).

202. See, e.g., Vance v. Rice, 524 F. Supp. 1297 (S.D. Iowa 1981).

203. Menefee v. Commonwealth, 55 S.E.2d 9, 15 (Va. 1949).

204. Hawkins v. United States, 358 U.S. 74, 79 (1958). See also Wolfle v. United States, 291 U.S. 7, 14 (1934).

5. Parent and Child

1. See generally Elizabeth S. Scott and Robert E. Scott, "Parents as Fiduciaries," 81 *Virginia Law Review* 2401 (1995).
2. Id. at 2413–14.
3. Barbara Bennett Woodhouse, "Who Owns the Child? *Meyers* and *Pierce* and The Child as Property," 33 *William and Mary Law Review* 995 (1992).
4. See, e.g., Tex. Human Resources Code, §40.002(b), effective September 1, 1997; Parental Rights and Responsibilities Act of 1996, S. 894.
5. 262 U.S. 390 (1923).
6. 268 U.S. 510 (1925).
7. Wisconsin v. Yoder, 406 U.S. 205 (1972).
8. Zablocki v. Redhail, 434 U.S. 374 (1978).
9. The United Nations Convention on the Rights of the Child (23/12/91) guarantees some of these rights to children.
10. Joseph Goldstein, Anna Freud, and Albert Solnit, *Beyond the Best Interests of the Child* (1973). See also Hilary Rodham Clinton, *It Takes a Village: And Other Lessons Children Teach Us* (1996).
11. See, e.g., Wendy A. Fitzgerald, "Maturity, Difference, and Mystery: Children's Perspectives and the Law," 36 *Arizona Law Review* 11, 40 (1994); Martha Minow, *Making All the Difference: Inclusion, Exclusion, and American Law* (1990).
12. But see Robert H. Mnookin, "Child-Custody Adjudication: Judicial Functions in the Face of Indeterminacy," 39 *Law and Contemporary Problems* 226, 227 (1975).
13. Parham v. J. R., 442 U.S. 584 (1979).
14. Mnookin, supra note 12; Scott and Scott, supra note 1, at 2431.
15. Judith Seltzer, "Consequences of Marital Dissolution for Children," 1994 *Annual Review of Sociology* 235.
16. Judith A. Seltzer, "Father by Law: Effects of Joint Legal Custody on Nonresident Fathers' Involvement with Children," NSFH Working Paper no. 75, University of Wisconsin, Center for Demography and Ecology (1997).
17. See Mary Ann Glendon, *The New Family and the New Property* (1981); Viviana A. Rotman Zelizer, *Pricing the Priceless Child: The Changing Social Value of Children* (1985); John Demos, "The American Family in Past Time," 43 *American Scholar* 422 (1974); John Demos, "Images of the American Family, Then and Now," in *Changing Images of the Family* 43 (Virginia Tufte and Barbara Myerhoff, eds., 1979).
18. Jon B. Minor, *Institutes of Constitutional and Statutory Law* 405 (1882).
19. See, for example, Buxton v. Bishop, 185 Va. 1, 37 S.E.2d 755 (1946); Jamil Zainaldin, "The Emergence of a Modern American Family Law: Child Custody, Adoption, and the Courts, 1796–1851," 73 *Northwestern University Law Review* 1038 (1979).
20. Sanford Katz, William Schroeder, and Lawrence Sidman, "Emancipating Our

Children: Coming of Legal Age in America," 7 *Family Law Quarterly* 211, 212, 214 (1973).

21. This comes directly from the Fourth Commandment, Exodus 20:12.

22. See John R. Sutton, "Stubborn Children: Law and Socialization of Deviance in the Puritan Colonies," 15 *Family Law Quarterly* 31 (1981).

23. For example, see 1 Hening [Va. Session Laws] 434 (March 1657–58); and 2 Hening [Va. Session Laws] 165–166 (December 1662, art. 4).

24. Lamentations 5:7.

25. See, e.g., John Rawls, *A Theory of Justice* 284–293 (1971). See also Carl E. Schneider, "The Channelling Function in Family Law," 20 *Hofstra Law Review* 495, 511 (1992).

26. Rosalind C. Barnett and Grace K. Baruch, "Determinants of Fathers' Participation in Family Work," 49 *Journal of Marriage and the Family* 29, 37 (1987); see generally Nancy Chodorow, *The Reproduction of Mothering* (1978). But see Judith Rich Harris, *The Nurture Assumption: Why Children Turn Out the Way They Do; Parents Matter Less Than You Think and Peers Matter More* (1998).

27. See, e.g., Greg J. Duncan and Saul D. Hoffman, "Welfare Benefits, Economic Opportunities, and Out-of-Wedlock Births among Black Teenage Girls," 27 *Demography* 519 (1990), and the discussion in Chapter 3. See also Judith Havemann and Barbara Vobejda, "A Job Program Tries to Tackle the Intangibles: As Limits on Welfare Loom, Barrier Often Is an Attitude," *Washington Post*, A1 (June 16, 1997).

28. Gary S. Becker, *A Treatise on the Family,* chap. 8 (2d ed. 1981); Richard Epstein, "Justice across the Generations," in *The Dialogue of Justice: Toward a Self-Reflective Society* 84, 89 (Peter Laslett and James S. Fishkin, eds., 1992); Douglas Burnheim, Andrei Shleifer, and Lawrence Summers, "The Strategic Bequest Motive," 93 *Journal of Political Economy* 1045–46 (1985); James M. Buchanan, "Rent Seeking, Noncompensated Transfers, and Laws of Succession," 26 *Journal of Law and Economics* 71 (1983); Philippe Weil, "Love Thy Children: Reflections on the Barro Debt Neutrality Theorem," 19 *Journal of Monetary Economics* 377 (1987); Franco Modigliani, "The Role of Intergenerational Transfers and Life Cycle Saving in the Accumulation of Wealth," 2 *Journal of Economic Perspectives* 15 (1988).

29. Zainaldin, supra note 19; Katz, Schroeder, and Sidman, supra note 20; Glendon, supra note 17.

30. See, e.g., Philippe Ariès, *Centuries of Childhood: A Social History of Family Life* (1962); Michael Grossberg, *Governing the Hearth: Law and the Family in Nineteenth-Century America* 5 (1985).

31. John Charles Caldwell, *Theory of Fertility Decline* (1982); Gary Becker and H. Gregg Lewis, "On the Interaction between the Quantity and Quality of Children," 2 *Journal of Political Economy* S279 (1973).

32. Zainaldin, supra note 19. See also Joseph Kett, *Rites of Passage: Adolescence in America, 1790 to the Present* (1977); Daniel Vickers, "Working the Fields in a Developing Economy: Essex County, Massachusetts, 1630–1675," in *Work and Labor*

in Early America 49–69 (Stephen Innes, ed., 1988); Louis Green Carr and Lorena S. Walsh, "Economic Diversification and Labor Organization in the Chesapeake, 1650–1820," in *Work and Labor in Early America* 150–151, 167–168 (Stephen Innes, ed., 1988); David Stern, Sandra Smith, and Fred Doolittle, "How Children Used to Work," 39 *Law and Contemporary Problems* 93 (1975).

33. See, e.g., Fletcher v. Taylor, 344 F.2d 93, 95 (4th Cir. 1965); Buxton v. Bishop, 37 S.E.2d 744 (Va. 1946).

34. Compulsory education statutes were enacted in the 1860s (Wisconsin v. Yoder, 406 U.S. 205 [1972]); child labor laws in 1890–1910 (Stern, Smith, and Doolittle, supra note 32).

35. See, e.g., Buxton v. Bishop, 37 S.E.2d 755 (Va. 1946); Wright v. Wright, 191 S.E.2d 223 (Va. 1972).

36. Minow, supra note 11, at 284; see also Katharine T. Bartlett, "Re-expressing Parenthood," 98 *Yale Law Journal* 293, 298 (1988) (suggesting that parents earn authority by meeting support obligations).

37. See, e.g., Kathleen McGarry and Robert Schoeni, "Transfer Behavior: Measurement and the Redistribution of Resources within the Family," NBER Working Paper no. 4607 (January 1994). See also Barbara Bennett Woodhouse, "Hatching the Egg: A Child-Centered Perspective on Parents' Rights," 14 *Cardozo Law Review* 1747, 1818–19 (1993); compare C. Russell Hill and Frank R. Stafford, "Parental Care of Children: Time Diary Estimates of Quantity, Predictability, and Variety," 15 *Journal of Human Resources* 2 (1980).

38. See, e.g., Gary S. Becker, "The Economic Way of Thinking," 101 *Journal of Political Economy* 205 (1993).

39. Buchanan, supra note 28; Gary S. Becker and Kevin Murphy, "The Family and the State," 31 *Journal of Law and Economics* 1 (1988).

40. See, e.g., Margaret F. Brinig, "Finite Horizons: The American Family," 2 *International Journal of Children's Rights* 293 (1994); Donald Cox and Odel Stark, "Intergenerational Transfers and the Demonstration Effect," Working Paper, Boston College Department of Economics (1993).

41. Joseph Schumpeter, *Capitalism, Socialism, and Democracy* 157–158 (3d ed. 1975).

42. 443 U.S. 622, 634 (1979); see generally Fitzgerald, supra note 11, at n.33.

43. For a review of the literature, see Kingsley R. Browne, "Sex and Temperament in Modern Society: A Darwinian View of the Glass Ceiling and the Gender Gap," 37 *Arizona Law Review* 971 (1995).

44. Harvey J. Ginsburg and Shirley M. Miller, "Sex Differences in Children's Risk-Taking Behavior," 53 *Child Development* 426 (1982).

45. This is reported in Margaret F. Brinig, "Does Mediation Systematicallly Disadvantage Women?" 2 *William and Mary Journal of Women and the Law* 1 (1995).

46. In an article in *Nature,* David H. Skuse and others explain that men, more than women, might need a social "blank-slate" to facilitate the formation of hunting parties or armies. David H. Skuse et al. "Sex and Sensibility," 393 *Nature* 13

(1998). Women would therefore be quicker to interpret body language and to infer what another person is feeling or thinking. David H. Skuse et al., "Sex and Sensibility," *Nature* 13 (1998). The study is described in David Brown, "Girls May Inherit Intuition Gene from Fathers; Study Suggests Chromosomes Hold the Key to Social Skills," *Washington Post*, A3 (June 12, 1997).

47. For examples, see Rebecca Boney and Bonita Douville, "Are Today's Students More Selfish Than Students Used to Be?" 8 *NEA Today* 39 (1990); and Thomas J. Lasley, "Teaching Selflessness in a Selfish Society," 68 *Phi Delta Kappan* 674 (1987).

48. See, e.g., Ann Pleshette Murphy, "The Language of Time," *Parents' Magazine*, 8 (October 10, 1993). The child's different sense of time is a cornerstone of Goldstein, Freud, and Solnit, supra note 10.

49. John Locke, *Second Treatise on Civil Government*, 306 ("Of Paternal Power," para. 58) (1992).

50. See Michael S. Wald, "Children's Rights: A Framework for Analysis," 12 *University of California–Davis Law Review* 255 (1979).

51. Jennifer Roback Morse, "The Development of the Utility Function of the Child," presented at a Liberty Fund Conference on the Individual, the Family, and the State, Alexandria, Virginia, July 1995.

52. Planned Parenthood v. Danforth, 428 U.S. 52 (1976); Bellotti v. Baird, 443 U.S. 622 (1979).

53. H. L. v. Matheson, 450 U.S. 398 (1981); Planned Parenthood v. Casey, 505 U.S. 833 (1992).

54. See, e.g., Ala. Code §22–8–4 (age fourteen); Ore. Rev. Stat. §109.640 (age fifteen); S.C. Code Ann. §20–7–280 (Law. Coop. 1985)(age sixteen); In re Green, 292 A.2d 387 (Pa. 1972).

55. See, e.g., Va. Code. Ann. §20–107.2(7)(Michie Supp. 1993); Wis. Stat. §767.24 (1985–86)(2); see generally Ellen G. Garrison, "Children's Competence to Participate in Divorce Custody Decision Making," 20 *Journal of Clinical Child Psychology* 78 (1991); Kett, supra note 32; Elizabeth S. Scott, "Judgment and Reasoning in Adolescent Decisionmaking," 1992 *Villanova Law Review* 1607, 1608.

56. See, e.g., Minow, supra note 11, at 284. See also Arlene Skolnick, "The Limits of Childhood: Conceptions of Child Development and Social Context," 39 *Law and Contemporary Problems* 38, 43 (1975). See also Carol Sanger and Eleanor Willemsen, "Minor Changes: Emancipating Children in Modern Times," 25 *University of Michigan Journal of Law Reform* 239 (1992).

57. 107 So. 2d 885 (Ala. 1958).

58. Id.

59. Demos, supra note 17, at 100–101; Jana Singer, "The Privatization of Family Law," 1992 *Wisconsin Law Review* 1443, 1445; James Schouler, *A Treatise on the Law of the Domestic Relation* 299 (1870); Minow, supra note 11, at 270.

60. Fitzgerald, supra note 11, at 40.

61. See, e.g., D. H. S. v. Holland, 602 So.2d 652, 654 (Fla. Ct. App. 1992); Clay v. Clay, 358 So. 2d 649 (La. Ct. App. 1978); but cf. In re Marriage of Goldstein, 229 Ill. App. 3d 399, 593 N.E.2d 102 (1992)); In re Howe's Estate, 132 N.Y.S.2d 855 (N.Y. Surr. 1954); Drewen v. Bank of Manhattan, 31 N.J. 110, 155 A.2d 529 (1959); but see Smith v. Smith, 467 P.2d 723 (N.M. 1970); Prudential Insurance Co. v. Rader, 98 F Supp. 44 (D. Minn. 1951); Forman v. Forman, 17 N.Y.2d 274, 217 N.E.2d 645, 270 N.Y.S.2d 586 (1966); Reliance Life Ins. v. Jaffe, 263 P.2d 82 (Cal. Ct. App. 1953).

62. Yarborough v. Yarborough, 290 U.S. 202 (1933).

63. Yost v. Yost, 190 A. 753 (Md. 1937); In re Marriage of Goldstein, 593 N.E.2d 102 (Ill. Ct. App. 1992).

64. Hewelette v. George, 68 Miss. 703, 9 So. 855 (1891), see generally Comment, "Defining the Parent's Duty after Rejection of Parent-Child Immunity: Parental Liability for Emotional Injury of Abandoned Children," 33 *Vanderbilt Law Review* 755 (1980)[hereinafter, Comment, "Defining"]; Comment, "Intrafamily Tort Immunity: A Doctrine in Decline," 21 *William and Mary Law Review* 273 (1979).

65. Price v. Price, 197 S.W.2d 200, 202–203 (Tex. 1946). For examples of the same reasoning in torts, see, e.g., Wright v. Wright, 191 S.E.2d 223 (Va. 1972); Burnette v. Wahl, 588 P.2d 1105 (Ore. 1978); see generally Comment, "Defining," supra note 64.

66. Karen Czapanskiy, "Child Support and Visitation—Rethinking the Connections," 20 *Rutgers Law Journal* 619 (1989); see also Bethune v. Bethune, 399 N.Y.S.2d 902 (N.Y. Fam. Ct. 1977).

67. 527 Pa. 532, 537, 594 A.2d 649, 651 (1991). See also Bethune v. Bethune, 399 N.Y.S.2d 602 (N.Y. Fam. Ct. 1977); Parker v. Stage, 371 N.E.2d 513 (N.Y. 1977); Worthington v. Worthington, 179 S.W.2d 648 (Ark. 1944); Abrego v. Abrego, 812 P.2d 806, 810 (Okla. 1991)(dictum).

68. See In re Serena C., 650 A.2d 1343 (Me. 1994); In re Alyne E., 448 N.Y.S.2d 984 (N.Y. Fam. Ct. 1984).

69. Cf. Lloyd Cohen, "Marriage, Divorce, and Quasi-Rents, Or, 'I Gave Him the Best Years of My Life,'" 16 *Journal of Legal Studies* 267, 300 (1987) (husband and wife).

70. W. Va. Code Ann. §48–2–4; La. Civ. Code Art. 9, §229 (Amended 1997).

71. David M. Chambers, "Fathers, the Welfare System, and the Virtues and Perils of Child Support Enforcement," 81 *Virginia Law Review* 2575 (1995). See also Margaret F. Brinig and F. H. Buckley, "The Market for Deadbeats," 25 *Journal of Legal Studies* 201 (1996).

72. Although this might be an enforcement mechanism, it would cause the child to suffer not one but two evils: lack of support money and lack of contact with the absent parent. See Czapanskiy, supra note 66.

73. Rosenblatt v. Birnbaum, 212 N.E.2d 37 (N.Y. 1965).

74. Robert Cooter and Bradley J. Freedman, "The Fiduciary Relationship: Its Eco-

nomic Character and Legal Consequences," 66 *New York University Law Review* 1045, 1065–69 (1991).

75. See, e.g., Becker and Murphy, supra note 39.

76. See, e.g., Parker v. Stage, 371 N.E.2d 513 (N.Y. 1977).

77. Life expectancy at birth in 1920 was 54.1 years. Bureau of the Census, *Historical Statistics, 1790–1970* B116 (1973). In 1990, the life expectancy at birth was 75.4. United States Department of Commerce, Bureau of the Census, *Statistical Abstracts* (1992), table 104 at 76. The percentage of the population over eighty-five was 0.2 in 1920 and 3.0 in 1990. Barbara Vobejda, "Census: Elderly Population Growth Will Lead to 4-Generation Families," *Washington Post,* A3 (November 10, 1992). Although these gains have occurred primarily at the low end, through reduction of infant mortality, there has also been an extension of the life expectancy of the elderly through eradication of some diseases and advances in surgical technology. United States Department of Commerce, Bureau of the Census, *Our Aging World II,* International Population Reports P95/92–93, 23–30 (1993).

78. The average size of a family in 1920 was 6.0. *Historical Statistics,* supra note 77, at A355. In 1990 the figure was 3.18. *Statistical Abstracts,* supra note 77, at table 66, p. 53. See also Norman Daniels, "Family Responsibility Initiatives and Justice between Age Groups," 73 *Law, Medicine, and Health Care* 153, 157 (1985)(family was twice as large in 1900).

79. See also Paul Rubin, James Rau, and Edward Meeker, "Forms of Wealth and Parent-Offspring Conflict," 2 *Journal of Social and Biological Structures* 53, 54 (1972).

80. Karen C. Holder and Timothy M. Smeeding, "The Poor, the Rich, and the Insecure Elderly Caught in Between," 68(2) *Millbank Quarterly* 191 (1990). Statutes in some states do require some minimal support from working children if aged and infirm parents would otherwise be on state support or are in state institutions. See, e.g. Ark. Stat. Ann. §20–47–106 (1992); Cal. Fam. Code §4400 (1992); Burns Ind. Code Ann. §31–16–17–1; Md. Fam. Law Code Ann. §13–102 (1991); Mont. Code Ann. §40–6–301 (1992); Nev. Rev. Stat. Ann. §428.070 (1991); N.J. Stat. Ann. §44:1–140 (West Supp. 1991); 62 P.S. §1973 (1968 and Supp. 1990); S.D. Cod. Laws §25–7–27 (1992); Va. Code Ann. §20–88 (Michie 1991); W. Va. Code §9–5–9 (1990). See generally Terrance A. Kline, "A Rational Role for Filial Responsibility Laws in Modern Society?" 26 *Family Law Quarterly* 195, 200 and n.47 (1992).

81. See, e.g., Charles Y. Horioka, *The Applicability of the Life Cycle Model of Saving to Japan* (1972), cited in Burnheim, Shleifer, and Summers, supra note 28, at 1074.

82. See, e.g., State ex rel. Williams v Marsh, 626 S.W.2d 223, 226 (Mo. 1982); D. C. Kolko, "Characteristics of Child Victims of Physical Violence: Research Findings and Clinical Implications," 7 *Journal of Interpersonal Violence* 244–276 (June 1992); Raymond H. Starr., Jr., D. C. MacLean, and D. P. Keating, "Life-Span De-

velopmental Outcomes of Child Maltreatment," in *The Effects of Child Abuse and Neglect: Issues and Research* 1–32 (Raymond H. Starr, Jr., and David A. Wolfe, eds., 1991); L. Y. Zaidi, J. F. Knutson, and J. G. Mehm, "Transgenerational Patterns of Abusive Parenting: Analog and Clinical Tests," 15 *Aggressive Behavior* 137–152 (1989).

83. See, e.g., Becker and Lewis, supra note 31; Gary Becker and Nigel Tomes, "Child Endowments and the Quantity and Quality of Children," *Journal of Political Economy* S143 (1976).

84. Becker and Lewis, supra note 31; Becker and Tomes, supra note 83.

85. See sources cited at note 31 supra.

86. See Brinig, supra note 40, at 303 and n.37; cf. Martin Zelder, "Inefficient Dissolutions as a Consequence of Public Goods: The Case of No-Fault Divorce," 22 *Journal of Legal Studies* 503 (1994).

87. Yoram Weiss and Robert Willis, "Children as Collective Goods and Divorce Settlements," 3 *Journal of Labor Economics* 268 (1985); see, e.g., Rosenblatt v. Birnbaum, 212 N.E.2d 37 (N.Y. 1965).

88. See discussion in Brinig, supra note 40, at 309–310.

89. The National Education Goals Panel, *The National Education Goals Report: Building a Nation of Learners* (1992).

90. Divorce itself, while it may be the best alternative for the adults involved, frequently has a negative effect on their children. See, e.g., Barbara Dafoe Whitehead, "Dan Quayle Was Right: Harmful Effects of Divorce on Children," 271 *Atlantic* 47 (April 1993); Mavis Hetherington, Martha Cox, and Roger Cox, "Effects of Divorce on Parents and Children," in *Nontraditional Families: Parenting and Child Development* 233 (Michael E. Lamb, ed., 1982); Mavis Hetherington, Martha Cox, and Roger Cox, "Long-Term Effects of Divorce and Remarriage on the Adjustment of Children," 24 *Journal of the American Academy of Child Psychiatry* 518 (1985); Judith S. Wallerstein, *Second Chances: Men, Women, and Children a Decade after Divorce* (1989); Judith S. Wallerstein, *Surviving the Breakup: How Children and Parents Cope with Divorce* (1980); Judith S. Wallerstein, "The Long-Term Effects of Divorce on Children: A Review," 30 *Journal of the American Academy of Child and Adolescent Psychiatry* 349 (1991).

91. For a discussion of dependence, see Martha A. Fineman, "Masking Dependency: The Political Role of Family Rhetoric," 81 *Virginia Law Review* 2181–15 (1995).

92. The full results and data sources are explored in Brinig, supra note 40.

93. See Fumio Hayashi, "Why Is Japan's Saving Rate So Apparently High?" in National Bureau of Economic Research, *Macroeconomics Annual* 147, 176 (Stanley Fischer, ed., 1986)(67 percent of persons sixty-five or over lived with their children in 1983).

94. Becker, supra note 38, at 24. See also Burnheim, Shleifer, and Summers, supra note 28, at 1074; see also Epstein, supra note 28, at 1466.

95. See Mary Ann Glendon, *Rights Talk: The Impoverishment of Political Discourse*

126 (1991)(noting the economic argument, but adopting a communitarian approach).

96. Victor Fuchs and Diane M. Reklis, "America's Children: Economic Perspectives and Policy Options," 255 *Science* 41, 44 (1992). See also Peter Laslett, "Is There a Generational Contract?" in *Justice between Age Groups and Generations* 24 (Peter Laslett and James S. Fishkin, eds., 1992).

97. Cox and Stark, supra note 40.

98. Whitehead, supra note 90, at 57.

99. Woodhouse, supra note 37. See also Schneider, supra note 25, at 526–529 (1992).

100. Martha Fineman, *The Neutered Mother, the Sexual Family, and Other Twentieth-Century Tragedies* (1995). See also Fineman, supra note 91.

101. See, e.g., Jerry Mishan, "Pareto Optimality and the Law," 19 *Oxford Economic Papers* 255, 272 n.2 (1967); Richard Posner, "The Economic Approach to Law," 53 *Texas Law Review* 757, 776 (1975).

102. This concept endorses all measures where the sum of the benefits exceeds the sum of the costs. See, e.g., Posner, supra note 101, at 11–13.

103. See, e.g., Czapanskiy, supra note 66.

104. Married women who do not work outside the home have the poorest mental health of any group of normal adults. As noted in Lois Verbegge and Jennifer Madans, "Women's Roles and Health," *American Demographics* 36 (March 1985). See also Margaret F. Brinig, "The Law and Economics of No-Fault Divorce: A Review of *No-Fault Divorce: What Went Wrong?*" 26 *Family Law Quarterly* 453, 466–467 and n.87 (1993). But cf. Linda J. Waite, "Does Marriage Matter?" 32 *Demography* 483, 499 (1995)(physical health benefits for women as well as men).

105. See Douglas W. Allen, "What's at Fault with No-Fault?" presented at Canadian Law and Economics Association Annual Meeting, Toronto, September 1992; Ira Ellman, "The Theory of Alimony," 77 *California Law Review* 1 (1989); and Zelder, supra note 86.

106. See, e.g., David Chambers, "Rethinking the Substantive Rules for Custody Disputes in Divorce," 83 *Michigan Law Review* 477, 504 (1984); sources cited supra note 90.

107. See, e.g., 23 Pa. Cons. Stat. §4327.

108. Va. Code Ann. §20–107.2.

109. See, e.g., Kujawinski v. Kujawinski, 376 N.E.2d 1382 (Ill. 1978).

110. Scott and Scott, supra note 1, at 2405–14.

111. Zelder, supra note 86.

112. 9 So. 885–886 (Miss. 1891).

113. Judith Areen, "Intervention between Parent and Child: A Reappraisal of the State's Role in Child Neglect and Abuse Cases," 63 *Georgetown Law Journal* 887, 908–909 (1975).

114. See, e.g., Worrell v. Worrell, 174 Va. 11, 19, 4 S.E.2d 343, 346 (1939); and Yost v. Yost, 172 Md. 128, 134, 190 A. 753, 756 (1937).

115. Wright v. Wright, 213 Va. 177, 179, 191 S.E.2d 223, 225 (1972).

116. Cates v. Cates, 156 Ill.2d 76, 619 N.E.2d 715 (1993).

117. See generally Samuel Mark Pipino, "In Whose Best Interest? Exploring the Continuing Viability of the Parental Immunity Doctrine," 53 *Ohio State Law Journal* 1111 (1992).

118. 36 N.Y.2d 35; 324 N.E.2d 338; 364 N.Y.S.2d 859 (1974).

119. Compare Scott and Scott, supra note 1 ("parental judgment rule").

120. 3 Cal.3d 914, 479 P.2d 648, 92 Cal. Rptr. 288 (1971).

121. 213 Va. 177, 191 S.E.2d 223 (1972). See also DeMarco v. DeMarco, 274 N.J. Super. 257, 643 A.2d 1053 (1992).

122. 284 Or. 705, 588 P.2d 1105 (1978); see generally Comment, "Defining," supra note 64. Compare Ankenbrandt v. Richards, 502 U.S. 1023 (1992); Mahnke v. Moore, 77 A.2d 923 (Md. 1951).

123. 107 So. 2d 885 (Ala. 1958).

124. See Jed Rubenfeld, "The Right of Privacy," 102 *Harvard Law Review* 737 (1989); see also Woodhouse, supra note 3.

125. For a critique of this approach, see Singer, supra note 59.

126. Becker and Murphy, supra note 39.

127. Compare Scott and Scott, supra note 1, at 2438 (advocating a parental judgment rule).

128. For example, a criminal conviction for sexual conduct with other minors will constitute such harm even if the child is not physically endangered. Both the child's image of proper parental conduct and his or her reputation in the community will be tarnished by the parent's activities. See, e.g., L. C. S. v. S. A. S., 453 S.E.2d 580 (Va. Ct. App. 1995).

129. Janet Moore, "Covenant and Feminist Reconstructions of Subjectivity within Theories of Justice," 55 *Law and Contemporary Problems* 159, 171 (1992).

130. See, e.g., Matthew 20:1–16 (laborers in the vineyard all paid the daily wage, even though they began at different times); the Parable of the Prodigal Son, Luke 15:11–32. See also Moore, supra note 129, at 172, citing Jon Levenson, "Covenant and Commandment," 21 *Tradition* 42, 50 (1983).

131. William J. Everett, "Contract and Covenant in Human Community," 36 *Emory Law Journal* 557, 567 (1987); Moore, supra note 129, at 186–196. Cf. Katharine T. Bartlett, "Feminist Legal Methods," 103 *Harvard Law Review* 829, 886 (1990).

132. See, e.g., Reid v. Reid, 429 S.E.2d 208 (Va. 1993).

133. See, e.g., Green v. Sollenberger, 656 A.2d 773 (Md. 1995); Huckaby v. Huckaby, 393 N.E.2d 1256 (Ill. Ct. App. 1979); Alig v. Alig, 255 S.E.2d 494 (Va. 1979).

134. See, e.g., Suire v. Miller, 363 So. 2d 945 (La. Ct. App. 1978); Wulff (Tierney) v. Wulff, 500 N.W.2d 845 (Neb. 1993).

135. See, e.g., Elizabeth S. Scott, "Rational Decisionmaking about Marriage and Divorce," 76 *Virginia Law Review* 9, 12 (1990); Robert Scott, "Conflict and Cooperation in Long-Term Contracts," 75 *California Law Review* 2005 (1987).

136. Cf. Becker and Murphy, supra note 39.

137. Scott and Scott, supra note 1, at 2460. Compare Alan Schwartz, "Unconscionability and Imperfect Information: A Research Agenda," 19 *Canadian Business Law Journal* 437 (1991).

138. Compare Margaret F. Brinig and Steven M. Crafton, "Marriage and Opportunism," 23 *Journal of Legal Studies* 869, 879–881 (1994) (unintended consequences of no-fault divorce).

139. Becker, supra note 28.

140. See also Yoram Ben-Porath, "Economics and the Family—Match or Mismatch? A Review of Becker's *A Treatise on the Family*," *Journal of Economic Literature* 52, 54 (1982).

141. Everett, supra note 131, at 562. See also William Everett, "Shared Parenthood in Divorce: The Parental Covenant and Custody Law," 2 *Journal of Law and Religion* 85–99 (1984). When the modern promise under seal is enforced, the appropriate remedy is expectation of damages. Melvin Eisenberg, "Donative Promises," 47 *University of Chicago Law Review* 1 (1979).

142. Lon Fuller, "Consideration and Form," 41 *Columbia Law Review* 799 (1941); Michael Trebilcock, *The Limits of Freedom of Contract* 12 (1993).

143. Everett, supra note 131, at 566. See also June R. Carbone and Margaret F. Brinig, "Rethinking Marriage: Feminist Ideology, Economic Change, and Divorce Reform," 65 *Tulane Law Review* 953, 1005–8 (1991).

144. See Francis G. Morrisey, "Proposed Changes in Canonical Matrimonial Legislation," 20 *Catholic Lawyer* 30 (1974). See also Joseph Allen, *Love and Conflict: A Covenantal Model of Christian Ethics* 17 (1984). Older religious discussions of covenant appear in Genesis 9:8–17 (covenant with Noah); Psalms 89:1; Hosea 2:19–23 (opposed to unfaithfulness); 1 Kings 8:16 and 2 Samuel 7:9–37 (Davidic covenant). See generally Geoffrey P. Miller, "Contracts of Genesis," 22 *Journal of Legal Studies* 15, 23–27 (1993). In the New Testament, Christ is seen as the new covenant between God and man. See, e.g., Matthew 26:28. Daniel Elazar, *American Federalism: A View from the States* (3d ed. 1984).

145. See Milton C. Regan, *Family Law and the Pursuit of Intimacy* 131–139 (1993); Scott and Scott, supra note 1, at 2460–62.

146. Beginning with Stanley v. Illinois, 405 U.S. 645 (1972) and Lehr v. Robertson, 463 U.S. 248 (1982), the cases include In re Petition of Otaker Kirchner, 164 Ill. 2d 468, 649 N.E. 2d 324 (1995); In re Clausen, 501 N.W.2d 193 (Mich. Ct. App. 1993); Augusta Co. Dep't. Soc. Serv. v. Unnamed Mother, 3 Va. App. 40, 348 S.E.2d 26 (1986); and Robert O. v. Russell K., 578 N.Y.S.2d 594 (App. Div.) 1990, aff'd., 604 N.E.2d 99 (N.Y. 1992).

147. See Everett, supra note 131; Jerry McCant, "The Cultural Contradiction of Fathers as Nonparents," 21 *Family Law Quarterly* 127 (1987); Schneider, supra note 25, at 526–528; Woodhouse, supra note 37, at 1772–75.

148. See, e.g., Malpass v. Morgan, 192 S.E.2d 794 (Va. 1972); Flowers v. Cain, 237 S.E.2d 111 (Va. 1977).

149. See Laura E. Montgomery et al., "The Effects of Poverty, Race, and Family Struc-

ture on U.S. Children's Health: Data from the NJIS," 86 *American Journal of Public Health* 1401 (1996); (1978–1980 and 1989–1991); Woodhouse, supra note 37, at 1755, 1815 (1993). See also Bartlett, supra note 36, at 294–295.

150. Regan, supra note 145.

151. Id. at 187.

152. Id.

153. Id. at 186.

154. "A diamond is forever" has long been the slogan of DeBeers, the South African diamond exporting monopoly. See Margaret F. Brinig, "Rings and Promises," 6 *Journal of Law, Economics, and Organization* 203 (1990).

155. Compare Miller, supra note 144, at 23–24 (1993): "It formalizes and bonds a promise by invoking the deity as witness or even as cobeneficiary of the promise." See also Moore, supra note 129, at 183.

156. See Chapter 3.

157. Seltzer, supra note 15, at 235.

158. See also Carbone and Brinig, supra note 143, at 1007; June Carbone, "Income Sharing: Redefining the Family in Terms of Community," 31 *Houston Law Review* 359 (1994).

159. Compare Fineman, supra note 91.

160. See Gary S. Anderson and Robert Tollison, "A Theory of Rational Childhood," 7 *European Journal of Political Economy* 199 (1991). The "lumping together" phenomenon is my characterization of Becker's treatment of children, supra note 28. See especially chap. 8 on the "Rotten Kid Syndrome."

161. Martha Minow, "Lawyering for the Child: Principles of Representation in Custody and Visitation Disputes Arising from Divorce," 87 *Yale Law Journal* 1126 (1978); Woodhouse, supra note 37.

162. See, e.g., In re Baby M., 537 A.2d 1227 (N.J. 1988). See generally Matt Ridley, *The Red Queen: Sex and the Evolution of Human Nature* (1993).

163. Huddleston v. Infertility Center, 700 A.2d 453 (Pa. Super. Ct. 1997); Davan Maharak, "Man Must Resume Payments in Surrogacy Case," *Los Angeles Times*, 5 (October 9, 1997).

164. See Jane Maslow Cohen, "Legal Claims of Coercive and Exploitative Agreement: Introducing Coercion-Feel," 94 *American Philosophical Association Newsletter* 99 (1994); and Lori B. Andrews, "Surrogate Motherhood: The Challenge for Feminists," *Law, Medicine, and Health Care* 72 (1988).

165. Margaret F. Brinig, "A Maternalistic Approach to Surrogacy: Comment on Richard Epstein's *Surrogacy: The Case for Full Contractual Enforcement*," 81 *Virginia Law Review* 2377 (1996).

166. 345 U.S. 528 (1953). Cf. Perry v. Ponder, 604 S.W.2d 306, 313 (Tex. Civ. App. 1980).

167. 502 N.W.2d 649 (Mich. 1993). See also In re Petition of Otaker Kirchner, 649 N.E.2d 324 (Ill. 1995), cert. denied, 515 U.S. 1152 (1995). For a comment, see Scott and Scott, supra note 1, at 2405–9.

168. Id. at 657, 687, 502 N.W.2d at 652, 665–666. The dissent noted that the majority had focused exclusively on the concerns of the competing adults; id. at 697–698, 502 N.W.2d at 670–671 (Levin, J., dissenting).

169. Bennett v. Jeffreys, 356 N.E.2d 277 (N.Y. 1976). See also DeShaney v. Winnebago Co. Dep't. of Soc. Servs., 489 U.S. 189 (1989).

170. Hogge v. Hogge, 16 Va. App. 520, 431 S.E.2d 656 (1993); see also Pappas v. Pappas, 75 N.W.2d 264 (Iowa 1956); Huckaby v Huckaby, 393 N.E.2d 1256 (Ill. Ct. App. 1979); Green v. Sollenberger, 656 A.2d 773 (Md. Ct. App. 1995).

171. Malpass v. Morgan, 192 S.E.2d 794 (Va. 1972).

172. Stanley v. Illinois, 405 U.S. 645 (1972).

173. Santosky v. Kramer, 455 U.S. 745 (1982); Lassiter v. Dep't. Soc. Servs., 452 U.S. 18 (1981).

174. This has occurred in part because of the increase in drug usage by parents, in part because of the new abuse reporting requirements. See, e.g., Va. Code Ann. §2.1–380, mandating investigation of any abuse complaint.

175. Geoffrey Cowley, "The Biology of Beauty," 127 Newsweek 60 (June 3, 1996).

176. See, e.g., Mary I. Benedict et al., "Reported Maltreatment in Children with Multiple Disabilities," 14 Child Abuse and Neglect 207–217 (1990); William N. Friedrich and Jerry A. Boriskin, "The Role of the Child in Abuse: A Review of the Literature," 46(4) American Journal of Orthopsychiatry 580–590 (1976); Ann L. Frodi, "Contribution of Infant Characteristics to Child Abuse," 85 American Journal of Mental Deficiency 341–349 (1981); Roger White et al., "Physical Disabilities as Risk Factors for Child Maltreatment: A Selected Review," 57 American Journal of Orthopsychiatry 93–101 (1987).

177. See, e.g., Diane Ackerman, "The Magic Touch: Nothing May Be More Important to a Baby than Physical Contact," 12 American Health 70 (1993); Tim Beardsley, "Different Strokes: Premature Infants Gain from Being Handled," 261 Scientific American 34 (1989); Bruce Bower, "Different Strokes: The Touch of a Hand and Sway of a Bed Can Have Far-Reaching Effects on Premature Babies Encased in Incubators," 128 Science News 301 (1985); Mary Lou Hulseman and Lee A. Norman, "The Neonatal ICU Graduate Part II: Fundamentals of Outpatient Care," 45 American Family Physician 1696 (1992); Saull M. Schanberg and Tiffany Field, "Sensory Deprivation Stress and Supplemental Stimulation in the Rat Pup and Preterm Human Neonate," 58 Child Development 1431–47 (1987). Premature infants are at increased risk for physical abuse and neglect. Bower, supra, at 301; K. K. Minde, "The Impact of Prematurity on the Later Behavior of Children and on Their Families," 11 Clinical Perinatology 227–233 (1984).

178. See, e.g., Ridley, supra note 162, at 297–306; Cohen, supra note 69.

179. See, e.g., Bd. of Curators of Univ. of Missouri v. Horowitz, 435 U.S. 78 (1978); Daniel S. Hamermesh and Jeff E. Biddle, "Beauty and the Labor Market," 84 American Economic Review 1174–94 (1994); Peter Passell, "An Ugly Subject: The Prejudice Against Hiring Homely People," New York Times, 2 (January 27, 1994).

180. Ridley, supra note 162, at 146–149.

181. Brinig, supra note 40; and Richard A. Posner, *Aging and Old Age* 220–222 (1995).
182. Harmatz v. Harmatz, 457 A.2d 399 (D.C. 1983).
183. For example, an eleven-year old boy was killed by his father for being unable to tell time. The child's great-grandmother said that he was a slow learner and was attending special education classes. Sari Hurwitz, "Father Is Charged in Beating Death of District Boy," *Washington Post,* A1 (May 1, 1997).
184. Hulseman and Norman, supra note 177.
185. Martin Daly and Margo Wilson, "Child Abuse and Other Risks of Not Living with Both Parents," 6 *Ethology and Sociobiology* 197 (1985); Joy L. Lightcap et al., "Child Abuse: A Test of Some Predictions from Evolutionary Theory," 3 *Ethology and Sociobiology* 61 (1982).
186. Abuse by stepparents, who have no genetic relationship to the child, and its connection with the second marriage is discussed in Owen D. Jones, "Evolutionary Analysis in Law: A Model for Analysis and Its Application to Child Abuse," 75 *North Carolina Law Review* 1117 (1997).
187. This competition with parents forms the basis of many of the child's actions, according not only to Sigmund Freud, *Basic Writings of Sigmund Freud* (A. A. Brill, trans. and ed., 1995), but also to Anderson and Tollison, supra note 160.
188. See, e.g., Edmund Wilson, *Sociobiology: The New Synthesis* (1975); Ridley, supra note 162.
189. William N. Friedrich and Allison J. Einbender, "The Abused Child: A Psychological Review," 12 *Journal of Clinical Child Psychology* 244–256 (1983) (ugly children).
190. Daly and Wilson, supra note 185; Lightcap et al., supra note 185.
191. *The Maltreatment of Children with Disabilities and Child Maltreatment in Substance Abusing Families* (1991), SIB-068, from the National Data Archive on Child Abuse and Neglect, Family Life Development Center, Cornell University.
192. The sample consisted of thirty-six agencies, or "primary sampling units," in which a total of two thousand substantiated instances of abuse had occurred over a period of four to six weeks.
193. The records we obtained contained 168 variables in the child-level file and 223 in the adult (case-level) file.
194. Margaret F. Brinig and F. H. Buckley, "Child Abuse and the Ugly Duckling," 1 *Journal of Family Studies* 41 (1999).
195. There were 432 such families.
196. DeShaney v Winnebago Co. Dep't. of Soc. Servs., 489 U.S. 189 (1989).
197. Richard Delaney and Frank Kunstal, *Troubled Transplants: Unconventional Strategies for Helping Disturbed Foster and Adoptive Children* (1993); see Audrey Gillan, "Controversial Disorder Raised as Defense in Boy's Death," *Washington Post,* A1 (September 19, 1997).
198. See, e.g., Brian Mooar, "Fla. Jury Convicts Man in Stepdaughter's Death; 7-Year-Old Formerly Lived in Md.," *Washington Post,* B1 (November 19, 1996).

199. DeShaney v. Winnebago Co. Dep't. of Soc. Servs., 489 U.S. 189 (1989).

200. 455 U.S. 745 (1982).

201. 452 U.S. 18 (1981).

202. 117 S. Ct. 555, 136 L. Ed. 2d 473 (1996) (right to transcript on appeal from termination).

203. Thus the spouse could grossly deviate from the marital contract and be disciplined by extralegal social norms. The parent who violates his fiduciary obligations may be subject to greater state control. Scott and Scott, supra note 1.

204. Margaret F. Brinig, "Equality and Sharing: Views of Households across the Iron Curtain," 7 *European Journal of Law and Economics* 55 (1998).

6. Families in Transition

1. Gary S. Becker, Elisabeth Landes, and Robert Michael, "An Economic Analysis of Marital Instability," 85 *Journal of Political Economy* 1141 (1977).

2. Douglas W. Allen and Margaret F. Brinig, "Sex, Property Rights, and Divorce," 5 *European Journal of Law and Economics* 211 (1998).

3. See id. We base our figures on more than twenty thousand divorces granted in 1995. See also Larry Bumpass, James Sweet, and Andrew Cherlin, "National Estimates of Cohabitation," 26 *Demography* 615 (1989), for earlier data.

4. Robert Wright, *The Moral Animal* (1994).

5. Matt Ridley, *The Red Queen: Sex and the Evolution of Human Nature* (1994).

6. See Richard A. Epstein, "The Varieties of Self-Interest," 8 *Social Philosophy and Policy* 103 (1990).

7. See also Theodore Bergstrom, "Economics in a Family Way," 34 *Journal of Economic Literature* 1903 (1996); Linda R. Hirshman, *Material Girls: A Game Theoretic Revision of the Social Contract Exercise with Women Present* 101–109 (1995).

8. Allen and Brinig, supra note 2.

9. William Everett, "Contract and Covenant in Human Community: Perspectives in Covenant, Contract, and the Resolution of Disputes," 36 *Emory Law Journal* 557, 560, 562 (1987); Daniel Elazar, *American Federalism: A View from the States* (1972); but compare Max Rheinstein, "The Law of Divorce and the Problem of Marriage Stability," 9 *Vanderbilt Law Review* 633, 660 (1956).

10. William Blackstone, 1 *Commentaries* 358, 408 (John B. Gifford, ed., 1823).

11. Edward Shorter, *The Making of the Modern Family* 255–268 (1975); June Carbone and Margaret F. Brinig, "Rethinking Marriage: Feminist Ideology, Economic Change, and Divorce Reform," 65 *Tulane Law Review* 953, 962–965 (1991); Roderick Phillips, *Putting Asunder: A History of Divorce in Western Society* 364–369, 378–382 (1988); Carl Schneider, "Moral Discourse and the Transformation of American Family Law," 83 *Michigan Law Review* 1803, 1842–45 (1986).

12. Michael Grossberg, "Guarding the Altar: Physiological Restrictions and the Rise of State Intervention in Matrimony," 26 *American Journal of Legal History* 198,

208 (1982); Shorter, supra note 11, at 5; Mary Ann Glendon, *The New Family and the New Property,* chap. 1 (1975).

13. State v. Rhodes, 61 N.C. 349, 353 (1868); but see Apitz v. Dames, 205 Ore. 242, 306, 287 P.2d 585 (Ore. 1955).

14. Elizabeth Scott and Robert Scott, "Marriage as Relational Contract," 84 *Virginia Law Review* 1225 (1998).

15. See Elizabeth Scott, "Rational Decisionmaking about Marriage and Divorce," 76 *Virginia Law Review* 9, 12, 72–76 (1990). See also Jeffrey Stake, "Mandatory Planning for Divorce," 45 *Vanderbilt Law Review* 397 (1992).

16. See, e.g., James Leitzel, "Reliance and Contract Breach," 52 *Law and Contemporary Problems* 87 (1989); Steven Shavell, "The Design of Contracts and Remedies for Breach," 99 *Quarterly Journal of Economics* 121 (1984). See generally Margaret F. Brinig and June Carbone, "The Reliance Interest in Marriage and Divorce," 62 *Tulane Law Review* 855, 870–82 (1988); Allen Parkman, "Remedies for Breach of the Marriage Contract," presented at the George Mason Law and Economic Center Conference honoring Judge Richard Posner, January 28, 1993.

17. See, e.g., Sidney v. Sidney, 4 Sw. and Tr. 178, 164 Eng. Rep. 1485 (1865).

18. Id. at 180; 164 Eng. Rep. 1485.

19. Gary S. Becker, *Treatise on the Family,* chap. 2 (2d ed. 1981).

20. Scott, supra note 15, at 12; Everett, supra note 9, at 558; Phillips, supra note 11, at 17.

21. Hendrik Hartog, "Marital Exits and Marital Expectations in Nineteenth-Century America," 80 *Georgetown Law Journal* 95 (1991).

22. Rheinstein, supra note 9, at 654; Lawrence Friedman and Robert Percival, "Who Sues for Divorce? From Fault through Fiction to Freedom," 5 *Journal of Legal Studies* 61, 76–77 (1976).

23. Michael Trebilcock and Rosemin Keshvani, "The Role of Private Ordering in Family Law: A Law and Economics Perspective," 41 *University of Toronto Law Journal* 533, 539–40, 544 (1991).

24. Lee Teitelbaum, "Placing the Family in Context," 22 *University of California–Davis Law Review* 801, 810–811 (1989); Daphne Spain and Susan Bianchi, "How Women Have Changed," 5 *American Demographics* 18, 23 (May 1983); and Glenna Spitze and Susan South, "Women's Employment, Time Expenditure, and Divorce," 6 *Journal of Family Issues* 307 (1987).

25. Rheinstein, supra note 9, at 643; Friedman and Percival, supra note 21, at 65 and n.11; and Herbert Jacob, *Silent Revolution: The Transformation of Divorce Law in the United States* 33–36, 47–51 (1988).

26. Friedman and Percival, supra note 21, at 67.

27. This is sometimes called unilateral, as opposed to bilateral, divorce. See, e.g., H. Elizabeth Peters, "Marriage and Divorce: Informational Constraints and Private Contracting," 76 *American Economic Review* 437 (1986); Allen W. Parkman, *No-Fault Divorce: What Went Wrong?* (1992).

28. See, e.g., Martha Albertson Fineman, *The Illusion of Equality: The Rhetoric and Reality of Divorce* 53–75 (1991); Martha Fineman, "Implementing Equality: Ideology, Contradiction, and Social Change: A Study of Rhetoric and Results in the Regulation of the Consequences of Divorce," 1983 *Wisconsin Law Review* 789; Grace Blumberg, "Reworking the Past, Imagining the Future: On Jacob's Silent Revolution," 16 *Law and Social Inquiry* 115, 130–131 (1991). But see Jacob, supra note 25, at 85–86.

29. See also Friedman and Percival, supra note 21.

30. Id.

31. B. G. Gunter and Doyle P. Johnson, "Divorce Filing as Role Behavior: Effect of No-Fault on Divorce Filing Patterns," 40 *Journal of Marriage and Family* 571 (1978).

32. Lynn D. Wardle, "No-Fault Divorce and the Divorce Conundrum," 1991 *Brigham Young University Law Review* 79.

33. Sanford L. Braver, Marnie Whitley, and Christine Ng, "Who Divorced Whom? Methodological and Theoretical Issues," 20 *Journal of Divorce and Remarriage* 1 (1993). For a discussion of women's filing patterns, see Margaret F. Brinig and Douglas W. Allen, "'These Boots Are Made for Walking': Why Wives File for Divorce," *American Economics and Law Review* (forthcoming).

34. Jacob, supra note 25, at 122. The "clean break" concept is criticized by Milton Regan in "Market Discourse and Moral Neutrality in Divorce Law," 1994 *Utah Law Review* 605, 606.

35. See Michael Vaughn, "The Policy of Community Property and Interspousal Transactions," 19 *Baylor Law Review* 20 (1967); Susan Prager, "Sharing Principles and the Future of Marital Property Law," 25 *UCLA Law Review* 1 (1977).

36. Suzanne M. Bianchi and Daphne Spain, "Women, Work, and Family in America," 51 *Population Bulletin* 2 (December 1996); Paula England and George Farkas, *Households, Employment, and Gender: A Social, Economic, and Demographic View* (1986); Victor Fuchs, *Women's Quest for Economic Equality* 44–45 (1988).

37. See, e.g., Gary Crippen, "Stumbling beyond Best Interests of the Child: Reexamining Child Custody Standard-Setting in the Wake of Minnesota's Four-Year Experiment with the Primary Caretaker Preference," 75 *Minnesota Law Review* 427, 453 (1990); Elizabeth Scott and Andre Derdeyn, "Rethinking Joint Custody," 45 *Ohio State Law Journal* 455, 468 and n.58 (1984); Michael Ellsworth and Robert Levy, "Legislative Reform of Child Custody Adjudication: An Effort to Rely on Social Data in Formulating Legal Policies," 4 *Law and Society Review* 167, 202 (1969).

38. See, e.g., Lenore Weitzman, *The Divorce Revolution: The Unexpected Social and Economic Consequences for Women and Children in America* (1985); Lenore Weitzman, "The Economics of Divorce: Social and Economic Consequences of Property, Alimony, and Child Support Awards," 28 *UCLA Law Review* 1181 (1981); Fineman, supra note 28; Peters, supra note 27; Heather Wishik, "Economics of Divorce: An Exploratory Study," 20 *Family Law Quarterly* 79 (1986). But

compare Marsha Garrison, "The Marriage Contract," 131 *University of Pennsylvania Law Review* 1039 (1983).

39. See Margaret F. Brinig and Steven M. Crafton, "Marriage and Opportunism," 23 *Journal of Legal Studies* 869 (1994); Marjorie Maguire Shultz, "Contractual Ordering of Marriage: A New Model for State Policy," 70 *California Law Review* 204, 207 (1982); Lloyd Cohen, "Marriage, Divorce, and Quasi-Rents or 'I Gave Him the Best Years of My Life,'" 16 *Journal of Legal Studies* 267 (1987); Stake, supra note 14; Scott, supra note 15; Douglas W. Allen, "An Inquiry into the State's Role in Marriage," 13 *Journal of Law, Economics, and Organization* 171 (1990); Parkman, supra note 27.

40. Carl E. Schneider, "The Contract in Family Life and Business Practice," presented at the International Society for Family Law North American Conference, Moran, Wyoming, June 11, 1993.

41. This is the articulated basis for the new American Law Institute's compensatory awards. See American Law Institute, *Principles of the Law of Marital Dissolution,* §5.03 (Proposed Final Draft, 1997).

42. See O'Brien v. O'Brien, 489 N.E.2d 712 (N.Y. 1985); but see, e.g., Graham v. Graham, 574 P.2d 75 (Colo. 1978); Stern v. Stern, 331 A.2d 257 (N.J. 1975); In re Marriage of Sullivan, 691 P.2d 1020 (Cal. 1984); In re Marriage of Weinstein, 470 N.E.2d 551 (Ill. Ct. App. 1984); Mahoney v. Mahoney, 453 A.2d 527 (N.J. 1982).

43. Trebilcock and Keshvani, supra note 23, at 556–559.

44. Thomas Marvell, "Divorce Rates and the Fault Requirement," 23 *Law and Society Review* 543 (1989); Margaret F. Brinig and F. H. Buckley, "No-Fault Laws and At-Fault People," 5 *International Review of Law and Economics* 211 (1998).

45. Brinig and Crafton, supra note 39.

46. See, e.g., Stake, supra note 15, at 405–406.

47. Scott and Scott, supra note 14.

48. Id. The Scotts argue that the couple will be disciplined by relational norms and exogenous (outside) social norms.

49. For a listing of the states offering only no-fault divorce or permitting fault to be considered at least in granting alimony, see Brinig and Crafton, supra note 39, at 880 and n.62.

50. Charles Meyers and Steven Crafton, "The Covenant of Further Exploitation—Thirty Years Later," 32 *Rocky Mountain Mineral Law Institute* 1, 6 (1968).

51. Anthony Kronman, "Paternalism and the Law of Contracts," 92 *Yale Law Journal* 763, 783 (1983).

52. Gerhard Mueller, "Inquiry into the State of a Divorceless Society," 18 *University of Pittsburgh Law Review* 545, 577–578 (1957).

53. See, e.g., Amy Stanley, "Conjugal Bonds and Wage Labor: Rights of Contract in the Age of Emancipation," 75 *Journal of American History* 471 (1988). See, e.g., Hetrick v. Apollo Gas Co., 608 A.2d 1074 (Pa. Super. Ct. 1992).

54. Mueller, supra note 52, at 559, 567, 572.

55. See cases cited in Brinig and Crafton, supra note 39, at 881 and n.68.

56. Joel Bishop, *Commentaries on the Law of Marriage and Divorce, with the evidence, practice, pleading, and forms: also of Separations without Divorce, and of the evidence of Marriage in all Issues* (6th ed. 1881) (calling marriage a status once celebrated), id. §3.

57. Charles Goetz and Robert Scott, "Principles of Relational Contracts," 67 *Virginia Law Review* 1089, 1091 (1981).

58. Basically all states now allow marriage to be terminable at will. See Scott, supra note 15, at 17.

59. Elizabeth Peters distinguishes between "unilateral" and "mutual" divorce states according to 1978 divorce laws, supra note 27. She does not classify according to fault and no-fault.

60. Compare American Law Institute, supra note 41, Reporter's Notes 50–51. The ALI does not take account of the role that fault grounds play in negotiations, but does consider fault-based systems determining fault in property or alimony decisions.

61. See, e.g., Sally C. Clarke, "Advance Report of Final Marriage Statistics, 1989 and 1990," 43(12) *Monthly Vital Statistics Report* (1995).

62. See Regan, supra note 34. See also Chapter 4.

63. Martha R. Mahoney, "Legal Images of Battered Women: Redefining the Issue of Separation," 90 *Michigan Law Review* 1 (1991), suggests it may be the threat of leaving that in fact triggers spouse abuse.

64. See, e.g., Cohen, supra note 39. Spousal "investments" in professional degrees are specifically considered in Cal. Fam. Code §4320(2)(b) and Wis. Stat. §767.26(9), in order to reduce incentives for opportunism.

65. Brinig and Crafton, supra note 39. See also Leona Friedberg, "Did Unilateral Divorce Raise Divorce Rates? Evidence from Panel Data," 88 *American Economic Review* 608 (1998).

66. Peters, supra note 27. See also Jacob, supra note 24; William J. Goode, *World Changes in Divorce Patterns* 144 (1993); Scott J. South, "Economic Conditions and the Divorce Rate: A Time-Series Analysis of the Postwar United States," 47 *Journal of Marriage and Family* 31, 37 (1985).

67. Brinig and Buckley, supra note 44.

68. See Peters, supra note 27.

69. Douglas W. Allen, "Marriage and Divorce: Comment," 82 *American Economic Review* 679 (1992). See Peters, supra note 27. See also Marvell, supra note 44, at 544.

70. See Brinig and Buckley, supra note 44.

71. See Margaret F. Brinig and Michael V. Alexeev, "Trading at Divorce," 8 *Ohio State Journal on Dispute Resolution* 279, 294 and table 2 (1993). See also Marygold Melli, Howard Erlanger, and Elizabeth Chambliss, "The Process of Negotiation: An Exploratory Investigation in the Context of No-Fault Divorce," 40 *Rutgers Law Review* 1133 (1988).

72. Richard A. Posner, *Sex and Reason* 249 (1992); Brinig and Crafton, supra note 39.

73. See, e.g., Scott and Scott, supra note 14; Amitai Etzioni, *The Spirit of Community: Rights, Responsibilities, and the Communitarian Agenda* 27 (1993).

74. "On such theories, it is unsurprising that modern American legal culture weigh[s] in heavily on the side of individual self-fulfillment." Mary Ann Glendon, *Abortion and Divorce in Western Law* 108 (1987).

75. See Marvell, supra note 44, at 557; Becker, supra note 19, at 228–229; Phillips, supra note 11, at 619.

76. Mean Divorce Rates, United States, United States Department of Health and Human Services, Bureau of Health Statistics, Marriage and Divorce Branch, various years, 1949–71.

77. Robert H. Mnookin and Lewis Kornhauser, "Bargaining in the Shadow of the Law: The Case of Divorce," 88 *Yale Law Journal* 950 (1979).

78. Peters, supra note 27.

79. Jacob, supra note 25, at 3–36, 47–51, 67. One judge noted that co-respondents always seemed to be caught in a pink negligée. See *New York Herald Tribune,* 19 (October 1, 1965); A. P. Herbert, *Holy Deadlock* (1934), reprinted in Carl E. Schneider and Margaret F. Brinig, *An Invitation to Family Law* 72 (1996).

80. Allen, supra note 69, at 148. See also Friedberg, supra note 65.

81. Martin Zelder, "The Economic Analysis of the Effect of No-Fault Divorce Law on the Divorce Rate," 16 *Harvard Journal of Law and Public Policy* 241 (1993).

82. Paul A. Nakonezny, Robert D. Shull, and Joseph Lee Rodgers, "The Effect of No-Fault Divorce Law on the Divorce Rate across the Fifty States and Its Relation to Income, Education, and Religiosity," 57 *Journal of Marriage and Family* 477 (1995). See also Marvell, supra note 44, showing a temporary increase.

83. Brinig and Buckley, supra note 44.

84. Elisabeth M. Landes, "The Economics of Alimony," 7 *Journal of Legal Studies* 35 (1978). See also Becker, Landes, and Michael, supra note 1.

85. Weitzman, "The Economics of Divorce" and *The Divorce Revolution,* both supra note 38.

86. Richard R. Peterson, "A Re-evaluation of the Economic Consequences of Divorce," 61 *American Sociological Review* 528 (1996); Greg Duncan and Saul Hoffman, "A Reconsideration of the Economic Consequences of Marital Dissolution," 22 *Demography* 485 (1985). Weitzman's rejoinder to Peterson is Lenore J. Weitzman, "The Economic Consequences of Divorce Are Still Unequal: Comment on Peterson," 61 *American Sociological Review* 537 (1996).

87. Marsha Garrison, "Good Intentions Gone Awry: The Impact of New York's Equitable Distribution Law on Divorce Outcomes," 57 *Brooklyn Law Review* 621 (1991).

88. Yoram Weiss and Robert Willis, "Transfers among Divorced Couples: Evidence and Interpretation," 11 *Journal of Labor Economics* 629 (1993). See also Eleanor Maccoby and Robert H. Mnookin, *Dividing the Child: Social and Legal Dilemmas of Custody* (1992).

89. Margaret F. Brinig and Michael V. Alexeev, "Legal Rules, Bargaining, and Transactions Costs: The Case of Divorce," in *Systematic Analysis in Dispute Resolution* 91, 98 and table 6.1 (Stuart S. Nagel and Miriam K. Mills, eds., 1991).

90. See Friedman and Percival, supra note 22, at 69, 75.

91. Landes, supra note 84.

92. Brinig and Carbone, supra note 16, at 863–864; Chester G. Vernier and John B. Hurlbut, "The Historical Background of Alimony Law and Its Present Statutory Structure," in 6 *Law and Contemporary Problems* 197, 198 (1939).

93. Brinig and Allen, supra note 33.

94. Brinig and Crafton, supra note 39.

95. South, supra note 66.

96. Austin Sarat and William L. F. Felstiner, "Lawyers and Legal Consciousness: Law Talk in the Divorce Lawyer's Office," 98 *Yale Law Journal* 1663 (1989); Brinig and Alexeev, supra note 71; and Brinig and Buckley, supra note 44.

97. Zelder, supra, note 81; Peters, supra note 27; Robert Mnookin, "Divorce Bargaining: The Limits on Private Ordering," 18 *University of Michigan Journal of Law Reform* 1015 (1985); Melli, Erlanger, and Chambliss, supra note 71, at 1142.

98. Mnookin and Kornhauser, supra note 77.

99. Stephen B. Goldberg, Eric D. Green, and Frank E. A. Sander, *Dispute Resolution* 91 (1985).

100. Jessica Pearson and Nancy Thoennes, "Mediating and Litigating Custody Disputes: A Longitudinal Evaluation," 17 *Family Law Quarterly* 497, 498 (1984).

101. Id. Most divorcing couples have children, so the parties must co-parent for at least a time.

102. Jessica Pearson et al., "The Decision to Mediate: Profiles of Individuals Who Accept and Reject the Opportunity to Mediate Child Custody and Visitation Issues," 6 *Journal of Divorce* 17, 20 (1982).

103. See, e.g., Janet Rivkin, "Mediation from a Feminist Perspective," 2 *Law and Inequality* 21, 23 (1984); Carrie Menkel-Meadow, "Portia in a Different Voice: Speculations on a Woman's Lawyering Process," 1 *Berkeley Women's Law Journal* 39, 53 (1985).

104. See, e.g., Arthur R. Miller, Note, "The Attorney as Mediator—Inherent Conflict of Interest? 32 *UCLA Law Review* 986, 989, 1006 (1985); see also Comment, "Lay Divorce Firms and the Unauthorized Practice of Law," 6 *University of Michigan Journal of Law Reform* 423, 443 (1973).

105. Stephen J. Bahr et al., "An Evaluation of a Trial Mediation Program," 18 *Mediation Quarterly* 37 (1987).

106. See, e.g., Wardle, supra note 32.

107. Milton C. Regan, *Family Law and the Pursuit of Intimacy* 139 (1993).

108. Trina Grillo, "The Mediation Alternative: Process Dangers for Women," 100 *Yale Law Journal* 1545, 1547 (1991); but cf. Joshua Rosenberg, "In Defense of Mediation," 33 *Arizona Law Review* 467 (1991); Beverly Horsburgh, "Redefining the

Family: Recognizing the Altruistic Caretaker and the Importance of Relational Needs," 25 *University of Michigan Journal of Law Reform* 423 (1992).

109. See, e.g., Jane Ellis, "Surveying the Terrain: A Review Essay of *Divorce Reform at the Crossroads*," 44 *Stanford Law Review* 471 (1992); Mnookin and Kornhauser, supra note 76; Jon Elster, "Solomonic Judgments: Against the Best Interest of the Child," 54 *University of Chicago Law Review* 1 (1987).

110. See, e.g., Joseph Folger and Sydney Bernard, "Divorce Mediation: When Mediators Challenge the Divorcing Parties," 10 *Mediation Quarterly* 5, 20 (1985); Laurie Woods, "Mediation: A Backlash to Women's Progress on Family Law Issues," 19 *Clearinghouse Review* 431, 435 (1985). See also Martha Shaffer, "Divorce Mediation: A Feminist Perspective," 46 *University of Toronto Faculty of Law Review* 162, 181, 185 (1988); and Penelope E. Bryan, "Killing Us Softly: Divorce Mediation and the Politics of Power," 40 *Buffalo Law Review* 441 (1992). But see Joan Kelly, "Mediated and Adversarial Divorce: Respondents' Perceptions of Their Processes and Outcomes," 24 *Mediation Quarterly* 71, 78 (table 1) (1989).

111. See Margaret F. Brinig, "Does Mediation Systematically Disadvantage Women?" 2 *William and Mary Journal of Women and the Law* 1 (1995).

112. Grillo, supra note 108, at 267.

113. See Mnookin and Kornhauser, supra note 77.

114. Id. This concept is further explored in Richard Neely, *The Divorce Decision: The Legal and Human Consequences of Ending a Marriage* 13 (1984).

115. See, for example, Scott and Derdeyn, supra note 37.

116. For a review of the literature, see Brinig and Buckley, supra note 44.

117. Melli, Erlanger, and Chambliss, supra note 71.

118. Carrie Menkel-Meadow, "Toward Another View of Legal Negotiation: The Structure of Problem Solving," 31 *UCLA Law Review* 754 (1984). See also her "Lawyer Negotiations: Theories and Realities—What We Learn from Mediation," 56 *Modern Law Review* 361 (1993).

119. John Ilich and Barbara S. Jones, *Successful Negotiating Skills for Women* (1981).

120. Grillo, supra note 108; Bryan, supra note 110; Wanda Wiegers, "Economic Analysis of Law and Private Ordering: A Feminist Critique," 42 *University of Toronto Faculty of Law Review* 170 (1992).

121. In addition to Mnookin and Kornhauser, supra note 77, see Mnookin, supra note 97, at 1016; Roger Fisher and William Ury, *Getting to Yes: Negotiating Agreement without Giving In* (1985).

122. See, e.g., Elster, supra note 109.

123. Mnookin, supra note 97, at 1025–26.

124. See, e.g., Va. Code Ann. §20–107.2 (1992).

125. See Garska v. McCoy, 278 S.E.2d 357 (W. Va. 1981); David Chambers, "Rethinking the Substantive Rules for Custody Disputes in Divorce," 83 *Michigan Law Review* 477, 493 (1984). But cf. Scott, supra note 15; and Crippen, supra note 37.

126. Brinig and Alexeev, supra note 71, at 294 and table 2, found that only 5 percent of

the cases in Wisconsin went to trial, while 10 percent of the Virginia divorces did. Twenty percent of the Virginia divorces involved pretrial motions, compared to 5 percent in Wisconsin.

127. Brinig and Alexeev, supra note 71, at 283.

128. See, e.g., Gary S. Becker and Gregg Lewis, "On the Interaction between the Quantity and Quality of Children," 81 *Journal of Political Economy* S 279 (1973); and Allen, supra note 39.

129. Lewis A. Kornhauser, "The Great Image of Authority," 36 *Stanford Law Review* 349, 360 and n.38 (1984).

130. Elster, supra note 109, at 4; Chambers, supra note 125, at 557.

131. Visitation would be denied only if the father was shown to be unfit. See, e.g., L. C. S. v. S. A. S., 453 S.E.2d 580 (Va. Ct. App. 1995).

132. See Jeremy Bulow, "Durable-Goods Monopolists," 90 *Journal of Political Economy* 314 (1982). This section is amplified in Margaret F. Brinig, "Property Distribution Physics: The Talisman of Time and Middle-Class Law," 31 *Family Law Quarterly* 93 (1997).

133. Aufmuth v. Aufmuth, 152 Cal. Rptr. 668 (Cal. Ct. App. 1979).

134. American Law Institute, supra note 40, at §4.02.

135. Bussewitz v. Bussewitz, 248 N.W.2d 417, 420 (Wis. 1977).

136. See American Law Institute, supra note 41, §4.07.

137. Joan Krauskopf, "Recompense for Financing Spouse's Education: Legal Protection for the Marital Investor in Human Capital," 28 University of *Kansas Law Review* 379 (1980). See also Allen M. Parkman, supra note 27, and "The Recognition of Human Capital as Property in Celebrity Divorces," 29 *Family Law Quarterly* 141 (1995). Gary Becker did the pioneering work on human capital; see his *Human Capital; A Theoretical and Empirical Analysis, with Special Reference to Education* (3d ed. 1993).

138. Parkman, supra note 137, at 146; Paul T. Heyne, *The Economic Way of Thinking* 204 (4th ed. 1983).

139. But see Graham v. Graham, 574 P.2d 75, 77 (Colo. 1978); and see O'Brien v O'Brien, 489 N.E.2d 712 (N.Y. 1985); see also Ciobanu v. Ciobanu, 409 S.E.2d 749, 751 (N.C. Ct. App. 1981).

140. Mahoney v. Mahoney, 453 A.2d 527 (N.J. 1982).

141. Thus, Lenore Weitzman calls them the "diamonds" of marital property; see *The Divorce Revolution*, supra note 38, at 109. They are "often the most valuable assets a couple owns." Id. at 141.

142. Parkman, supra, note 27.

143. See also Parkman, supra note 137, at 147.

144. See Lehmincke v. Lehmincke, 339 Pa. Super. 571, 573, 389 A.2d 786, 788–789 (Weiland, J., concurring and dissenting).

145. The expected value of an asset (good) P currently worth $100 is calculated as follows. Say we want to know its expected value in a year. There is a 80 percent prob-

ability that it will have a normal rate of return and be worth $110. There is a 10 percent probability that it will do exceptionally well and be worth $120, and a 10 percent probability that it will do badly and be worth only $105. $EV(P) = (.8 \times \$110) + (.1 \times \$120) + (.1 \times \$105) = \$88 + \$12 + \$10.50 = \$110.50$. See John von Neumann and Oskar Morgenstern, *Theory of Games and Economic Behavior* (1964).

146. Cases include Piscopo v. Piscopo, 557 A.2d 1040 (N.J. Super. Ct. 1989); Golub v. Golub, 627 N.Y.S.2d 926 (N.Y. Misc. 1988); Meinholz v. Meinholz, 678 S.W.2d 348 (Ark. 1984).

147. See, e.g., "A Prize Ex-husband; Divorce Doesn't Doom a Wife's Stake in a Nobel," *Pittsburgh Post Gazette*, A14 (October 30, 1995).

148. O'Brien v. O'Brien, 489 N.E.2d 712 (N.Y. Ct. App. 1985).

149. See, e.g., McSparron v. McSparron, 662 N.E.2d 745 (N.Y. 1995).

150. Compare Shultz, supra note 39, at 264; Brinig and Crafton, supra note 39, at 883.

151. June Carbone, "Economics, Feminism, and the Reinvention of Alimony: A Reply to Ira Ellman," 43 *Vanderbilt Law Review* 1463 (1990); Ira Ellman, "The Theory of Alimony," 77 *California Law Review* 1 (1989). Another critical comment is Schneider, supra note 11.

152. See Golub v. Golub, 139 Misc. 2d 440, 527 N.Y.S.2d 946 (1988).

153. Brinig, supra note 132, at 100 and n. 33.

154. Douglas W. Allen, "'What Does She See in Him?' The Effect of Sharing on the Choice of Spouse," 30 *Economic Inquiry* 57 (1992).

155. See Alfred Chandler, *Scale and Scope: The Dynamics of Industrial Capitalism* (1990).

156. William A. Klein, *Business Organization and Finance: Legal and Economic Principles* 145–146 (1980).

157. See Richard Brealey and Stewart C. Myers, *Principles of Corporate Finance* 137–140 (1981); Jeffrey Gordon and Lewis Kornhauser, "Efficient Markets, Costly Information, and Securities Research," 60 *New York University Law Review* 761, 825–827 (1985); Parkman, supra note 139, at 146.

158. Although explicit trading does not occur directly in the marital situation, the couple may make an informal deal to account for a move or a graduate school education. See generally Brinig and Carbone, supra note 16, at 877–882 (1988); Cohen, supra note 39.

159. Gary S. Becker, "On the Allocation of Time," 75 *Economic Journal* 492, 512 (1991); Becker, supra note 18, at 1145–46.

160. Carol Bruch, "Property Rights of De Facto Spouses, Including Thoughts on the Value of Homemaker's Services," 10 *Family Law Quarterly* 101 (1976).

161. Regan, supra note 107; Margaret F. Brinig, "Status, Contract, and Covenant," 79 *Cornell Law Review* 1573 (1994).

162. England and Farkas, supra note 36, at 31–42.

163. See Scott and Scott, supra note 14.

164. Becker, supra note 19, at 30.

165. Cohen, supra note 39.

166. Michael H. Trebilcock, "Marriage as Signal," in *The Fall and Rise of Freedom of Contract* (F. H. Buckley, ed., 2000); William Bishop, "Is He Married? Marriage as Information," 34 *University of Toronto Law Journal* 245 (1984). See also Yoram Ben-Porath, "The F-Connection: Families, Firms, Friends, and the Organization of Exchange," 3 *Population Development Review* 1, 6 (1985).

167. See, e.g., Jean Utz Griffin, "Marriage, Health, Still a Twosome," *Chicago Tribune,* C8 (November 16, 1988); Linda J. Waite, "Does Marriage Matter?" 32 *Demography* 483, 499 (1995).

168. Bea Smith, "The Partnership Theory of Marriage: A Borrowed Solution Fails," 68 *Texas Law Review* 689 (1990). See also Rothman v. Rothman, 320 A.2d 496 (N.J. 1974); Sally B. Sharp, "Equitable Distribution of Property in North Carolina: A Preliminary Analysis," 67 *North Carolina Law Review* 247 (1983); Jana B. Singer, "Divorce Reform and Gender Justice," 78 *North Carolina Law Review* 1103, 1117–18 (1989); Cynthia Starnes, "Divorce and the Displaced Homemaker: A Discourse on Playing with Dolls, Partnership Buyouts, and Dissociation under No-Fault," 60 *University of Chicago Law Review* 67 (1993).

169. Armen A. Alchian and Harold Demsetz, "Production, Information Costs, and Economic Regulation," 62 *American Economic Review* 777 (1972).

170. Ronald W. Coase, "The Nature of the Firm," 4 *Economica* 386 (November 1937); Steven N. S. Cheung, "The Contractual Nature of the Firm," 26 *Journal of Law and Economics* 1 (1983).

171. See Amy Tan, "The Rice Husband," in *The Joy Luck Club* (1989); compare Singer, supra note 168.

172. See Frank Knight, *Risk, Uncertainty, and Profit* (1921).

173. See Starnes, supra note 168; and Nancy Staudt, "Taxing Housework," 84 *Georgetown Law Journal* 1571 (1996).

174. West Virginia Code §48–1–12b.

175. Margaret F. Brinig and Michael V. Alexeev, "Fraud in Courtship: Annulment and Divorce," 2 *European Journal of Law and Economics* 45 (1994).

176. Allen, supra note 154.

177. Allen Parkman, "Why Are Married Women Working So Hard?" 18 *International Review of Law and Economics* 41 (1998).

178. Cf. American Law Institute, supra note 40, at 10–11.

179. See, e.g., DeWitt v. DeWitt, 296 N.W.2d 761, 768 (Wis. 1980).

180. See, e.g., Va. Code Ann. §20–107.3 (G).

181. See, e.g., Owen v. Owen, 14 Va. App. 623, 419 S.E.2d 267 (1992).

182. Va. Code Ann. §20–107.3(G).

183. See, e.g., Regan, supra note 107, at 143. Herma Hill Kay, "An Appraisal of California's No-Fault Divorce Law," 75 *California Law Review* 291, 313 (1987); and Ellman, supra note 151.

184. To make up for uncertainty, the stock price will be lower if the risk is higher. See Brealey and Myers, supra note 157.
185. See, e.g., Kay, supra note 183, at 298, 313; Ellman, supra note 151. For a British example, see Pamela Symes, "Indissolubility and the Clean Break," 48 *Modern Law Review* 44 (1984). Criticizing the clean break concept are Fineman, supra note 28; and June Carbone, "Income Sharing: Redefining the Family in Terms of Community," 31 *Houston Law Review* 359 (1994).
186. See, e.g., England and Farkas, supra note 36, at 65, 67–68 (1987).
187. Carol Bruch, supra note 160, Frances Olsen, "The Family and the Market: A Study of Ideology and Legal Reform," 96 *Harvard Law Review* 1497 (1983).
188. Parkman, supra note 177; W. Keith Bryant, "The Family and Technology," 20 *Human Ecology Forum* 11 (1992); Cathleen D. Zick and Jennifer Geurer, "Family Composition and Investment in Household Capital: Contrasts in the Behavior of Husband-Wife and Female-Headed Households," 21 *Journal of Consumer Affairs* 21 (1987); and "Trends in Married Couples' Time Use: Evidence from 1977–78 and 1987–88," 24 *Sex Roles* 459 (1991); Carol Rose, "Women and Property: Gaining and Losing Ground," 78 *Virginia Law Review* 421 (1992).
189. Gillian Hadfield, "Households at Work: Beyond Labor Market Policies to Remedy the Gender Gap," 82 *Georgetown Law Journal* 89 (1993); Mary O'Connell, "On the Fringe: Rethinking the Link between Wages and Benefits," 67 *Tulane Law Review* 1421 (1993).
190. Bruch, supra note 160; Starnes, supra note 168.
191. Staudt, supra note 173.
192. Some economists see the investment as quite a small one. See, e.g., Parkman, supra note 137, at 147.
193. George A. Akerlof and Janet L. Yellin, eds., *Efficiency Wage Models of the Labor Market* (1986).
194. See, e.g., Jones & Laughlin Steel Corp. v. Pfeifer, 462 U.S. 523 (1983); see also American Bank and Trust Co. v. Community Hospital, 683 P.2d 670 (Cal. 1984).
195. See, e.g., Delta Airlines v. Ageloff, 552 So. 2d 1089 (Fla. 1989); Stuart M. Speiser, *Recovery for Wrongful Death* (2d ed. 1975), where a present value table appears in §8.4 at 713–718. See generally Michael T. Brody, "Inflation, Productivity, and the Total Offset Method of Calculating Damages for Lost Future Earnings," 49 *University of Chicago Law Review* 1003 (1982).
196. Parkman, supra note 137, at 147.
197. California requires equal division. Cal. Fam. Code §2550. Wisconsin, among others, presumes it. Wis. Stat. §767.255. See also American Law Institute, supra note 40, §4.15; Herma Hill Kay, "Beyond No-Fault: New Directions in Divorce Reform," in *Divorce Reform at the Crossroads* 6, 13 (Stephen Sugarman and Herma Hill Kay, eds., 1990). But some states reject even the presumption. See, e.g., Rothman v. Rothman, 320 A.2d 496 (N.J. 1974).
198. See, e.g., Mullen v. Mullen, 188 Va. 259, 49 S.E.2d 349 (1948).

199. In re Marriage of Graham, 574 P.2d 75, 77 (1978).

200. Risk adjustment at the outset, while in some ways more certain, fixes the obligations of the earning spouse in a way that many think undesirable. Daniel D. Polsby and Martin Zelder, "Risk-Adjusted Valuation of Professional Degrees in Divorce," 23 *Journal of Legal Studies* 273 (1994); DeWitt v. DeWitt, 98 Wis. 2d 44, 296 N.W.2d 761, 768 (1980).

201. Alimony and child support are typically exempt; property division is not. See, e.g., In re Calhoun, 715 F.2d 1103 (6th Cir. 1983); 11 U.S.C. §522(d)(10)(D); Cal. Family Code §916, §3592. See generally Sheryl Scheible, "Defining 'Support' Under the Bankruptcy Law: Revitalization of the 'Necessaries' Doctrine," 41 *Vanderbilt Law Review* 1 (1988).

202. Supra note 41, §4.07(1), Comment A, at 167.

203. See, e.g., dela Rosa v. dela Rosa, 309 N.W.2d 755 (Minn. 1981), and Haughan v. Haughan, 343 N.W.2d 796 (Wis. 1984).

204. Brinig and Carbone, supra note 16. Interest was in fact awarded in Inman v. Inman, 578 S.W.2d 266, 269 (Ky. Ct. App. 1979).

205. See Marriage of Graham, 574 P.2d at 78; and Gagliano v. Gagliano, 211 S.E.2d 62 (Va. 1975).

206. See e.g., Srinivasan v. Srinivasan, 396 S.E.2d 675 (Va. Ct. App. 1990).

207. See, e.g., Antonelli v. Antonelli, 409 S.E.2d 117, 119 (Va. 1991); Matter of A.I., 435 N.Y.S.2d 928 (N.Y. Fam. Ct. 1981).

208. Cal. Fam. Code §3650 (alimony); Va. Code Ann. §20–109 (1994).

209. Discounting to present value requires that the decision maker calculate how much a sum today is likely to appreciate into the future (when the full amount would be due). The present value for a $300 payment to be made in three years, given 3 percent interest, is $300/(1.03 \times 1.03 \times 1.03) = \$282.86$.

210. For example, see G. K. Chesterton, "The Superstition of Divorce," in 4 *Collected Works* (1987).

211. Scott and Scott, supra note 14.

212. Both Ira Ellman's *Theory of Alimony,* supra note 151, and the American Law Institute, supra note 41, provide for children.

213. This seems one of my students' primary objections to Becker, supra note 19. See Margaret F. Brinig, "A Comment on Jana Singer's 'Alimony and Efficiency,'" 82 *Georgetown Law Journal* 2461 (1994). See, e.g., Wisner v. Wisner, 631 P.2d 115 (Ariz. Ct. App. 1981).

214. See Ellman, supra note 151. But see Jennifer Morse Roback, "Wages, Rents, and Amenities: Differences among Workers and Regions," 26 *Economic Inquiry* 23 (1988).

215. See, e.g., In re Marriage of Yantis, 629 P.2d 883 (Or. Ct. App. 1981). Using this approach, the partnership model and a lost career opportunities model would produce similar results.

216. See Becker, supra note 19, at 21.

294 Notes to Pages 173–174

217. Singer, supra note 168, at 1118.

218. Parkman, supra note 27.

219. For an amplification of this discussion, see Brinig, supra note 132.

220. Becker, supra note 19; Jacob Mincer and Solomon Polacheck, "Family Investments in Human Capital: Earnings of Women," 397; Arleen Leibowitz, "Home Investments in Children," 432; and Reuben Gronau, "The Effect of Children on the Housewife's Value of Time," 457; all in *Economics of the Family: Marriage, Children, and Human Capital* (Theodore W. Schultz, ed., 1974).

221. Glendon, supra note 12.

222. Krauskopf, supra note 137; Margaret F. Brinig, "The Law and Economics of No-Fault Divorce: A Review of *No-Fault Divorce: What Went Wrong?*" 26 *Family Law Quarterly* 453, 459 and n.36 (1993).

223. Parkman, supra note 27, at 41.

224. Id. at 92.

225. New York, which also goes the furthest in making professional degrees marital property (O'Brien v. O'Brien, 489 N.E.2d 712 [N.Y. 1985], also equitably distributes other career gains that occurred as a result of the marriage; see Golub v. Golub, 527 N.Y.S.2d 946 (N.Y. Misc. 1988).

226. Richard Epstein, "Why Restrain Alienation?" 85 *Columbia Law Review* 970 (1985); Schneider and Brinig, supra note 79, at 387; see also Margaret Friedlander Brinig, "A Maternalistic Approach to Surrogacy: Comment on Richard Epstein's 'Surrogacy: The Case for Full Contractual Enforcement,'" 81 *Virginia Law Review* 2377 (1995); and June R. Carbone, "The Role of Contract Principles in Determining the Validity of Surrogacy Contracts," 28 *Santa Clara Law Review* 581, 590–597 (1988).

227. Maynard v. Hill, 125 U.S. 190, 205 (1988); Regan, supra note 107.

228. Both insurers and employers prefer married to single men. See, e.g., "Why Do Married Men Earn More Than Unmarried Men?" 20 *Social Science Resources* 29 (1991); Fuchs, supra note 36, at 78; Waite, supra note 167, at 492–493.

229. Around 60 percent of divorces. United States Department of Commerce, Bureau of the Census, Child Custody and Child Support, in *Current Population Reports,* Special Series 8 (Series P-23, no. 84) (1979).

230. Compare Jeffrey Parker, "Structural Unemployment in the United States: The Effects of Interindustry and Interregional Dispersion," 30 *Economic Inquiry* 101 (1992).

231. See, e.g., Barbara Dafoe Whitehead, "Dan Quayle Was Right: Harmful Effects of Divorce on Children," 271 *Atlantic* 47 (1993); Mavis Hetherington, Martha Cox, and Roger Cox, "Effects of Divorce on Parents and Children," in *Nontraditional Families: Parenting and Child Development* 233 (M. E. Lamb, ed., 1982); Mavis Hetherington, Martha Cox, and Roger Cox, "Long-Term Effects of Divorce and Remarriage on the Adjustment of Children," 24 *Journal of the American Acad-*

emy of Child Psychiatry 518 (1985); Judith S. Wallerstein, *Second Chances: Men, Women, and Children a Decade after Divorce* (1989); Judith S. Wallerstein and Joan B. Kelly, *Surviving the Breakup: How Children and Parents Cope with Divorce* (1989); Judith S. Wallerstein, "The Long-Term Effects of Divorce on Children: A Review," 30 *Journal of the American Academy of Child and Adolescent Psychiatry* 349 (1991).

232. Barbara Dafoe Whitehead, *The Divorce Culture* 94 (1997).

233. Sara McLanahan and Irwin Garfinkel, "Single Mothers, the Underclass, and Social Policy," 501 *Annals, APSS* 92, 98–99 (1989); Sara McLanahan and Gary D. Sandefer, *Growing Up with a Single Parent: What Hurts, What Helps* (1994).

234. Carbone, supra note 185; McLanahan and Garfinkel, supra note 233.

235. Paul R. D'Amato, "Life-Span Adjustment of Children to Their Parents' Divorce," 4 *The Future of Children: Children and Divorce* 143, 145 (1994).

236. Susan Gettleman and Janet Markowitz, *The Courage to Divorce* 86–87 (1974).

237. Sharon Kraus, "The Crisis of Divorce: Growth Promoting or Pathogenic?" 3 *Journal of Divorce* 111 (1979).

238. Mel Krantzler, *Creative Divorce: A New Opportunity for Personal Growth* 211 (1974).

239. J. Guideubaldi et al., "The Impact of Parental Divorce on Children: Report of the Nationwide NASP Study," paper presented at the annual convention of the National Association for School Psychologists, 1983.

240. American Academy of Pediatrics, "The Pediatrician's Role in Helping Children and Families Deal with Separation and Divorce" (July 1994).

241. Kristin A. Moore and Alma A. Driscoll, "Report to Congress on Out-of-Wedlock Childbearing," *Child Trends* (1997).

242. Hetherington, Cox, and Cox, "Long-Term Effects," supra note 231.

243. E. Mavis Hetherington, "Effects of Father Absence on Personality Development," 7 *Developmental Psychology* 313, 316 (1972).

244. Wallerstein and Kelly, supra note 231, at 21–209.

245. Id. at 219.

246. Elizabeth S. Scott and Robert E. Scott, "Parents as Fiduciaries," 81 *Virginia Law Review* 2401, 2444 (1995).

247. D'Amato, supra note 235, at 146.

248. M. Anne Hill, and June O'Neill, "Family Endowments and the Achievement of Young Children with Special Reference to the Underclass," 29 *Journal of Human Resources* 1064 (1994).

249. David L. Featherman and Robert M. Hauser, *Opportunity and Change* 242–246 (1978).

250. See Martha Fineman, "Masking Dependency: The Political Role of Family Rhetoric," 81 *Virginia Law Review* 2181 (1995). See also Becker, supra note 19, at 43.

251. Saul D. Hoffman, "Divorce and Economic Well-Being: The Effects on Men,

Women, and Children," *Delaware Lawyer* (Spring 1987), suggests that 40 percent of the wage gap between men and women may be due to such reductions. See also Donald Cox, "Panel Estimations of the Effects of Career Interruptions on the Earnings of Women," 22 *Economic Inquiry* 386 (1984); Thomas J. Oldham, "Putting Asunder in the 1990s," 80 *California Law Review* 1091, 1108 and n.82 (1992).

252. Thus I disagree with American Law Institute, supra note 41, which counts only sacrifices made during the marriage itself.

253. See, e.g., Abby v. Strange, 924 S.W.2d 623 (Tenn. 1996); see generally Karen Czapanskiy, "Child Support and Visitation: Rethinking the Connections," 20 *Rutgers Law Journal* 619 (1989).

254. Ira Lupu, "Separation of Powers and the Protection of Children," 61 *University of Chicago Law Review* 1317 (1994); Weiss and Willis, supra note 87; Margaret F. Brinig and F. H. Buckley, "Joint Custody: Monitoring and Bonding Theories," 73 *Indiana Law Journal* 393 (1998); Mnookin and Kornhauser, supra note 77, at 956–957; Shultz, supra note 39, at 264.

255. Lupu, supra note 254.

256. Hal Varian, *Intermediate Microeconomics* 103 (1987).

257. Margaret F. Brinig, "The Family Franchise: Elderly Parents and Adult Siblings," 1996 *Utah Law Review* 393.

258. It should come as no surprise that the Catholic marriage service includes children as an important factor and canon law as an important ingredient in a sacramental marriage. See, e.g., William C. Morrisey, "Proposed Changes in Canonical Matrimonial Legislation," 20 *Catholic Lawyer* 30 (1974).

259. Ross W. Beales, "In Search of the Historical Child: Miniature Adulthood and Youth in Colonial New England," in *Growing Up in America* 7, 22–23 (N. Ray Hiner and Joseph M. Hawes, eds., 1985).

260. U.S. Const., Amend. 26. Subsequently, forty-five states lowered the age of majority to eighteen. Homer Clark, *Domestic Relations* §9.1, at 530 (2d ed. 1987).

261. Sanford Katz, William Schroeder, and Lawrence Sidman, "Emancipating Our Children: Coming of Legal Age in America," 7 *Family Law Quarterly* 211 (1973).

262. Carol Sanger and Eleanor Willemsen, "Minor Changes: Emancipating Children in Modern Times," 25 *University of Michigan Journal of Law Reform* 239, 244 (1992). Some states, unlike California, do provide for counsel in statutory emancipation.

263. Id. at 248.

264. Id. at 244.

265. See, e.g., Parker v. Stage, 371 N.E.2d 513 (N.Y. 1977); Anthony v. Anthony, 196 S.E.2d 66, 67 (Va. 1973).

266. Parental permission is necessary for a minor to marry or to enlist. 10 U.S.C. §505(a) (1988); Cal. Fam. Code §302(a); Cal. Mil. and Vet. Code §389.

267. See, e.g., Suire v. Miller, 363 So. 2d 945 (La. Ct. App. 1978); Bennett v. Bennett, 18 S.E.2d 911, 913 (Va. 1942).

268. See, e.g., Iroquois Iron Co. v. Industrial Commission, 128 N.E. 289 (Ill. 1920); Va. Code §8.01–229.

269. See, e.g., Buxton v. Bishop, 37 S.E.2d 755 (Va. 1946).

270. See, e.g., Cal. Civ. Code §§7600 et seq.; Conn. Gen. Stat. §46b–150d; Ill. Comp. Stat. Ann. ch. 750, act 30/1 et seq.; La. Civ. Code art. 365; Mich. Comp. L. Ann. §722.4; Nev. Rev. Stat. §129.080; N.M. Stat. §32A-21–3; Ore. Rev. Stat. §419B.552; Va. Code §8.01–229, §§16.1–309 et seq., Wyo. Stat. §14–1–201. But see Sanger and Willemsen, supra note 262.

271. Kingsley v. Kingsley, 623 So. 2d 780, 783 (Fla. Ct. App. 1993). See generally Georgia Sargeant, "'Parental Divorce' Cases Highlight Need for Children's Advocates," 29 *Trial* 88 (1988); Herri A. Blair, "Gregory K. and Emerging Children's Rights," 29 *Trial* 22 (1993); Mark Hansen, "Boy Wins 'Divorce' from Mom; Critics Claim Ruling Will Encourage Frivolous Suits by Dissatisfied Kids," 78 *American Bar Association Journal* 16 (1992).

272. 623 So. 2d at 784.

273. Mays v. Twigg, 1993 WL 330624 (Fla. App. 1993).

274. Id. at 3, 6.

275. Id. at *5.

276. See, e.g., Cal. Fam. Code §§7050, 7052.

277. Suire v. Miller, 353 So.2d 945 (La. Ct. App. 1978); Stern v. Stern, 473 A.2d 56 (Md. 1984); Fauser v. Fauser, 271 N.Y.S.2d 59, 61 (N.Y. Fam. Ct. 1966).

278. See, e.g., Harmatz v. Harmatz, 457 A.2d 399 (D.C. 1983).

279. See, e.g., In re Marriage of Vrban, 293 N.W.2d 198, 202 (Iowa 1980). See generally Robert M. Washburn, "Post-majority Support: Oh Dad, Poor Dad," 44 *Temple Law Quarterly* 319 (1971).

280. Sanger and Willemsen, supra note 262, at 308.

281. Id. at 313–314.

282. John L. Langbein, "The Twentieth-Century Revolution in Family Wealth Transmission," 85 *Michigan Law Review* 722, 726 (1988).

7. Winding Up the Firm

1. See Mary Ann Glendon, *Rights Talk: The Impoverishment of Political Discourse* 121–130 (1991).

2. See, e.g., Margaret F. Brinig and Michael V. Alexeev, "Fraud in Courtship: Annulment and Divorce," 2 *European Journal of Law and Economics* 45 (1995); Margaret F. Brinig, "The Effect of Transactions Costs on the Market for Babies," 18 *Seton Hall Legislative Law Journal* 553 (1994); Margaret F. Brinig and Steven M. Crafton, "Marriage and Opportunism," 23 *Journal of Legal Studies* 869 (1994); and Margaret F. Brinig, "Rings and Promises," 6 *Journal of Law, Economics, and Organization* 203 (1990).

3. See Margaret F. Brinig, "Status, Contract, and Covenant," 79 *Cornell Law Review*

1573 (1994); Margaret F. Brinig, "The Family Franchise: Adult Siblings and Elderly Parents," 1996 *Utah Law Review* 393.

4. In addition to the articles cited in note 2, supra, see Marjorie Maguire Shultz, "Contractual Ordering of Marriage: A New Model for State Policy," 70 *California Law Review* 204 (1982).

5. See, e.g., Margaret F. Brinig and June Carbone, "The Reliance Interest in Marriage and Divorce," 62 *Tulane Law Review* 855 (1988); June Carbone, "Economics, Feminism, and the Reinvention of Alimony: A Reply to Ira Ellman," 43 *Vanderbilt Law Review* 1463 (1990); Arthur Cornell, "When Two Become One and Then Come Undone: An Organizational Approach to Marriage and Its Implications for Divorce Law," 26 *Family Law Quarterly* 103 (1992); Brinig and Crafton, supra note 2.

6. See Margaret F. Brinig, "The Nature of the Contract between Parent and Child," paper prepared for the Liberty Fund Symposium, "The Family, the Person, and the State," July 1995.

7. See, for example, Milton C. Regan, *Family Law and the Pursuit of Intimacy* 4 (1993); Brinig, supra note 3, at 1573; Carl E. Schneider, "Moral Discourse and the Transformation of American Family Law," 83 *Michigan Law Review* 1803, 1832 (1985).

8. Brinig, supra note 3, at 1601.

9. Id. Regan, supra note 7; see also William Everett, "Contract and Covenant in Human Community," 36 *Emory Law Journal* 557 (1987); Bea Ann Smith, "The Partnership Theory of Marriage: A Borrowed Solution Fails," 68 *Texas Law Review* 689 (1990); Cynthia Starnes, "Divorce and the Displaced Homemaker: A Discourse on Playing with Dolls, Partnership Buyouts, and the Dissociation under No-Fault," 60 *University of Chicago Law Review* 67 (1993).

10. Brinig, supra note 3, at 1597–99.

11. See Robert Jervis, *Perception and Misperception in International Politics*, chap. 3 (1976); and "Hypothesis on Misperception," in *The War System: An Interdisciplinary Approach* (Richard A. Falk and Samuel S. Kim, eds., 1980).

12. See, e.g., Edward H. Dance, *History the Betrayer: A Study in Bias* (1975); Stephen Van Evera, "Hypothesis on Nationalism and War," 18 *International Security* 5 (1994).

13. See, e.g., John Barry, "Portraits in Oil: *The Prize*" (book review), *Los Angeles Times*, 7 (December 9, 1990). But see "A Great Nation Must Be Philanthropic" (editorial), *Japan Economic Journal*, 8 (July 4, 1987).

14. Paul Kennedy, "The Rise of Anglo-German Antagonism, 1860–1914," 24 *History Journal* 999 (1983).

15. See Edward J. Valaushas, "On the Nets and on the Streets," 16 *Online* 41 (1992).

16. Thomas Schelling, *The Strategy of Conflict* (1960).

17. See, e.g., Thomas C. Schelling, "An Essay on Bargaining," 46 *American Economic Review* 281, 299–301 (1956); see also Robert Axelrod, *The Evolution of Cooperation* 21 (1984); Brinig, supra note 3, at 1592; Carrie Menkel-Meadow, "Pursuing

Settlement in an Adversary Culture: A Tale of Innovation Co-opted or 'The Law of ADR,'" 19 *Florida State Law Review* 1, 36 (1991); Eric Rasmusen, *Games and Information: An Introduction to Game Theory* (1989).

18. Thomas Hobbes, *Leviathan* [1651], in *Philosophy of Right*, (T. M. Knox, ed., 1952).

19. See David Charny, "Nonlegal Sanctions in Commercial Relationships," 104 *Harvard Law Review* 375 (1990); Stewart Macaulay, "Non-contractual Relations in Business: A Preliminary Study," 28 *American Sociological Review* 55 (1963).

20. Anthony T. Kronman, "Contract Law and the State of Nature," 1 *Journal of Law, Economics, and Organization* 5, 9 (1985).

21. Id. at 12–14.

22. Id. at 16.

23. See discussion in Chapter 2, supra.

24. Kronman, supra note 20, at 20–21.

25. Id. at 18–19.

26. Jon Elster, *Ulysses and the Sirens: Studies in Rationality and Irrationality* 37–47 (1984). See also Thomas C. Schelling, "Enforcing Rules on Oneself," 1 *Journal of Law, Economics, and Organization* 357 (1985). In the context of marriage, see Elizabeth S. Scott, "Rational Decisionmaking in Marriage and Divorce," 76 *Virginia Law Review* 9, 49 (1990).

27. See, e.g., John Umbeck, "A Theory of Contract Choice and the California Gold Rush," 20 *Journal of Law and Economics* 421 (1978). In the context of trusts and estates, see, e.g., Adam J. Hirsch and William K. S. Wang, "A Qualitative Theory of the Dead Hand," 68 *Indiana Law Journal* 1, 51 (1992). For a description of specific investments by spouses, see Lloyd Cohen, "Marriage, Divorce, and Quasi-Rents: Or, 'I Gave Him the Best Years of My Life,'" 16 *Journal of Legal Studies* 267–268 (1987). The specific investments cause the damage to follow breach automatically, or nearly so. Kronman, supra note 20, at 19.

28. Yoram Ben-Porath, "The F-Connection: Family, Friends, and Firms, and the Organization of Exchange," 6 *Population and Development Review* 1 (1980).

29. See, e.g., Lassiter-Geers v. Reichenbach, 492 A.2d 303 (Md. 1985); Stuart v. Board of Sups. of Elections, 295 A.2d 223 (Md. 1972).

30. Kronman, supra note 20, at 21.

31. Id.

32. James M. Buchanan, "Rent Seeking, Noncompensated Transfers, and Laws of Succession," 26 *Journal of Law and Economics* 71 (1983).

33. See Ronald Coase, "The Nature of the Firm," 4 *Economica* 386 (1937); Oliver Williamson, *The Economic Institutions of Capitalism: Firms, Markets, Relational Contracting* (1985); Richard N. Langlois, "The New Institutional Economics: An Introductory Essay," in *Economics as a Process: Essays in the New Institutional Economics* 1 (Richard Langlois, ed., 1986). For a complete discussion in the context of franchising, see Gillian K. Hadfield, "Problematic Relations: Franchising and the Law of Incomplete Contracts," 42 *Stanford Law Review* 927 (1990); Paul H. Rubin,

"The Theory of the Firm and the Structure of the Franchise Contract," 21 *Journal of Law and Economics* 223 (1978).

34. Hadfield, supra note 33, at 931–932.
35. Id. at 949. See generally Robert S. Pindyck and Daniel L. Rubinfeld, *Microeconomics* 617–623 (1989).
36. Hadfield, supra note 33, at 931–938.
37. Benjamin Klein, Robert G. Crawford, and Armen Alchian, "Vertical Integration, Appropriable Rents, and the Competitive Contracting Process," 21 *Journal of Law and Economics* 297 (1978).
38. Harry M. Kursch, *The Franchise Room* 118–119 (rev. ed. 1968).
39. John J. Hooker, "The Story of Minnie Pearl—A Case History of One New Company's Trials, Tribulations, and Triumphs," in *Franchising Today: Report on the Fifth International Management Conference on Franchising* 176 (C. Vaughn, ed., 1970).
40. Barry E. Adler, "A Theory of Corporate Insolvency," 72 *New York University Law Review* 343 (1997).
41. Karen Gross, "Taking Community Interests into Account in Bankruptcy: An Essay," 72 *Washington University Law Quarterly* 1031 (1994).
42. Alan Schwartz, "A Contract Theory Approach to Business Bankruptcy," 107 *Yale Law Journal* 1807 (1998).
43. See, e.g., Va. Code Ann. §§16.1–290, 16.1–252F(3).
44. Elizabeth S. Scott and Robert E. Scott, "Marriage as Relational Contract," in *The Fall and Rise of Freedom of Contract* (F. H. Buckley, ed., 2000).
45. Brinig and Crafton, supra note 2.
46. See, e.g., Judith S. Wallerstein and Joan Berlin Kelly, *Surviving the Breakup: How Children and Parents Cope with Divorce* 5–6 (1980); David Chambers, "Stepparents, Biologic Parents, and the Law's Perceptions of 'Family' after Divorce," in *Divorce Reform at the Crossroads* 102–103 (Stephen D. Sugarman and Herma Hill Kay, eds., 1990). For couples' reactions, see Wallerstein and Kelly at 193.
47. Research suggests that even if joint custody is awarded, in practice one parent, usually but not always the mother, will have physical custody the vast majority of the time. Eleanor Maccoby and Robert H. Mnookin, *Dividing the Child: Social and Legal Dilemmas of Custody* (1992).
48. Yoram Weiss and Robert Willis, "Children as Collective Goods and Divorce Settlements," 3 *Journal of Labor Economics* 268, 269 (1985). See, e.g., Victor Fuchs, *How We Live: An Economic Perspective on Americans from Birth to Death* 73 (1983).
49. Weiss and Willis, supra note 48, at 270.
50. Id. at 270. See also Martin Zelder, "Inefficient Dissolutions as a Consequence of Public Goods: The Case of No-Fault Divorce," 22 *Journal of Legal Studies* 503 (1993).
51. Weiss and Willis, supra note 48, at 270.
52. Id. at 272.

53. Id. at 288.

54. See, e.g., Judith A. Seltzer, "Legal Custody Arrangements and Children's Economic Welfare," 96 *American Journal of Sociology* 895 (1991).

55. Weiss and Willis, supra note 48, at 279.

56. Douglas Bernheim, Andre Shleifer, and Lawrence Summers, "The Strategic Bequest Motive," 93 *Journal of Political Economy* 1045, 1049 (1985). See also Gary Becker, "A Theory of Social Interactions," 82 *Journal of Political Economy* 1063 (1974); Wendy Fitzgerald, "Maturity, Difference, and Mystery: Children's Perspectives and the Law," 36 *Arizona Law Review* 11, 71 (1994).

57. See, e.g., Conway v. Conway, 395 S.E.2d 464 (Va. Ct. App. 1990).

58. See, e.g., In the Matter of Burgess, 913 P.2d 473 (Cal. 1996); Tropea v. Tropea, 665 N.E.2d 145 (N.Y. 1996); Gordon v. Goertz, 134 D.L.R.4th 321 (S.Ct. Canada 1996).

59. See, e.g., Margaret F. Brinig and Michael V. Alexeev, "Trading at Divorce: Preferences, Legal Rules, and Transaction Costs," 8 *Ohio State Journal on Dispute Resolution* 279 (1993); Robert H. Mnookin and Lewis Kornhauser, "Bargaining in the Shadow of the Law: The Case of Divorce," 88 *Yale Law Journal* 950 (1979); Marygold Melli et al., "The Process of Negotiation: An Exploratory Investigation in the Context of No-Fault Divorce," 40 *Rutgers Law Review* 1133, 1154 (1988); Elizabeth S. Scott, "Pluralism, Parental Preference, and Child Custody," 80 *California Law Review* 615 (1992). Garska v. McCoy, 278 S.E.2d 357 (W. Va. 1981), suggests that the father may threaten litigation to get a favorable financial result. See also Jon Elster, "Solomonic Judgments: Against the Best Interests of the Child," 54 *University of Chicago Law Review* 1 (1987).

60. See, e.g., Block v. Block, 112 N.W.2d 923, 927 (Wis. 1961); Radford v. Matczuk, 164 A.2d 904 (Md. 1960); Judith Wallerstein and Sandra Blakeslee, *Second Chances: Men, Women, and Children: A Decade after Divorce* 233, 235, 237–239 (1989).

61. David M. Chambers, "Fathers, the Welfare System, and the Virtues and Perils of Child-Support Enforcement," 81 *Virginia Law Review* 2575 (1995).

62. Karen Czapanskiy, "Child Support and Visitation: Rethinking the Connections," 20 *Rutgers Law Journal* 619 (1989).

63. Rosenblatt v. Birnbaum, 264 N.Y.S.2d 521, 212 N.E.2d 37 (N.Y. 1965).

64. See Brinig and Crafton, supra note 2.

65. Yarborough v. Yarborough, 290 U.S. 202 (1933).

66. Yost v. Yost, 190 A. 753 (Md. 1937); Goldstein v. Goldstein, 593 N.E.2d 102 (Ill. Ct. App. 1992).

67. See Hewlett v. George, 9 So. 855 (Miss. 1891). Although spouses can generally sue each other in tort today, see, e.g., Merenoff v. Merenoff, 388 A.2d 951 (N.J. 1978), Va. Code Ann. §8.01–220.1; Homer Clark, *The Law of Domestic Relations in the United States* §10.1 at 372 and n.21 (2d ed. 1987) (for torts other than automobile negligence the intrafamilial immunity doctrine remains intact in most states.) See

generally Comment, "Defining the Parent's Duty after Rejection of Parent-Child Immunity," 33 *Vanderbilt Law Review* 755 (1980); Comment, "Intrafamilial Immunity," 21 *William and Mary Law Review* 273 (1979).

68. Price v. Price, 197 S.W.2d 200, 202–203 (Tex. Ct. App. 1946); see generally Comment, "Defining the Parent-Child Immunity," supra note 67.

69. See, e.g., Conway v. Conway, 395 S.E.2d 464 (Va. Ct. App. 1990).

70. See, e.g., Flowers v. Cain, 237 S.E.2d 111 (Va. 1977).

71. Czapanskiy, supra note 62, claims that if child support payments are not made, noncustodial parents should not be able to visit the child; see also Bethune v. Bethune, 399 N.Y.S.2d 902 (N.Y. 1977).

72. For a case in which a noncustodial father sued his former wife for intentional infliction of emotional distress (and lost), see Hetfield v. Bostwick, 901 P.2d 986 (Ore. App. 1995).

73. In fact, in some cases the father has successfully avoided child support responsibility on the ground that the child has effectively abandoned him. See, e.g., Oehler v. Gross, 594 A.2d 649 (Pa. 1991). See also Bethune v. Bethune, 399 N.Y.S.2d 602 (App. Div. 1977); Parker v. Stage, 371 N.E.2d 513 (N.Y. 1977); Angel v. McLellan, 16 Mass. 28, 31 (1819).

74. See Sandra Evans, "For Va. Woman, Welfare Wasn't an Easy Ride," *Washington Post*, B1 (February 2, 1995). See generally F. H. Buckley and Margaret F. Brinig, "The Market for Deadbeats," 25 *Journal of Legal Studies* 201 (1996).

75. See Glenda Riley, *The Female Frontier: A Comparative View of the Prairie and the Plains* 81 (1988). The pressure for lax divorce laws in the West was hastened by informal "remarriages," without the benefit of a formal divorce. Like the informal corporation, bigamous marriages were a "shadow" institution in matrimonial law with much lower transaction costs. See Henry Butler, "Nineteenth-Century Jurisdictional Competition in the Granting of Corporate Privileges," 14 *Journal of Legal Studies* 129 (1985); Lawrence Friedman and Robert Percival, "Who Sues for Divorce?" 5 *Journal of Legal Studies* 61, 69 (1976).

76. See, e.g., Owens v. Owens, 31 S.E. 72, 74 (Va. 1898).

77. See, e.g., Buchanan v. Buchanan, 197 S.E. 426, 432 (Va. 1938).

78. See, e.g., Pennsylvania v. Warren, 105 A.2d 488, 489 (1954).

79. See, e.g., L. 1952, c. 516 (Virginia); Md. Laws [1957] art. 89C, §1. The more modern version of the Virginia law is the Uniform Reciprocal Enforcement of Support Act, Va. Code Ann. 20–88–12—20–88.31, now replaced by the Interstate Family Support Act, Va. Code Ann. §§20–88.32 et seq., mandated by the federal Social Security Act, Child Support Enforcement Assistance Amendments, 42 U.S.C. §658, which also imposed guidelines for child support awards.

80. See, e.g., Fleming v. Fleming, 271 S.E.2d 584 (N.C. Ct. App. 1980); Sandra Evans, "Candidates' Positions on Social Services Reflect Differences of National Parties," *Washington Post*, B1 (October 24, 1989). State barriers to enforcement of support

obligations explain why many plaintiffs vigorously pursue substitute mechanisms with much higher transaction costs, such as long-arm jurisdiction. See, e.g., Kulko v. Superior Court, 436 U.S. 84 (1978). In addition, states continue to enact legislation extending jurisdiction so that the forum state will be able to render final judgments that merely need execution in the obligor's state. See, e.g., Va. Code Ann. §8.01–328.1(8) and (9).

81. Department of Health and Human Services, Office of Child Support Enforcement, *Twenty-second Annual Report to Congress,* table 2 (1997).

82. Id. at 136, table 76.

83. Margaret F. Brinig and F. H. Buckley, "The Market for Deadbeats," 25 *Journal of Legal Studies* 201 (1996).

84. See Barbara Vobejda, "Gauging Welfare's Role in Motherhood: Sociologists Question Whether Family Caps Are a Legitimate Solution," *Washington Post,* A1 (June 2, 1994).

85. More than 90 percent of the children of divorcing parents live with their mothers. The number is even higher for the children of parents who have never been married.

86. See Weiss and Willis, supra note 48.

87. See Brinig and Alexeev, supra note 59; Judith A. Seltzer, "Father by Law: Effects of Joint Legal Custody on Nonresident Fathers' Involvement with Children," NSFH Working Paper no. 75, University of Wisconsin, Center for Demography and Ecology (1997).

88. See, e.g., Philippe Ariès, *Centuries of Childhood: A Social History of Family Life* (1962); John Demos, "The American Family in Past Time," 43 *American Scholar* 422 (1974); Viviana Zelitzer, *Pricing the Priceless Child: The Changing Social Value of Children* (1985); Margaret F. Brinig, "Finite Horizons: The American Family," 2 *International Journal of Children's Rights* 293 (1994).

89. Bureau of the Census, Current Population Survey, various years.

90. See also Margaret F. Brinig and F. H. Buckley, "Joint Custody: Monitoring and Bonding Theories," 73 *Indiana Law Journal* 393 (1998).

91. See Margaret F. Brinig, "Does Mediation Systematically Disadvantage Women?" 2 *William and Mary Journal of Women and the Law* 1, 2–3 (1995).

92. Trina Grillo, "The Mediation Alternative: Process Dangers for Women," 100 *Yale Law Journal* 1545, 1547 (1991).

93. Jessica Pearson et al., "The Decision to Mediate: Profiles of Individuals Who Accept and Reject the Opportunity to Mediate Child Custody and Visitation Issues, 6 *Journal of Divorce* 17, 20 (1982); see also Joyce Hauser-Dann, "Divorce Mediation: A Growing Field?" 43 *Arbitration Journal* 15, 17 (1988).

94. June Carbone and Margaret F. Brinig, "Rethinking Marriage: Feminist Ideology, Economic Change, and Divorce Reform," 65 *Tulane Law Review* 953, 962–965 (1991); see also Roderick Phillips, *Putting Asunder: A History of Divorce in Western*

Society 364–369, 378–382 (1988); Carl Schneider, "Moral Discourse and the Transformation of American Family Law," 83 *Michigan Law Review* 1803, 1842–44 (1985).

95. For some examples of parting couples who could not overcome their animosity, think of Mia Farrow and Woody Allen, 626 N.Y.S.2d 125 (N.Y. Ct. App. Div. 1995), appeal dismissed, 655 N.E.2d 696 (1995); Elizabeth Morgan and Eric Foretich, 564 A.2d 1 (1989), cert. denied, 488 U.S.1007; see also Foretich v. CBS, Inc., 619 A.2d 48 (D.C. 1993); Foretich v. Capital Cities/ABC, 37 F.3d 1541 (4th Cir. 1994); and the less well known Helene and David Stainback, 396 S.E.2d 686 (Va. Ct. App. 1990), all of whom have used custody battles to prolong their partner's suffering.

96. Brinig and Buckley, supra note 90.

97. Among these are Karen Czapanskiy, "Volunteers and Draftees: The Struggle for Parental Equality," 38 *UCLA Law Review* 1415 (1991); Carol Sanger, "M Is for the Many Things," 1 *Southern California Review of Law and Women's Studies* 15 (1992); and Scott, supra note 59.

98. Joseph Goldstein, Anna Freud, and Albert Solnit, *Beyond the Best Interests of the Child* (1973).

99. Ira Lupu, "The Separation of Powers and the Protection of Children: Beyond the Public/Private Debate," 61 *University of Chicago Law Review* 1317 (1994).

100. American Law Institute, "Principles of the Law of Marriage Dissolution," §2.02, Tentative Draft no. 3 (1998).

101. John S. Murray, "Improving Parent-Child Relationships within the Divorced Family: A Call for Legal Reform," 19 *University of Michigan Journal of Law Reform* 563 (1986); Scott, supra note 26.

102. A biblical example is the book of Hosea. Legal examples include In re Estate of Atherley, 119 Cal. Rptr. 41 (Cal. Ct. App. 1975); and In re Soper's Estate, 264 N.W. 427 (Minn. 1935).

103. Carl Schneider and I describe such a wife as Mrs. Appleby in our *Invitation to Family Law* 59 (1996). See generally Margaret F. Brinig, "The Economics and Law of Covenant Marriage," 16 *Gender Issues* 4 (1998), and Chapter 2, supra.

104. For an early proposal suggesting that income sharing be tied to the length of the marriage, see Jana B. Singer, "Divorce Reform and Gender Justice," 67 *North Carolina Law Review* 1103 (1989).

105. Statistically this is unlikely; only 40 percent of divorced women over forty remarry, and the percentage decreases with age, while the life expectancy for women is five years longer than for men. Barbara F. Wilson and Sally C. Clarke, "Remarriages: A Demographic Profile" 13 *Journal of Family Issues* 123 (1992).

106. Even the strongest advocates of a non-dependence model would allow this. See Herma Hill Kay, "Equality and Difference: A Perspective on No-Fault Divorce and Its Aftermath," 56 *University of Cincinnati Law Review* 1 (1987); Marsha Garrison,

"The Economics of Divorce: Changing Rules, Changing Results," in *Divorce Reform at the Crossroads* 75 (Stephen Sugarman and Herma Hill Kay, eds., 1990); Vicki Schultz, "Telling Stories about Women and Work: Judicial Interpretations of Sex Segregation in the Workplace in Title VII Cases Raising the Lack of Interest Argument," 103 *Harvard Law Review* 1749 (1990).

107. To a limited extent, Virginia's divorce statute maintains such a difference. Va. Code Ann. §20–91(a)(9) (six months separation if no children; one year when there are children).

108. See also Starnes, supra note 9; and Jeffrey Stake, "Mandatory Planning for Divorce," 45 *Vanderbilt Law Review* 397 (1992).

109. This implicit contract is the subject of Brinig, supra note 88.

110. For discussions of quasi-rents in the context of marriage and divorce, see Cohen, supra note 27; and Margaret F. Brinig and Douglas W. Allen, "'These Boots Are Made for Walking': Why Wives Usually File for Divorce," 2 *American Economics and Law Review* (forthcoming).

111. See Kronman, supra note 20.

112. John Locke, *Second Treatise on Government*, §§95 et seq. (rev. ed.). See also Adam Smith, "Of the Order in Which Individuals are Recommended by Nature to Our Care and Attention," in *Theory of Moral Sentiments*, pt. 6, §2, chap. 1, 355, 369 (E. G. West, ed., 1976).

113. Locke, supra note 112, at §119.

114. Buchanan argues that this currying of favor may not be what the elderly parent wants. Buchanan, supra note 32, at 77. The parent wants good behavior to be spontaneous and any gift to be a gift, not something earned.

115. See Charny, supra note 19; Benjamin Klein and Keith B. Leffler, "The Role of Market Forces in Assuring Contractual Performance," 89 *Journal of Political Economy* 615 (1981); Lester G. Telser, "A Theory of Self-Enforcing Agreements," 53 *Journal of Business* 27 (1980); and Oliver Williamson, "Credible Commitments: Using Hostages to Support Exchange," 73 *American Economic Review* 519 (1983).

116. Ted Bergstrom, "Economics in a Family Way," 34 *Journal of Economic Literature* 1903 (1996), maintains, however, that the siblings still have incentives to cooperate because they possess common genes.

117. See, e.g., Nora Underwood, "Mid-life Panic: Thousands of Canadians Are Caught between Children and Elderly Parents," *Maclean's*, 30 (August 19, 1991); Lee Smith, "What Do We Owe to the Elderly?" *Fortune*, 55 (March 27, 1989); Merril Silverstein, "Stability and Change in Temporal Distance between the Elderly and Their Children," 32 *Demography* 29 (1995); Herbert S. Donow, "Am I My Father's Keeper? Sons as Caregivers," 31 *Gerontologist* 709 (1991); Marshall B. Kapp, "Elder Law: Who's the Parent Here? The Family's Impact on the Autonomy of Older Persons," 41 *Emory Law Journal* 773 (1992); Beverly Horsburgh, "Redefining the Family: Recognizing the Altruistic Caregiver and the Importance of Relational

Needs," 25 *University of Michigan Journal of Law Reform* 423 (1992); Christine L. Himes, "Future Caregivers: Projected Family Structures of Older Persons," 47 *Journal of Gerontology and Social Sciences* 17 (1992).

118. See Richard Posner, *Aging and Old Age* 51–65 (1995).

119. See Silverstein, supra note 117, at 35 (31 percent of elderly persons studied lived farther from their children after the four years that elapsed during the study; she attributes all moves to parent moves, however).

120. See, e.g., Charny, supra note 19, at 393; Klein and Leffler, supra note 115, at 615–616; Lewis Kornhauser, "Reliance, Reputation, and Breach of Contract," 26 *Journal of Law and Economics* 691, 695 (1983); Carl Shapiro, "Premiums for Higher-Quality Products as Returns to Reputations," 98 *Quarterly Journal of Economics* 659, 662–666 (1983); Telser, supra note 115, at 35–36.

121. For example, see Ben-Porath, supra note 28, at 3–4.

122. Ben-Porath, supra note 28, at 3, 4.

123. Kapp, supra note 117, at 782.

124. John L. Langbein, "The Twentieth-Century Revolution in Family Wealth Transmission," 86 *Michigan Law Review* 722 (1988).

125. The corollary, of course, is that parents will not feel as obligated to support the children when they are young. See Brinig, supra note 88.

126. Luke 15:25–32. He is angry at his brother for engaging in loose living and returning to be rewarded, and even more at his father for what he sees as ignoring his own good traits while favoring the brother.

127. See Kronman, supra note 20, at 22 and nn. 12 and 13. But note that occasionally siblings vie not to sacrifice for one another. See, e.g., In re Guardianship of Pecinski, 67 Wis. 2d 4, 226 N.W.2d 180 (1975); and State v. Hale and Hossler, 44 Md. App. 376, 408 A.2d 772 (1979).

128. Bergstrom, supra note 116, suggests a genetic motivation.

129. Gary S. Becker, "The Economic Way of Thinking," 101 *Journal of Political Economy* 385 (1993). See also J. David Lewis and Andrew Weingert, "Trust as a Social Reality," 63 *Social Forces* 967, 968–974 (1985); Robert L. Sutton and Anita L. Callahan, "The Stigma of Bankruptcy: Spoiled Organizational Image and Its Management," 30 *Academic Management Journal* 405, 412–422 (1987).

130. See, e.g., *Elder Abuse: Conflict in the Family* (Karl Pillemer and Rosalie Wolfe, eds., 1986).

131. Smith, supra note 112, at 359–360.

132. Posner, supra note 118, at 27, notes that "[a]lthough the young may be less selfish than the old when the cost of being selfless is the same, the cost of voting selflessly may be higher for the young because they have more to gain or lose from the governmental policies at issue in the election, having a much longer period over which gains and losses can accrue to them."

133. See Comment, "The Coming Of Age of Grandparent Visitation Rights," 43 *American University Law Review* 563, 564 (1994). See, e.g., Williams v. Williams, 485

S.E.2d 651 (Va. Ct. App. 1997); In re Adoption of A. M. R., 527 N.W.2d 565 (Minn. Ct. App. 1995); Beckman v. Boggs, 655 A.2d 901 (Md. 1995).

134. See, e.g., Williams v. Williams, 256 Va. 19, 501 S.E.2d 417 (1998); Beckman v. Boggs, 655 A.2d 901 (Md. 1995); see also In re Nearhoof, 359 S.E.2d 587 (W. Va. 1991).

135. Hawk v. Hawk, 855 S.W.2d 573 (Tenn. 1993); Herndon v. Tuhey, 857 S.W.2d 203 (Mo. 1993); Williams v. Williams, 256 Va. 19, 501 S.E.2d 417 (1998).

136. See, e.g., Layton v. Foster, 460 N.E.2d 1351 (N.Y. 1984); Picker v. Barnes, 236 S.E.2d 715 (N.C. Ct. App. 1977); see generally Peter Zabolotsky, "To Grandmother's House We Go: Grandparent Visitation after Stepparent Adoption," 32 *Wayne Law Review* 1 (Fall 1985); Kathleen S. Bean, "Grandparent Visitation: Can the Parent Refuse?" 24 *University of Louisville Journal of Family Law* 393 (1985–86); Edward M. Burns, "Grandparent Visitation Rights: Is It Time for the Pendulum to Fall?" 25 *Family Law Quarterly* 59 (Spring 1991); Samuel V. Schoonnaker et al., "Constitutional Issues Raised by Third-Party Access to Children," 25 *Family Law Quarterly* 95 (Spring 1991); Note, "The Constitutional Constraints on Grandparents' Visitation Statutes," 86 *Columbia Law Review* 118 (1986).

137. 855 S.W.2d at 582.

138. Id. at 576.

139. Bottoms v. Bottoms, 457 S.E.2d 102 (Va. 1995).

140. See, e.g., Stainback v. Stainback, 396 S.E.2d 686 (Va. Ct. App. 1990); Watkins v. Watkins, 265 S.E.2d 750 (Va. 1980).

141. See, e.g., Roanoke Engineering Sales Co., Inc. v. Rosenbaum, 290 S.E.2d 882 (Va. 1982).

142. *King Lear* 1.1.39–42.

143. Id. at 1.1.60.

144. Id. at 1.1.72–78.

145. This last is pointed out by Cordelia. Id. at 1.1.101–106.

146. This story has its parallel in the British folk tale of "Caporushes," in Flora Annie Steele, *English Fairy Tales* (1918); and Jane Smiley, *A Thousand Acres* (1992).

147. *King Lear* 1.1.91–93.

148. As Buchanan notes, supra note 32, at 72, this type of rent-seeking behavior occurs only where the parties have done nothing to deserve the rents.

149. Arrow's "Voting Paradox" and the phenomenon of cycling are the subject of an article by my former colleague Maxwell Stearns, "The Misguided Renaissance of Social Choice," 103 *Yale Law Journal* 1219 (1994). We discovered only after our ideas were already in print that we had both used the *Lear* story.

150. In the play, the two eldest form the initial alliance.

151. Note, for example, the bargaining between the daughters and their father over how many servants he can bring along on his visits to them. *King Lear* 2.4.200–255.

152. Kronman, supra note 20.
153. Outside the family, game theorists have studied such behavior in a two-person game called "The Ultimatum Game," in which one participant is given a sum of money and can divide it (without conversation) with the other. The second participant has the option of accepting or rejecting the proffered amount. See Richard Thaler, "Anomalies: The Ultimatum Game," 2 *Journal of Economic Perspectives* 195 (Fall 1988). More recently, the game has been played by men and women in a series of studies by Catherine Eckel and Philip Grossman, "Chivalry and Solidarity in Ultimatum Games" and "The Relative Price of Fairness: Gender Differences in a Punishment Game," Department of Economics, Virginia Polytechnic Institute and State University (1994). Women tend to expect less from the men who offer them shares in the initial endowment, though on average they offer approximately the same amount.
154. Buchanan, supra note 32, at 78.
155. Buchanan maintains that it is the predictability of the rules for succession rather than any particular rule itself that is relevant for eliminating rent seeking. Id.
156. Genesis 25:28–34. Ben-Porath, supra note 28, at 8.
157. See, e.g., Sundin v. Klein, 269 S.E.2d 787 (Va. Ct. App. 1980); Va. Code Ann. §55–401.
158. See, e.g., Bruere v. Mullins, 320 S.W.2d 274 (Ark. 1959); Urban v. House, 1190 WL 284364 (Conn.Super. Ct.); Wingate v. Beatty, 1995 WL 749718 (Neb. Ct. App. 1995).
159. See Brinig, supra note 88.
160. Life expectancy increased from 54.1 years in 1920 to 75.4 in 1990. United States Department of Commerce, Bureau of the Census, *Statistical Abstracts* (1992), table 104, at 76.
161. Posner, supra note 118, at 16 and figure 5.1, reports that approximately 10 percent of the population in any given age bracket says that they are not very happy. The portion of octogenarians stating they are very happy is about the same as for people between thirty and thirty-nine, approximately 30 percent.
162. See also Ben-Porath, supra note 28, at 7.
163. See, e.g., Land O' Lakes v. Fredjos, 1992 U.S. Dist. LEXIS 9224 (7th Cir.)
164. See, e.g., Picture Lake Campgrounds, Inc. v. Holiday Inns, 497 F. Supp. 858 (E.D. Va. 1980). See generally James M. Malcomson, "Work Incentives, Hierarchy, and Internal Labor Markets," 92 *Journal of Political Economy* 486, 486–487 (1984); Paul Weiler, *Governing the Workplace: The Future of Labor and Employment Law* 70 and n.43 (1990).
165. See, e.g, Ark. Stat. Ann. §20–47–106 (1992); Cal. Fam. Code 4400 (1992); Burns Ind. Code Ann. §31–16–7–1 (1992); Md. Fam. Law Code Ann. §13–102 (1991); Mont. Code Ann. §40–6–301 (1992); Nev. Rev. Stat. Ann. §428.070 (1991); N.J. Stat. Ann. §44:1–140 (West Supp. 1991); 62 Pa. Cons. Stat. Ann. §1973 (1968 and Supp. 1990); S.D. Cod. Laws §25–5–21 (1992); Va. Code Ann. §20–88 (Michie

1991); W. Va. Code §9–5–9 (1990). See generally Terrance A. Kline, "A Rational Role for Filial Responsibility Laws in Modern Society," 26 *Family Law Quarterly* 195, 200 and n.47 (1992); Catherine D. Byrd, "Relative Responsibility Extended: Requirements of Adult Children to Pay for Their Indigent Parents' Medical Needs," 22 *Family Law Quarterly* 98 (1988); Renae R. Patrick, "Honor Thy Father and Mother: Paying the Medical Bills of Elderly Parents," 19 *University of Richmond Law Review* 69 (1984); and Alison P. Barnes and Lawrence N. Frolick, "America the Aging," 16 *Family Advocate* 19, 22–23 (1993).

166. See Donald Cox and Odel Stark, "Intergenerational Transfers and the Demonstration Effect," presented at the Southern Economics Association annual meeting in New Orleans, November 21–23, 1992. Brinig, supra note 88, questions whether and how contacts with elderly parents may coincide with investment in one's own minor children.

167. Buchanan, supra note 32.

168. On a state level, data would include elder abuse per capita, the percentage of elderly living alone, average per capita income (adjusted for the cost of living), possibly the violent crime rate, and the state life expectancy of people over sixty-five.

169. Becker, supra note 129. See also Burnheim, Shleifer, and Summers, supra note 56, at 1074; and Brinig, supra note 88.

170. See also Richard Epstein, "Justice across the Generations," 67 *Texas Law Review* 1465, 1466, 1472, 1475 (1989).

171. See also Langbein, supra note 124; Posner, supra note 118, chap. 2.

172. Robert S. Lynd and Helen M. Lynd, *Middletown: A Study in American Culture* 220 (1929). See also Kyriakos S. Markides, Joanne S. Boldt, and Laura A. Ray, "Sources of Helping and Intergenerational Solidarity: A Three-Generations Study of Mexican Americans," 31 *Journal of Gerontology* 506 (1986).

173. The dangers of individualism in a family setting are explored by Regan, supra note 7, at 83–88.

174. As Regan, supra note 7, at 115 notes, family discourse "[m]akes available a 'middle distance' that creates the possibility of a relational sense of self that is nonetheless relatively stable." Compare Smiley, supra note 146, at 20, where she speaks of needing an optimum distance for viewing one's father. The healthy family permits a perspective of self from which all of us can grow to lead better lives.

175. Clearly fathers are hurt by such circumstances as well. See Gilbert A. Holmes, "The Tie That Binds: The Constitutional Right of Children to Maintain Relationships with Parent-Like Individuals," 53 *Maryland Law Review* 358 (1994); and Mary Shanley, "Unwed Fathers' Rights, Adoption, and Sex Equality: Gender-Neutrality and the Perpetuation of Patriarchy," 95 *Columbia Law Review* 60 (1995).

176. Amy Tan, "Queen Mother of the Western Skies," in *The Joy Luck Club* (1989).

177. Doan Thi Huong Anh v. Nelson, 245 N.W.2d 511 (Iowa 1976).

178. Elster, supra note 59.

179. Another familiar case comes from the story of Moses in Exodus 2.

180. See In re Adoption/Guardianship no. 2633, 646 A.2d 1036 (Md. App. 1994)(white foster parents cared for the child for eighteen months, until she was two, when she was placed with a black family that already had custody of her two brothers); In re T. J., 661 A.2d 1 (D.C. App. 1995).

181. See, e.g., Alma Society v. Mellon, 601 F.2d 1225 (2 Cir. 1979); see also In re Roger B., 418 N.E.2d 751 (Ill. App. 1981), app. dism'd., 454 U.S. 806 (1981).

182. See, e.g., N.D. Cent. Code §14–15.1–01—14–15.1–07; Va. Code Ann. 63.1–126.

183. See Leverett Millen and Samuel Roll, "Solomon's Mothers: A Special Case of Pathological Bereavement," 55 *American Journal of Orthopsychiatry* 411, 412–413 (1985).

184. See, e.g., Holmes, supra note 175; Laurie A. Ames, "Open Adoptions: Truth and Consequences," 16 *Law and Psychology Review* 137 (1992); Nancy E. Dowd, "A Feminist Analysis of Adoption," 107 *Harvard Law Review* 913, 931 (1994).

185. Annette Haselhoff, "Survey of New York Practice," 67 *Saint John's Law Review* 145, 169 (1993).

186. Robert Frost, *North of Boston* 20 (1915). Extended families are also featured in Moore v. City of East Cleveland, 431 U.S. 491 (1977).

187. See, e.g., Carol Gilligan, *In a Different Voice: Psychological Theory and Women's Development* 25 (1982); Carrie Menkel-Meadow, "Portia in a Different Voice: Speculations on a Woman's Lawyering Process," 1 *Berkeley Women's Law Journal* 39, 42 (1985).

8. The Role of Law Reform

1. Ankenbrandt v. Richards, 504 U.S. 689, 704 (1992). The case held that children could bring a federal diversity action against their father and his paramour for sexual and other abuse.

2. Swift and Co. v. United States, 196 U.S. 375, 398 (1905)(Holmes, J.).

3. Margaret F. Brinig and F. H. Buckley, "The Market for Deadbeats," 25 *Journal of Legal Studies* 201 (1996).

4. For reviews, see William J. Carney, "The Production of Corporate Law, 71 *Southern California Law Review* 715 (1998); William W. Bratton and Joseph MaCahery, "The New Economics of Jurisdictional Competition: Devolutionary Federalism in a Second-Best World," 86 *Georgetown Law Journal* 201 (1997).

5. Margaret F. Brinig and F. H. Buckley, "No-Fault Laws and At-Fault People," 16 *International Review of Law and Economics* 325 (1998).

6. Lawrence M. Friedman, "Rights of Passage: Divorce Law in Historical Perspective," 63 *Oregon Law Review* 649, 655 (1984).

7. See, e.g., Allen M. Parkman, *No-Fault Divorce: What Went Wrong?* 15 (1992). See also Margaret F. Brinig and June Carbone, "The Reliance Interest in Marriage and Divorce," 62 *Tulane Law Review* 859, 860–861 (1988).

8. Max Rheinstein, *Marriage Stability, Divorce, and the Law,* 35 (1972).

9. Friedman, supra note 6, at 653; Glenda Riley, *Divorce: An American Tradition* 40–44 (1991).

10. Friedman, supra note 6, at 635; Richard Chused, *Private Acts in Public Places: A Social History of Divorce in the Formative Era of American Family Law* (1994).

11. See Margaret F. Brinig and Michael V. Alexeev, "Trading at Divorce: Preferences, Legal Rules, and Divorce Settlements," 8 *Ohio State Journal on Dispute Resolution* 279 (1993); Lynn Wardle, "No-Fault Divorce and the Divorce Conundrum," 1991 *B.Y.U. Law Review* 79, 109 (1991).

12. See Brinig and Buckley, supra note 5.

13. Friedman, supra note 6, at 661.

14. Roderick Phillips, *Putting Asunder: A History of Divorce in Western Society* 455–456 (1988).

15. *New York Tribune* (March 1, 1860), cited in Riley, supra note 9.

16. Riley, supra note 9, at 64.

17. See Nelson M. Blake, *The Road to Reno: A History of Divorce in the United States* (1977).

18. Rheinstein, supra note 8, at 364.

19. 325 U.S. 226 (1945).

20. Kulko v. Superior Court, 436 U.S. 84 (1978).

21. Perry v. Ponder, 604 S.W.2d 306 (Tex. Ct. Civ. App. 1980).

22. May v. Anderson, 345 U.S. 528 (1953).

23. Uniform Child Custody Jurisdiction Act (see, e.g., Va. Code Ann. §§20–129 et seq.).

24. 28 U.S.C. §1738A.

25. 501 N.W.2d 193 (Mich. Ct. App. 1993), aff'd. in part, vac. in part, and remanded, 502 N.W.2d 649 (Mich. 1993).

26. In re Petition of Doe, 638 N.E.2d 181 (Ill. 1994).

27. Compare Roberta Romano, *The Genius of American Corporate Law* (1993).

28. See Frederick J. Turner, *The Frontier in American History* (1893) (reprint ed. 1986).

29. F. H. Buckley and Margaret F. Brinig, "Welfare Migrants: The Race for the Top," 5 *Supreme Court Economic Review* 141 (1997).

30. 852 P.2d 44 (Haw. 1993). On December 3, 1996, the district court, on remand, decided that the statute disallowing same-sex marriages unconstitutionally violated Hawaii's equal rights law. Baehr v. Miike, 1996 WL 694235, 65 USLW 2399, 96 Daily Journal D.A.R. 14,647, 96 CJ C.A.R. 2041 (Hawaii Cir. Ct., December 3, 1996) (No. Civ. 91–1394). For an account of the case, see Lyle Denniston, "Judge OKs Same-Sex Marriages; Ruling in Hawaii Applies Only to That State; Test Case Involved Three Couples, 1 Living in Baltimore," *Baltimore Sun,* 1A (December 4, 1996).

31. Haw. Rev. Stat. §572–1(3) (1985) (referring to "the man" and "the woman" as the applicants for marriage license).

32. A Bill for an Act Relating to Marriage, 1994 Hawaii Advance Legislative Service 217.

33. 1996 WL 694235 (Hawaii Cir. Ct.). See also Brause and Dugan v. ?,—P.2d— (Alaska Super. Ct. 1998), as reported in "Judge Says Choosing Partner Is a Right," *Washington Post*, A19 (March 1, 1998).

34. See Denniston, supra note 30.

35. 28 U.S.C.A. §1738C.

36. 1 U.S.C.A. §7.

37. See, e.g., Va. Code Ann. §20–45.2. An Internet site keeping track of the legislation for the Conference of Catholic Bishops is the Marriage Law Project, http://www.pono.net/policy/samesex-marriage/ssm-sub.html. Another is maintained by the Lambda Legal Defense Fund, http://ucc.gu.uwa.edu.au/~rod/gay/marriage.html.

38. Shahar v. Bowers, 114 F.3d 1097 (11th Cir. 1997).

39. Romer v. Evans, 517 U.S. 620 (1996).

40. Art. 6, §4.

41. See, e.g., In re May's Estate, 114 N.E. 4 (N.Y. 1953); Naim v. Naim, 90 S.E.2d 849 (Va.1956); Needam v. Needam, 33 S.E.2d 288 (Va. 1945).

42. Jennifer Gerardo Brown, "Competitive Federalism and the Legislative Incentives to Recognize Same-Sex Marriage," 68 *Southern California Law Review* 745 (1995).

43. See Milton C. Regan, *Family Law and the Pursuit of Intimacy* 118–122 (1993).

44. See, e.g., "D.C. Passes Citywide Recycling; . . . AIDS Law Repealed in Raucous Session," *Washington Post*, C8 (December 14, 1988).

45. A Web site containing information about these efforts is located at http://adams.patriot.net/~crouch/adr/index.html.

46. Margaret F. Brinig, "Rings and Promises," 6 *Journal of Law, Economics, and Organization* 203, 207–208 (1990). This paper was discussed in Chapter 2.

47. Margaret F. Brinig and Steven M. Crafton, "Marriage and Opportunism," 23 *Journal of Legal Studies* 869 (1994). This paper was discussed in Chapter 6.

48. Id. at 892 and n.104.

49. Parkman, supra note 7, at 61–63.

50. Herma Hill Kay, "Equality and Difference: A Perspective on No-Fault Divorce and Its Aftermath," 56 *University of Cincinnati Law Review* 1 (1987).

51. Parkman, supra note 7, at 83–85. But see Herbert Jacob, "Another Look at No-Fault Divorce and the Post-Divorce Finances of Women," 23 *Law and Society Review* 95 (1989); and Martha Albertson Fineman, *The Illusion of Equality: The Rhetoric and Reality of Divorce Reform* 11 (1991).

52. See Margaret F. Brinig, "The Law and Economics of No-Fault Divorce," 26 *Family Law Quarterly* 453, 461–462 (1993).

53. Margaret F. Brinig, "Does Mediation Systematically Disadvantage Women?" 2 *William and Mary Journal of Women and the Law* 1 (1995).

54. Compare Smith v. Lewis, 530 P.2d 589, (Cal. 1975) (attorney committed malpractice in failing to seek divisible military pension rights for his client).

55. See, e.g., Barnes v. Barnes, 1995 Va. App. LEXIS 319.

56. Domestic Relations Tax Reform Act of 1986, PL 99–514, 28 U.S.C. §71(b). See generally Bernard P. Ingold, "Recent Reforms in Divorce Taxation: For Better or for Worse?" 120 *Military Law Review* 203 (1988); Laurie L. Malman, "Unfinished Reform: The Tax Consequences of Divorce," 61 *New York University Law Review* 363 (1986); Ronald L. Hjorth, "Divorce, Taxes, and the 1984 Tax Reform Act: An Inadequate Response to an Old Problem," 61 *Washington Law Review* 151 (1986).

57. I.R.C. §1041, and §1042, overruling United States v. Davis, 370 U.S. 65 (1962). See Slawski v. United States, 6 Ct. Cl. 433 (1984).

58. Eileen Spring, *Law, Land, and Family: Aristocratic Inheritance in England, 1300–1800* (1991).

59. Friedman, supra note 6; Lawrence Friedman and Robert Percival, "Who Sues for Divorce? From Fault through Fiction to Freedom," 5 *Journal of Legal Studies* 67 (1976).

60. Friedman and Percival, supra note 59.

61. Eleanor Maccoby and Robert H. Mnookin, *Dividing the Child: Social and Legal Dilemmas of Custody* (1992).

62. Scott Altman, "Lurking in the Shadow," 68 *Southern California Law Review* 493 (1995).

63. Ira Lupu, "Separation of Powers and the Protection of Children," 61 *University of Chicago Law Review* 1317 (1994).

64. Minn. Stat. §259.255; see In re Petition to Adopt S. T. and N. T., 512 N.W.2d 894 (Minn. 1994).

65. This is the solution advocated by critics of transracial adoption such as Twila Perry. See, e.g., Twila L. Perry, "The Transracial Adoption Controversy: An Analysis of Discourse and Subordination," 21 *N.Y.U. Review of Law and Social Change* 33 (1993–94); Peter Hayes, "The Ideological Attack on Transracial Adoption in the U.S.A. and Britain," 9 *International Journal of Law and the Family* 1 (1995). Congress forbade the use of race in adoption as part of 1996 legislation. Small Business Jobs Protection Act, Pub. L. no. 104–188, §1808 (1996); see 110 *Harvard Law Review* 1352 (1997).

66. The act was found unconstitutional in Maldono v. Houston, 1997 U.S. Dist. LEXIS 15474 (E.D. Pa. 1977), on grounds it violated the privileges and immunities clause.

67. See Margaret F. Brinig and F. H. Buckley, "The Price of Virtue," 98 *Public Choice* 111 (1999).

68. Brinig and Crafton, supra note 47.

69. Victor Fuchs, *Women's Quest for Economic Equality* (1988).

70. Compare the Paul Simon song "I Am a Rock": "I am a rock, I am an island, / I

touch no one and no one touches me." Simon's lyrics are of course drawn from John Donne, "For Whom the Bell Tolls," in *Complete Poems of John Donne* (Alexander Ballock ed. 1872–73).

71. For an analysis of the effects of no-fault divorce, see Lynn D. Wardle, "No-Fault Divorce and the Divorce Conundrum," 1991 *B.Y.U. Law Review* 79.

72. Brinig and Crafton, supra note 47.

73. Brinig and Buckley, supra note 67.

74. See Wardle, supra note 71.

75. Margaret F. Brinig, "Finite Horizons? The American Family," 2 *International Journal of Children's Rights* 293 (1994).

76. Margaret F. Brinig, "The Family Franchise: Elderly Parents and Adult Siblings," 1996 *Utah Law Review.*

77. Mark Stodghill, "Cottage Sparks Fond Childhood Memories," *Duluth News-Tribune,* 1A (July 29, 1995).

78. Jacqueline L. Salmon, "With E-Mail, Absence Makes Families Fonder; Parents, Offspring in College Open Up Online," *Washington Post,* A1 (October 27, 1997).

79. Va. Code Ann. §20–91(9); Tenn. Code Ann. §36–4–101. See generally Elizabeth S. Scott and Robert E. Scott, "Marriage as Relational Contract," 84 *Virginia Law Review* 1225 (1998).

80. See, e.g., Carol Gilligan, *In a Different Voice: Psychological Theory and Women's Development* 25 (1982); Carrie Menkel-Meadow, "Portia in a Different Voice: Speculations on a Woman's Lawyering Process," 1 *Berkeley Women's Law Journal* 39, 42 (1985).

Index

Abortion, 46; effect on adoption, 47

Abuse, spousal, and covenant marriage, 32

Abuse of children, 134–138; ground for divorce, 32; and error, 113–115

Adoption: black market, 47; costs of regulation, 48–49; consent for and live birth requirement, 62–63; revocation of consent, 63–68; transaction costs, 63–68; voluntariness of consent, 64–68; rent-extraction in, 67; wrongful adoption, 68–70; fraud in, 68–70; special needs children, 69–70; and opportunism, 70–71; intermediary, 72–73; equitable, 78; open, 206–207

Adultery, 96

AFDC and unwed birth rate, 59–61

Affection, 19

Agency costs, 6

Agreements: firm, 5; antenuptial, 38–40; premarital, 38–40; terms of marriage contract, 39–40

Alimony: and specialization, 99–101; and no-fault, 33, 148–152; as damages, 148; as flow of earnings, 163–164

Altruism: and children, 119; and gender, 119; and covenant, 131

Annulment: history of, 22; contemporary reasons for, 23; fraud as ground for, 25–27; as rescission of marriage; and divorce, 26

Antenuptial agreements, 38–40; problems with negotiating, 39; and incomplete information, 39

Arbitration, same-sex couples, 36

Arranged marriage, 19

Assets, division at divorce, 163–166

Assortative mating, 19

Attachment disorder, 137

Autonomy, 102–104; investment in marriage, 106; children's, 120

Baby brokering, 76

Baby Jessica, 64, 134, 210

Baby Richard, 55, 210

Baker and Emery, 17–18

Bargaining, 11; and human capital, 91–92; in marriage, 91–97; and children, 92; and market power, 92–93; threat point, 93; and biology, 94; at divorce, 158–163

Bargaining equality, same-sex couples, 37

Becker, Gary, 11, 167–168; on markets, 19; division of labor, 85, 87–90

Becker, Landes, and Michael, 144

Best interests, parental presumption, 110–115

"Best interests of child" standard, 48

Biological fathers: consent for adoption, 134

Birth rate: and no-fault divorce, 46; and single parents, 58

Black market: in babies; 47; in surrogacy, 76–77

Bond, engagement ring as, 41

Bounded rationality, 103

Breach, 2, 18; and same-sex couples, 36; of